LEGISLATION AT WESTMINSTER

Legislation at Westminster

*Parliamentary Actors and Influence in
the Making of British Law*

MEG RUSSELL

and

DANIEL GOVER

OXFORD
UNIVERSITY PRESS

OXFORD
UNIVERSITY PRESS

Great Clarendon Street, Oxford, OX2 6DP,
United Kingdom

Oxford University Press is a department of the University of Oxford.
It furthers the University's objective of excellence in research, scholarship,
and education by publishing worldwide. Oxford is a registered trade mark of
Oxford University Press in the UK and in certain other countries

Published in the United States of America by Oxford University Press
198 Madison Avenue, New York, NY 10016, United States of America

British Library Cataloguing in Publication Data
Data available

Library of Congress Control Number: 2017945345

ISBN 978–0–19–875382–7

Printed and bound by
CPI Group (UK) Ltd, Croydon, CR0 4YY

Acknowledgements

Our ability to produce this book has relied upon the cooperation and support of numerous people and organisations, over a period spanning several years.

Meg Russell's programme of work on the policy impact of the UK parliament received initial support during a Research Fellowship funded by the Economic and Social Research Council (ESRC) for the period 2008-11 (RES-063-27-0163). This was followed by more targeted research grants from the Nuffield Foundation, including for a project specifically to study parliament's impact on government legislation, which ran from 2011 to 2015. Although much of the research in the book was funded by the Nuffield Foundation, and we are extremely grateful to its trustees and staff for their support, any views expressed are those of the authors and not necessarily those of the Foundation. This funding enabled the Constitution Unit (University College London) to employ Daniel Gover, originally alongside Kristina Wollter and Meghan Benton – both of whom contributed significantly to initial planning, as well as data collection and analysis. We are tremendously grateful to them for their contributions, and the happy times that we spent together as colleagues.

The book draws on a wide range of sources, including the parliamentary record and other published materials. However it is crucially reliant on information from research interviews that we conducted with well over 100 busy people. Without the generous cooperation of such individuals, good quality qualitative research would not be possible, and public understanding of the dynamics of political institutions would be greatly impoverished as a result. We therefore sincerely thank our interviewees for giving up the time to speak to us. Our conversations were often lively, sprinkled with valuable insights, occasionally spiked with emotion, and rarely dull – as hopefully reflected in various quotations throughout the book. Many of our interviewees are listed in Appendix B, but some chose not to be named, and we have also drawn in places from interviews on related projects.

To gain further insight beyond the written record we have also benefited greatly from the cooperation of others in parliament, government and the pressure group world. Specifically we are grateful to those holding the most senior staff roles in both chambers – David Natzler, Clerk of the House of Commons, and his predecessor Robert Rogers (now Lord Lisvane), alongside David Beamish, the recently retired Clerk of the Parliaments, and his successor Ed Ollard. All have demonstrated great commitment to cooperation with the academic research community and to enhancing public understanding of parliament. We have at times sought more specific advice and information from numerous staff in each chamber's Public Bill Office, the two parliamentary libraries, various other parliamentary offices, the Cabinet Office and the Office of the Parliamentary Counsel, for which we are very grateful. The traditions of the Study of Parliament Group, and the links that it provides between academics and parliamentary staff, remain extremely important and valuable.

At the Constitution Unit our research benefited significantly not only from Kristina and Meghan's input, but also that of many research volunteers. Over such a lengthy period they soon became too numerous to mention individually, though Elsa Piersig made a particularly important contribution through the analysis of select committee mentions in debate (see chapter 8). We have generally been very fortunate to work in such a vibrant intellectual environment, surrounded by clever and committed people – in the Unit itself and the wider UCL Department of Political Science. Particular thanks are due to Tom Semlyen for research support at the early stages, and to Roberta Damiani, Ruxandra Serban and Jack Sheldon for behind-the-scenes help in putting the book together. Daniel also owes thanks to his colleagues at Queen Mary University of London for their support, including Philip Cowley and Michael Kenny – and to the School of Politics and international Relations for generously providing funding which, together with Constitution Unit funds, contributed towards the compilation of the index.

When circulating draft chapters for comment, we have received useful support and insights from a wide range of other people – though clearly errors of fact and judgement remain our own. In addition to some of those already mentioned, they included Richard Chapman, Paul Evans, Oonagh Gay, Wyn Grant, Peter John, Amie Kreppel, Liam Laurence Smyth, Stephen Laws, Cristina Leston-Bandeira, Alan Renwick, Jack Simson Caird, Philippa Tudor, Albert Weale and Tom Wilson. We are grateful for feedback received on an early version of chapter 10 from attendees at a conference of the Political Studies Association specialist group on Parliaments and Legislatures, particularly including Stephen Bates and Sarah Childs.

We were delighted at the end of the process that Philip Cowley, Amie Kreppel and David Natzler wanted to provide such positive comments for the back cover. Natasha Flemming and Eve Ryle-Hodges at Oxford University Press were both efficient and tolerant throughout, and we are also grateful to Nancy Rebecca and the other members of the production team.

Finally, for even greater tolerance and kindness we thank our friends and family for their support. Meg, as ever, owes a particular debt of thanks to Philip Carter. Daniel in particular thanks Alan Francis, Mandip Lally and Andrew Bazeley.

Contents

List of Tables and Figures

Tables

Figures

1

Introduction

The legislative process matters. Every year the UK parliament agrees dozens of bills that go on directly to affect people's lives. These determine issues as diverse as employees' rights at work, the structure of welfare benefits, the creation and abolition of new criminal offences, and companies' responsibilities towards the environment. At Westminster, such changes are debated in the House of Commons and the House of Lords, and normally need the assent of both. But while the UK parliament is very visible, and ostensibly central to politics, people often suggest that it makes little impact on the legislation that gets agreed. Most successful bills are drafted in government departments and proposed by ministers, and the number explicitly rejected by parliament is very small. This can create an impression that government, not parliament, controls the process. Parliament may even be dismissed as relatively peripheral—as just a 'talking shop' or a 'rubber stamp'. Such claims are particularly prevalent with respect to Westminster, but equivalent legislatures in other democracies often face similar criticisms as well.

Despite the centrality of the parliamentary legislative process, there has been relatively little detailed study of its dynamics in recent years. This is at least partly because of the suspicion that government is dominant, and hence parliament unimportant. In addition, analysing the process carefully is very time-consuming. Huge numbers of legislative amendments are proposed to public bills—in the 2015–16 session alone, there were over 8,000 in the House of Commons and House of Lords combined—and to read and comprehend them all would be a mammoth task.[1] In addition, the many hours of parliamentary debate dedicated to every bill need to be studied. Plus, to really understand how the process works, and where influence lies, the important but less visible negotiation that goes on behind the scenes must be explored.

This book is the first detailed study of the Westminster legislative process for over 40 years. It analyses and explains what happens when a bill passes through parliament, and the roles that different actors play. Our primary objective is to improve understanding of how the law is made—where the dynamics of the parliamentary legislative process are clearly central. But Westminster's treatment of legislation also offers important indicators regarding the broader question of the extent to which parliament really matters in shaping public policy. Contrary to popular expectations, we conclude that it matters very much. Another core objective of the book is therefore to explore how legislative influence works.

Legislation at Westminster. First edition. Meg Russell and Daniel Gover. © Meg Russell and Daniel Gover 2017. Published 2017 by Oxford University Press.

We do this by tracing the passage of 12 specific pieces of government legislation through Westminster, and drawing on interviews with numerous people who were closely involved. This allows us to enliven what might otherwise be a rather dry, abstract topic with accounts of actual legislative influence, including words from those who helped to bring such change about. The chapters in the book are organized around the contributions made by different groups in parliament—such as members aligned with the government and opposition, independent members, and external pressure groups. Parliament serves as a forum for interaction between these different sets of actors, each of which have their own different motivations and strategies. We show that they all affect legislative outcomes in important ways.

A key context for the book is the significant change that has taken place at Westminster since the last major study of the process. This includes the creation of specialist select committees in the House of Commons, and subsequently in the House of Lords, and the wider changes to the Lords which have turned it from a hereditary-dominated institution into one largely made up of appointed members. The characteristics of members in both chambers have also altered significantly over time, and so has their behaviour—particularly through greater willingness to show independence from the party whip. The 2010–15 parliament then witnessed the first coalition government at Westminster since 1945. All of these developments potentially affect the dynamics of the legislative process.

Our study concerns lawmaking in the UK parliament, and will therefore be of particular interest to British readers. But, although there may be important differences of detail, many of the patterns that we observe will have resonance further afield. There is great diversity among legislative institutions around the world, but (as implied in the name) a central function that they all share is making the law. Nonetheless, legislatures in well-established democracies are often seen as fairly weak and executive-dominated. Among them, the Westminster parliament is characterized as particularly so. Hence if it turns out that the executive is actually less dominant at Westminster than commonly assumed, this may have wider-ranging implications for the understanding of legislative institutions and their policy contribution.

This book is designed for a wide range of readers who are interested in both politics and law. They most obviously include students and teachers, but also others with a less academic interest—who wish to understand better how parliament works, how different groups within the institution operate and interact, and how legislative influence operates. We hope that readers will include those within parliament itself, and others who interact with it professionally. The two chambers at Westminster comprise over 1,400 members, supported by even greater numbers of staff—each of whom necessarily plays only a small part in its work. Our research seeks, in contrast, to provide a full picture of how the machine functions as a whole—through documentary analysis, and talking to participants throughout the system. We therefore hope that the book will prove interesting both to those with very limited knowledge of Westminster, and to those who know aspects of its work very well. In short, anyone interested in how the policy process works, or in influencing that process through parliament, will potentially benefit from reading this book.

Common Views of Parliament and its Power in the Legislative Process

It is common to hear assertions in popular debate that the British parliament is relatively peripheral to policy-making, and particularly to the shaping of legislation. For example on 1 June 2009 an editorial in the respected *Financial Times* suggested that Westminster had 'become a rubber stamp', with '[t]oo many bills, allocated too little time after shoddy drafting … whipped through by the ruling party machine'.[2] A few years earlier the then Leader of the Opposition, William Hague, claimed in a speech that parliament 'nods through complicated and important legislation with only cursory investigation' and, instead of holding the government properly to account, simply 'bows and scrapes to ministers'.[3] Such comments do little to maintain faith in Britain's democratic institutions.[4]

The academic literature, even when providing a more nuanced account of parliament's role, often perpetuates such impressions. One recent textbook aimed at undergraduate students of British politics notes that 'it may be questioned whether Parliament effectively makes the law … [its] influence on the principles and even the details of government legislation is usually limited' (Leach, Coxall, and Robins 2011: 236). Another suggests that 'the House of Commons is misunderstood if viewed as a legislator' (Moran 2015: 111). Law students are exposed to similar arguments. One leading textbook in this field claims that 'parliamentary input into legislation is in practice rather modest', and that a notion of 'Parliament the lawmaker' would therefore be misplaced (Harlow and Rawlings 2009: 141).

The relatively younger academic discipline of public policy has also contributed to these debates in important ways, and similarly tends to downplay the role of formal legislative institutions. A recent comparative textbook in this field suggests that, '[i]n most political systems … it is the executive which tends to dominate the policy-making process'; and that '[d]espite the name "parliamentary democracy", the parliament plays only a limited role in decision-making in the British Westminster model' (Knill and Tosun 2012: 58, 139). Public policy scholars instead tend to emphasize the importance of informal processes and relationships to the agreement of policy—such as behind-the-scenes meetings between civil servants and representatives of interest groups, or the impact of the media. An early text in this tradition even made the eye-catching claim that Britain had become a 'post-parliamentary democracy', implying that while Westminster was perhaps powerful in the past its influence had since drained away (Richardson and Jordan 1979). This was just the latest in a long succession of texts espousing what some scholars refer to as the 'parliamentary decline thesis' (Flinders and Kelso 2011). For example, 75 years earlier Low (1904: 80) had complained that the 'House of Commons no longer controls the Executive; on the contrary, the Executive controls the House of Commons'.

This picture of Britain has influenced the views of comparative scholars, who often present Westminster as being at one end of a possible spectrum of legislative influence. For example, Polsby (1975) drew a distinction between 'transformative' legislatures, possessing clear ability to shape policy, and 'arena' legislatures which are primarily public discussion forums, of which Westminster was cited as a classic case. Likewise, Mezey (1979) distinguished between legislatures which were 'active' on policy, and those which were merely 'reactive', again with the UK falling into the latter group. In contrast, the US Congress was always seen very differently: as the classic 'transformative' or 'active' legislature. This partly reflects academic beliefs about the differing dynamics in presidential systems (where a strict 'separation of powers' exists between the legislature and the executive) versus parliamentary systems like the UK (where the executive depends on the confidence of the legislature to stay in office). In parliamentary systems power is more 'fused', and legislatures tend to be seen as merely reactive to what governments propose. This leads public policy scholars to claim that legislatures play only a 'small role in the policy process in parliamentary systems', where disciplined political parties mean that ministers can 'more often than not take legislative support for granted' (Howlett and Ramesh 2003: 68, 63). Even among these parliamentary democracies, Westminster is often presented as relatively weak (e.g. Martin and Vanberg 2011). While the contrast is well worn, and insufficiently tested, it remains the case that for most academics 'the US Congress and the British Parliament serve as the emblematic examples of a strong Congress and weak parliament respectively' (Kreppel 2014: 95).

Legislative institutions have many functions, including holding the government publicly to account and acting as a debating forum for the nation. In one classic account Bagehot (2001 [1867]: 100) particularly emphasized the House of Commons' 'elective function', given its decisive role in who should form the government, downplaying its lawmaking role. Likewise, John Stuart Mill (1998 [1861]: 282) suggested that 'instead of the function of governing, for which it is radically unfit, the proper office of a representative assembly is to watch and control the government: to throw the light of publicity on its acts'. It is these roles, rather than Westminster's contribution to legislation, that tend to be emphasized by its defenders. Explicitly responding to Richardson and Jordan's allegation of 'post-parliamentary democracy', Judge (1993) argued that Britain remained a fundamentally 'parliamentary state', where Westminster provided a legitimating frame within which the executive must take decisions. In asking whether parliament 'matters', Norton (1993: 205) similarly emphasized legitimation, and other key roles such as representation and executive oversight, while concluding that parliament's role in lawmaking was 'essentially at the margins'. More recently Tomkins (2003) has suggested that by focusing on policy decisions we have lost sight of what parliament is 'for'. But it is questionable in practice whether policy-making can be separated from these wider parliamentary roles. And while Westminster and other legislatures may not often publicly clash with their respective governments, they may still be central to how policy is set. Whether parliament is truly a 'legislator' hence depends very much on the interpretation of that term.

While specialist scholars frequently comment on the distinct functions of parliaments, there has been relatively less reflection on distinct forms of parliamentary influence or power. In the wider politics literature, in contrast, debates on power frequently note that it is multifaceted. Beyond the power to force change, the well-known power of 'anticipated reactions' (Friedrich 1968) recognizes that one actor may think through in advance what another actor is likely to accept, and adjust their plans accordingly. In a very widely cited text, Steven Lukes proposed that there were three 'faces' of power, of which the third was for one actor not even to contemplate certain courses of action, having internalized another actor's preferences—suggesting that 'the supreme exercise of power' is 'to get another or others to have the desires you want them to have' (1974: 23). Other authors have disputed Lukes's framework, variously suggesting that there are four faces (Digeser 1992), that power should be seen as persuasive, not just coercive (Scott 2008), that it can be exercised both positively and negatively (Haugaard 2012), and that too much attention has focused on 'power over', at the expense of 'power to' or indeed 'power with' (Allen 1998, Isaac 1987).

Despite widespread acknowledgement that there may be many complex forces at work in legislatures, these various concepts of power have rarely been applied (though for some emphasis on Lukes's three faces, see Norton 1993: 134, 203). The main exception is the potential importance of parliamentary 'anticipated reactions', which has long been noted (e.g. Blondel 1970, Mezey 1979). In a classic work on the US Congress, Mayhew (1974: 107) observed that 'presidents, bureaucrats and judges, anticipating trouble with Congress, take action to avoid it'. Such defensive action by governments seems likely to be even more important in parliamentary systems, where ministers depend on legislative support in order to survive. Hence parliament's impact on policy may occur partly at the early stages of policy formulation, before bills have been formally published and introduced.

These kinds of influence are very difficult to demonstrate. As John (2012: 41) notes, the counterfactual of what would have happened in the absence of parliament is not available, making a comprehensive assessment of parliamentary policy impact 'an almost impossible research task'. Nonetheless, scholars can at least partially get at such questions in certain settings. For example, Manow and Burkhart (2007) have shown that German governments facing hostile second chamber majorities exercise greater legislative self-restraint, by proposing fewer controversial bills. However, it is the first chamber, which possesses the confidence vote, that may induce far greater self-restraint—and this would be far harder to detect. The largest study of the legislative process at Westminster to date—described more fully in the next chapter—found that amendments moved in parliament by ministers in fact often responded to points raised at earlier stages of the process by non-government parliamentarians (Griffith 1974). This kind of influence is traceable with detailed study, and shows that on-the-record influence may not be all that it seems. Nonetheless, parliamentary influence is likely to take far less visible forms which can be extremely important.

If parliament exercises different forms of visible and less visible power, further questions arise—about which particular groups of parliamentary actors contribute and how. Parliament is not a unitary actor, but a complex organization within which exist many competing political groups. Indeed, the size and complexity of the legislature, and its difficulty in speaking with one voice, is often seen as a weakness in the face of the far more unified executive (Ekins 2012, Waldron 1999, Wright 2004). This book is organized according to groups of different actors, in order to explore the diverse roles that they play in the legislative process. The classic view in Britain suggests that government backbenchers are the key group at Westminster, and that their influence is primarily exercised behind the scenes (King 1976). Others such as the opposition have classically been seen as weak. But such analyses largely pre-date the kind of important changes outlined above. This makes assumptions about legislative power at Westminster worthy of re-examination.

Questions Answered by the Book

As should already be clear, this book is designed to serve various purposes. First, it provides a general text on the legislative process intended to be informative for those starting from a fairly low level of knowledge. Second, it reports on a major piece of research about that process, informed by study of 12 case study bills. These case studies allow us to illustrate the contribution of different actors, to aid understanding both about specific groups and how they interact. Third, the case studies allow us to address larger generic questions about the power of parliament and the dynamics of parliamentary influence. Although we draw on specific evidence and examples, our purpose is to illustrate fundamental dynamics of the Westminster parliament, which may also hold lessons for similar institutions in other settings.

Throughout the book, we seek in particular to address the questions set out below.

1. How is the legislative process structured at Westminster? This most basic question concerns straightforward facts about the Westminster legislative process. Particularly in Chapter 2, but also gradually in other places throughout the book, we set out the details of key procedures and legislative rules. By illustrating through case studies, we indicate differences, for example, between the various legislative stages and types of amendments that can be proposed, and between practices in the Commons and the Lords. We discuss the formal functions of different groups (such as ministers, civil servants, and committees), and how parliament interacts with others outside. These aspects of the book will be of most interest to those who are less familiar with the process but, through illustration with real policy examples, are intended to be engaging for both expert and non-expert readers.

2. What objectives do different actors in parliament pursue during the legislative process, and what strategies do they employ to achieve these? Different actors who take part in the legislative process clearly play diverse roles. Government ministers most obviously want to promote their legislation and see it pass through parliament. Other parliamentarians may wish to amend or block government bills.

But the motivations of those who contribute to the legislative process are more complex than many might expect, and are not limited simply to dealing with the bill at hand. We examine how the legislative process is used by actors in parliament to achieve various (often non-legislative) objectives, paying particular attention to the motivations behind non-government amendments. Drawing out these distinct perspectives and contributions is facilitated by structuring the book by different groups of parliamentary actors.

3. *To what extent do different actors wield influence in the legislative process? How do they work both together and separately to achieve policy change?* While the book emphasizes that actors use the legislative process for a variety of purposes, a key motivation for non-government parliamentarians is obviously achieving policy change. Through careful analysis of the passage of amendments we explore who is responsible for the ideas implemented through changes made to bills in parliament. Most amendments that succeed are formally proposed in the name of government ministers, but we trace the extent to which these are in fact responses to proposals from non-government parliamentarians, and who those parliamentarians are. This question is, however, not straightforward—MPs and peers from different groups often work together, either by accident or design. In addition, as captured in the next question, there are many other means of influencing legislation beyond amendments.

4. *What are the dynamics of legislative influence? To what extent is this visible (particularly through amendments), and how much instead occurs behind the scenes?* Although we draw on plentiful data about legislative amendments, we also demonstrate that it is crucial to look beyond these in order to understand how parliamentary influence works. If ministers propose amendments which were actually inspired by non-government parliamentarians, this already indicates some influence not easily visible from the public record. By drawing on evidence from interviews, in particular, we can trace the extent to which influence occurs behind the scenes. This includes not only amendments, but also—as discussed above—the power of 'anticipated reactions', plus the potential for one player (in this case parliament) to shape the ambitions of another (in this case government), even at unconscious levels. Interviews can help to tease out such dynamics at least to some extent. In addition, parliament can have other less tangible effects, for example through determining which aspects of bills get most public exposure.

5. *How do the politics of the legislative process differ between the Lords and the Commons, and between coalition and single-party government?* As well as looking at the contributions of specific political groupings in parliament, it is important to consider the effects of more structural factors. The legislative procedures of the two chambers of parliament differ substantially, but so too do their politics. In the House of Commons, the government generally has a partisan majority, but the post-1999 House of Lords is instead a 'no overall control' chamber where hostile majorities can far more easily form against the government. By tracing bills through both chambers, we can reflect on differences and similarities between them, as well as considering how they work together in shaping legislation. In addition, while single-party government is the norm at Westminster the book covers the

period 2005–12, hence spanning the end of the long period of Labour government and the first two years of the Conservative/Liberal Democrat coalition. The Conservatives won a majority by themselves in 2015, but in 2017 fell short of one, and many expect more coalitions in future. Our study allows some early reflections on how the political dynamics of the legislative process can differ between periods of single-party and coalition government.

6. Overall, how influential is parliament in the Westminster legislative process? Our final question is a very central one—of whether the Westminster parliament is genuinely influential on legislation or not. This is important not only for understanding UK politics, but also the dynamics of parliamentary systems in general, given Westminster's prominence in the comparative literature. By exploring the contributions of different groups and their interactions, the different forms of influence, its variation across the chambers and between different forms of government, we gradually build up a picture of parliament's influence overall. The case study bills underwent numerous changes during their passage through parliament, some of them very significant. This in itself suggests that parliament is far from marginal. In fact, putting all of the evidence together, in terms of the various stages of the policy process, and facets of visible and less visible influence, we conclude that Westminster is a very influential institution, and in very important ways a 'legislator'.

Research Methods

The results reported in this book are the product of a major research project, conducted at the Constitution Unit, University College London, over a period of several years.[5] This traced the progress of 12 government bills through all stages of their parliamentary passage at Westminster during the period 2005–12. We focus on government bills (rather than other sources of law such as private members' bills and 'secondary legislation'), because these account for the great majority of important legal changes agreed.[6] Our sampling strategy and methods are set out more fully in Appendix A.

In terms of sampling, the case studies were chosen to be as representative as possible, and are quite diverse, though clearly 12 bills cannot adequately capture all of the variety that exists. But the bills differed by parliamentary session, sponsoring department, size, and level of controversy. Seven were drawn from the period of Labour government 2005–10, and five from the first (two-year) parliamentary session under the coalition 2010–12. The 12 bills were as follows:

- Identity Cards Bill (Labour, 2005–06)
- Health Bill (Labour, 2005–06)
- Corporate Manslaughter and Corporate Homicide Bill (Labour, 2005–07)[7]
- Further Education and Training Bill (Labour, 2006–07)
- Employment Bill (Labour, 2007–08)
- Saving Gateway Accounts Bill (Labour, 2008–09)

- Energy Bill (Labour, 2009–10)
- Identity Documents Bill (coalition, 2010–12)
- Savings Accounts and Health in Pregnancy Grant Bill (coalition, 2010–12)
- Budget Responsibility and National Audit Bill (coalition, 2010–12)
- Public Bodies Bill (coalition, 2010–12)
- Welfare Reform Bill (coalition, 2010–12)

Our analysis was both quantitative and qualitative. Like Griffith (1974), a key element was tracing the source of successful amendments, using analysis based on the public record. A total of 4,361 amendments were proposed to the bills during their passage through the two chambers of parliament. We logged various key details of each amendment in a database. A crucial step was then identifying connections between similar amendments at different legislative stages, in order to trace the ultimate outcome of all proposals made. As already indicated, non-government amendments at one stage of the parliamentary legislative process may be followed by government concessionary amendments at a subsequent stage. To capture this, we linked amendments together in what we termed legislative 'strands'. Later in the book we present figures for these strands, as well as for amendments themselves.

While Griffith conducted some background interviews, we use this kind of qualitative evidence far more centrally than he did. We conducted over 120 interviews with key protagonists on the bills, including ministers, civil servants, opposition spokespeople, backbenchers, non-government parliamentarians, parliamentary staff, and representatives of outside groups. We also studied the parliamentary record for each bill, including all relevant debates, committee proceedings, and select committee reports—as well as other background information including government consultation documents. The interviews enabled us to get beyond all of the above and explore off-the-record developments, such as government's initial preparation of bills, and the numerous private meetings that go on between ministers, civil servants, and parliamentarians during their passage. Our interviews were conducted on a non-attributable basis, so individual sources are not named in the text. But a full list of interviewees is given in Appendix B. Interview evidence is frequently quoted throughout the book to demonstrate some of the nuances of how actors engaged with the process.

Organization, Style, and How to Use This Book

The remainder of the book comprises nine chapters. With the exception of the first and last of these, which are more general, each is focused on a particular type of actor in the legislative process. This enables us to explore the different roles that these actors have, as well as their contributions to shaping the bills. While the book is clearly intended to stand as a whole, we also recognize that some readers may wish to focus on only certain aspects. We have therefore structured each of our chapters as far as possible to stand alone. For example, those wanting a basic outline of the Westminster legislative process could read Chapter 2, while those interested in our conclusions about parliamentary influence could go directly to Chapter 10. Readers with interests in certain types of actor may wish to read selectively from Chapters 3 to 9.

Chapter 2 provides a basic summary of the legislative process at Westminster, and a more detailed overview of the case study bills. It starts with a short introduction to both chambers of parliament, and their membership during our period of study 2005–12. It then summarizes some of the previous studies of the legislative process, at Westminster and beyond, on which we build. This is followed by a short description of each of the 12 bills and their origins. The second half of the chapter provides more detailed discussion of the legislative process stage by stage, and the nature of legislative amendments. Here we present some summary statistics about the passage of the case study bills, including numbers of amendments proposed and agreed at each stage. This illustrates some of the diversity in the process, and provides key background on which subsequent chapters will draw.

Chapters 3–8 each discuss the contribution of one specific group of actors to the legislative process, including specifically through changes made to the bills in parliament. We begin in Chapter 3 with the government. Here we introduce the role of different government actors—such as ministers, civil servants, and government lawyers—and summarize what existing literature tells us about them. Because all of our case studies are government bills, we also focus here on government's preparation before bills are introduced to parliament, including for example the degree of consultation during the formulation of policy. We then discuss internal government negotiation over the introduction of bills to parliament, and the roles of government actors during the parliamentary legislative process itself. This leads to an initial discussion of government amendments and their sources.

In Chapter 4 we move on to the next most visible actor in parliament: the opposition. This chapter discusses how opposition parties organize themselves, and the classic presentation by scholars of the role that the Westminster opposition plays. We then summarize opposition frontbench responses to the 12 case study bills, showing that there is not one single 'opposition mode' of an adversarial kind, and that government bills can present opposition parliamentarians with some difficult dilemmas. After this we focus on opposition amendments and their motivations—emphasizing that not all of these are sincere attempts at legislative change. Nonetheless, opposition politicians clearly do also pursue legislative change, and we show that they played a role in many of the biggest changes made to the bills in parliament. The various means of opposition influence, illustrated with examples from the case study bills, are discussed in the final main section of the chapter.

The next two chapters are structured in quite similar ways to this, with respect to actors who can be central to decision-making in the Commons and the Lords respectively. Chapter 5 focuses on government backbenchers—who are less visible than the opposition, but often assumed by scholars to be far more influential. We explore backbench responses to the bills, amendments proposed by government backbenchers, and the central influence that they exert, often at a less visible level, as 'pivotal' actors in the Commons. Chapter 6 focuses on a less well-studied group—non-party parliamentarians. Very few independent MPs are elected to the

House of Commons, but the House of Lords includes large numbers of members who do not take a party whip. As we show, these members can be important—both through their legislative amendments and their more subtle influence on parliamentary culture and decisions.

Chapter 7 goes beyond the walls of Westminster, to consider the contribution to the legislative process of outside 'pressure groups'. Such actors have received much attention from scholars of public policy, but are generally thought to focus their attention primarily on government, not parliament. However, changes in parliament—such as the growth of committees, and increasing independence of government backbenchers—have provided new entry points for outside groups. We summarize the different kinds of pressure groups, briefly discuss their organization, and survey their contributions to the various forms of influence exercised by parliament on the case study bills. The analysis shows that groups are closely involved at all stages of the parliamentary legislative process, and that parliament is an important forum for them either to press for change, or to defend policies previously negotiated behind the scenes.

Chapters 8 and 9 focus on cross-party groupings at Westminster, which are traditionally seen as weak. We start in Chapter 8 with select committees, whose growth is widely cited as one of the most important recent changes made. Although these committees play little formal part in the legislative process (with the 'committee stage' of bills instead debated in other forums) we find their connections with it to be surprisingly extensive. Like pressure groups, the select committees crucially provide expertise which supports and strengthens other elementary actors. The chapter explores the extent to which they were cited during debates on the bills, and the ways in which they affected the policies finally agreed. Chapter 9 focuses instead on more informal cross-party working, and connections between the groups discussed in previous chapters. We discuss the different forms of cross-party working, the nature of cross-party amendments, and the extent to which cross-party groups influence legislative outcomes. We find that the degree of cross-party working at Westminster is in fact relatively high, which is crucial to parliament's policy influence.

Chapter 10 closes the book, and focuses on parliament's overall influence on government legislation. Here we draw the various analyses together, presenting our general conclusions—including on the six questions set out above. As well as building on examples in previous chapters we present some further evidence from our interviews about how those involved in the process inside and outside parliament view parliamentary influence. In summary, we find that Westminster's impact on government bills in terms of amendments is significant—many important changes were made to the case study bills—but its overall influence on the process goes far further. We suggest that forcing amendments is only one of six 'faces' of parliamentary power exercised by legislatures in the process of agreeing government bills. At Westminster, these apply to differing degrees to different parliamentary actors, who combine to subject government bills to scrutiny. Parliament has a significant power of conscious anticipated reactions, and its concerns are also likely to be taken into account relatively unconsciously in the preparation of government bills. Even when provisions in bills pass largely intact, parliament hence cannot be assumed to be powerless. Parliamentarians also have agenda-setting power, which can influence policy-making at earlier stages and determine which topics within bills receive the greatest attention. Once an issue is on the agenda, parliamentarians then have a power to require government to account for its decisions publicly. Finally, when members choose to support the government's position, this must also be seen as an active choice. We conclude that once all six forms of power are taken into account, the Westminster parliament is indeed a 'legislator' of a surprisingly effective kind.

Notes

1. In the Lords 3,678 amendments were tabled (House of Lords Legislation Office 2016). In the Commons, over 4,600 amendments were tabled, although this figure excludes ping-pong stages and may include a small number on private and hybrid bills (figures provided by House of Commons Public Bill Office).
2. 'Rebalancing power in British politics', *Financial Times*, 1 June 2009.
3. House of Commons Hansard, 13 July 2000, column 1084.
4. Perhaps connectedly, research by the Hansard Society (2016) consistently shows that only one-quarter to one-third of people are satisfied with how parliament works.
5. For fuller details of the project, see the Acknowledgements at the beginning of the book. Earlier outputs based on this research include Russell, Gover, and Wollter (2016) and Russell et al. (2017).
6. For a brief explanation of secondary legislation, see Chapter 3. This has become markedly more controversial in recent years, particularly since the end of our study period. For an academic review of delegated legislation processes, see Page (2001). On private members' bills, see Brazier and Fox (2010).
7. The Corporate Manslaughter and Corporate Homicide Bill began its passage during the 2005–06 session, and was 'carried over' to complete its passage during the 2006–07 session.

2

Overview of the Legislative Process and Case Studies

In this first substantive chapter of the book we introduce key aspects of the legislative process at Westminster, and give a brief summary of our 12 case study bills. Those already familiar with parliament may feel able to skip some sections; but for others the chapter will provide essential background to understanding the processes described in the rest of the book—or may even serve as a useful standalone introduction. The descriptions of the case study bills in this chapter provide essential background for all readers, and start to demonstrate the diversity of legislative proposals that parliament is asked to consider.

The chapter begins with a very basic summary of the structure of the Westminster parliament, and how the institution works—particularly with respect to legislation. This describes both the House of Commons and the House of Lords, and how the two chambers work together. It thus begins to address one of the central questions in the book, in terms of the differences and similarities between them. Aside from the obvious difference of one being elected while the other is not, the chambers are also quite distinct both politically and procedurally. Having introduced these basics, we then turn to a discussion of how the legislative process tends to be viewed by academics, and what previous studies have shown. As already indicated in Chapter 1, the dominant view is that the Westminster parliament is relatively non-influential. But that has been challenged to some extent by specialist scholars, and may also have been affected by recent changes in parliament. This question of legislative influence is one of the central themes in the book.

In the second half of the chapter we introduce the 12 case study bills, which had very different origins, attracted different levels of controversy, and (partly as a consequence) received different treatments in parliament. We summarize the nature of the bills and provide some key indicators—such as their timing and size. Using them for illustration, we then provide a more detailed general summary of the Westminster legislative process stage by stage, followed by a discussion of legislative amendments. Here we begin to introduce some more detailed data on the bills—including the varying amounts of time devoted to debate, the number of amendments proposed and agreed, and the outcome of amendments and legislative 'strands'. The detail of what happened during these debates, and who was responsible for change resulting from these amendments and strands, is further explored throughout the remainder of the book.

Legislation at Westminster. First edition. Meg Russell and Daniel Gover. © Meg Russell and Daniel Gover 2017. Published 2017 by Oxford University Press.

Westminster and the Legislative Process

In order to reach the statute book (i.e. become law), all bills must normally be explicitly approved by both chambers of parliament: the House of Commons and the House of Lords. The House of Commons, whose members are known as MPs (i.e. Members of Parliament) is wholly elected, and enjoys certain privileges in the legislative process. The majority of bills begin there, passing to the Lords afterwards, and by convention bills dealing wholly with financial matters always do so. But just under one-third of government bills during our study period began in the Lords, passing to the Commons afterwards.[1] For bills starting in the Commons, any objections by the Lords can *in extremis* be overridden (as described later in the chapter). But although disputes arise fairly frequently between the chambers over the detail of legislation, these are usually resolved instead by negotiation, during a process colloquially known as 'ping-pong' (whereby a bill shuttles backwards and forwards until a final version is agreed).

Members of the House of Commons are elected at least every five years using the electoral system commonly referred to as 'first past the post'.[2] In the 2005 parliament there were 646 constituencies and in the 2010 parliament there were 650, each returning one candidate on the basis of who won the largest number of local votes. The resulting party make-up of the Commons in 2005 and 2010 is shown in Table 2.1. In 2005 Labour won a comfortable majority of seats and was thus able to form a single-party government; in contrast in 2010 no party won an overall majority, and a coalition government was formed between the Conservatives and Liberal Democrats. Historically, single-party government has been the norm (and was returned to in 2015). Arrangements in the Commons are therefore built to some extent on this expectation, and privilege in particular the government and the largest opposition party. Nonetheless, coalition government was relatively easily accommodated in 2010–15 (see Yong 2012). Compared to many other parliaments, Commons procedures also allow significant freedom for individual backbenchers to participate—for example through tabling amendments, asking parliamentary questions, and sponsoring debates.[3]

The House of Lords is not elected, and instead contains members chosen via three different routes. The majority are 'life peers', having been appointed to membership for life by the monarch, on advice of the Prime Minister. The chamber hence includes members proposed by consecutive Prime Ministers, many of whom are considered to be subject experts.[4] An additional 92 members are chosen as representatives of the hereditary peers (i.e. those who have inherited titles)—a group which dominated the chamber's membership until 1999.[5] Third, the chamber includes 26 Church of England bishops and archbishops (further discussed in Chapter 6). While the number of hereditary peers and bishops is limited, there is no limit on the number of life peers, so the overall size of the chamber is not fixed. Because there were numerous appointments to the chamber after both the 2005 and 2010 general elections, Table 2.1 gives membership for the following January, by which point these members had taken their seats. As shown, neither the 2005 nor the 2010

Table 2.1 Party breakdown of the House of Commons and House of Lords in the 2005 and 2010 parliaments

	House of Commons, May 2005		House of Lords, January 2006*		
	N	%	N	%	% of party members
Labour	355	54.9	208	29.0	42.6
Conservative	198	30.7	205	28.6	42.0
Liberal Democrat	62	9.6	74	10.3	15.2
SNP	6	0.9	—	—	—
DUP**	9	1.4	—	—	—
UUP**	1	0.2	—	—	—
Sinn Fein	5	0.8	—	—	—
Plaid Cymru	3	0.5	—	—	—
SDLP	3	0.5	—	—	—
Green	—	—	1	0.1	0.2
Respect	1	0.2	—	—	—
Crossbench**	—	—	193	26.9	—
Bishop	—	—	26	3.6	—
Other†	3	0.5	10	1.4	—
Total	**646**		**717**		

	House of Commons, May 2010		House of Lords, January 2011*		
	N	%	N	%	% of party members
Labour	258	39.7	233	30.9	44.0
Conservative	306	47.1	204	27.1	38.6
Liberal Democrat	57	8.8	83	11.0	15.7
SNP	6	0.9	—	—	—
DUP	8	1.2	4	0.5	0.8
UUP	—	—	3	0.4	0.6
Sinn Fein	5	0.8	—	—	—
Plaid Cymru	3	0.5	—	—	—
SDLP	3	0.5	—	—	—
Alliance	1	0.2	—	—	—
Green	1	0.2	—	—	—
UKIP	—	—	2	0.3	0.4
Crossbench	—	—	182	24.2	—
Bishop	—	—	25	3.3	—
Other†	2	0.3	17	2.2	—
Total	**650**		**753**		

* Date chosen to allow post-election appointments to have come into effect. Excludes members disqualified or on leave of absence.

** In 2006 members of Northern Ireland parties sat in the House of Lords as Crossbenchers, but by 2011 the group had tightened its membership criteria to exclude any party representatives.

† Other in House of Commons comprised the Speaker and two independents (Peter Law and Richard Taylor) in 2005, and the Speaker and one independent (Lady Sylvia Hermon) in 2010. In the House of Lords this group includes various nonaffiliated members, many of whom have split from their parties.

Sources: House of Commons Library, House of Lords Information Office.

government had a majority in the Lords, partly due to the presence of numerous independent 'Crossbenchers'. However, the coalition was relatively stronger in the Lords than Labour had been, since it had the support of two political parties.

This difference in party make-up is probably the most crucial one between the two chambers, as it means that the government can generally depend on the support of the House of Commons, but the same does not apply to the Lords. In the 2005 parliament, Labour could be easily outnumbered in the Lords by the two opposition parties combined, and Liberal Democrat votes were usually crucial to the outcome of Lords 'divisions' (i.e. recorded votes). As further discussed in Chapter 6, when the Liberal Democrats entered government after the 2010 election, independent Crossbenchers instead became the chamber's key 'pivotal voters'. While the government's partisan majority makes defeats on the floor of the House of Commons extremely unusual (there were just eight in the period 2005–12), both Labour and the coalition were defeated fairly frequently in the Lords in this period. During the 2005–10 parliament there were 175 such government defeats and during the 2010–12 session there were 48. All but 12 of these were on legislation (Russell 2013: 135).

The two parliamentary chambers perform broadly similar functions. Both hold regular question times with ministers, host different kinds of debates, and organize members into specialist 'select committees' which conduct inquiries and produce reports containing policy recommendations. All of these activities contribute to holding the government to account for its actions, and all differ significantly in terms of detailed procedure between the chambers. Both chambers also spend a substantial amount of their time dealing with legislation. Most of this concentrates on bills proposed by the government, though members of both chambers can also introduce their own bills, few of which reach the statute book.[6]

The period between general elections is referred to as a 'parliament', which is in turn split into 'sessions', generally lasting one year (although the session immediately after the 2010 election was unusual, lasting two years).[7] The breakdown of time in the chambers themselves is shown in Table 2.2 for the fairly typical session 2008–09. We see that the two chambers sat for a similar number of hours, and that the proportion of time dedicated to government bills in both was quite dominant, but far more so in the Lords than the Commons. The norm remains for most bills to pass through parliament in a single legislative session (though the capacity does now exist for a bill to be 'carried over' from one session to the next—see Kelly 2015a). It is primarily because of this that legislation can start in either chamber—if it all started in the Commons, then that chamber would be overburdened at the beginning of each session, and the Lords very quiet, while the Lords would be overburdened at the end. But the option of a Commons override does not exist on bills introduced via the Lords (as discussed further below), so ministers try to start only less controversial bills in that chamber. Nonetheless as our case studies—particularly the Public Bodies Bill—show, such bills do not always prove as uncontroversial as ministers would like.

As with other activities, the procedures for legislation in the two chambers are similar, but nonetheless differ in important ways. Bills go through a series of 'stages', where the 'first reading' is purely formal, the 'second reading' focuses largely on the

Table 2.2 Distribution of time between broad categories of business in the Commons chamber and Lords chamber 2008–09

Category of business	House of Commons		House of Lords	
	Hours spent	% of total	Hours spent	% of total
Government bills	258	25	479	53
Private members' bills and motions	78	7	31	3
Delegated legislation	20	2	40	5
Ministerial statements	90	9	52	6
Oral questions	117	11	63	7
Debates	342	33	202	22
Procedural matters	11	1	5	1
Miscellaneous other business	132	13	35	3
Total	1,049	100	907	100

Sources: House of Commons Sessional Return 2008–09; House of Lords Sessional Statistics on Business and Membership 2010–12.

Figures exclude time spent in Westminster Hall in the Commons, grand committee in the Lords, and any other committees 'off the floor' in both chambers.

broad themes in the bill, while the 'committee stage' and 'report stage' concentrate more closely on the detail. Finally, there is a 'third reading', which differs slightly between the two chambers. These stages are outlined more fully later in the chapter. A key difference between the chambers is that the Lords is often described as being 'self-regulating', whereas the Commons is more closely governed by the Speaker and by formal rules. Notably, in the House of Commons the Speaker or committee chair can 'select' and 'call' amendments for debate; in the Lords this does not apply, so all amendments may be debated. Likewise, there is no formal system of 'programming' legislation (i.e. setting a rigid timetable for the stages of a bill) in the Lords. Especially when added to the lack of a government majority, these factors make it a far less certain environment than the Commons for ministers to navigate.

Established Understanding of the Legislative Process, and Previous Studies

The legislative process is central to policy-making, and hence widely reported in the academic literature, though often at a fairly general level. We saw in Chapter 1 that summaries in textbooks covering British politics (e.g. Leach, Coxall, and Robins 2011, Moran 2015) and law (e.g. Harlow and Rawlings 2009) often give the impression that Westminster's impact on government bills is relatively small, and this is also true of the comparative literature. Specialist texts on the workings of parliament aimed at both academic and more general readers (e.g. Blackburn and Kennon 2003, Norton 2013, Rogers and Walters 2015, Rush 2005) provide significantly greater procedural detail, and some texts for lawyers focus on legislation in particular (e.g. Greenberg 2011, Zander 2015).[8] But all of these have relatively little up-to-date research about the parliamentary legislative process on which to draw.

The classic study of the process remains J. A. G. Griffith's (1974) *Parliamentary Scrutiny of Government Bills*, which comprised very close analysis of all bills passing through parliament in the sessions 1967–68, 1968–69, and 1970–71. Griffith was particularly interested in questions of parliamentary influence, and explored these primarily through study of the success of amendments in the House of Commons. He included some coverage of the House of Lords, though without systematically tracing links between amendments in the two chambers. Other scholars subsequently applied similar methods to analyse in detail the passage of government bills through the Lords in the 1988–89 session (Drewry and Brock 1993, Miers and Brock 1993).

Griffith concluded that parliament's influence on legislation was 'by no means negligible' (1974: 256); for example, he suggested that at least 15 per cent of government amendments agreed at House of Commons report stage responded to policy demands from backbench or opposition MPs at the previous committee stage.[9] But he nonetheless argued that concessions were made 'largely on [the government's] own terms'. In addition, it is quite clear from these early studies that the government had significant freedom to use amendments to rewrite its own legislation following introduction to parliament—with very many not inspired by parliamentary pressure at all. Miers and Brock did not attempt to quantify the number of government amendments in the Lords that responded to earlier suggestions from non-government peers, though they made clear that this happened fairly frequently. However, they also found that peers were frustrated by government's 'legislate as you go' approach, citing two bills that had over 100 pages of new material added in the Commons (1993: 134). This suggested a disregard for the importance of parliamentary scrutiny, and an assumption by ministers that their legislation would ultimately always be accepted.

These studies were important and insightful but are clearly now dated. Since their publication, a good deal in the British parliament has changed—as scholars widely acknowledge. In the late 1970s the House of Commons select committee system was significantly boosted, and has subsequently continued to develop in important ways (Drewry 1985b, Kelso 2009, Norton 1998b, Russell 2011). As further discussed in Chapter 8, while the select committees primarily have responsibility for executive oversight and investigations, rather than the scrutiny of legislation, they may have significant effects—including on parliament's wider culture. Since the changes in the Commons, a distinct system of select committees has gradually developed in the Lords as well (Russell 2013, Shell 1992, Torrance 2012). More recently—as further described later in the chapter—important changes were made to Commons public bill committees in 2006, to introduce evidence-taking from outside experts (Levy 2010, Thompson 2015). Another development, carefully charted by Norton (1975, 1980) and subsequently Cowley (2002, 2005), is the growing independence of voting (or 'rebelliousness') among government backbench MPs. On top of this came the transformation of the House of Lords, from a largely hereditary institution long dominated by the Conservative Party, which used its power very cautiously (Bromhead 1958, Shell 1992, Shell and Beamish 1993), to a far more politically balanced chamber where members feel more confident to challenge government policy (Russell 2010, 2013).

Hence there are persuasive reasons to return to the question of legislation at Westminster, the dynamics of which may well have changed. Both the workings of parliament and academic approaches to the study of parliaments have developed significantly since Griffith's book was published. Nonetheless, in a comparative context the ambition of his study continues to stand up remarkably well. The cataloguing of thousands of amendments without access to modern computing power is truly impressive, as is his focus on the original sources of ideas in government amendments. Even today, the measures of legislative influence quoted in the wider comparative literature are often far more crude. Olson's (1994: 84) '90% rule' is often cited, which suggests that '[i]n most democratic legislatures . . . the cabinet proposes at least 90% of the legislative agenda, and at least 90% of what it proposes is adopted'. Various studies have got little further than exploring such claims by cataloguing the success rates of government and non-government bills in different settings (e.g. Arter 1985, Capano and Giuliani 2001, Maurer 1999, Pettai and Madise 2006, Zubek 2011), while others have dug deeper to explore the success of government and non-government amendments (e.g. Damgaard and Jensen 2006, Kerrouche 2006). But it is decades since Blondel (1970) pointed out that both opposition and government amendments can indicate legislative 'viscosity'—that is, the policy resistance demonstrated by parliament—because government amendments might be driven by pressures from others in the legislature. Further complication comes from the fact that not all amendments are equal—some make relatively trivial changes while others can be outright policy reversals. Plus, as Griffith (1974: 37) noted in relation to non-government actors, '[a]mendments may have one or more of a great variety of purposes'—so cannot necessarily be interpreted as sincere attempts to change a bill. We seek to address all of these elements of complexity in our analysis.

Such factors mean that assessing who has influence in the legislative process requires careful study. Detailed amendment analyses similar to Griffith's have since been applied in some other settings, most notably the European Parliament. These have accounted, for example, for policy substantiveness of different amendments, and the links between those at one legislative stage and the next (e.g. Häge and Kaeding 2007, Kasack 2004, Kreppel 1999, Tsebelis et al. 2001). At the domestic level, Shephard and Cairney (2005) demonstrated how roughly one-quarter of substantive executive-sponsored amendments in the Scottish Parliament were inspired by non-executive parliamentarians, while O'Dowd (2010) conducted a more limited analysis in the Irish Oireachtas with similar conclusions. In the US, Barrett (2008) and Barrett and Eshbaugh-Soba (2007) have applied slightly different techniques to explore the extent to which legislation is subject to detailed amendment in the legislature. But in most national domestic settings there has been remarkably little detailed study of this kind.

As discussed in Chapter 1, one of the reasons that parliaments are dismissed as relatively powerless is that their influence may be largely invisible from the public record—even with careful research that tracks legislative amendments. A framework commonly used in the public policy literature (though also commonly disputed: see John 2012: 18–20, 28), describes the policy-making process as a series of distinct phases or stages: such as agenda setting, policy formulation, decision-making, implementation, and evaluation. This perspective is helpful when thinking about where legislatures fit in the process. Their classic role is at the 'decision-making' stage, when approval must be given to legislation. But in a relatively rare study bringing together theories from public policy with legislative studies, Olson and Mezey (1991: 20) hypothesized that '[t]he policy activity of parliaments will be most extensive at the implementation stage, intermediate at the stages of gestation and deliberation and decision, and least at the proposal stage'. This was tested with reference to several country case studies using largely qualitative methods, and the authors concluded that the evidence was mixed (Mezey 1991). The chapter in this volume on the UK emphasized the cyclical nature of the policy process—and how parliamentary scrutiny of implementation may help to set the future policy agenda (Wood 1991).

Since Griffith's (1974) work, no equivalent large-scale quantitative analysis of legislative amendments has been conducted at Westminster.[10] Nonetheless, some researchers have brought parts of his study up to date, or explored questions of legislative influence that he did not address. Russell (2013), and Russell and Sciara (2007, 2008), have traced and analysed the effects of government defeats in the House of Lords, finding that—although government could in principle overturn all such defeats in the House of Commons—almost half of those during the period 1999–2012 went on to be wholly or largely accepted. Most recently, Thompson (2013, 2015) conducted an impressive study of House of Commons public bill committees over the period 2000–10, including analysis of some 30,000 amendments. She found that only 0.6 per cent of non-government amendments were agreed to in committee—which appears to be a significantly lower proportion than that recorded by Griffith (1974)—but that there had been an 'enormous increase in the number of undertakings' given by ministers to consider change following backbench and opposition proposals (Thompson 2015: 124).[11] In total almost a thousand such undertakings were traced, demonstrating that 'the persuasive impact of committees is often seen long after a bill has been reported back to the House' (ibid.: 8). Nonetheless, this analysis was limited almost entirely to the House of Commons committee and report stages, not accounting for any links to the House of Lords. In more qualitative terms, a major analysis conducted by the Hansard Society analysed the passage of five case study bills through both chambers, and suggested that parliament was indeed influential. The authors specifically drew attention to links between the chambers, noting how 'the government resists amendments in the Commons and deliberately saves up concessions for the Lords' (Brazier, Kalitowski, and Rosenblatt 2008: 185). Other qualitative studies have tended to be limited to single bills (e.g. Crewe 2015, Kettell and Cairney 2010).

So, there are reasons to suspect that the British parliament may be more influential on legislation than in the past, and specifically that it may be taken more seriously by ministers than in Griffith's day. But a full bicameral analysis has never actually been conducted.[12] Additionally, studies have tended to be either largely quantitative or largely qualitative, while a combination of these methods is required to understand the dynamics of the process fully. In particular, insights from government insiders are needed. As emphasized in Chapter 1, parliament may have significant power through 'anticipated reactions', and shaping bills before they are submitted to the legislature. Brazier, Kalitowski, and Rosenblatt (2008: 175) noted such dynamics, suggesting that '[t]his intangible aspect of the legislative process is frequently Parliament's most potent tool'. But such effects are of course impossible to trace by only looking at amendments. Hence our analysis uses a combination of quantitative amendment analysis and more qualitative evidence from interviews and other sources.

The 12 Case Study Bills

As already indicated, our 12 case study bills were chosen as far as possible to be representative of the breadth of government bills considered by parliament. The means by which we selected the bills was summarized in Chapter 1, and is detailed fully in Appendix A. Some basic information on the bills is shown in Table 2.3, which groups them separately for the 2005–10 parliament and the 2010–12 session. This shows that they had varying lengths, came from a range of government departments, and that (in line with the broader population of government bills) one-third were introduced via the House of Lords. They include some 'flagship' bills which were high profile and considered central to the government's legislative programme, alongside some lower-profile bills which proved less controversial in parliament. In two cases the coalition's bill in the 2010–12 session reversed changes made by a Labour bill that we studied in the previous parliament: the Identity Documents Bill ended the scheme introduced by the Identity Cards Bill, and the Savings Accounts and Health in Pregnancy Grant Bill did the same with respect to the provisions in the Saving Gateway Accounts Bill.

The remainder of this section summarizes the policy content of the bills, and gives some indication of their reception inside and outside parliament. It also touches on the circumstances of their introduction, such as whether the policy had been explicitly mentioned in a governing party manifesto or (post-2010) coalition agreement. This not only provides context for the discussions in subsequent chapters, but also demonstrates the key ways in which government bills can differ from each other. Further background to the bills, in terms of the extent of government consultation on the policies that they contained, is included in Chapter 3.

The 2005–10 Bills

Seven of the 12 bills were drawn from the 2005–10 parliament, with a spread across the sessions of that parliament. Three began in the immediate post-election session of 2005–06, one of which was carried over to the 2006–07 session. The remaining four bills were, in turn, drawn from the other four sessions of the parliament. This was Labour's third term in office post-1997; at the start of the period Tony Blair was

Table 2.3 Summary information about the 12 case study bills

	Session	Responsible government department	Length at introduction (pages)
2005–10 parliament			
Identity Cards	2005–06	Home Office	47
Health	2005–06	Health	92
Corporate Manslaughter and Corporate Homicide	2005–07*	Home Office**	20
Further Education and Training [HL]	2006–07	Education and Skills***	30
Employment [HL]	2007–08	Business, Enterprise and Regulatory Reform	23
Saving Gateway Accounts	2008–09	Treasury	17
Energy	2009–10	Energy and Climate Change	31
2010–12 session			
Identity Documents	2010–12	Home Office	16
Savings Accounts and Health in Pregnancy Grant	2010–12	Treasury	6
Budget Responsibility and National Audit [HL]	2010–12	Treasury	44
Public Bodies [HL]	2010–12	Cabinet Office	30
Welfare Reform	2010–12	Work and Pensions	175

* Carried over from 2005–06 to 2006–07 session.
** Transferred to newly established Ministry of Justice in 2007.
*** Renamed Innovation, Universities and Skills in 2007.
'[HL]' indicates that the bill was introduced via the Lords.

still Prime Minister, but Gordon Brown succeeded him in June 2007. Two of the bills were considered by parliament wholly under Blair's premiership, three wholly under Brown's premiership, and two began their passage under Blair but completed the very last stages of their passage under Brown.

Identity Cards Bill 2005–06

The first bill to be introduced, on 25 May 2005, was the Identity Cards Bill, which sought to introduce a system of identity cards to the UK. This was a high-profile issue, and could be seen as one of Tony Blair's 'flagship' bills. The pledge to introduce identity cards had been included in Labour's 2005 election manifesto, though the wording with respect to whether these would become compulsory for citizens was ambiguous—which helped to fuel parliamentary resistance on this question.[13] As outlined in Chapter 3, the possible introduction of identity cards had been under consideration for many years. Ministers claimed that the cards would be beneficial for demonstrating entitlement to access public services (such as welfare and the

NHS), and for combating identity fraud. This policy was ostensibly popular—with polls indicating public support—but it was also highly controversial. As discussed in Chapters 4 and 5, the bill created dilemmas for opposition parties, and was resisted by some Labour backbenchers. It was significantly amended in parliament, with a key point of contention being the degree of compulsion in the scheme. It was ultimately overturned by the coalition's Identity Documents Bill.

Health Bill 2005–06

The Health Bill was introduced into the Commons on 27 October 2005. This large bill also included some 'flagship' elements, but dealt with a wide range of fairly disconnected issues, in five main parts. The most high-profile matter—which was to prove the most controversial during its parliamentary passage—was the introduction of a ban on smoking in enclosed public places. Labour's manifesto had promised to introduce such a ban, with limited exceptions for private members' clubs and licensed premises (i.e. pubs or bars) not serving food. These exemptions were initially contained in the bill, but were removed following parliamentary pressure. Other aspects of the bill mentioned in the manifesto included measures to deal with healthcare associated infections, and tighter regulation of dangerous or harmful drugs. Both of these responded to recent perceived crises. The first targeted increasing incidence of antibiotic-resistant infections (such as MRSA)[14] contracted by patients in hospital. The second responded to crimes by the GP Harold Shipman, who was convicted in 2000 of multiple murders, after allegations that he had killed over 200 of his patients. Other less noted elements of the bill dealt with regulation of pharmacists, ophthalmic services, NHS auditing arrangements, and the status of the NHS Appointments Commission. These matters received relatively less attention in parliament.

Corporate Manslaughter and Corporate Homicide Bill 2005–07

This third bill also introduced a policy that was high profile in Labour circles, and had long been called for by various external groups, implementing a manifesto promise to 'legislate for a new offence of corporate manslaughter' (Labour Party 2005: 51). The offence could occur where an organization owed a duty of care to an individual, but had contributed to the individual's death due to a gross breach of that duty by senior managers. If an organization was convicted, courts would be able to impose an unlimited fine, and require remedial action. This change was considered important by trade unions in order to ensure that employers took seriously their responsibility for the safety of employees. But it had also been called for by groups representing those affected by disasters whose victims went beyond employees, such as passengers killed in the Zeebrugge ferry disaster of 1987, or the sinking of the Marchioness pleasure boat on the Thames in 1989. The issues were hence highly emotive, but there were nonetheless some concerns from industry groups. Objections were also raised by some supporters of the bill to the exclusion of certain public bodies (most notably prisons) from the offence—which became the subject of a long parliamentary argument. Although the bill formally began in the 2005–06 session it was introduced only in July 2006, with an understanding from the start that it would be carried over into 2006–07.

Further Education and Training Bill 2006–07

This bill was introduced via the House of Lords on 20 November 2006, and hence completed its stages there before passing to the Commons. It was far lower profile than the previous three bills, as is typical of much legislation introduced into the Lords. Nonetheless, it did implement manifesto commitments (which were worded in quite general terms), to reform further education colleges. And it did arouse significant controversy among organizations in the sector—particularly over new powers for the Learning and Skills Council to intervene in colleges perceived to be failing, and for further education colleges to be given their own power to award 'foundation degrees'. These topics received significant attention when the bill was in the Lords.

Employment Bill 2007–08

The Employment Bill was also introduced via the Lords, on 6 December 2007. Rather like the Health Bill, it contained a series of only loosely connected measures. By this point in the parliament many of the party's manifesto commitments had already been implemented, and none of the relatively detailed measures in this bill had been mentioned. One matter covered by the bill was enforcement mechanisms for the national minimum wage (including clarification of when employment could be considered exempt), and changes to penalties. Another aspect changed arrangements for dispute resolution between employers and employees. This reversed statutory changes introduced in the previous parliament, and allowed for more informal settlements. A third aspect, which attracted particular attention during Lords debates, responded to a ruling in the European Court of Human Rights over the ability of trade unions to expel people from membership who belonged to extremist political parties.

Saving Gateway Accounts Bill 2008–09

The sixth Labour government bill was likewise relatively uncontroversial. It was introduced into the Commons in Labour's penultimate session, on 4 December 2008. The bill's central purpose was to encourage a savings habit among those on lower incomes, by introducing Saving Gateway Accounts which would be available to people either in receipt of 'tax credits' or certain welfare benefits (as specified in the bill). The measure did not feature in the 2005 manifesto, but had appeared in the 2001 manifesto and after this local pilot projects had been introduced. The bill allowed ministers to establish a national scheme, with regulations initially allowing account holders to deposit up to £25 per month for a term of two years, and the government to top up the account at a rate of 50p for each £1 saved (i.e. requiring maximum government expenditure of £300 per saver). There was relatively little resistance to the bill in parliament, aside from some questioning of the detail, and some scepticism that the target group would have sufficient ability to save and thus to benefit from the scheme.

Energy Bill 2009–10

This final Labour bill was introduced in the short session preceding the May 2010 general election, on 19 November 2009. It was again relatively small and uncontroversial. The bill made changes to the regulation of gas and electricity markets, including clarifying the responsibilities of the regulator, Ofgem, towards tackling climate change. It also provided for carbon capture and storage projects, and required energy suppliers to reduce fuel poverty. These broad objectives all had cross-party support. The bill did not complete its Commons stages and pass to the Lords until late February 2010, leaving insufficient time for all of the Lords stages to be taken in the usual way. It thus became subject to the pre-election 'wash-up' procedures, as discussed in Chapter 4.

The 2010–12 bills

The 2010–12 session marked both the beginning of a new parliament and a new government. Gordon Brown's Labour government had been lagging in the polls since 2008, and Labour's loss of power had come to look inevitable, with the possibility of a 'hung parliament'—where no party had a majority in the House of Commons—widely predicted (Hazell et al. 2009, Kavanagh and Cowley 2010). When these predictions proved correct, the Conservatives and Liberal Democrats entered talks, and reached agreement on forming a coalition. The new government's policy programme was cemented in two coalition agreements, drawing on the two parties' manifestos, published in short succession in May (Conservative Party and Liberal Democrats 2010, HM Government 2010). The new parliament thus began with a sharply different policy agenda.

Identity Documents Bill

The Identity Documents Bill, introduced to the Commons on the day after the Queen's Speech, was symbolic of this change of direction. The initial coalition agreement had pledged to 'reverse the substantial erosion of civil liberties under the Labour Government ... [including] scrapping [the] ID card scheme' (Conservative Party and Liberal Democrats 2010: 6). This echoed the almost identical wording in the two parties' manifestos, to 'scrap ID cards' (Conservative Party 2010: 79) and 'scrap intrusive Identity Cards' (Liberal Democrats 2010: 94). The cards had by that time still not been introduced for the general population (due to the changes wrought by parliament to Labour's bill, as discussed in subsequent chapters). There had been only limited pilot schemes, resulting in issue of approximately 15,000 identity cards to UK citizens. This bill repealed the Identity Cards Act, abolishing the National Identity Register on which the scheme was based, and ending both the issuing of cards and the validity of cards already issued. However, compulsory identity cards for foreign nationals, introduced in November 2008, were retained.

Savings Accounts and Health in Pregnancy Grant Bill

This short bill was introduced to the Commons on 15 September 2010, and repealed not only the Saving Gateway Accounts Act (see above), but also two other schemes. The better known of these was the Child Trust Fund which, like Saving Gateway Accounts, was seen as part of 'asset-based welfare' that encouraged a savings habit (Collard and McKay 2006, Finlayson 2009). Children born after September 2002 were entitled to a Child Trust Fund (i.e. a specific form of savings account), into which the government would pay an initial deposit at birth, and another at age 7, with the ability for others to also make contributions. The funds were to be made accessible to children when they reached age 18.[15] Both the Conservative and Liberal Democrat manifestos had promised to reduce government payments into this scheme, and the bill ended eligibility for the scheme for children born after 2 January 2011.[16] The third change in the bill was to abolish the Health in Pregnancy Grant—a tax-free lump sum of £190 payable to expectant mothers—which had been introduced by Labour in 2008.

Budget Responsibility and National Audit Bill

This bill, to establish the new Office for Budget Responsibility (OBR) in statute, was introduced into the House of Lords on 21 October 2010. The Conservative manifesto had promised to create such a body, 'to restore trust in the government's ability to manage the public finances' and 'ensure that no Labour government can ever attempt to bankrupt our public finances again' (Conservative Party 2010: 7).[17] The OBR would have responsibility for producing independent forecasts for the economy and public finances, replacing those previously produced by the Treasury in the Budget and Pre-Budget Report. To try to demonstrate their fiscal prudence in the wake of the 2008–09 financial crisis the Conservatives had set up a 'shadow' OBR when in opposition in late 2009; an interim OBR was then established on a non-statutory basis immediately after the 2010 election. This bill formalized the arrangements and—despite the initial political rhetoric—proved relatively non-controversial in parliament. Aside from the OBR, it also included some minor provisions on the Comptroller and Auditor General and the National Audit Office that had appeared in Labour's Constitutional Reform and Governance Bill 2010, but had been lost in the pre-election wash-up.

Public Bodies Bill

The Public Bodies Bill was also introduced via the House of Lords, on 28 October 2010. Although somewhat technical in nature, it actually proved hugely controversial, particularly in the Lords. The bill implemented promises by the two coalition parties to 'cut the unaccountable quango state and root out waste' (Conservative Party 2010: 69) and '[r]eplace wasteful quangos' (Liberal Democrats 2010: 39), by allowing for the abolition, merger, or restructuring of numerous public bodies. Both before and after the election this had been dubbed a 'bonfire of the quangos', suggesting that the degree of change would be dramatic.[18] The main body of the bill was relatively short (15 pages), setting out generalized ministerial powers to make changes to bodies via future secondary legislation without naming the bodies concerned, with most of the bodies under threat listed in schedules at the back of the bill.[19] These included at least 44 bodies and offices identified for abolition, eight identified for merger, and 21 for other specified changes.[20] But Schedule 7 of the bill included a list of 150 bodies which could potentially be moved in future to one of the other schedules, and which therefore faced a very uncertain future. The bodies listed were extremely diverse: everything from the Advisory, Conciliation and Arbitration Service (ACAS) to the Health and Safety Executive, Public Records Office, and United Kingdom Atomic Energy Authority (AEA).[21] The bill was subject to major changes during its passage through parliament, including complete removal of this schedule.

Welfare Reform Bill

The final bill, which was the longest by far in our sample, was introduced almost a year into the coalition's term, on 16 February 2011. Like several others above this could be considered a 'flagship' bill, contributing to the coalition's overall promise to reduce the public deficit, 'with the main burden of deficit reduction borne by reduced spending' (HM Government 2010: 15). As well as contributing to this objective the bill introduced substantial structural changes to welfare benefits. It provided for the introduction of a new Universal Credit to replace various pre-existing allowances (e.g. Income Support, Housing Benefit, and Child Tax Credit), and for replacement of Disability Living Allowance with a new Personal Independence Payment. It also introduced greater 'conditionality' for working age benefits, including mandatory work placement and tougher sanctions (such as withdrawal of benefit), and made changes to the system for claiming child maintenance from absent parents. Two of the most controversial elements in the bill were the introduction of an overall household 'benefit cap' of £500 per week, and provisions for an 'underoccupancy penalty' (which opponents came to dub the 'bedroom tax'), whereby council or housing association tenants would have their benefits restricted if their home was deemed larger than required.[22] The bill overall attracted a high degree of controversy, though (as discussed in Chapter 4) it also presented significant challenges to the Labour opposition, as many of the measures were seen to have public support.

The Legislative Process Stage by Stage

Having outlined the bills, we now turn to a more detailed overview of how the legislative process works at Westminster. Obviously, much will be explored in depth in later chapters of the book. But this section introduces some key terms and processes, illustrated with data about the 12 bills. We start by describing the legislative process stage by stage across the two chambers, before turning in the next section to summarize key points about legislative amendments.

Pre-introduction, and first reading

The first reading of a bill takes a similar form in both chambers, and is a pure formality which immediately precedes its publication. It comprises no more than the title of the bill being read out, and there is no debate. As well as being able to examine the bill itself, publication gives those inside and outside parliament access to associated documents, including the 'explanatory notes' which set out its structure and purpose in less technical terms.

The first reading of a government bill is not of course normally the first time it has been brought to parliament's attention. As we have seen, legislation will often have been promised in a party manifesto. As discussed in the next chapter, policies are also often subject to pre-legislative consultation by government. The publication of a government consultation document, or the end of such a consultation, will often be accompanied by a statement from a minister to parliament, allowing members to ask questions. Other opportunities to ask ministers about legislative plans include regular departmental question times, Prime Minister's Questions, and general debates. Where a bill has been promised by government and not introduced, or where members wish to encourage ministers to consider introducing a bill, there are various other mechanisms that backbenchers can use to press their case—such as private members' bills (in both chambers) and 'early day motions' (in the Commons).

Preceding a bill's formal first reading, it will often have been signalled in the speech read by the monarch at the opening of the parliamentary session. These speeches are relatively short (and are actually written by government officials), hence references to specific bills are brief. For example at the start of the 2005–06 session the Queen's Speech included only the words '[l]egislation will be taken forward to introduce an identity cards scheme' and '[m]y Government will take forward proposals to introduce an offence of corporate manslaughter'—though the words dedicated to the Health Bill were rather longer.[23] In the days following the speech, debates are held in both chambers on the session's legislative programme, allowing members to raise more detailed points with ministers and begin to set out their positions.

Second reading

The first certain opportunity to debate a bill takes place at its second reading, which generally occurs two weeks or so after the first reading. In both chambers, this debate focuses on the broad principles of the bill, and no amendments to it may be formally proposed. The debate is opened by a minister (generally in the Commons the cabinet minister responsible for the bill, and in the Lords a more junior minister), who will explain the intentions behind the bill and its main provisions. A speech from the opposition shadow spokesperson will follow. Further speakers can then contribute from the party backbenches, smaller parties, and (in the Lords) non-party benches. Like most debates in Westminster, it closes with 'winding up' speeches from the opposition frontbench and then the government.

The second reading debate thus serves various purposes. It can be an opportunity for the main party groups to set out their political positions, and often includes a degree of adversarial 'party politicking'—particularly in the Commons, which is more prone to such behaviour than the Lords. It presents an opportunity for backbenchers to speak in support of their party's frontbench line, but also (even on the government side) to raise any specific concerns that they have about the bill. This can bring matters of concern to the attention of those who participate in the subsequent committee stage. In the Commons, where committee stage usually takes place 'off the floor', a backbench speech may also signal that the member is interested in serving on the bill committee.

For major bills the second reading debate often takes up a full day of parliamentary debate, and sometimes more. The amount of time dedicated to this, and subsequent stages, for the 12 case study bills in both chambers is shown in Tables 2.4 and 2.5. As the tables demonstrate, the shortest second reading was an hour and a half on the Saving Gateway Accounts Bill, and the longest over eight hours, on the Public Bodies Bill, both in the Lords.

At the end of the second reading debate, members will be asked to agree to a motion that 'the bill be now read a second time'. If no objection is raised, this is taken as agreed, and the bill may proceed to its committee stage. Should the motion fail to be agreed, the bill would die. In the Commons, there will often (but by no means always) be an objection, forcing a division on the motion. A 'reasoned amendment' to the motion is sometimes moved, typically by the opposition, setting out any key objections to the bill; but the government's Commons majority can almost invariably defeat this.[24] In the Lords, the so-called 'Salisbury convention' holds that the unelected chamber should not block government bills outright which implement manifesto commitments, and in practice divisions of any kind at second reading are rare.[25] However, very occasionally peers use an amendment to the second reading motion to express concerns about a bill. Such an amendment was proposed by the

Table 2.4 Debating time and number of amendments proposed to the eight bills starting in the Commons, by legislative stage

	Identity Cards	Health	Corporate Manslaughter	Saving Gateway	Energy	Identity Documents	Savings Accounts	Welfare Reform	Total (all eight bills)
Time (hours: minutes) spent at:									
Commons second reading	07:10	05:53	05:25	03:06	05:31	05:46	04:31	06:23	43:45
Commons committee	26:35	28:35	12:44	13:26	26:43	07:32	19:59	72:27	208:01
Commons report	05:22	05:04	04:39	02:19	04:21	02:57	03:46	11:10	39:38
Commons third reading	00:44	00:53	00:40	00:18	00:24	00:34	00:49	00:30	04:52
Lords second reading	06:42	04:12	04:22	01:29	03:13	02:03	03:02	07:30	32:33
Lords committee	34:53	21:12	12:57	05:49	00:12	03:33	00:00	63:53	142:29
Lords report	17:02	07:30	05:07	01:30	00:00	01:56	00:00	35:10	68:15
Lords third reading	02:51	01:09	00:32	00:01	00:00	00:01	00:00	02:54	07:28
Commons consideration of Lords amendments (CCLA)	12:36	00:41	07:43	00:36	—	00:06	—	08:06	29:48
Lords consideration of Commons amendments (LCCA)	07:58	—	05:37	—	—	01:37	—	09:36	24:48
Total time	121:53	75:09	59:46	28:34	40:24	26:05	32:07	217:39	601:37
Stages of CCLA/LCCA	11	1	10	1	1	2	0	4	n/a
Government defeats in the Lords*	12	0	5	0	0	2	0	8	27

Amendments proposed [and agreed] at:

Commons committee	242 [1]	148 [37]	147 [39]	43 [2]	55 [0]	8 [0]	53 [0]	313 [33]	1,009 [112]
Commons report	68 [4]	56 [19]	89 [25]	13 [0]	62 [41]	12 [4]	55 [0]	84 [22]	439 [115]
Lords committee	316 [1]	137 [10]	99 [3]	49 [3]	9 [9]	20 [0]	0 [0]	373 [45]	1003 [71]
Lords report	176 [58]	57 [39]	53 [32]	19 [5]	0 [0]	6 [1]	0 [0]	244 [59]	555 [194]
Lords third reading	21 [15]	11 [9]	2 [0]	0 [0]	0 [0]	0 [0]	0 [0]	15 [11]	49 [35]
Commons consideration of Lords amendments	28 [27]	0 [0]	48 [48]	0 [0]	0 [0]	1 [1]	0 [0]	26 [14]	103 [90]
Lords consideration of Commons amendments	14 [14]	0 [0]	34 [33]	0 [0]	0 [0]	0 [0]	0 [0]	21 [8]	69 [55]
Total	865 [120]	409 [114]	472 [180]	124 [10]	126 [50]	47 [6]	108 [0]	1,076 [192]	3,227 [672]

Note: Here, and throughout the book, our definition of 'amendments' is slightly wider than that used by the parliamentary authorities (for further information, see Appendix A). Number of amendments in parentheses is the number agreed to.

* Defeats figure reflects only the number of divisions, not the number of amendments involved (any consequential and related amendments will generally be agreed to without further divisions following a defeat).

Sources: Calculated from House of Commons and House of Lords Hansard; House of Commons Sessional Information Digests; House of Commons and House of Lords amendment papers; and House of Commons public bill committee and report stage proceedings documents.

Table 2.5 Debating time and number of amendments proposed to the four bills starting in the Lords, by legislative stage (and totals for all 12 bills)

	Further Education	Employment	Budget Responsibility	Public Bodies	Total (all four bills)	Grand total (all 12 bills)
Time (hours: minutes) spent at:						
Lords second reading	04:55	03:38	02:41	08:37	19:51	52:24
Lords committee	06:48	13:07	08:46	45:25	74:06	216:35
Lords report	03:49	03:50	01:50	17:51	27:20	95:35
Lords third reading	00:38	01:16	00:04	03:17	05:15	12:43
Commons second reading	05:35	04:18	02:19	03:40	15:52	59:37
Commons committee	09:28	07:32	09:54	21:01	47:55	255:56
Commons report	04:23	04:07	02:28	04:50	15:48	55:26
Commons third reading	01:02	00:32	00:25	00:45	02:44	07:36
Lords consideration of Commons amendments (LCCA)	01:43	00:11	—	03:32	05:26	30:14
Commons consideration of Lords amendments (CCLA)	00:33	—	—	01:01	01:34	31:22
Total time	38:54	38:31	28:27	109:59	215:51	817:28
Stages of CCLA/LCCA	3	1	1	2	n/a	n/a
Government defeats in the Lords*	2	0	0	4	6	33
Amendments proposed [and agreed] at:						
Lords committee	72 [3]	43 [3]	44 [0]	334 [39]	493 [45]	1,496 [116]
Lords report	66 [44]	38 [16]	15 [10]	135 [67]	254 [137]	809 [331]
Lords third reading	10 [8]	10 [4]	0 [0]	10 [4]	30 [16]	79 [51]
Commons committee	44 [8]	30 [5]	35 [1]	82 [34]	191 [48]	1,200 [160]
Commons report	33 [0]	34 [0]	9 [0]	64 [29]	140 [29]	579 [144]
Lords consideration of Commons amendments	7 [6]	0 [0]	0 [0]	12 [5]	19 [11]	88 [66]
Commons consideration of Lords amendments	6 [6]	0 [0]	0 [0]	1 [0]	7 [6]	110 [96]
Total	238 [75]	155 [28]	103 [11]	638 [178]	1,134 [292]	4,361 [964]

For notes and sources, see Table 2.4.

Labour frontbench on the Public Bodies Bill, to send it to a select committee for detailed consideration before its formal committee stage, but this was defeated.

Four other decisions may also be taken at the end of the second reading debate. First, in the Commons it is now the norm for a 'programme motion' to be agreed, setting out a timetable for the bill's remaining stages. Programming replaced the old system of moving individual 'guillotine' motions from the start of the 1997 parliament, and although initially intended to be consensual, these timetable motions are often contested and subject to a division. In the Lords, programming does not apply. Second, in both chambers there is a decision to be made at this point about where the committee stage will be taken (which in the Commons usually forms part of the programme motion). Third, if a bill requires spending or taxation the Commons must also agree a 'money resolution' or a 'ways and means resolution'. Fourth, in the relatively rare cases where a bill is to be 'carried over' from one parliamentary session to the next, the carry-over motion may be agreed at this stage. Among our bills, only the Corporate Manslaughter and Corporate Homicide Bill was carried over. This bill had no money resolution, so at the end of its Commons second reading there could therefore have been divisions on three matters: the second reading itself (and any reasoned amendments), the programme motion, and the carry-over motion. In fact, there were only two, as the second reading itself was simply agreed with no objections.

Committee stage

At committee stage in both chambers, members work their way more methodically through the bill discussing points of detail. This stage generally starts at least one week after second reading in the Commons, and two weeks in the Lords. Detailed amendments can be proposed and made and—as discussed below—structure much of the debate. Tables 2.4 and 2.5 show that where the committee stage takes place it is invariably the lengthiest stage, and tends to attract the largest number of amendments. On major bills, many days may be spent 'in committee'. For the largest bill in our sample, the Welfare Reform Bill—as shown in Table 2.6—there were 26 sittings (on 13 separate days) in Commons committee and 17 committee sittings (each on a separate day) in the Lords. This amounted to over 136 hours in total. In contrast, two of the bills notably spent very little or no time in committee in the Lords: Labour's Energy Bill and the coalition's Savings Accounts and Health in Pregnancy Grant (SAHPG) Bill. The Energy Bill was rushed through its final stages as a result of the pre-election 'wash-up'—meaning that after the election had been called there was a quick behind-the-scenes agreement between the parties, and the bill was passed with just a handful of government amendments proposed and agreed to. The SAHPG Bill was, in contrast, certified as a 'money bill' by the Speaker at the end of its Commons stages, meaning that it was judged to deal only with taxation and spending.[26] By convention money bills and certain other types of financial legislation are not fully debated in the Lords.[27] The Speaker's decision—which necessarily resulted in a curtailment of debate—proved somewhat controversial, as further discussed in Chapter 4.

Table 2.6 Nature of committee stage by bill

	Commons						Lords	
	Committee membership					No. sittings	Type of Committee	No. sittings
	Lab	Con	Lib	Other*	Total			
Identity Cards	10	5	2	0	17	11	CWH	6
Health	10	5	2	0	17	12	GC	6
Corporate Manslaughter	10	5	2	0	17	7	GC	4
Further Education	10	5	2	0	17	4	GC	2
Employment	9	5	2	0	16	4	GC	4
Saving Gateway	9	5	2	0	16	5	GC	2
Energy	10	5	2	1	18	12	CWH	1
Identity Documents	7	8	2	1	18	5	GC	2
Savings Accounts	7	8	2	1	18	8	n/a	0
Budget Responsibility	7	8	2	1	18	4	GC	4
Public Bodies	7	9	2	1	19	8	CWH	9
Welfare Reform	10	13	2	1	26	26	GC	17

* DUP on Identity Documents Bill, Budget Responsibility and National Audit Bill, Welfare Reform Bill; SNP on Energy Bill; SDLP on Savings Accounts and Health in Pregnancy Grant Bill, Plaid Cymru on Public Bodies Bill.

For financial legislation, procedure in the Commons and the Lords differs dramatically, but there are also standard day-to-day differences between how the two chambers operate at committee stage. As already indicated, the norm in the Commons is to commit bills to a relatively small public bill committee, which meets 'off the floor' of the chamber in a separate committee room. This applied to all of our bills—with numbers of committee members ranging from 16 to 26 (see Table 2.6).[28] Usually only bills considered to be of 'first class' constitutional importance, extremely urgent or (in contrast) very uncontroversial are taken in a 'committee of the whole house' on the floor of the Commons. The use of public bill committees allows the committee stage of several bills to be taken at once, and frees up the chamber to deal with other matters (since committees can meet when the chamber is in session). But arrangements in the Lords are rather different. Here committee stage is taken either in a committee of the whole house or in a parallel 'grand committee', both of which allow all peers to participate.

Comparing the two chambers, the 'off the floor' arrangements in the Commons are closer to the European norm, but nonetheless have distinctive features widely seen as disadvantageous to legislative scrutiny (for a review, see Russell, Morris, and Larkin 2013). First, Commons bill committees are temporary, being drawn together only to consider the bill in question and then disbanding. Second, there is no requirement on their members to be subject experts. Bill committees are thus very different to the Commons' select committees (further discussed in Chapter 8), which have a permanent membership that allows both expertise and relationships across party lines to develop. Since 2010 there has also been a major difference in how members of these two kinds of Commons committees are chosen: select committee members are now elected, while bill committee members are in effect (like select committee members used to be, pre-2010) chosen by party whips.[29] This risks 'awkward' members (who may even be subject experts) being kept off the committees. The public bill committee will include among its members the bill minister and main shadow spokespeople, as well as government and opposition whips, alongside backbenchers. It is chaired by a senior MP who is a member of the 'Panel of Chairs' (selected by the Speaker), and who acts as a neutral arbiter. The chair, and committee in general, receives support and expert procedural advice from a clerk based in the Commons Public Bill Office.

As indicated above, a new evidence-taking stage was incorporated in 2006, which applies to all bills that begin their passage in the Commons and have not previously been subject to evidence-taking in draft form.[30] It is generally seen as having improved the process—though criticisms remain over the fact that whips, via the committee's programming subcommittee, have primary control over the timetable and which witnesses are called (see Levy 2010). Evidence-taking occurs before the line-by-line scrutiny, providing an opportunity for outside groups to feed into the process (as discussed further in Chapter 7). Thompson (2015) has calculated that in the period 2007–12 committees attracted an average of 26 witnesses, and she found that MPs frequently cited this evidence during the later stages.

The dynamics of committee stage in the Lords are rather different. Clearly the number of members taking part is potentially larger, and certainly less predictable than that in the Commons. Any member may participate by moving an amendment or speaking in debate. Given the breadth of Lords membership, this means that serious subject experts often contribute—which can prove challenging for ministers. In addition, as already indicated, all amendments are liable to be debated, since—unlike in the Commons—the member presiding has no power to 'select' those for debate.

Aside from differences to the Commons, there are also key differences between committee stages taken on the floor of the Lords and in grand committee. Most importantly, while divisions can be held in Commons public bill committees, and in either chamber when meeting as a committee of the whole house, these cannot occur in Lords grand committee. Here amendments can only be agreed by consensus—meaning that an amendment which proves controversial must either be dropped, or decided upon at the report stage. But, actually, divisions at committee stage in either chamber occur only on a minority of amendments (e.g. there were 1,200 amendments considered in Commons committee on the 12 bills, but only 81 divisions). In both chambers proposers of amendments often conclude by simply asking the minister to reflect on their proposal, leaving the option open to return to the issue.

Report stage

The report stage in both the Commons and the Lords takes place on the floor of the chamber—in the Lords two weeks must normally elapse after the end of the committee stage, but there is no fixed interval in the Commons. The bill as amended in committee is 'reported', not (as it would be in many other parliaments) by a neutral 'rapporteur' on behalf of the committee, but in a debate led by the minister. This is another opportunity to discuss details of the bill, when amendments can be proposed and agreed, and where all members can potentially take part. Members consider the amended version of the bill produced by the committee, and may adjust or even reverse changes made there. The report stage can also be an opportunity to discuss new proposals, or to take decisions on proposals which were discussed, but not agreed, in committee.[31] As seen in Tables 2.4 and 2.5, the amount of time spent on the report stage is significantly shorter than that in committee, and there is less variation between bills.

We have already seen that members will sometimes withdraw their amendments at committee in the hope that a similar amendment can be agreed at report. As discussed throughout the book, it is fairly common that a government backbencher, opposition member, or non-party parliamentarian proposes a committee stage amendment, which is then responded to with a government amendment at report. Nonetheless, report stage is also a further opportunity for non-government amendments to be discussed and potentially agreed.

In the Commons, report stage is the final opportunity for a bill to be amended. In the Lords, in contrast, bills remain amendable at third reading. The Commons report stage also tends to be more pressurized, as it is usually programmed, and many amendments may fail to be selected or called for debate. In the Commons, it is unlikely—given the government's partisan majority—that an amendment will be agreed if it does not have ministerial support. In the Lords, where the government has no inbuilt majority, non-government amendments are far more likely to be agreed. It is at this stage that by far the largest number of Lords divisions, and defeats, take place.[32]

Third reading

Third reading likewise takes place on the floor of the chamber in both the Commons and the Lords. In the Commons, it tends to be very short, given that the opportunity to agree amendments has passed, and usually happens straight after report stage.[33] In the Lords, in contrast, the *Companion to the Standing Orders* specifies that there should normally be a gap of at least three sitting days, and third reading is a last opportunity to amend the bill. However, the *Companion* explicitly states that practice 'is normally to resolve major points of difference by the end of report stage, and to use third reading for tidying up the bill', so '[a]n issue which has been fully debated and voted on or negatived [i.e. rejected] at a previous stage of a bill may not be reopened by an amendment on third reading' (House of Lords 2015: 152–3). Third reading amendments are hence generally responses to debates that were not resolved at earlier stages. A government amendment may be brought forward in response to amendments proposed by other peers, or the debate can provide a final chance for peers to defeat the government. In addition, particularly in the Commons, there is an opportunity for members to comment on the bill as a whole, and for closing statements by the minister and main opposition frontbencher. Like at second reading, the minister in charge of the bill will move that it be read for a third time, and the chamber may divide on that proposition—that is, have a final vote on the question of whether the bill, as amended at earlier stages, should pass. In the Commons, such votes are largely a formality, as the government's majority should be enough to secure the passage of the bill.[34] In the Lords, votes on the principle of third reading are even more unusual than at second reading.[35]

The 'ping-pong' stages

Third reading is not necessarily the last time either chamber sees a bill. After having passed through the chamber into which it was introduced, a bill must repeat the same stages in the other chamber. If that results in any amendments being made, it must return to the initial chamber for those to be considered. So, for example, if a bill begins in the Commons it passes to the Lords after all of its Commons stages, and if the Lords makes amendments these must be put to the Commons before the bill can finally be agreed. Under normal circumstances, the bill will only reach the statute book once the two chambers agree to it in identical form. Hence in the example just given, any Lords amendments will spark an additional stage, called Commons consideration of Lords amendments (CCLA). At that point if the Commons agrees the amendments the bill can proceed to royal assent. But if the Commons rejects any of the Lords' amendments, makes amendments to them, or passes alternative 'amendments in lieu', the bill must return to the Lords again for an equivalent Lords consideration of Commons amendments (LCCA) stage. This process of to and fro—colloquially known as 'ping-pong'—can continue an unspecified number of times until the two chambers agree.[36] Given that it is quite normal for a bill to be amended in both chambers, at least one round of CCLA or LCCA is commonplace, and need not indicate disagreement. Particularly if the amendments have government backing, they may be readily accepted by the other chamber.

Protracted ping-pong occurs only when there is a disagreement—generally in terms of the Lords seeking to make amendments opposed by the government. Among our bills this occurred on the Identity Cards Bill and the Corporate Manslaughter Bill, where there were 11 and 10 CCLA or LCCA stages respectively (and eventually a deal was struck, as discussed later in the book). There was also some, less protracted, disagreement on the Public Bodies Bill, the Further Education and Training Bill, the Identity Documents Bill, and the Welfare Reform Bill. The latter two of these again illustrated a key difference between the chambers, as the Commons rejected Lords amendments citing 'financial privilege'—which caused some controversy among peers. This means that the Lords amendments were judged by Commons officials to have financial implications. The scope of the Commons' financial privilege remains somewhat ill-defined, as is the extent to which it can be asserted, but the convention is that when presented with such a claim the Lords will back down (although it may propose an alternative). This constitutes part of the Commons' overall claim to financial primacy, as also indicated by the special procedures for money bills and other purely financial bills (see Gover and Russell 2015, Russell and Gover 2014).

Faced with hostile amendments, the Commons does usually have the ultimate power to overrule the Lords. These provisions are included within the Parliament Acts 1911 and 1949. If the Lords does not back down in its disagreement, and the Commons is unwilling to compromise, a bill which began its passage in the Commons can be reintroduced in the subsequent session and passed even without the Lords' assent.[37] In fact since the 1949 Parliament Act was passed, just four bills have reached the statute book in this way, and it is far more common for a compromise to be reached.[38] Notably the Parliament Acts do not apply to bills which begin their passage in the Lords, where the chamber retains a final veto.

Amendments and their Outcomes

A key part of our analysis focuses on amendments proposed to the 12 case study bills during their passage through parliament. Amendments are essentially proposals to change the text of the legislation under consideration, through deleting, adding to, or substituting some of its content. As we have seen, they can be tabled in both chambers, at seven distinct legislative stages. Tables 2.4 and 2.5 disaggregate the 4,361 amendments proposed to the case study bills by both stage and bill. Some bills were subject to many more proposed amendments than others, and the greatest number of amendments (2,696, or 62 per cent) were tabled at committee stage (in either chamber), while most of the rest (1,388, or 32 per cent) were on report.

Illustrative examples of amendments are given in Figure 2.1, and begin to demonstrate their diversity. Some make only minor 'technical' changes (e.g. amendment A), whereas others would affect policy outcomes. We refer to this as the amendment's 'substantiveness', as discussed further in Chapter 3. Some amendments are relatively easy to understand (e.g. B), but others are more legalistic and cross-reference to existing statutory provisions (e.g. C). Most propose to alter the text of existing clauses or schedules, but others add entire new clauses (e.g. D) or new schedules. A specific category of more minor technical change comprises 'consequential' amendments (e.g. E), which bring the rest of the bill into line with other changes made by more substantive amendments. In this case, the substantive amendment had widened the scope of the original provision by adding a second part—requiring a subsequent cross-reference to the original part to be updated.

The legislative process is supported in parliament by impartial clerks in each chamber's Public Bill Office, through which members must submit (i.e. 'table') most amendments. The Public Bill Office publishes lists of amendments submitted, both in hard copy and on the parliamentary website. In the Commons, amendments must normally be tabled three sitting days before a debate; in the Lords, those tabled only a day before debate will still be printed.[39] Any member may table an amendment, though in a Commons public bill committee only a member of the committee can 'move' it for debate. Once tabled, other members of the chamber can indicate their support for an amendment by adding their names.[40]

A. Identity Cards Bill

Page 19, line 43, leave out 'for being' and insert 'to be'.

B. Budget Responsibility and National Audit Bill

Page 3, line 23, at end insert—
'( ) At a time when a report is published, the Office must publish, in a readily accessible form, the data, methods, and costings used to compile the report.'

C. Welfare Reform Bill

Clause 47, page 27, line 45, at end insert—
'(2) In section 37 of the Jobseekers Act 1995 (Parliamentary control), in subsection (1) at end insert—
"(d) regulations made under sections 19, 19A, 19C, 6J, or 6K."'

D. Further Education and Training Bill

Insert the following new Clause-
'Sector Skills Council
After section 17 of LSA 2000 (use of information by Council) insert—
"17A Sector Skills Council
The Council must have regard to the Sector Skills Council when preparing guidance or publishing a plan relating to the needs of employers regarding education and training of their employees and potential employees."'

E. Public Bodies Bill

Page 4, line 27, leave out '(2)' and insert '(2)(a)'

Figure 2.1 Examples of amendments tabled to the case study bills

Given that legislation can be complicated, one of the functions of the Public Bill Office clerks is to advise MPs and peers—particularly backbenchers and non-party parliamentarians, who have relatively little other support—on drafting of amendments. In the Commons in particular not all proposals are admissible. An amendment must reasonably be judged to be within the 'scope' of the bill (i.e. to be clearly related to its content—here the 'long title' of the bill offers some guidance).[41] It must also not be purely frivolous, or deal with a matter already decided earlier at the same stage (this matters particularly during lengthy committee stages). In the Commons the clerks specifically advise the chair, including on the 'selection' of amendments, and some may be ruled 'out of order' and hence blocked from debate.[42] In the Lords the chair has no such power and members are largely expected to regulate themselves.[43] In the Commons the clerks also advise on the 'grouping' of amendments for debate, which is decided by the chair. In the Lords, groupings are relatively more informal and negotiated through the government whips' office. Once all of the amendments related to a particular clause have been dealt with at committee stage there is generally an opportunity to debate the clause as a whole. This is referred to as a 'stand part' debate, because it is on the motion

'That the clause [as amended] stand part of the Bill'. This can be pressed to a division if MPs or peers wish to delete the clause.

A key feature of the Westminster process is that debate in both chambers is very much structured around amendments, and the allocation of debating time to different parts of the bill will thus relate closely to the number of amendments tabled. For example, on Labour's Health Bill, which had five main 'parts', almost half of the amendments (188 of 409) related to the part about smoking. Hence a disproportionate amount of debating time (when compared to the length of the bill) was focused on this part. In both the Commons and the Lords, more than half the committee stage sittings were spent debating smoking and tobacco.

The immediate outcomes of the 4,361 amendments tabled to the case study bills are presented in Table 2.7. This shows that a large majority (75 per cent) were neither agreed nor disagreed, for various reasons. In the Commons 12 per cent of amendments were 'not selected'. A further 41 per cent were 'not called' by the chair, meaning that, although they were selected, MPs were not invited to formally move them (though some will nonetheless have been debated as part of a group of amendments where only the lead amendment was called). The equivalent process in the Lords helps to explain why almost half (44 per cent) of amendments were 'not moved' by peers. Even after an amendment has been moved, the mover may request to 'withdraw' it after debate rather than pushing it to a decision, which applied to around one-fifth of all amendments proposed. A relatively smaller number of amendments were withdrawn by their sponsor prior to debate.

This leaves only one-quarter of amendments which were subject to a formal decision, of which the vast majority were agreed. Only a small number of amendments on the bills (just 3 per cent of the total) were formally 'negatived'—that is, disagreed to. A minority were agreed 'on division' (usually indicating either opposition objections to a government amendment, or else a government defeat in the

Table 2.7 Amendments and their outcomes by chamber

House	Commons		Lords		Total	
	N	%	N	%	N	%
Agreed on division	29	1.5	35	1.4	64	1.5
Agreed without division*	371	19.6	529	21.4	900	20.6
Negatived on division	87	4.6	38	1.5	125	2.9
Negatived without division	8	0.4	2	0.1	10	0.2
Not selected	227	12.0	n/a	n/a	227	5.2
Not called	774	41.0	n/a	n/a	774	17.7
Not moved	17	0.9	1,096	44.3	1,113	25.5
Withdrawn	346	18.3	585	23.7	931	21.3
Withdrawn prior to debate	30	1.6	187	7.6	217	5.0
Total	1,889	100	2,472	100	4,361	100

* Includes 83 amendments agreed alongside others on a division during ping-pong.

Lords). But most were agreed 'without division'. This category includes amendments (particularly government proposals) which are genuinely non-contentious and are approved without objection, plus consequential amendments to those agreed on division (which are generally accepted without further divisions being held). Agreed amendments are incorporated into the text of the bill before the next legislative stage.

We know, however, that the immediate on-the-record outcome of amendments can be misleading. Some (particularly Lords defeats, and related consequential amendments) may go on to be overturned at subsequent stages. Those that are not agreed at one stage are often re-tabled in identical or modified form at a subsequent stage, either by non-government parliamentarians who wish to press a point, or sometimes in the name of ministers. Amendments from non-government parliamentarians may have been withdrawn specifically because the government promised to respond with its own proposals. It was to capture these relationships that we recorded links between similar amendments at different stages in the two chambers, creating what we refer to as legislative 'strands' (as described in Appendix A). This enabled us to establish not only how legislation was amended between its introduction and royal assent, but also which parliamentary actors contributed to these changes.

A summary of legislative strands, broken down by bill and outcome, is shown in Table 2.8. We see that the 4,361 amendments can be summarized as 2,050

Table 2.8 Amendments proposed and outcome of legislative strands by bill

	Amendments proposed to bill	Strands of amendments on bill				
		Total initiated	Not agreed	Neither agreed nor disagreed	Agreed	% agreed of initiated
2005–10 parliament						
Identity Cards	865	508	464	4	40	8
Health	409	212	161	6	45	21
Corporate Manslaughter	472	144	113	4	27	19
Further Education	238	96	64	12	20	21
Employment	155	79	63	3	13	16
Saving Gateway	124	63	50	6	7	11
Energy	126	59	38	4	17	29
Total (2005–10)	2,389	1,161	953	39	169	15
2010–12 session						
Identity Documents	47	18	15	1	2	11
Savings Accounts	108	36	36	0	0	0
Budget Responsibility	103	58	47	4	7	12
Public Bodies	638	290	129	111	50	17
Welfare Reform	1,076	487	394	21	72	15
Total (2010–12)	1,972	889	621	137	131	15
Grand total	4,361	2,050	1,574	176	300	15

strands. Of these, 300 (or 15 per cent) resulted in a change to the bill—that is, at least one amendment which was agreed and not subsequently overturned. An additional 176 (9 per cent) neither resulted in clear success or failure, most commonly because a strand containing similar provisions was agreed. There is some clear variation between the bills, both in terms of number and proportion of agreed strands. The extent to which such changes demonstrate genuine parliamentary influence—as opposed, perhaps, to ministers simply amending their own bills at whim—requires further investigation. This is one of the key questions for the rest of the book.

Notes

1. As outlined in Appendix A, we excluded certain types of bill when selecting our case studies, most of which always begin in the Commons. Of the 170 bills that remained, 113 (66 per cent) were introduced into the Commons and 57 (34 per cent) into the Lords.
2. More properly this is what political scientists refer to as a single member plurality (SMP) system.
3. For a discussion, see Russell and Paun (2007). While Westminster is often seen as party-dominated, it maintains traditions that pre-date the party system in terms of the rights of individual members. Hence daily questions and adjournment debates in the Commons are allocated by nonpartisan parliamentary officials using a random 'shuffle', while equivalent decisions in many parliaments are taken within parties by whips. In addition, a change was made at the start of the 2010 parliament to introduce 'backbench business', whereby groups of backbenchers can propose debates on a cross-party basis (Foster 2015, Russell 2011).
4. The Prime Minister by convention makes appointments from across the political spectrum, though generally with a bias towards the governing party (or parties). There is also an independent House of Lords Appointments Commission which vets party appointments for propriety and recommends independent members to serve as Crossbenchers. For a longer discussion, see Russell (2013).
5. In 1999 the Labour government legislated to remove the hereditary peers, but by cross-party agreement 92 were allowed to remain. For detail see Russell (2013) and Shell (2000, 2007).
6. For further discussion, see Brazier and Fox (2010). Out of 808 private members' bills introduced in either chamber in the six sessions between 2005–12, just 29 were passed. Both government and private members' bills are 'public bills', meaning that they concern public policy. They are distinct from 'private bills', which give powers to particular individuals or groups.
7. Sessions previously ran from one autumn to the next, meaning that spring general elections were preceded by a short session, and followed by a longer one. The Fixed-term Parliaments Act 2011 instead required general elections to be held every five years in May (with early elections possible, as occurred in 2017). In preparation for this the 2010 election was followed by a two-year session. In 2017 another two-year session was announced for 2017–19.
8. In addition, those seeking reliable factual summaries can access high-quality briefing papers on parliament's own website (http://www.parliament.uk).

9. Despite the very impressive nature of Griffith's study, it is often difficult to interpret his figures with certainty—which presents significant challenges if wishing to compare his quantitative results with ours. In this case, he found 365 government report stage amendments which responded to points raised in committee by other actors, out of 2,414 which were moved. But Griffith (1974: 167) explicitly states that his figures for responsive amendments 'exclude a number of consequential amendments formally moved and agreed to'. How large that number was is not stated.

10. In published work, an exception is our own findings drawing from the same case studies as those used in this book (Russell and Cowley 2016, Russell, Gover, and Wollter 2016, Russell et al. 2017).

11. For the difficulty of making direct comparisons with Griffith, see note 9. As a proportion of all non-government amendments agreed, negatived, or withdrawn his equivalent would be 5 per cent (Griffith 1974: 93); but his appendices indicate that there were several thousand other such amendments discussed which do not fall into these three categories—suggesting that the figure might be closer to 2 per cent.

12. Again, with the exception of our own earlier papers based on this research—see note 10.

13. For precise wording, and discussion of the difficulties which ensued, see Chapter 5.

14. Methicillin-resistant staphylococcus aureus.

15. The starting levels for this initial payment were between £250 and £500 per child, dependent on family income (Edmonds and Kennedy 2010).

16. Payments to existing account holders had already been reduced by secondary legislation, in July 2010.

17. This could be seen as part of an international trend towards establishment of arm's-length 'fiscal councils' (Calmfors and Wren-Lewis 2011, Wren-Lewis 2011).

18. For example, ' "Bonfire of the Quangos" Revealed', *Channel 4 News*, 14 October 2010, available at http://www.channel4.com/news/bonfire-of-the-quangos-promised [accessed 18 April 2016].

19. For a brief explanation of secondary legislation, see Chapter 3. As discussed there, the degree of power delegated in this particular case led to complaints that it was a 'skeleton bill'.

20. In several cases the 'body' listed had various counterparts—for example operating in different parts of the UK. These are therefore minimum figures.

21. A full list can be found in the original bill as introduced (HL Bill 25 of session 2010–12) available at http://www.publications.parliament.uk/pa/ld201011/ldbills/025/2011025.pdf [accessed 8 August 2014].

22. The same rule already applied to those in privately rented property.

23. 'My Government will continue to reform the National Health Service in a way that maintains its founding principles. Measures will be brought forward to introduce more choice and diversity in health care provision and to continue to improve the quality of health services and hospital hygiene. Legislation to restrict smoking in enclosed public places and workplaces will also be introduced' (House of Commons Hansard, 17 May 2005, column 29). The words on ID cards and corporate manslaughter appeared in columns 29 and 30 respectively.

24. For example, the Labour opposition tabled a lengthy reasoned amendment at Commons second reading on the Welfare Reform Bill (House of Commons Hansard, 9 March 2011, column 934). In total, five of the 12 bills faced divisions on second reading, either on the motion itself or on a reasoned amendment (or both): Identity Cards,

Further Education and Training, Savings Accounts and Health in Pregnancy Grant, Public Bodies, and Welfare Reform.

25. See Joint Committee on Conventions (2006). During the entire period 1999–2012 there were only 12 divisions in the Lords at second reading, just two of which explicitly sought to reject the bill (Russell 2013).

26. A 'money bill' is a bill judged by the Commons Speaker to contain only national taxation or spending provisions, as set out in the Parliament Act 1911. The Act allows such bills to be sent for royal assent without the approval of the Lords one month after being passed by the Commons. In practice this provision has never been used, and the Lords does not usually seek to amend such bills. For discussion, see Constitution Committee (2011), Greenberg (2013).

27. The main other category comprises 'bills of aids and supplies'. Not all Finance Bills (i.e. bills implementing the annual Budget) will be classified as money bills, but all fall into this other category.

28. Standing orders allow these committees to be as large as 50 members, but they are usually significantly smaller.

29. The membership of public bill committees is decided by the Commons Committee of Selection, most of whose members are party whips. This is in fact an even more closed process than used to apply to the select committees, as Committee of Selection proposals for select committee membership pre-2010 required endorsement by the chamber, while the membership lists for public bill committees do not.

30. This kind of reform had long been called for (e.g. Hansard Society 1992). Evidence-taking does not apply to bills arriving in the Commons having already been scrutinized by the Lords. For discussion of bills published in draft form, see Chapter 3.

31. In the Lords, amendments disagreed on division at committee stage 'may not be retabled on report', although a substantively different amendment on the same topic may be submitted (House of Lords 2015: 150). By contrast, there is no such rule in the Commons.

32. For example, in the 2010–12 session there were 128 divisions at report stage, compared to 34 at committee stage and 26 at third reading—of which 27, six and six respectively resulted in defeat (Russell 2013).

33. Under the 'English Votes for English Laws' reforms, introduced in October 2015, government legislation containing any clause or schedule certified as relating only to England (or to England and Wales) now has its 'legislative grand committee' stage(s) in-between Commons report and third reading. This change took effect after our period of study, but is described in Gover and Kenny (2016).

34. Five of the 12 bills faced divisions on third reading: Identity Cards, Health, Savings Accounts and Health in Pregnancy Grant, Public Bodies, and Welfare Reform.

35. An attempt to defeat the coalition's Health and Social Care Bill in the 2010–12 session was the first such vote since at least 1970.

36. Some other bicameral systems instead enforce a fixed number of rounds, or some other stopping rule (Tsebelis and Money 1997). One limitation on this is the so-called 'double insistence rule', which prevents repeated disagreement on the precise same words—but this is usually easily avoided procedurally (see House of Lords 2015: 159–60).

37. To qualify under the Acts, a bill must have been rejected by the Lords in both sessions, and a year must have elapsed between its initial Commons second reading and its final Commons approval. The extent of delay that would be caused hence varies, according to the length of the session and the timing of the bill's introduction.

38. The War Crimes Act 1991, European Parliamentary Elections Act 1999, Sexual Offences (Amendment) Act 2000, and Hunting Act 2004.
39. In both chambers there is also the ability to propose a 'manuscript' amendment on the day of debate, which is not printed. But these are strongly discouraged, and rare.
40. The exception is 'motions' during the ping-pong stages (counted in our figures as amendments), which in the Lords may be proposed in the name of only one member.
41. For example the long title of the Welfare Reform Bill was 'to make provision for universal credit and personal independence payment; to make other provision about social security and tax credits; to make provision about the functions of the registration service, child support maintenance and the use of jobcentres; and for connected purposes'.
42. The rules for amendments judged out of order in the Commons are specified in Erskine May (2011: 576–7).
43. The Lords rules are set out in the *Companion to the Standing Orders* (House of Lords 2015: 132); peers are advised by the clerks not to table amendments that are out of order, and on very rare occasions they have rejected this advice.

3

Government Drafting and Handling of Legislation

This book focuses on the legislative process as applied to government bills. Hence when considering the role of different actors, the natural place to start is with the government itself.

Government bills begin their life in (what is generally referred to as) 'Whitehall', being prepared by government departments—for example, the Home Office or Department of Health—in conjunction with government lawyers.[1] Within parliament, their progress is overseen by government ministers in both the Commons and the Lords, supported by their officials. As discussed below, many of the amendments made to bills in parliament are also drafted and proposed by the executive. Hence understanding government processes with respect to parliament is absolutely central to understanding how legislation is made.

But the passage of a bill through parliament also tells only part of the story. Where public policy scholars describe the policy-making process as a cycle, or a series of stages, parliament's input might be expected to occur at the decision-making stage. But before a bill is presented to parliament, the issue that it deals with must first have been brought to government's attention ('agenda setting'), and the policy been formulated. These prior stages often require much preparation—and frequently also consultation—on the part of government. The extent of discussion at this point is potentially important to the later parliamentary passage of a bill. Indeed, when preparing its policy government may well seek to anticipate parliament's likely reaction. Hence this chapter also discusses the early stages of policy formulation with respect to the 12 bills studied in the book, to provide context for their parliamentary passage.

In a pattern that will be repeated in subsequent chapters, we begin by identifying precisely who we are talking about when discussing the role of 'government'— as there are many different kinds of government actors involved. We then briefly explore what the existing literature has to say about the role of these actors, and of government in general, in the legislative process. Next, we work our way through the development of legislation from the point of view of government, illustrated throughout with material about the 12 bills. We start by considering the source of bills (which may formally 'originate' with government, but often result from pressure by external forces), and the early policy formulation process, including the degree of government consultation. We next briefly outline the procedure for

Legislation at Westminster. First edition. Meg Russell and Daniel Gover. © Meg Russell and Daniel Gover 2017. Published 2017 by Oxford University Press.

actually drafting a bill before its parliamentary introduction, and how ministers and officials prepare strategies for handling bills in parliament. This is followed by a discussion of the government's role during the parliamentary process itself. In the final substantive section we consider the question of government amendments—why they are made, the pattern of amendment to the case study bills, and the extent to which government amendments are actually driven by external demands—particularly from actors inside parliament. This provides useful context for future chapters, which focus on how each of these non-government forces—the opposition, government backbenchers, and other groups—contribute to the process.

The Government: Who Are They?

When considering the passage of a bill through parliament, by far the most visible representatives of government are ministers. But supporting them are myriad other people working for the government in different capacities—both from the department sponsoring the bill, and holding more central coordinating roles.

Starting with the visible face, several ministers will be involved in the preparation and parliamentary passage of any bill. Ultimately the Secretary of State or other cabinet-level equivalent (e.g. the Chancellor of the Exchequer for Treasury bills) is responsible for all of the work of their department. They will be key in deciding whether to bid to have a bill in the government's legislative programme, and may need to make the case for departmental legislation at the highest level—in Cabinet, with the Treasury and the Prime Minister's office in 10 Downing Street. When the bill is prepared, this senior departmental minister will have some oversight, and ultimately approve it on the department's behalf. In most cases they also speak in the highest-profile parliamentary debates—such as the bill's Commons second and third reading. But the day-to-day work on most bills takes place below cabinet level. Usually a more junior minister in the department is tasked with coordinating work on a bill—including during its preparation and its parliamentary stages. Most often this is a Commons minister, whose duties will include piloting the bill through its committee stage in that chamber and contributing in the chamber debates—for example by giving the closing speech at the second reading. In the Lords the bill must likewise be piloted by a minister, but Lords ministers are less numerous and also generally more junior. This often means that ministers from outside the lead department must contribute—as occurred for example on Labour's Health Bill, where Baroness (Jan) Royall (at the time a junior whip) supported the Minister of State in the Department of Health Lord (Norman) Warner. The senior minister responsible for the bill in the Commons, and the lead bill ministers in both chambers, are shown in Table 3.1 for the 12 case study bills.

Ministers have two obvious sources of support during the passage of a bill. The first is the general support of their Private Office—for example in organizing meetings and correspondence. The second is the more focused support which comes from the 'bill team', consisting of policy civil servants—who manage the preparation of the bill as well as its passage through parliament. This group is headed by the

Table 3.1 Lead ministers on the 12 case study bills

Bill	Commons senior minister	Commons bill minister	Lords minister
Identity Cards	Charles Clarke, Home Secretary	Tony McNulty, Minister of State	Bns. Scotland of Asthal, Minister of State
Health	Patricia Hewitt, Secretary of State for Health	Caroline Flint, Parliamentary Under-Secretary of State	Lord Warner, Minister of State
Corporate Manslaughter	John Reid, Home Secretary	Gerry Sutcliffe, Parliamentary Under-Secretary of State	Bns. Scotland of Asthal, Minister of State
Further Education	Alan Johnson, Secretary of State for Education and Skills	Bill Rammell, Minister of State	Lord Adonis, Parliamentary Under-Secretary of State
Employment	Pat McFadden, Minister of State, DBERR	Pat McFadden	Lord Jones of Birmingham, Minister of State
Saving Gateway Accounts	Yvette Cooper, Chief Secretary to the Treasury	Ian Pearson, Economic Secretary to the Treasury	Lord Myners, Financial Services Secretary to the Treasury
Energy	Ed Miliband, Secretary of State for Energy and Climate Change	Joan Ruddock, Minister of State	Lord Hunt of Kings Heath, Minister of State
Identity Documents	Theresa May, Home Secretary	Damian Green, Minister of State	Bns. Neville-Jones, Minister of State
Savings Accounts	Mark Hoban, Financial Secretary to the Treasury	Mark Hoban	Lord Sassoon, Commercial Secretary to the Treasury
Budget Responsibility	Justine Greening, Economic Secretary to the Treasury	Justine Greening	Lord Sassoon, Commercial Secretary to the Treasury
Public Bodies	Francis Maude, Minister for the Cabinet Office	Nick Hurd, Minister of State	Lord Taylor of Holbeach, Government Whip
Welfare Reform	Iain Duncan Smith, Secretary of State for Work and Pensions	Chris Grayling, Minister of State	Lord Freud, Parliamentary Under-Secretary of State

Note: In all cases the junior minister is drawn from the same department as the senior minister, unless stated.

Abbreviations: Bns. = Baroness; DBERR = Department of Business, Enterprise and Regulatory Reform; DEFRA = Department for Environment, Food and Rural Affairs.

Bill Team Leader, and usually comprises only a handful of members. Depending on the nature of the bill, other policy civil servants beyond the bill team (including some from other departments) will often also feed into this process—as will ministers' special advisers.

Both during initial preparation and a bill's parliamentary passage, officials more centrally located in government are also crucial. Primary responsibility for drafting government bills (and government amendments) lies with 'parliamentary counsel'—the specialist lawyers employed for this specific purpose. The Office of the Parliamentary Counsel comprises around 50 lawyers, is formally part of the Cabinet Office, and is headed by the First Parliamentary Counsel—who has a status similar to a departmental Permanent Secretary. Within the Cabinet Office there is also a Parliamentary Business and Legislation Secretariat, which coordinates introduction and management of bills and supports the cabinet committee which oversees the process (as further set out below). Both they and the department managing the bill must coordinate with other central officials—including in Number 10 and the Treasury, and in the whips' offices in both chambers.

Established Understanding of Government and the Legislative Process

As already outlined in previous chapters, the common assumption is that government dominates the legislative process in parliamentary democracies, and particularly in Britain. For example, the well-known comparativist Arend Lijphart (1999: 127, 34) suggests that Britain is an example of 'clear executive dominance' and that 'there is no good reason to judge any cabinets to be more dominant than the British Cabinet'. In most parliamentary systems legislatures are seen as merely 'reactive', while the main policy initiative lies with the executive (Mezey 1979, Norton 1998a). As discussed in Chapter 2, scholars emphasize the dominance of government legislation, and government amendments, at the expense of those proposed by non-government actors in the legislature (e.g. Olson 1994). Specifically, with respect to Britain, Norton (2013: 77) suggests that 'MPs and peers are not involved centrally in the initiation and formulation of legislation. It is overwhelmingly a government-centred activity.'

Public policy scholars, who have a strong interest in influence within the policy process, tend to focus on the executive's policy decisions, and emphasize its interaction with forces external to parliament—such as pressure groups, the media and public opinion—while giving relatively little attention to the formal legislative process (John 2012, Knill and Tosun 2012). A dominant theme has been the notion of 'policy networks' or 'policy communities' which draw together government insiders and pressure group representatives in deciding policy direction (Rhodes and Marsh 1992, Richardson and Jordan 1979). In line with Richardson and Jordan's alleged 'post-parliamentary democracy', parliamentarians—with the exception of ministers themselves—are seen as largely external to these networks. This contrasts to the

USA, where it has long been considered that 'Congress ... plays an integral role in many policy communities' (Baumgartner and Jones 1993: 195).

We saw in Chapter 2 that public policy scholars often characterize the policy process in terms of distinct phases or stages. Their attention often focuses on the earlier stages (i.e. agenda setting and policy formulation), or the later stages (i.e. implementation and evaluation), rather than the decision-making stage where parliament's main contribution might be expected. As Chapter 2 indicated, scholars who have explicitly sought to link legislative studies to public policy have noted that parliament's contribution might also be significant at these other stages (Mezey 1991). Nonetheless Wood's study of industrial policy at Westminster suggested that 'the policy *preparation* stage is dominated by civil servants and essentially outside the realm of parliamentary influence' (1991: 121, emphasis in original).

While most public policy scholars do not pay close attention to the legislative process, the same is true to some extent of legal scholars—albeit for different reasons. They are clearly interested in legislation, but often more in its drafting and its interpretation than in the political processes that help to bring it about. An interesting exception is the recent book by Greenberg (2011), a former government parliamentary counsel. It is, like this book, structured around the roles of different actors who participate in the legislative process, evaluating the contribution of each. Greenberg understandably—given both his background and the dominant understanding of the process—focuses most attention on those inside government itself. He places particular emphasis on the importance of officials, suggesting for example that 'on most Bills the involvement of Ministers ... is occasional and peripheral' while 'the personal influence of the senior drafter on an Act is potentially immense' (ibid.: 11, 24).

Such close attention on the role of government insiders in managing legislation (rather than formulating policy in the broader sense), is relatively unusual in the academic literature. A useful exception is the work of Page, which has included detailed focus on the roles of parliamentary counsel and of bill teams. He for example charts the very substantial growth in numbers of parliamentary counsel, from only 18 members in 1961, and 28 in 1994, to 40 in 2000 and 60 by 2007 (Page 2009). Such growth might be expected to have a positive impact on preparedness of government legislation prior to parliamentary introduction—though it is also associated with a greater volume of legislation overall. In his study of bill teams Page (2003: 651) analysed in detail the progress of four bills in 2002, concluding that the 'role of civil servants in preparing legislation is far more important than is generally assumed' and that such teams—despite often being made up of relatively junior civil servants—'work with considerable autonomy' from ministers (ibid.). Also crucial to the passage of legislation are the government whips and respective Leaders of the two chambers, collectively known as the 'business managers', who meet with their opposition counterparts privately through the so-called 'usual channels'. These have received relatively little academic attention, but were thoroughly catalogued by Rush and Ettinghausen (2002), and are also discussed by Cowley (2002, 2005).

Where authors focus on the detailed preparation of legislation, and the actual interaction between government insiders and parliament, they often note that the government is not as dominant as it seems. As already discussed in Chapter 2, Griffith (1974) explored the extent to which amendments moved by ministers in parliament in fact responded to objections raised by other parliamentary actors, such as opposition members and government backbenchers. With respect to the Commons committee stage this work has since been updated by Thompson (2013, 2015). Griffith demonstrated that although the great majority of amendments actually made to legislation in parliament were proposed by ministers, '[m]ost Government amendments moved in committee in the Commons are the result of extra-Parliamentary activity or of pressure exerted by Members [of Parliament] privately' (1974: 94). Likewise, both authors found that government amendments at the Commons report stage often responded to points raised by other non-government parliamentarians in committee. Their focus was the Commons, but similar dynamics operate in the Lords, where ministers must also often prepare compromise amendments—both in response to defeats, and also in order to avoid them (Russell 2013, Russell and Sciara 2008). Page (2003) noted that significant effort by bill teams during the parliamentary stages went into drafting ministerial amendments following points raised by non-government parliamentarians. So, the relatively few studies that exist show a consistent pattern: parliament may in fact have significant impact on government legislation at the decision-making stage, but much of this remains hidden if you consider only the official sponsors of successful amendments.

Nonetheless, as already emphasized in Chapter 1, parliament's prior influence through 'anticipated reactions' may be even greater. Mezey (1979: 26) pointed out that 'government proposals [may] appear to pass the legislature unopposed and unamended simply because the government avoids introducing those things which may provoke legislative resistance, or because it has acceded to changes privately'. If the government introduces legislation that has been formulated in order to be acceptable to parliament, subsequent amendment may prove unnecessary. Very little is written about this dynamic, though Page (2003: 653) cites a bill team member as saying that one of the key objectives in government's preparation of bills is 'to get the legislation in a form that would actually go through parliament'. Former First Parliamentary Counsel George Engle (1983) has specifically emphasized this imperative, as has his successor Stephen Laws (2016b). As discussed later in this chapter, there are increasingly sophisticated internal mechanisms to achieve it. Given this likely action by governments at the early stages specifically to avoid legislative conflict one scholar has recently suggested, from a comparative perspective, that the central question is '[w]hy does executive-initiated legislation ever get defeated?' (Saiegh 2011: 5).

A close focus on government's handling of legislation enables us to explore various questions about influence in the legislative process. At the most basic level, the mechanisms for government preparation and introduction of legislation are not often discussed, and we describe them. Our particular interest is the extent to which parliament is taken into account during this preparatory phase, as well as during the subsequent parliamentary passage of bills; few studies have previously questioned government insiders about such dynamics. This focus helps us to address questions set out at the start of the book, about visible and less visible legislative influence, and the motivations behind legislative amendments—starting with those proposed by ministers themselves. We explore how responsive ministers are to parliament, at what policy stage(s), and to which actors in particular—for example, the extent to which government both seeks to anticipate, and responds to, the views of the Commons versus the Lords. Reviewing the pre-parliamentary preparation and formulation of policy also enables us to consider later in the book whether bills introduced into parliament in a rushed manner without careful planning become subject to greater parliamentary pressure, and perhaps to greater change. Hence we begin our consideration of the 12 case study bills with a summary of this policy formulation stage.

Government and Policy Formulation

There are many different potential triggers for government legislation. The public policy literature gives significant attention to 'agenda setting', and it is far from straightforward to trace the original sources of policy ideas (Page 2006, Rose 1980). To attempt to do this for the case study bills would be beyond the scope of our study, though we are clearly interested in whether parliament contributed—which is touched upon at various points throughout the book. At a basic level, some bills are strongly backed by the party (or parties) forming the government, and may implement policies that appeared in an election manifesto—even sometimes helping to distinguish the party very publicly from its competitors. Other bills may have been pressed heavily on the government by outside interest groups, or respond to external events. Such legislation may be partly declaratory, to signal that the government is taking action. Some bills are relatively less ideological and lower profile—often representing incremental changes to existing government programmes. These categories are, of course, not mutually exclusive. For example a bill may respond to interest groups but also have the strong public backing of the governing party, while even many 'flagship' bills contain some additional content which is far more routine.[2]

The case study bills demonstrated a wide variety of influences prior to introduction (as already touched upon in Chapter 2). Labour's Identity Cards Bill implemented a flagship policy which had appeared in the party's manifesto. Its Health Bill contained the flagship provision to ban smoking in public places, but also a number of proposals responding to recent events—such as the inquiry into the murder of numerous patients by GP Harold Shipman—and various lower-profile matters. The Employment Bill made mostly incremental changes, but also responded to a court ruling. Under the coalition, the bills were quite strongly manifesto-related, as they appeared in the first parliamentary session of the new government. But even here some lower-profile policies crept in: most notably the provisions on the National

Audit Office in the Budget Responsibility and National Audit Bill, which had previously been dropped from Labour's Constitutional Reform and Governance Bill in the previous parliament.

In formulating policy, provisions in many of the case study bills were subject to consultation, some dating back years before the bill was introduced. The classic means by which government consults is via a 'green paper' which explicitly invites comments on future policy direction and/or a 'white paper' which sets out policy intentions that are more concrete. Such papers may elicit parliamentary responses—particularly from select committees, which frequently base inquiries around them. Upon a green or white paper's publication, there will also often be a government statement to parliament, allowing members to question the minister, while other formal parliamentary mechanisms, such as oral and written questions, may be used to tease out the detail. All of this feeds into the process before a bill is published and introduced. In recent years, the government has also adopted a practice of publishing some bills in 'draft' form for 'pre-legislative scrutiny' before their formal introduction, often explicitly inviting select committees to comment (but this remains the exception rather than the rule).[3] Consultation papers and draft bills also obviously allow others outside parliament—particularly pressure groups, as discussed in Chapter 7—to feed into the policy formulation process.

The variation between the bills is illustrated in Table 3.2, which summarizes some of the key consultations and other events which fed into their preparation. Notably, there was relatively little consultation on policy in the coalition's bills prior to their introduction—unsurprisingly, as the change of government meant that the coalition parties had not been able to commission such reviews. But it is worth noting that because two of the bills (the Identity Documents Bill and Savings Accounts and Health in Pregnancy Grant Bill) reversed previous Labour legislation there had been substantial recent discussion on the issues concerned, including in parliament. The coalition sought in part to respond to previous criticisms made. With respect to the Budget Responsibility and National Audit Bill, the Conservative Party had announced the establishment of a 'shadow' Office for Budget Responsibility (OBR) in 2009, and immediately upon assuming office the coalition established an interim OBR with the same chair, Sir Alan Budd. While there was no formal consultation, the interim OBR went on to be examined by the Treasury Select Committee, at the same time that the government was preparing its bill (as discussed further in Chapter 8). The remaining two coalition bills—the Welfare Reform Bill and Public Bodies Bill—were subject only to brief consultations, some of which overlapped their parliamentary passage. Some of these documents were examined by parliamentary committees; one of them (on the future of public forests) was actually withdrawn before its closing date, as the government abandoned the policy.

The example of the coalition's forestry policy indicates how lack of prior government consultation can lead to difficulties in parliament. But the Labour bills illustrate that extensive consultation does not necessarily prevent parliamentary controversy. The gestation of all of these bills was longer, as our study period covered the government's third term in office. The most striking example is the Identity Cards Bill, where discussion of the central policy can be traced back well

Table 3.2 Key examples of pre-legislative consultation on the 12 case study bills

Bill	Key central government publications and any draft bills	Key external inquiries and reviews
Identity Cards	• *Entitlement Cards and Identity Fraud: A Consultation Paper* (Jul. 2002) • *Identity Cards: The Next Steps* (Nov. 2003) • *Legislation on Identity Cards: A Consultation* (Apr. 2004) • Draft Identity Cards Bill (2003–04)	
Health	• *Choosing Health: Making Healthy Choices Easier* (Nov. 2004) • *Consultation on the Smokefree Elements of the Health Improvement and Protection Bill* (Jun. 2005) • *Making the Best Use of the Pharmacy Workforce: A Consultation Paper* (Dec. 2004) • *Action on Health Care Associated Infections in England* (Jul. 2005) • *Proposals to Reform and Modernise Pharmaceutical Services Legislation in England* (Jul. 2005)	• Office of Fair Trading: *The Control of Entry Regulations and Retail Pharmacy Services in the UK* (Jan. 2003) • Shipman Inquiry: *The Regulation of Controlled Drugs in the Community* (Jul. 2004)
Corporate Manslaughter	• *Reforming the Law on Involuntary Manslaughter: The Government's Proposals* (May 2000) • Draft Corporate Manslaughter Bill (2004–05)	• Law Commission: *Legislating the Criminal Code: Involuntary Manslaughter* (Mar. 1996)
Further Education and Training	• *Further Education: Raising Skills Improving Life Chances* (Mar. 2006)	• Sir Andrew Foster: *Realising the Potential: A Review of the Future Role of Further Education Colleges* (Nov. 2005)
Employment	• *Success at Work: Protecting Vulnerable Workers, Supporting Good Employers* (Mar. 2006) • *Success at Work: Resolving Disputes in the Workplace: A Consultation* (Mar. 2007) • *National Minimum Wage and Employment Agency Standards Enforcement: Consultation Document* (May 2007) • *National Minimum Wage and Voluntary Workers: Consultation Document* (Jun. 2007) • *Success at Work: Consultation on Measures to Protect Vulnerable Agency Workers* (Feb. 2007) • *ECHR Judgment in ASLEF v. UK Case—Implications for Trade Union Law: Consultation Document* (May 2007)	• Michael Gibbons: *Better Dispute Resolution: A Review of Employment Dispute Resolution in Great Britain* (Mar. 2007) • Low Pay Commission: *National Minimum Wage Low Pay Commission Report 2005* (Feb. 2005)

Table 3.2 *Continued*

Bill	Key central government publications and any draft bills	Key external inquiries and reviews
Saving Gateway Accounts	• *Saving and Assets for All: The Modernisation of Britain's Tax and Benefit System, Number Eight* (Apr. 2001) • *Delivering Saving and Assets: The Modernisation of Britain's Tax and Benefit System, Number Nine* (Nov. 2001) • *The Saving Gateway: Operating a National Scheme* (Mar. 2008)	
Energy	• *Towards Carbon Capture and Storage: A Consultation Document* (Jun. 2008) • *A Framework for the Development of Clean Coal: Consultation Document* (Jun. 2009) • *The UK Low Carbon Transition Plan: National Strategy for Climate and Energy* (Jul. 2009)	
Identity Documents	None	
Savings Accounts	None	
Budget Responsibility	None	
Public Bodies	None prior to bill's introduction • *The Future of the Public Forest Estate in England: A Public Consultation* (Jan. 2011) (published after bill's introduction) • *Consultation on Reforms Proposed in the Public Bodies Bill: Reforming the Public Bodies of the Ministry of Justice* (Jul. 2011) (published after bill's introduction)	
Welfare Reform	• *21st Century Welfare* (Jul. 2010) • *Universal Credit: Welfare That Works* (Nov. 2010) • *Disability Living Allowance Reform* (Dec. 2010) • *Strengthening Families, Promoting Parental Responsibility: The Future of Child Maintenance* (Jan. 2011)	

Note: Excludes consultations and other documents published after the bill was introduced to parliament, unless otherwise stated.

over a decade—which did not prevent the bill being hotly debated in parliament.[4] From the late 1980s, Conservative backbench MPs had urged the Thatcher government to introduce identity cards, including through a number of unsuccessful private members' bills (see Chapter 5). In October 1994 the Home Secretary Michael Howard announced the government's intention to pursue such a scheme, and subsequently issued the green paper *Identity Cards: a Consultation Document* (Home Office 1995). The House of Commons Home Affairs Committee (1996) reported in favour of a voluntary ID cards scheme, and the government promised a draft bill, which never appeared.

Labour was initially opposed to ID cards, and the 1997 government took no action. But in 1999 Home Secretary Jack Straw commented that while he could 'see no arguments to convince me in favour of compulsory identity cards', he could 'fully understand the arguments in favour of voluntary identity cards'.[5] Arguments at first concentrated on how cards might help prove 'entitlement' to public services (such as the NHS) and tackle identity fraud. But interest grew in their potential security benefits following the terrorist attacks in the USA in September 2001. Thus the government issued a consultation paper the following July, stating that it had 'already ruled out the option of a compulsory scheme and does not wish to consult on it', but favouring a voluntary scheme, whereby it 'was entirely at the discretion of the individual whether they registered with the scheme and obtained a card' (Home Office 2002: 20, 18). A white paper followed in November 2003, and a draft bill—which was subject to pre-legislative scrutiny by the Home Affairs Committee (see Chapter 8)—in April 2004. A bill was formally introduced later that year, but failed to complete its parliamentary passage before the 2005 election. The policy was high profile throughout, and a vocal umbrella organization, 'NO2ID', was formed in May 2004 to coordinate opposition.

Policies in other Labour bills were also subject to prior discussion and consultation, but none to the same extent. Just one other bill—the Corporate Manslaughter and Corporate Homicide Bill—was published in draft form for consultation. This policy had also been under consideration for a long time, following a review by the Law Commission which recommended a new 'special offence of corporate killing' (1996: 110).[6] Home Secretary Jack Straw pledged action to the Labour Party conference in 1997, but none followed in that parliament. Labour committed to the policy in its 2001 manifesto, but the draft bill was not published until March 2005. The Commons committee which considered it, made up of members of the Home Affairs Committee and Work and Pensions Committee, heard evidence from numerous groups. One of its most notable recommendations (in the light of subsequent events) was that the offence of corporate manslaughter should be applicable to deaths in police and prison custody—which the government instead proposed should be excluded under Crown immunity. As discussed in Chapter 7, key groups were split in their evidence to the committee on this point, with some wanting the exclusion lifted. This offered an indication of parliamentary battles to follow.

Other bills offer further clear examples of legislation sparked, at least in part, by independent external inquiries. The Health Bill and the Employment Bill both had wide scope and dealt with a number of somewhat disconnected issues. With respect to health, the inquiry chaired by Dame Janet Smith into the deaths caused by Harold Shipman published six reports, including one covering regulation of controlled drugs, which strongly informed Part 3 of the bill. Several of its more technical aspects (e.g. on pharmaceutical regulation) had been subject to government reviews. The most high-profile element, on smoking in public places, had also been exposed to much prior discussion—including in parliament. As with identity cards, this included pressure expressed through numerous private members' bills (see Chapter 5). A white paper in 2004 made proposals for smoke-free public places, and a more detailed consultation followed in June 2005.[7]

Similarly the Employment Bill followed the Gibbons review on dispute resolution in the workplace, and was unusual in overturning aspects of previous Labour legislation—where some provisions of the 2002 Employment Act were seen as problematic. The bill also responded to proposals from the Low Pay Commission on enforcement of the national minimum wage. The government issued its own consultation papers on how to respond to several of these issues. A final part of the bill responded to the European Court of Human Rights judgment in the *ASLEF v. UK* decision of February 2007. This related to trade unions' right to expel members belonging to extremist parties, and was triggered by the trade union ASLEF expelling a British National Party member. Previously, British law had forbidden trade unions from barring members on the basis of political party activism, but the judgment held that this breached article 11 of the European Convention on Human Rights on freedom of assembly and association. The government subsequently consulted on two options to implement the decision. One was to simply remove the previous legal exemption, and the other included clear safeguards. The government preferred the former—that is, giving trade unions freedom to expel members on the basis of their party affiliations, leaving protections to individual trade union rules. This was written into the bill, but proved controversial in parliament.

Legislation is also sometimes informed by the results of pilot studies—designed specifically to test the effectiveness of the policy. This occurred on Labour's Saving Gateway Accounts Bill, where there were consultations and then two waves of studies in five locations.[8] These tested different levels of contribution and government match funding. The pilots were deemed a success, including by the House of Commons Treasury Committee (2007), which issued a report encouraging the government to proceed with a national scheme. By the time the bill was introduced this was what one official described as 'a well-gestated policy'.

Government and the Pre-Parliamentary Preparation of Legislation

Having formulated its policy in broad terms, the government must develop its detailed ideas to present to parliament in the shape of a bill. But before this the relevant department must get cross-governmental agreement that such a bill should be introduced. The government's legislative programme is formally coordinated by the Leader of the House of Commons, who chairs a cabinet committee with oversight of such matters—currently entitled the Parliamentary Business and Legislation (PBL) committee.[9] This committee includes the other parliamentary business managers—that is, the Leader of the House of Lords and Chief Whips in both chambers—and additional ministers. As much as a year before each Queen's Speech the Commons Leader—supported by the PBL secretariat in the Cabinet Office—invites bids from departments for slots in the programme, which are considered by the committee. In practice, other central departments—particularly Number 10—have a very large influence in this process. There are usually many more bids than space, and those at the centre also want to ensure that the annual programme is balanced and communicates the right external messages. They thus want some 'flagship' bills which signal the government's key priorities, around which can be fitted various lower-profile bills.

Legislative drafting

Once a department has won a slot in the programme, it must provide parliamentary counsel with a detailed specification (known as 'instructions') to allow them to begin their work.[10] Policy staff work alongside departmental lawyers to put the instructions together, coordinating input from individual policy teams—of which there may be several for a large bill. The bill team provides the central point of contact between them, the minister, and other parts of government, and ensures that the bill is prepared on time. On large high-profile bills (such as the Corporate Manslaughter and Corporate Homicide Bill, or Public Bodies Bill) there will be significant coordination between departments and with Number 10; on lower-profile and more specialist policies (such as the Energy Bill) there may be relatively little. Where spending is involved (particularly in large quantity, as in the Welfare Reform Bill) such coordination will centrally involve the Treasury. On some policies, consultation with the devolved administrations (in Scotland, Wales, and Northern Ireland) will also be important. Discussion of major policies will involve ministers directly, but most occur at the official level.

When the government changes after a general election these well-organized processes face some disruption. Whitehall does its best to prepare for different eventualities, with opposition frontbenchers invited in to speak to officials about their plans in the preceding months. But their plans are often not well advanced, and the election outcome can remain uncertain (as was very clearly the case in 2010). The Queen's Speech of 17 May 2010 was based on the coalition agreements which had been hastily put together by the two parties. As a senior minister explained, preparation of the first session's legislative programme 'had to be done very quickly because we had just a matter of days before the Queen's Speech'. Hence 'officials worked heroically in the opening months of the government in order to get the bills through'.

Once the instructions are ready, parliamentary counsel can begin their work. Development of the bill itself will often be an iterative process, where counsel raise questions about the instructions and how to interpret them, offering choices to the department—mostly through departmental lawyers and policy officials, and only where necessary being referred to ministers. As a member of parliamentary counsel explained:

We will, in principle, try to draft something which makes the legal changes that the department have set out. Very often in the process of this we will question whether the changes that the department has envisaged are necessarily the right ones to give effect to the policy. A lot of that will be terribly technical stuff about the way that the statute book works. So they will say 'you need to repeal section 95', or whatever it is, and we'll say 'actually, we're not sure why section 95 gives you the effect that you think it will have'. So there's a lot of legal technical questioning going on, but also questions about what appear to us to be gaps in a policy, how it will work in practice.

This process of elaboration continues once the drafting itself has begun. In the words of the same official:

[Sometimes] in the process of trying to express it you realize you don't know what it is you're trying to express. So you might start to draft something, realize actually you can't do it because there are too many unanswered questions, and then you put the draft to one side and write [to the department]. Then once you've got the answers you pick up the draft and have another go.

In most cases this process will involve setting out the policy to a high level of detail in the bill. However, it is also quite normal for there to be gaps, where detail will be filled in later via government regulations. A classic example is in welfare policy, where the bill (i.e. 'primary legislation') sets out the broad principles of a social security benefit, while the details of benefit levels or eligibility will be left to regulations (or 'secondary legislation'). This maintains flexibility, for example to allow annual benefit uprating, because secondary legislation is subject to less stringent parliamentary scrutiny than primary legislation (Fox and Blackwell 2014). Subsequent regulations may be subject to the 'affirmative' parliamentary procedure, whereby they must be approved by both chambers but cannot be amended (and get no more than minimal debate), or the 'negative' procedure where there is no debate or vote unless parliamentarians explicitly request it. Although use of these procedures is essential to modern government, it can cause controversy. Most notably in 2015 the government sought major changes to the tax credits regime via secondary legislation, which the House of Lords objected to, causing the government in turn to suggest that the Lords had overreached its powers. The boundary between what belongs in primary and secondary legislation has thus become somewhat blurred, and recently been hotly contested.[11]

Where significant policy details are left out of a bill this often causes controversy during its passage through parliament. Such arguments applied particularly to two of our case studies—the Identity Cards Bill and Public Bodies Bill—both of which were widely seen as 'skeleton bills'. This style of drafting can be a result of lack of clarity on the part of ministers about what precisely they are seeking to achieve, and/or of undue haste in preparing the legislation. The Welfare Reform Bill was also seen as stretching the principle of delegated power over the detail of benefits quite far. As an official said with respect to the Identity Cards Bill, 'it was a skeleton in that the precise details of how they were going to implement it was not settled to start with. So they had a number of options and wanted a bill that covered all the options'. Likewise, on the coalition's Public Bodies Bill an official explained that 'a lot of departments, and DEFRA [responsible for the forestry provisions] was certainly guilty of this ... of not actually knowing what they wanted to do, and what they would use the powers for'. These characteristics became controversial during the subsequent parliamentary stages, as described in later chapters.

It is during the drafting process that consideration of the bill's likely reception in parliament begins in earnest. On the technical side, parliamentary counsel will make contact with parliamentary clerks about procedural points—such as whether the bill will need a 'money resolution', and potentially whether it might even be certified by the Commons Speaker to be a 'money bill' (and thus have an expedited passage through the House of Lords—as applied to the Savings Accounts and Health in Pregnancy Grant Bill, discussed in Chapter 4). Contact between these officials will continue throughout the bill's passage, for example regarding whether amendments are 'in scope' or engage financial privilege (see Greenberg 2011). More substantively, both the bill team and ministers will think ahead during the drafting stages to the necessary parliamentary 'handling' of the bill.

Parliamentary handling

Once the bill is more or less fully drafted, the minister must attend a meeting of the PBL committee to obtain approval for its parliamentary introduction. This second discussion focuses on the detail of the bill, rather than an in-principle out-line, and it is considered alongside its explanatory notes and other related documents such as the delegated powers memorandum. A key concern will be any difficulties envisaged during the bill's passage through parliament, and how these will be managed. The meeting decides whether the bill should be published at all, whether it might be better suited to draft publication for pre-legislative scrutiny, and—if it is to be formally introduced to parliament—whether this should happen via the Commons or the Lords. This can be a tough meeting for the bill minister, who must attend without supporting officials, and faces questioning from the business managers—particularly the whips—who are in contrast supported by theirs. A key player here is the Private Secretary to the Commons Chief Whip—a permanent civil servant with a central coordinating function over the government's parliamentary business; but input from the Lords is very important as well.[12]

In the late 1990s the Labour government introduced greater formality to the process of preparing bills for parliamentary introduction, requiring all departments to draft a written 'handling strategy', to be scrutinized by the cabinet committee. Such documents originally related only to the Lords, but now apply to both chambers. As set out in the Cabinet Office *Guide to Making Legislation*, the handling strategy must indicate 'which areas are likely to be contentious, based on an awareness of the mood of the House', plus members 'likely to take a particular interest and what engagement with them is planned', and details of 'possible concessions and fallback positions' (Cabinet Office 2015: 136–7). The preparation of this document rests with the bill team, who work with officials in the whips' offices in both chambers, using a template provided by the Cabinet Office secretariat. Departmental policy officials are often fairly unfamiliar with the dynamics of parliament, so the input of these latter groups is important. Once the document has been agreed between officials it is circulated to members of the PBL committee for discussion with the minister.

This formal process reinforces a more general dynamic whereby consideration of parliamentarians' views occurs right from the early stages. As a former Labour minister explained, 'when government starts drafting legislation it already has to have a view in its mind as to what it can get through parliament'. A civil servant likewise described parliament as part of the 'climate of opinion which shapes how the legislation is framed'.

An interesting question is which of the two chambers is the primary focus when thinking through the bill's parliamentary reception. This frequently came up during our interviews, and was somewhat disputed among interviewees. One senior Conservative commented that 'the priority for bills and the structure for proposals are pretty much done alongside Commons members'. Most ministers are likely to be more attuned to the Commons, where they know that they must retain support of their backbenchers if the bill is to pass. In contrast, this interviewee continued, there is a 'deliberate exercise to understand what the Lords think about legislation and then try to anticipate it, even before the point at which legislation is introduced'. Such consideration is necessary, because, as a former Labour minister in the Lords put it, you should 'never underestimate the ignorance of Commons ministers about the Lords'. This interviewee suggested that:

The Secretary of State's life is spent making sure that MPs from his own party are supporting what he or she is intending, and they have very little time for the Lords; but the best Secretaries of State always took a lot of notice when legislation was being prepared to consider what the Lords' reaction would be.

It is this kind of conscious planning that the original introduction of 'Lords handling strategies' sought to institutionalize. While these now extend formally to both chambers, officials frequently observed that when preparing the legislation and handling strategy, 'it was the Lords that we had in mind'. The deliberate and conscious consideration of the Lords' likely view is a clear example of the classic 'power of anticipated reactions'. In contrast, the views of MPs are much more likely to be internalized by ministers, and considered relatively automatically—in something closer to Steven Lukes's (1974) third face power, as mentioned in Chapter 1. The Commons and the Lords thus play complementary roles in shaping government proposals.

The extent of this kind of behind-the-scenes thinking in government may appear surprising to those who assume that parliament, and the legislative process, is executive-dominated. But ministers and officials that we interviewed consistently emphasized its importance. Putting it simply, in the words of one former minister, 'the fact that parliament exists means that legislation is drafted in a way that you can get through parliament'. Where such consideration is not carried out, ministers can find themselves in trouble. Another former minister recalled a bill (not one of our case studies) where government was forced in parliament to change course, suggesting that 'nobody had done enough to anticipate the alliance of very well-informed members of both Houses'.

A key element of this careful planning is to identify changes that it may be necessary to make to the bill in order to navigate it through parliament. Hence various officials explained that 'you do have really quite a rigorous and detailed concessions strategy thought out in advance'. This meant that ministers would need a 'certain amount of discretion', 'had to have something in reserve', and needed to be 'ready to give certain things'. A concession strategy is officially required for the PBL approval meeting, but in quite broad terms—at this stage no concessionary amendments are actually drafted. Drafting occurs only if needed later in the process, with separate approval for any concessionary amendments subsequently sought from PBL members, usually via correspondence.

The cabinet committee must decide the bill's chamber of introduction. For a number of reasons Lords introduction is generally reserved for lower-profile, less controversial bills, with high-profile ones introduced via the Commons. Senior ministers are concentrated in the Commons, the chamber receives more media attention, and the government's primary accountability is to elected MPs. But also, bills introduced via the Lords are not subject to the Parliament Acts, meaning that ministers have no means of forcing them through without the Lords' consent—clearly leaving government more vulnerable. Among our case studies four bills were introduced via the Lords—the Employment Bill, Further Education and Training Bill, Budget Responsibility and National Audit Bill, and Public Bodies Bill. The first three of these were fairly typical Lords bills, being described by those in government as 'not frightfully controversial politically' or 'of insufficient gravity in the overall bill programme'. But reflecting on the Public Bodies Bill one peer with government experience suggested that it was 'very stupid to start it in the House of Lords'. This decision disappointed the ministers concerned, as officials suggested that 'they didn't think it would have the impact' in terms of drawing public attention to the promised 'bonfire of the quangos'. Plus, Lords introduction contributed greatly to the difficult passage of the bill. But it was a decision born of necessity, since management of the legislative programme requires some bills to be introduced via the Lords, and in the coalition's first session few other candidates were available.

Although the PBL committee can ultimately block a bill from introduction, we were told that this is 'very rare'. Generally, if problems cannot be ironed out in the preparations and negotiations prior to the committee meeting, the bill will merely be delayed. Yet we learned that there was, for example, a 'robust debate' about handling of the coalition's Welfare Reform Bill. Likewise, on the Public Bodies Bill, 'there was a recognition early on that was going to be a very difficult bill—[though] not as difficult as it turned out to be'. One official suggested that 'it would not have got through [PBL] committee if there had been any other bill ready'. This was a rapidly prepared bill on which there had been virtually no consultation and little parliamentary planning. Its reception in parliament—as described in subsequent chapters—showed the risks to government of such an approach.

Government's Role During the Parliamentary Process

Once a bill has been introduced into parliament, the question of 'handling' becomes very real. The same core government actors will remain involved in this process. Ministers guide the bill through each of its legislative stages in both chambers, publicly defending its content and responding to parliamentarians' questions and proposed amendments. They do this with the support of officials from the bill team, who will always be present—including to hand notes to the minister as and when required during debates. Behind the scenes, the bill team continues to work closely with parliamentary counsel, particularly in preparing responses to amendments, or drafting any amendments of the government's own. In terms of garnering votes, the whips in both chambers will also listen carefully to what members say, and seek to ensure that those on the government side attend and support the legislation. All of these groups work closely together throughout.

Government briefing and handling in parliament

Although the first formal discussion of a bill in both chambers takes place at its second reading, opportunities to communicate with parliamentarians generally start beforehand. In some cases these occur through formal channels, such as the debate on the Queen's Speech, or parliamentary questions. But many important informal channels exist as well. Ministers tend to engage in numerous behind-the-scenes meetings with parliamentarians during the passage of their bill, as further discussed below.

Throughout the parliamentary legislative process the bill team works hard to produce background briefing, to enable the minister to answer any questions that arise. For example, the 'second reading briefing pack', even for a relatively small and uncontroversial bill such as the Saving Gateway Accounts Bill, may run to several hundred pages. At the despatch box, the minister will retain a short version of this document, while supporting officials (who sit on benches to the side in a specially designated 'box') retain the longer version for additional backup. As one official explained, 'you try to think of every question you can' so that when sitting in the box a page can if necessary simply be torn out and passed to the minister by a Parliamentary Private Secretary (PPS) or whip.

At the committee stage, briefing and background work becomes more elaborate. Before the amendment process begins, ministers piloting bills that begin in the Commons are now likely to face questioning by the public bill committee. In these cases officials attend alongside the minister, and may also contribute to the evidence. For example on the Energy Bill ministers Joan Ruddock and David Kidney were formally questioned at the third sitting of the public bill committee. Both were members of the committee, which had heard evidence from outside groups at its previous two sittings. They were questioned for two and a half hours, alongside three officials (including the bill team manager)—one of whom responded to a small number of the questions. This is clearly a potentially testing environment, requiring much preparation on the detail of the bill.

In both chambers the committee stage is also when large numbers of non-government amendments are likely to be proposed, and these structure much of the debate on the bill. Here officials will prepare separate briefings on every amendment tabled. This requires fast work: as noted in Chapter 2, only three sitting days' notice is required for tabling amendments ahead of debates in the Commons, and even less in the Lords. Bill team officials may be required to work late nights or over the weekend, in close collaboration with government lawyers, with briefing work shared among them in what one described as a 'chaotic' process.[13] The finished documents, which may need further revision once the final grouping of amendments is available, must arrive with the minister in time to be absorbed before the committee meets.

The briefing on each non-government amendment will give a short interpretation of what it does, information about who is proposing it, and some speaking notes. Crucially it will also give advice on how the minister should respond to the amendment. This advice falls into fairly fixed categories, including 'resist', 'agree to consider', or 'agree in principle'. By default, most amendments will be resisted, as the government has clearly drafted the legislation in the form that it wants. Some amendments will run strongly counter to the government's policy or seek to reverse it. But where an amendment seeks clarification, highlights flaws, or makes constructive suggestions, ministers will wish to be more open—especially if it comes from an influential parliamentarian and/or one on their own side. For civil servants, this process is primarily technical and legal, while for ministers it is a job of political management. As one minister explained, when presenting a bill and facing parliamentary resistance, you need to:

ask yourself the basic question: 'why are these people so discomforted about what I see as being very reasonable?'. And then you've got to think 'well, I've got a job to do here, to try and make them at ease with what I'm trying to do'.

Where the member's case is strong (in which case contact may well have been made before the amendment is debated) the minister can indicate an intention to respond with a government amendment at a later stage—as further discussed in the next section. In Commons committee, parliamentary clerks will take a note when this occurs, making it likely that related non-government amendments tabled on report will be called. But a minister may be able to respond sympathetically in various other ways.[14] Sometimes a member may be reassured by a verbal account of the government's intent on the spot; if not, the minister may offer to write to them, or offer a private meeting to discuss the matter. An assurance on the record in Hansard can be important—since such statements potentially have legal force, being able to inform judicial interpretation under the *Pepper v. Hart* case of 1993.[15] As one official explained, 'with an eye to Pepper–Hart ministers are made to explain what legislation means, and subsequently ... [the courts] do refer back to what ministers thought they were advising parliament'. An example of such ministerial assurance was the government's response to amendments proposed by Labour's Lord (Larry) Whitty to the Public Bodies Bill, to ensure that employees would have their employment rights preserved where bodies were merged or functions transferred. This safeguard did not reach the face of the bill, but following behind-the-scenes discussions a form of words for the minister to use was agreed with Whitty in advance of the debate.[16] Such non-legislative concessions may be somewhat less troublesome for ministers to give than proceeding with amendments.[17] In addition to explanations, other forms of concession short of amending the bill itself include promises that something will be written into guidance circulated to officials implementing the policy, or that increased funding will be provided.

Intragovernmental tensions

It might be assumed that government behaves as a cohesive bloc when managing the parliamentary stages of legislation. But there are many internal tensions that can occur, and be played out through the legislative process—with parliament sometimes providing an important forum for their resolution.

Ministers and civil servants generally work harmoniously together to achieve the government's goals. But each faces different pressures, and sometimes tensions can arise between the two professional groups—including over responses to non-government parliamentarians. Ministers are in effect the interface between the government machine and parliament, with one foot in both. As political members of government, who are drawn from parliament and accountable to it, ministers will often be relatively more sympathetic to parliamentarians' views. As one former minister put it:

Parliament's important because these are elected representatives in all their glorious technicolour and diversity from all corners of the island that elects people, and I think with that what you also get is quite frankly a little bit more of real life than sometimes you get from within government departments.

Several interviewees suggested that ministers will sometimes take a more pragmatic attitude to legislation than their officials. A former minister claimed that 'having done the work on it civil servants want it to go through the way they drafted it', while politicians are 'more realistic'. As further discussed below, it is of course ministers who must smooth over difficulties in order to ensure that bills will pass. Another interviewee suggested that 'everybody thinks they are arguing with the government: you're not actually, you're arguing with the civil service'; hence 'what you often need is a strong minister who is prepared to overrule their civil servants'.

But tensions within government in the face of parliamentary pressure are not limited to professional ones between ministers and officials—far bigger interpersonal conflicts can arise among ministers themselves. One key example, which was fairly widely reported in the media at the time, occurred over the smoking ban in Labour's Health Bill.[18] Here the party manifesto had promised a partial ban on smoking in public places, with exclusions for licensed premises serving food and for private members' clubs—a policy negotiated by the then Health Secretary, John Reid. But after the election he was succeeded in post by Patricia Hewitt, who had greater sympathy with health professionals and parliamentarians who were calling for a total ban. Those close to the process told us that the change in Secretary of State 'made a significant difference', and allowed a move away from what some considered a 'frankly wholly unsatisfactory compromise in the manifesto'. Behind the scenes there was what one described as a 'bloody great row', which was elevated to the Cabinet, where it proved impossible to get agreement either to stick to the existing policy or to move to a total ban. As one protagonist explained (and as further discussed in Chapter 8) the government ultimately allowed a free (i.e. unwhipped) vote on the matter:

> We tried to get agreement at the [Cabinet] sub-committee and couldn't and then it basically went—I mean it didn't go to Cabinet, but it kind of went to the Prime Minister—and so we sort of thrashed it out there and just agreed, a free vote was the only way to go.

A particularly obvious form of internal tension occurred during the period of coalition government, where the two partners needed to reach agreement on policy. This too had the potential ultimately to be resolved in parliament. While a Liberal Democrat minister told us that 'it would be pretty dishonest to achieve collective agreement on a policy [within government] and quietly be trying to undermine it', there were some clear signs of this happening on the case study bills. A notable example was the Welfare Reform Bill where, as discussed in Chapter 5, Liberal Democrat backbenchers worked hard to argue for concessions, sometimes with the covert support of ministers. One interviewee told us that, during the row about the benefit cap proposals within the bill, members of the 'Quad' (which brought together the Conservative Prime Minister and Chancellor, and the Liberal Democrat Deputy Prime Minister and Chief Secretary to the Treasury) was divided. But such divisions inside coalition were not always along party lines, with interparty tensions intersecting in complex ways with more familiar interdepartmental conflicts. Most notably, interviewees reported disagreements between the Department for Work and Pensions and the Treasury over elements of this bill. For example we were told that the benefit cap was particularly pushed by the Treasury, and that 'certainly [DWP] officials hated it and I think ... to some extent that was true with ministers'. One key protagonist has written that relations between the two departments were 'often bad and sometimes awful' (Laws 2016a: 98). These tensions surfaced publicly in 2016 under the single-party Conservative government, when Secretary of State for Work and Pensions Iain Duncan Smith ultimately resigned from the Cabinet.

On the Public Bodies Bill, internal government negotiation over how much to concede to parliament proved particularly complex, given that many different departments were involved—each with interest in a particular body or bodies. Although the bill was managed by the Cabinet Office, tensions occurred for example over provisions 'owned' by the Ministry of Justice regarding the future of the Chief Coroner and the Youth Justice Board. Despite pressure from the Lords on these provisions, the department 'came across as more intransigent than anywhere else', and was described as 'literally prepared to hold the rest of the bill to ransom' by refusing to concede. In the end, Number 10 again got involved, and a meeting of interested departments was held to, as one official put it, 'face down the MoJ'. Compromise was ultimately reached in the Lords' favour on both provisions.

This leads to another source of internal government tension—of an intercameral kind, in terms of ministers handling the bill in the Commons and the Lords. While behind-the-scenes discussion (as further described below) takes place in both, debate in the Commons places greater emphasis on differentiation from the opposition, while the government's lack of a majority in the Lords means that—in the words of one former minister—a key objective is to 'forge the maximum degree of consensus'. As another said, 'you get brownie points in the Lords if you show you're listening to people'. Yet while facing an environment where government is numerically weaker, and therefore having to deploy significant negotiating skills, Lords ministers are generally junior within their departments. Hence one, who faced a particularly difficult reception in the Lords, confessed that 'the actual bill I didn't see until after it had been written'. Any changes normally have to be channelled through the lead minister in the Commons. As one such interviewee explained, 'this was my bill, so the Lords wouldn't agree anything without me saying "yes"'. Reflecting on the challenges Lord (John) Taylor faced in taking the Public Bodies Bill through the Lords, a former Labour minister suggested:

He will have been saying to Francis Maude [the Commons minister] and to other members of the Cabinet 'this bill is not going to get through the House of Lords in its present state, if you want to get some of it through you're going to have to change it'. And they'll have said, just like [name] used to say to me all the time, 'no, no, no, don't worry, don't be ridiculous, it will go through, it will be absolutely fine, you're just reading it wrong, you do not understand'.

Others close to the process on this bill recalled 'being very surprised just how unsighted the Commons ministers were as to what was going on in the Lords, because they didn't seem to have any idea just how difficult it was'. Despite all the emphasis placed on preparing handling strategies, such misunderstandings between the two chambers remain surprisingly common. In the end the Lords Chief Whip is central to advising what is feasible, not just with respect to the bill at hand, but in terms of implications for the whole legislative programme—because protracted arguments on one bill can limit the parliamentary time available for others. Hence, we were told, the Chief Whip will sometimes need to take a minister aside and warn that 'the session isn't going to be extended just because you want to keep fighting on x'.

Informal contact and meetings

Throughout a bill's parliamentary passage ministers and officials engage in numerous behind-the-scenes meetings with parliamentarians in both chambers, both individually and in groups. Meetings of various kinds generally form a key part of the government's 'handling strategy' for the bill. As explored at various points later in the book, these involve not just government backbenchers, as might be expected, but frequently also opposition frontbenchers and others. They range from large open meetings in the Lords to which all peers are invited, to small private meetings; from informal conversations with ministers in corridors to more formal scheduled meetings attended by their officials. Even on a relatively noncontroversial bill, a civil servant involved described extensive meetings, of both a 'purely political' kind (with officials absent) and 'on official government terms' (i.e. the reverse), including with opposition frontbenchers in both chambers. Such discussions allow members to air concerns, and gather information and assurances from the minister, away from the glare of publicity. As the same official suggested, off-the-record meetings allow you to have 'more helpful conversations than you can either in committee or on the floor of the House'. A minister likewise described how she would 'talk to people endlessly, square them off, explain when you can't and why you can't [meet their concerns]'.

Such meetings may be requested by non-government parliamentarians, or promised during debate by ministers in order to smooth over concerns expressed; but they are also often instigated by the government. Officials are frequently put into direct contact with members to discuss their concerns, or to consult on the wording of forthcoming government amendments or statements. Hence a member who has tabled an amendment might receive a phone call from a minister or departmental officials to discuss it. Exactly how these processes work on each bill depends on the personality of the minister (some are known for being more consultative than others), the degree of freedom that the minister has to negotiate (within the constraints set by the Secretary of State, or other departments including the Treasury), the culture of the department sponsoring the bill, and the degree of controversy surrounding the bill itself.

Among our case studies probably the most extensive behind-the-scenes discussions occurred on the coalition's troubled Public Bodies Bill. Lord Taylor was described as 'having discussions all over the House'. These began at an open meeting for peers before the bill's second reading, where we were told that there were 'gasps of amazement' at some of the officials' responses to questions, such that the event (in the words of another interviewee present) 'shook the bill team rigid'. Taylor subsequently held numerous meetings with peers, while one member of the bill team reported having personally met with two or three groups per week throughout the whole of the Lords committee stage—which lasted from late November to early March. Meetings continued thereafter, including during the Commons and ping-pong stages. These not only included Francis Maude, as cabinet minister with overall responsibility for the bill, but also ministers and officials from various other departments (including for example Secretary of State for Justice Ken Clarke), and parliamentary counsel. In addition, parallel meetings were occurring between government and outside groups. This illustrates how the debates on the official record in Hansard reflect only a very small part of the discussion that occurs during a bill's parliamentary stages.

Government Amendments and their Motivations

It is well established that the great majority of amendments made to legislation at Westminster are sponsored by government ministers. This is often taken as an indication that government dominates the legislative process. The first of these statements is undoubtedly correct; the second is far more open to question.

The next two tables show the number of amendments proposed and agreed to on the case study bills, by whether they were government or non-government-sponsored. Table 3.3 breaks these down by bill, while Table 3.4 does so by stage in the legislative process. The majority of amendments with explicit government backing are proposed solely in the name of ministers, but small numbers are co-sponsored with members of other groups. This is often a sign that government lawyers drafted the amendment in order to respond to parliamentary concerns—with non-government parliamentarians adding their name to a government amendment to show their approval, or a minister adding their name to an amendment formally sponsored by a non-government parliamentarian.[19] But to avoid the risk of overstating non-government influence, we class these as government amendments (which is also how they are treated in the official record).

The first feature obvious from the tables is that almost all government amendments (on these bills nearly 95 per cent) go on to be agreed, while this is true only a tiny minority (less than 4 per cent) of non-government amendments. Furthermore, the overall success rate of government amendments was really only dragged down by the Public Bodies Bill—where numerous such amendments were withdrawn in the Lords once it became clear that whole sections of the bill would be sacrificed. Only three government amendments on other bills failed to be agreed, all for fairly trivial administrative reasons.[20] This already makes government look dominant. In addition, it is important to acknowledge that of the 125 non-government amendments initially agreed, ninety-nine went on to be overturned at subsequent stages of the process. This is not reflected in the table, and is one reason why we base much of the analysis in the book on legislative 'strands'—as introduced in Chapter 2 and set out more fully in Appendix A—rather than just amendments.

Beyond this obvious factor, we see that the number of government amendments varied considerably by bill—from none on the Savings Accounts and Health in Pregnancy Grant Bill to over 200 on the Public Bodies Bill. On most bills the number of non-government amendments greatly outweighed that proposed by ministers. The variation by legislative stage is less pronounced. Notably, while the number of non-government amendments at committee stage greatly exceeds that at report, this is not true of government amendments. In the Commons, the number of government amendments at these two stages is broadly similar; the Lords the number at report is roughly double that in committee. This is one crude indication of government responsiveness to points raised by parliamentarians. We also see that 121 of the 125 agreed non-government amendments were in the Lords, and only four were in the Commons. Most of these occurred at the report and Lords consideration of Commons amendments (LCCA) stages, and most were a result of government defeats.[21]

Table 3.3 Government and non-government amendments proposed and agreed by bill

	Government amendments					Non-government amendments		
	Proposed			Agreed		Proposed	Agreed	% Agreed
	Govt alone	Govt & others	Total proposed	Total agreed	% Agreed			
2005–10 parliament								
Identity Cards	86	0	86	86	100.0	779	34	4.4
Health	106	7	113	112	99.1	296	2	0.7
Corporate Manslaughter	137	6	143	142	99.3	329	38	11.6
Further Education	65	1	66	66	100.0	172	9	5.2
Employment	24	4	28	28	100.0	127	0	0.0
Saving Gateway	10	0	10	10	100.0	114	0	0.0
Energy	50	0	50	50	100.0	76	0	0.0
Total (2005–10)	478	18	496	494	99.6	1,893	83	4.4
2010–12 session								
Identity Documents	4	0	4	4	100.0	43	2	4.7
Savings Accounts	0	0	0	0	n/a	108	0	0.0
Budget Responsibility	11	0	11	11	100.0	92	0	0.0
Public Bodies	185	18	203	159	78.3	435	19	4.4
Welfare	167	5	172	171	99.4	904	21	2.3
Total (2010–12)	367	23	390	345	88.5	1,582	42	2.7
Grand total	845	41	886	839	94.7	3,475	125	3.6

Table 3.4 Government and non-government amendments proposed and agreed by legislative stage

	Government amendments					Non-government amendments		
	Proposed			Agreed		Proposed	Agreed	% Agreed
	Govt alone	Govt & others	Total proposed	Total agreed	% Agreed			
In Commons at:								
—committee	168	2	170	158	92.9	1,030	2	0.2
—report	139	7	146	144	98.6	433	0	0.0
—CCLA	94	0	94	94	100.0	16	2	12.5
Commons total	401	9	410	396	96.6	1,479	4	0.3
In Lords at:								
—committee	124	12	136	107	78.7	1,360	9	0.7
—report	275	15	290	286	98.6	519	45	8.7
—third reading	41	5	46	46	100.0	33	5	15.2
—LCCA	4	0	4	4	100.0	84	62	73.8
Lords total	444	32	476	443	93.1	1,996	121	6.1
Total in both Houses	**845**	**41**	**886**	**839**	**94.7**	**3,475**	**125**	**3.6**

Before turning to the reasons for ministers to propose amendments, it is worth reflecting further on the extent to which such amendments can be considered substantive in policy terms—a concept already briefly touched upon in Chapter 2. This is a particularly prescient question when considering government amendments.

It is widely noted among those who have sought to analyse the legislative process quantitatively that not all amendments are equal. A single amendment can range from the trivial—for example renumbering a provision—to extremely major—for example deleting an entire section of a bill. Scholars have hence generally distinguished between different classes of amendment in terms of policy importance (e.g. Häge and Kaeding 2007, Herman 1972, Kasack 2004, Kreppel 1999, Thompson 2013, 2015, Tsebelis and Kalandrakis 1999). We built on the categories employed by Shephard and Cairney (2005) by assigning each amendment to one of three categories. The least substantive was that of 'technical or consequential' amendments (as illustrated in Chapter 2). The second comprised 'clarificatory' amendments, which make little change to the legislation's effect but are intended to limit its interpretation (e.g. by adding detail). The third category comprised 'substantive' amendments, which would actually change the policy in the bill.

Table 3.5 shows government and non-government amendments to the 12 case study bills broken into these three categories. We see that over half of government-sponsored amendments fall into the least substantive category, while only one-third can be considered genuinely substantive. In contrast the pattern for non-government amendments is quite different. Here more than two-thirds of amendments are substantive, and only around one-sixth are technical or consequential.

To explore the reasons for this difference we must start thinking about why the government seeks to amend its own legislation in parliament. As previous authors have noted, there are various such motivations (Griffith 1974, Thompson 2015).[22] These can be summarized in terms of four basic categories, each discussed in turn below. The first is simply to 'tidy up' the bill in drafting terms—if it was introduced without careful enough review or if technical flaws are pointed out by others. The second is a desire to alter the policy in the bill due to a straightforward government change of heart. The third is to change policy in response to external events, rather than purposeful government decision, and the fourth is to change it under pressure from parliament. Notably in all four cases the government does actually intend that

Table 3.5 Government and non-government amendments proposed by substantiveness

	Technical/ consequential		Clarificatory		Substantive		Total	
	N	%	N	%	N	%	N	%
Government alone	473	56	114	13	258	31	845	100
Government & others	17	41	1	2	23	56	41	100
Government total	**490**	**55**	**115**	**13**	**281**	**32**	**886**	**100**
Non-government total	597	17	423	12	2455	71	3475	100
Grand total	**1,087**	**25**	**538**	**12**	**2,736**	**63**	**4,361**	**100**

its amendments will change the bill—which may seem obvious, but when considering amendments from other parliamentary actors (as we will see in later chapters) is not always true.[23]

Tidying-up amendments

The first government objective, to simply 'tidy up' a bill, helps explain the large number of non-substantive amendments proposed by ministers. Clearly it might be expected that the government would hold back its legislation until it was absolutely technically watertight, but this is not always the case. Parliamentary counsel resources are limited, government bills are complex, and political imperatives (e.g. the start of a new parliamentary session or, as in 2010, a new government) can require bills to be introduced before government lawyers are completely content. Plus, of course, it is only once the bill is published that it attains a wider readership. As a former minister explained in interview, 'parliamentary draftsmen are not perfect, and you will always find that their first draft of the legislation, experts will say, "well hold on a minute, that doesn't make sense, it's not consistent with this, what about that", and [on] any bill you will have technical amendments that the government will table'. Tidying-up amendments were very numerous in Griffith's (1974) day, and their extent has almost certainly declined due to better government preparation.

The relatively trivial nature of such amendments is clear from some examples. In the Energy Bill the definition of a 'licensed gas supplier' was updated to refer to section 7A(1) rather than 7A of the Gas Act 1986. Likewise, in the Health Bill a government amendment changed the definition of 'licence', from 'authorising the consumption of alcohol' to 'authorising sale by retail of alcohol for consumption'. Ministers will often explicitly introduce such changes in debate as 'technical amendments'. For example when introducing fifteen amendments to the Welfare Reform Bill, Chris Grayling told members that they 'simply tidy up a few references that need to be made to previous pieces of legislation', stating that while government seeks to get such references right before bills are introduced, 'a few always slip through the net'.[24] Such explanations are generally taken at face value by parliamentarians, who agree the changes without controversy.[25] While the opportunity might exist, we were assured by officials that ministers would never 'try and pull the wool over people's eyes' by passing off a more substantive amendment as purely technical.

Government changes of heart

The second reason for government amendments is a straightforward change of heart on the part of ministers. This can occur because a bill was introduced before the substance of the policy was fully agreed, or because government actors subsequently decide to include matter which had not been considered before. These are the kinds of government changes that can infuriate parliamentarians, and lead to allegations that the government is abusing its position. If late government amendments with real policy substance are introduced, some provisions in a bill may not receive full scrutiny. As noted in Chapter 2, the study by Miers and Brock (1993) of the legislative process in the 1980s found examples of some bills being largely rewritten in parliament. Such stories fuel cynicism about government's control of the legislative process, and of parliament's powerlessness, but we found little evidence of this kind of activity on the case study bills. In the intervening years, the legislative process has become far more rigorous. Inside government, processes such as those described above increasingly force ministers to introduce bills in a better state. This is partly a response to changes such as the introduction of public bill committees, greater backbench independence, and the increasingly demanding environment of the House of Lords—which all enhance parliament's ability to scrutinize. One government insider with long experience explained that, 'the internal procedures have been tightened, so we are very often told that the bill must be in a state where no government amendments will be needed', though he added that this is 'pretty impossible to achieve'.

Despite this, some bills are still amended following government changes of heart, albeit usually in minor ways. Such changes on the case study bills were generally pre-planned, typically because bills were introduced when the response to government consultations was still awaited. For example, the consultations about enforcement of the national minimum wage, including on its likely effect on voluntary workers, ended only shortly before the Employment Bill's introduction into the Lords. Some charities expressed concerns that the rules could make them liable for paying volunteers, which they could not afford to do. Hence at the bill's Lords committee stage the minister introduced a government amendment 'to broaden the type of expenses that can be reimbursed to voluntary workers without triggering eligibility for the minimum wage', citing the 'compelling arguments' of respondents to the consultation.[26] Ideally this material would have been included in the bill as introduced (with the consultation timed accordingly), but its insertion at this early stage of legislative proceedings provoked no controversy.

Some more major changes were made to the coalition's bills at the government's own initiative, necessitated by this being its first parliamentary session, with bills introduced before policy was fully worked out. For example, on the Welfare Reform Bill a set of government amendments was proposed in Commons committee to establish a new Social Mobility and Child Poverty Commission in place of the previously existing Child Poverty Commission. In proposing the changes, the minister explained that they were the result of responses to the government's consultation on child poverty, which ended in February 2011, and therefore could not have been included in the original version of the bill.[27] Unlike the changes to the Employment Bill this new material proved controversial, and there were several subsequent attempts to amend it. New material was likewise added to the coalition's Public Bodies Bill, with the most substantial change concerning the abolition of the nine Regional Development Agencies (RDAs) previously created by Labour. The original version of the bill included the RDAs in the schedule listing bodies due for abolition, which required consultation before the change could be made. After the bill's Lords stages, government amendments were introduced at Commons committee to instead put the abolition of the RDAs on the face of the bill. In introducing the amendments, the minister explicitly stated that this was to allow abolition to proceed more quickly.[28] The opposition had previously declared abolition of the RDAs 'fundamentally the wrong decision'.[29] Yet this had been a clear commitment in the coalition agreement, and opposition attempts to remove it from the bill in the Lords had failed. By this point it was clear that the bodies were doomed, and amendments to accelerate the process were not strongly opposed.

Responding to events

Amendments to implement purely government-initiated changes of heart were however very much the exception. Some other government amendments responded to external events which were less within ministers' control. For example, ministers proposed amendments to the Welfare Reform Bill both to accommodate changes to the devolution settlement following a referendum in Wales in March 2011, and in response to a decision of the Scottish Parliament to withhold 'legislative consent' on certain matters. At the Lords report stage of the Public Bodies Bill over twenty-five government amendments were agreed altering provisions for Wales, as a result of the referendum and requests from Welsh ministers. Amendments such as these are clearly not made as a result of parliamentary pressure, but cannot be considered a result of government initiative either.

Responding to parliament

The final category of government amendments are those considered 'concessionary', which do respond to pressure from parliament.[30] We have already noted that previous authors—most notably Griffith (1974), and more recently Thompson (2013, 2015)—have found that significant numbers of government amendments respond to earlier non-government proposals. Our own figures are not directly comparable to theirs—most notably because we take account of amendments tabled at all stages throughout the bicameral legislative process. Our summary results are given in Table 3.6, which expresses responsiveness in two ways. First, through the number of government amendments to each bill—and substantive amendments, shown separately—which responded to some kind of parliamentary pressure. Second, through the number of distinct legislative strands on each bill which were initiated by one or more government amendments, compared to the total number of agreed strands (i.e. including those initiated by amendments from other actors).

Of the 839 government amendments to the 12 bills that were formally agreed, 111 either simply overturned a previous amendment and/or were themselves over-turned by a subsequent one. This typically applies during ping-pong on House of Lords defeats. It would overstate non-government influence to code such government amendments as 'responsive', since they either simply reversed changes made in parliament to return the bill to its original state, or were themselves reversed; but it would also overstate government influence to code them as government-initiated changes to a bill. Hence Table 3.6 excludes such cases, and shows only 728 government amendments. Of these, 297 (41 per cent) responded to some form of prior

Table 3.6 Government amendments agreed (excluding overturned and overturning) and success of government-initiated strands

| | Total amendments | | | Substantive amendments | | | Strands | | Total agreed | Govt initiated as % of total agreed |
| | Agreed | Responded | | Agreed | Responded | | Govt initiated | Govt initiated agreed | | |
	N	N	%	N	N	%	N	N	N	%
2005–10 parliament										
Identity Cards	62	58	94	19	19	100	12	12	40	30
Health	112	33	29	18	8	44	35	35	45	78
Corporate Manslaughter	104	39	38	20	14	70	20	19	27	70
Further Education	47	15	32	8	8	100	12	12	20	60
Employment	28	7	25	7	3	43	9	9	13	69
Saving Gateway	10	7	70	4	4	100	2	2	7	29
Energy	50	20	40	8	7	88	12	12	17	71
Total (2005–10)	413	179	43	84	63	75	102	101	169	60
2010–12 session										
Identity Documents	4	4	100	2	2	100	2	2	2	100
Savings Accounts	0	0	n/a	0	0	n/a	0	0	0	n/a
Budget Responsibility	11	10	91	6	6	100	1	1	7	14
Public Bodies	144	53	37	56	24	43	44	24	50	48
Welfare Reform	156	51	33	46	22	48	37	37	72	51
Total (2010–12)	315	118	37	110	54	49	84	64	131	49
Grand total	728	297	41	194	117	60	186	165	300	55

parliamentary pressure. If we disregard technical/consequential and clarificatory amendments (i.e. restricting to those in category three above), 60 per cent of substantive government amendments responded to pressure from parliament.[31]

Some bills saw particularly large numbers of government amendments in response—on each of the Identity Cards, Public Bodies, and Welfare Reform bills there were over fifty, nearly half of which were substantive. The great majority of responsive government amendments (250 of 297) were traceable to one or more amendments from non-government parliamentarians, and the dynamic of this process is discussed frequently throughout the remainder of the book. A handful (13) responded to points raised in debate, without the pressure of non-government amendments, while (as we explore in Chapter 8) 114 responded to proposals made by parliamentary select committees—a form of pressure that barely existed in Griffith's day.[32]

Our primary means of tracking government responsiveness is through legislative strands, as shown in the right-hand side of the table. These capture influence through non-government amendments only.[33] We see that of the 2,050 legislative strands, 186 were initiated by government amendments, and unsurprisingly, almost all of these (165) were agreed. But there were 300 strands agreed in total, meaning that nearly half (45 per cent) were triggered by non-government amendments. The typical pattern is for non-government amendments early in a strand not to be agreed, but followed by agreed government amendments (less commonly a non-government amendment is agreed against the government's wishes, followed by government tidying-up or compromise amendments). The two sets of figures in the table—for amendments and for legislative strands—hence essentially tell us the same thing: that many government amendments respond to pressure from non-government actors in parliament. This is particularly true of those with policy substance. Notably, 57 of the agreed government-initiated strands (i.e. just over one-third) contained only minor technical amendments, whereas the same was true of only three non-government initiated strands. Once this factor is taken into account, a clear majority of substantive changes made to the bills were traceable to non-government pressure in parliament—usually attained through 'concessionary' government amendments. In the remainder of this section we describe some general aspects of this concession-giving process, as seen from the government's point of view.

We noted that ministers receive civil service advice on all non-government amendments, and that often this will be to 'resist'. Alternatively, the minister may 'agree in principle' or 'agree to consider'. Page (2003: 667–8) comments that resistance may be encouraged in particular by parliamentary counsel, who view amendments 'as threatening the coherence of the carefully crafted structure that their drafting has produced'. But he quotes a bill team interviewee who conceded—like several of ours—that the passage through parliament 'if it works properly, will uncover things not right in the bill'. This will often result in government amendments.

As indicated above, tensions can arise between ministers and officials over the appropriate response to non-government amendments. While officials have primary responsibility for the detailed drafting of legislation, it is ministers who have to defend it publicly, and to navigate pressures from parliament. As parliamentarians themselves, ministers are sensitive to the concerns of their colleagues, and to what parliament will ultimately accept. Hence a former minister said of discussions with civil servants:

In the Lords I had to say to them, 'you tell me to resist this amendment, I'm actually going to take it back because I cannot get my resistance through', and they would argue with me, and I would say, 'look, I can't do it, you do it if you think you can win the House of Lords, but I know this place'.

Another former minister from the Commons made a similar point even more colourfully, recalling being told by a civil servant to propose a particular response, which he refused to do:

I said to the official: 'Well if you want me to move the amendment, I suggest why don't you stand for election, get 330 people elected, get appointed by the Prime Minister to be the minister, and then you go and move it, because I'm not [going to]!'

Yet even where ministers are sympathetic to the point being made in a non-government amendment, it is extremely unusual for them to agree that it should be accepted into the bill as it stands. As one official told us, 'as a bill manager, it would never be going through my mind "shall we just accept that?"—it's not in the repertoire'.[34] There are various reasons for this. Most obviously, government may not wish non-government actors to appear to be winning. But in fact the technical and procedural obstacles are usually more important. Parliamentary counsel tend to assume that drafting of non-government amendments is technically flawed, so they will prefer to draft their own version. In addition, ministers do not actually have the authority to change policy 'on the hoof'—since the bill was formally approved by a cross departmental cabinet committee, similar approval is required for subsequent changes, and a 'write-round' to relevant ministers to get agreement to an amendment takes time. Hence the default is to return to the matter at the subsequent legislative stage.

Non-government amendments are generally drafted by parliamentarians themselves, or their staff, or sometimes by outside groups, often with some support from parliamentary clerks—none of whom have the expert drafting skills of government lawyers. Since it is widely recognized that non-government amendments will not make it into a bill without being changed, a government insider explained that 'very often amendments aren't drafted in order to make the bill work, they are drafted … in order to enable the member to debate the policy change he wants'. If the principle is accepted by government, a new amendment will be brought forward.[35] Indeed, the government will often respond with a package of amendments including various consequential ones that non-government parliamentarians rarely attempt to think through fully—which is the other key reason for the large number of nonsubstantive government amendments agreed.

The extent to which this process can become a game of arguing over the merits of particular wording is occasionally humorous. On the smoking provisions in the

Health Bill, a Conservative amendment in Commons committee sought to change a clause allowing restrictions to be applied in areas where people would be 'likely to be exposed to smoke' to specify that this must be 'significant amounts of smoke'. The minister resisted the amendment, arguing that '[w]e do not think this is about levels per se, but about harm' and doubting that 'the word "significant" adds anything meaningful to the Bill'.[36] At the Lords committee stage, the Conservative frontbench proposed that 'smoke' be replaced with 'a risk of significant harm from smoke', seemingly in line with the minister's previous suggestion. This was also resisted, but at the next stage the government brought forward an amendment to introduce the words 'significant quantities of smoke', effectively reverting to the opposition's previous suggestion. This was agreed. Similarly the Employment Bill provided an example of a government amendment identically worded to the previous non-government amendment, which the proposer had been asked to withdraw.[37]

There are various reasons why the government may offer concessions in response to non-government amendments. One is simply seeing the merits of the case. A former minister, presented with a list of changes made to a bill that he had piloted, commented that most of them were 'stuff that ... we hadn't thought through properly that needed to be amended'. An official who worked on the same bill said that 'there were many times when we thought "that's not a bad idea" '. But there is often also an element of ministers wanting to stifle dissent, and to avoid awkward divisions and possible defeats. Discussing the changes on one bill, a former minister suggested that ideas in non-government amendments were accepted 'largely because we saw some merit in what they were saying, but also we probably were actually worried at that point that we'd go inevitably to a defeat on that group of amendments so we'd make a concession to try and buy them off'. However, government insiders indicated that giving ground can be problematic. Another former minister recalled having to ask herself 'will a concession satisfy, or will it feed demand for more?'. A third indicated that this was a reason for not giving concessions 'too soon, because otherwise, obviously, if they've taken half your arm off they can take the other half'.

An important question—addressed throughout the book—is which groups of parliamentarians ministers are most likely to concede to, and why. A particularly obvious example is whether the government is more likely to concede to members of the Commons or the Lords. Engagement over non-government amendments generally begins at committee stage in the chamber of introduction, and then continues at report and in the other chamber, with possible government concessionary amendments at these subsequent stages. For the majority of bills that begin in the Commons, this means that proposals raised in Commons committee may be responded to either at Commons report or in the Lords. Table 3.4 showed that the number of government amendments made at Lords report stage was particularly high. As already indicated, the need for clearance means that ministers may not be able to respond to pressure immediately. But there are also political reasons for holding back concessions. One government official suggested that the 'golden rule is don't amend in committee, save it for report'. Likewise, 'if you can wait for the Lords, then wait for the Lords'; in short 'don't amend until you have to amend'. Another official suggested that 'the culture of the Commons is one in which any minor concession would be trumpeted as a major climbdown or humiliating U-turn, and I just don't think that the rhetoric that is used is the same in the Lords'. Nonetheless, saving concessions for the Lords can prove very aggravating for MPs, who complain that their voices are being ignored. Another interviewee suggested that 'as a minister in the Commons, one's preference would often be to give the concession in the Commons ... [because] you're hopefully building a bit of credit with people who can be helpful to you'. However, he admitted that 'significant concessions were invariably held back for the Lords'. Hence while the government may sometimes look more responsive to peers than MPs, concessions given in the Lords are frequently at least in part responses to the Commons.

We have seen that ministers are likely to have a pre-prepared concession strategy, and may have anticipated some of the concerns raised by non-government parliamentarians. For example, we were told that the pressure to add recipients of Carer's Allowance to those eligible for the scheme introduced by the Saving Gateway Accounts Bill was always anticipated. The government preferred not to include this benefit, but when pressed on the matter by a government back-bencher (as described in Chapter 5), brought forward amendments to do so. Various changes to the coalition's Welfare Reform Bill were likewise assumed by non-government parliamentarians to have been anticipated. This raises the question of whether some concessions are in fact 'manufactured', and built into bills in order to allow ministers to look more responsive to parliament—in which case our analysis might overstate parliamentary influence. A few interviewees did suggest that this occurs. One kind of manufactured concession would be to allow very small changes, with little or no legal effect. A former minister referred to these as 'apparent concessions', around which you can 'create theatre', and give ground on 'second-order questions that aren't of tremendous importance'. Another former minister drew an analogy with international diplomacy, where you build in 'negotiating fat'; so you 'go for the top whack of a proposition but be ready to moderate it'. Yet the notion of building in concessions on substantive matters was dismissed by most interviewees. Thus if the government had really wanted to extend the saving gateway scheme to those in receipt of Carer's Allowance it would have been risky to leave this provision out. As one government official suggested, 'it would be dangerous to design it tougher than you wanted because, if you didn't get the pressure that you were expecting, you'd ... have to make government amendments and then you'd look a bit silly'. Another senior official commented that 'if we were told "please draft this, we don't actually want it but it's part of some wider political game" I think we would certainly protest about that'. In these circumstances, ministerial plotting would need to be extremely underhand and complex. Hence one frontbencher suggested that this idea was 'excessively cynical' and that 'certainly nothing in my experience would actually suggest that it happened'.

Conclusions

The common perception, both in much of the academic literature and in more popular accounts, is that government dominates the legislative process. Indeed the Westminster parliament is often presented as an archetypal case of such dominance. But closer study of government's handling of legislation, both before a bill's introduction to parliament and subsequently, demonstrates the need for a more nuanced view. Government actors are central to the making of legislation, and fundamentally responsible for coordinating and managing this process. Nonetheless they remain responsive at all stages to other actors, including those in parliament. In various and often subtle ways parliamentarians have significant influence on the legislation that is made. To really understand the process, it is necessary to look well beyond the government.

This chapter has summarized some of the key processes in government for managing legislation. Numerous actors are involved in legislative production, including departmental civil servants and lawyers, ministers and whips in both chambers, parliamentary counsel, and others at the heart of government in the Treasury, Cabinet Office, and Number 10. The process of planning legislation begins long before its introduction to parliament—with some bills having a very long gestation indeed. Commonly this includes wide consultation on the direction and detail of policy, and often government legislates in direct response to external intervention. This is seen among our case study bills, for example, in the Law Commission's report on corporate manslaughter, the Shipman inquiry on the Health Bill, and the Gibbons review on dispute resolution in the workplace. As will be further illustrated in later chapters, parliament is not excluded from these early policy formulation stages, and often provides a key forum for discussion. As one interviewee put it, 'the most influential period in the making of legislation is before it is published' but 'parliamentarians are part of that process'.

As will be further discussed in later chapters, parliamentarians can use mechanisms such as parliamentary questions, early day motions (EDMs), and private members' bills to put policy issues on the agenda, and to keep up pressure on ministers during the policy formulation stage. Conversely, where prior consultation and discussion on a policy has been limited, difficulties in parliament may follow. A former cabinet minister suggested that 'to a large extent the quality of the bill you introduce depends critically on the work you do at green paper and white paper stage ... and by "quality" I mean the extent to which you are likely to produce a bill which is likely to be enacted'. Nonetheless the constraints of electoral timetables, in particular, mean that such planning cannot always take place. The most obvious problems among our case studies occurred on the Public Bodies Bill, introduced shortly after a general election with little prior consultation. Meanwhile, as shown by the Identity Cards Bill, a long gestation is not a guarantee of an easy passage through parliament if a policy remains controversial.

At the next stage, when policy is developed into concrete legislative plans, elaborate processes now exist inside government to ensure that parliamentarians' likely response is thought through in advance. The internal system of 'handling strategies' is designed to avert difficulties in parliament—and particularly in the Lords, with which most senior ministers (and civil servants) are less familiar. This demonstrates parliament's 'power of anticipated reactions', which was strongly emphasized to us by many interviewees. While the power of the Lords in this regard is quite explicit, the power of the Commons operates more subconsciously in the minds of ministers when policy proposals are devised, in something akin to Lukes's (1974) third face of power—as summarized in Chapter 1. Hence, responsiveness to the Lords may be more visible, but responsiveness to the Commons nonetheless exists, and is ultimately more important—given that the government depends on the confidence of that chamber to remain in office. Indeed, even once the formal legislative process has begun, concessions to the Lords often respond to (or anticipate) points raised in the Commons.

It is a quirk of the process that the Lords is less comprehensible to most government insiders, and provides a more obviously risky environment for government legislation, yet Lords ministers are generally junior within their departments. Major decisions on bills are taken by Commons ministers, which can result in misunderstanding and complications. But these intercameral tensions are only one kind of division that can occur inside government in the handling of legislation. An important factor when considering the power of parliament is that government is not monolithic, and various internal tensions can exist. Ministers provide the interface between government and parliament, with one foot in each, which can sometimes generate professional tensions with civil servants. There are also often interpersonal tensions among ministers, interdepartmental tensions within Whitehall, and there were additional interparty tensions under coalition. Parliament frequently provides a final very public forum in which these various kinds of differences are resolved.

Once a bill has been introduced to parliament it is likely to be amended, with the great majority of successful amendments being proposed in the name of ministers. Of the 964 amendments agreed to the 12 case study bills, 839 (87 per cent) were government amendments. Furthermore, 99 of the 125 non-government amendments agreed went on to be overturned later in the process, and an additional two served only to overturn other amendments. Excluding these two 'overturning' categories there were 752 amendments agreed to the bills in total, of which 728 (97 per cent) were proposed by ministers. This might appear to be clear evidence that the government is dominant. But there are also some obvious 'reasons for doubt' (Russell, Gover, and Wollter 2016). We have identified four motivations for government amendments, only one of which is a spontaneous desire to change policy direction. Many such amendments in fact have little policy substance: half are merely technical, or consequential on other more substantive amendments. Only one-third of government amendments (compared to over two-thirds of those from non-government parliamentarians) fall into the most substantive category. Some government amendments with substance represent genuine changes of heart, while some others respond to external events; but the majority on the case study bills responded to visible pressure from parliament, usually expressed through amendments from non-government parliamentarians. Our construction of 'legislative strands' allows us to trace this influence. The typical pattern is for proposals made in non-government amendments to be addressed through government concessionary amendments.

Our conclusions therefore differ from those of earlier scholars, in that we found relatively few examples of genuine government changes of heart. We also saw fewer government 'tidying-up' amendments, due to better bill preparation. Current guidance indeed strongly discourages government amendments unless they are 'essential to ensure that the bill works properly; to avoid a government defeat or otherwise significantly ease handling in Parliament' (Cabinet Office 2015: 152). This attitude is clearly very different to the 'legislate as you go' approach found by Miers and Brock (1993: 134).

Instead our evidence strongly demonstrates that government is responsive to non-government actors in parliament. Exploring who those parliamentarians were, and what changes they negotiated, forms an important part of the discussion in subsequent chapters of the book.

Notes

1. Whitehall is a road adjacent to parliament on which many UK government departments are based. However, the term has come to refer much more widely to the central offices of the main UK government departments and their civil servants, regardless of their physical location. The government is also frequently referred to as the 'executive', and these two terms are used interchangeably throughout the book.
2. Rose (1980) for example distinguished between legislation resulting from manifesto promises and from the 'ongoing Whitehall process'; but Page (2003: 656) points out that this is a distinction 'hard to sustain in reality', not least because civil servants can play a part in legislation which reaches the manifesto.
3. For example, in 2010–12, the government published 11 draft bills (Kelly 2015b), while 47 government bills were formally introduced.
4. For a lengthier discussion of the gestation of this policy, see King and Crewe (2013).
5. House of Commons Hansard, 14 June 1999, column 3.
6. For further background on development of the policy, see Gobert (2005).
7. For a broader perspective on development of this policy, see Cairney (2007, 2009).
8. Cambridge, Cumbria, East London, Manchester, and Hull. The identity cards scheme was also piloted with 1,500 staff at Manchester airport, following the passage of Labour's bill. But this cannot be seen as influencing the coalition's subsequent bill in any meaningful way. Indeed, one of the arguments over the Identity Documents Bill in parliament concerned whether the pilot scheme should be completed and assessed. Amendments proposing this were sponsored by the Labour frontbench in both the Commons and the Lords, but rejected by the government.
9. Previous names for the committee have included the Legislative Programme Committee (informally known as 'LP'), and the Legislation Committee ('LegCo').
10. For a more detailed discussion of these processes, see Greenberg (2011), Cabinet Office (2015).
11. Because the Lords has an absolute veto on secondary legislation it has in practice exercised restraint and used its power only very rarely (Joint Committee on Conventions

2006, Russell 2013). For recent arguments, which sparked a review of the House of Lords' power in this area, see Constitution Committee (2016) and Delegated Powers and Regulatory Reform Committee (2016).

12. For a discussion of these roles, see Rush and Ettinghausen (2002). The Commons post has famously been held by only four individuals since 1919, and its current holder Roy Stone has been in post since 2000. In the Lords the Chief Whip's Private Secretary is a parliamentary clerk, on temporary secondment.

13. One official complained of the extreme inefficiency of preparing detailed briefing on numerous non-government amendments which are likely to be withdrawn. But, as discussed in subsequent chapters, many amendments seek primarily to test whether the government can defend its policy, so the ability to construct an argument against change plays an important part in parliamentary accountability.

14. As discussed at greater length by Thompson (2015).

15. For a brief description of *Pepper v. Hart*, see Littleboy and Kelly (2005). For discussion of its rights and wrongs, see Greenberg (2011).

16. See Lord Taylor of Holbeach, House of Lords Hansard, 9 May 2011, column 676.

17. But even in these cases cross-departmental clearance—as described below with respect to amendments—will often have to be obtained.

18. See for example 'Ministers at War Over Plan to Ban Smoking', *Daily Mail*, 26 October 2005; 'Hewitt Admits Cabinet Split on Smoking Ban', *Guardian*, 27 October 2005.

19. In this respect, practice in the House of Commons and the House of Lords differs. In the Lords, if the minister adds their name to a non-government amendment, it will be added at the end—making clear the original source of the amendment. In the Commons in the same circumstances the minister's name is automatically added at the top—which makes it difficult after the event to discern the amendment's original source.

20. On each of the Health Bill and the Welfare Reform Bill one government amendment was withdrawn and brought back at a subsequent stage and passed; while on the Corporate Manslaughter and Corporate Homicide Bill one became redundant as a result of another amendment.

21. Table 3.4 shows only four government amendments proposed at LCCA stage. This is because, at this stage, Lords ministers typically move that peers accept the Commons' proposals. As explained in Appendix A, at Commons consideration of Lords amendments (CCLA) and LCCA stages we did not count as amendments proposals that simply accepted the other chamber's decisions.

22. For some nice illustrations from a former First Parliamentary Counsel, see Engle (1983).

23. A similar but not identical set of four categories of amendment is recognized in the government's own *Guide to Making Legislation*. Here the categories are 'minor and technical', 'desirable', 'essential', and 'concessionary' respectively (Cabinet Office 2015: 153–4).

24. Public Bill Committee (Welfare Reform Bill), 28 April 2011, column 558.

25. Where changes are really minute, and clearly have absolutely no substance, they can also be accepted by parliamentary clerks as 'printing amendments' which need not be formally agreed during parliamentary proceedings. Examples could include correction of obvious typos. But this is not without controversy; Greenberg (2011:103) in particular opposes the practice.

26. Lord Jones of Birmingham, House of Lords Hansard, 13 March 2008, column GC265.

27. House of Commons Hansard, 9 May 2011, column 967.

28. Public Bill Committee (Public Bodies Bill), 13 September 2011, columns 129–30.

29. Baroness Royall of Blaisdon, House of Lords Hansard, 23 March 2011, column 829.
30. As freely admitted by the government: see note 23.
31. We have already noted in Chapter 2 the difficulty of comparing our figures with those of Griffith. However, in some respects our figures here do appear similar: he found 365 government amendments at Commons report stage which responded to non-government amendments, of which 125 were judged 'important in varying degrees' (Griffith 1974: 206). Some of his figures seem to exclude technical and consequential amendments, and of course they cover a great many more bills. But we found 297 government amendments overall to be responsive, of which 117 had policy substance.
32. Note that these figures do not add up to 297 because, as discussed in Chapter 8, 80 government amendments responded to proposals made both in a select committee recommendation and in non-government amendments.
33. Strands are by definition composed of amendments, which may be initiated by a proposal either from government or from non-government actors. Where government amendments responded to a select committee recommendation, but there were no related amendments from non-government actors, these are hence counted here and throughout most of the book as 'government-initiated' (as seen in Chapter 8, there were 12 such strands). Strands where government amendments responded only to points raised in debate, in the absence of non-government amendments (of which there were six), are likewise counted as government-initiated. Hence these figures if anything somewhat understate non-government influence.
34. This does appear to be a clear change from when Griffith was writing. As noted in Chapter 2, the proportion of non-government amendments agreed in committee appears to have dropped sharply in this period. This is at least in part due to the nature of those amendments. Griffith (1974: 112) for example found that in 1967–68 there were 46 opposition amendments agreed without division in committee, of which 38 were 'drafting, clarificatory or of very minor significance'. Very few opposition drafting amendments are proposed today.
35. The government's own *Guide to Making Legislation* advises that 'Opposition and backbench amendments are very often defective in some degree; but it is for the Opposition and backbenchers to propose changes to the bill and for the Government, which alone has drafting resources, to clean up the drafting' (Cabinet Office 2015: 212).
36. Caroline Flint, Standing Committee E (Health Bill), 8 December 2005, column 152.
37. The amendment concerned the circumstances in which certain employment tribunal cases could be held without a hearing. The bill stated that one circumstance was where all parties had given 'consent' to the arrangement. This amendment (proposed by a government backbencher in the Lords) added just two words, to specify that this must be 'in writing'. The minister promised to consider the amendment, and an identical two-word government amendment was agreed without division on report. See House of Lords Hansard 4 February 2008, column GC477-81 and 19 May 2008, column 1265 respectively. Thompson (2015: 65–6) even cites examples of ministers refusing to accept amendments that attempted to correct spelling mistakes.

4

The Role of the Opposition

Aside from government ministers, the most visible actors in parliament are oppos-ition parties. Westminster is often described as an 'adversarial' parliament, as reflected both in its procedures and its traditional debating style, and this adversari-alism is most clearly played out between government and opposition. The largest non-government party forms 'Her Majesty's Official Opposition', and has a central role in holding the government to account. The layout of both chambers, with government and opposition benches facing each other, emphasizes the centrality of this relationship.

We therefore begin our analysis of non-government actors at Westminster by exploring the role of opposition parties in scrutinizing and amending government bills. We ask about the opposition's strategies and motivation, how they organize, and the extent to which they achieve their goals. The popular perception is that opposition politicians at Westminster may generate a lot of noise, but have relatively little policy impact. However, we suggest that the picture is actually rather more complex. Opposition parties do seek to change legislation, though the legislative process also offers them opportunities to pursue other political goals. This means that their 'success' cannot be measured only in terms of the number of amendments agreed. Nonetheless, our research shows that the number of opposition proposals adopted is far from negligible. Opposition parties played a central role in negoti-ating major changes to several of the case study bills. This is in part because the opposition, while at a numerical disadvantage in the Commons, has always been able to call on other resources such as the power of publicity. But it also results from recent changes at Westminster, not accounted for in older analyses: in particular, the changed composition and greater confidence of the post-1999 House of Lords.

The chapter starts by briefly describing the opposition parties in the 2005 and 2010 parliaments, and how they were numerically distributed. We then look at what existing academic analyses say about the role of parliamentary opposition, and summarize opposition organization. The remainder of the chapter is based on analysis of the 12 case study bills. We discuss the attitudes of opposition parties to the bills, illustrating some of the strategic dilemmas that such parties can face in deciding how to respond to government legislation. We then look at opposition party amendments, both reviewing their distribution and explor-ing, largely based on interview evidence, what motivates them. This question of motivations is a theme taken up in subsequent chapters, demonstrating that non-government parliamentarians use the legislative process for various purposes,

Legislation at Westminster. First edition. Meg Russell and Daniel Gover. © Meg Russell and Daniel Gover 2017. Published 2017 by Oxford University Press.

only one of which is achieving change to the bill at hand. The last main section of the chapter analyses the policy influence exerted by the opposition, which takes various forms. Opposition frontbenchers have a classic 'issue politicization' role in parliament, determining to a large extent which topics in bills get discussed and reach wider attention. This function is important and influential on the process. But, additionally, many opposition amendments helped to trigger policy changes to the bills. We explore both the quality and quantity of these changes, suggesting that they challenge traditional views of opposition policy weakness at Westminster.

The Opposition: Who Are They?

The term 'opposition' most commonly describes the largest non-government party in the House of Commons. Britain has traditionally been seen as having a two-party system—implying that Westminster's main players are two distinct government and opposition blocs, with few other actors of interest. In the twentieth century, that conception arguably oversimplified matters (Bogdanor 2004); in the twenty-first century things have become more complicated still. Since the 1990s the third party—until recently the Liberal Democrats—has been strongly represented at Westminster, and representation of other minor parties has also grown since the 1970s. Following the 2010 election, the government itself was formed of two parties. Among party and electoral system specialists Britain has thus come to be described as having a 'two-and-a-half-party system', a 'two-party plus system', or even the beginnings of a multiparty system (Dunleavy 2005, Quinn 2013). These changes have had an important effect on Westminster.

Throughout the period 1997–2010 the Labour government faced two main opposition parties: the Conservatives and Liberal Democrats. The former held by far the larger number of seats, and the status as Her Majesty's Official Opposition (see Table 2.1 in Chapter 2). Standing orders give this group certain privileges, including control over 17 of the 20 'opposition days' for debate in the Commons each session, and the right to chair a proportion of select committees, including the prestigious Public Accounts Committee. In practice, its privileges go far further, for example through opposition frontbenchers' established right to speak at the start and end of most debates, and to intervene during oral question times, plus an expectation that the Commons Speaker will select the most important opposition amendments for debate at report stage of government bills. Commons standing orders also recognize the 'second largest opposition party', which enjoys similar benefits at a reduced level. Hence under Labour the Liberal Democrats had control over three opposition days per session, and enjoyed rights to some (albeit fewer) interventions by frontbenchers during debates and question times. In practice the largest opposition party also exerts significant influence via the so-called 'usual channels', essentially facilitated by the whips, which informally discuss matters such as timetabling in the chamber (Rush and Ettinghausen 2002). Smaller opposition parties have far less access.

Post-2010 the situation changed, with a reduction from two main opposition parties to one. As the Liberal Democrats entered government with the Conservatives, Labour became the official opposition. Initially there was uncertainty as to what would happen regarding the privileges of the 'second largest opposition party' (some Liberal Democrats considered the loss of these rights a high price to pay for entry into government). But things settled into a position where Labour for most purposes was the principal opposition voice. The gap between its number of MPs (258) and that of the next largest opposition party (the Northern Ireland Democratic Unionist Party—DUP—with just eight) was so great that any other arrangement would have given disproportionate privileges to a tiny party.

This summarizes the primary arrangements in the Commons. But there are two further important dimensions when considering the opposition parties' role. The first is the very different nature of arrangements in the House of Lords. As was shown in Table 2.1, while Labour enjoyed a comfortable majority in the Commons from 2005 to 2010 it was heavily outnumbered in the Lords. For example in January 2006 the Conservatives and Liberal Democrats combined had 279 peers, to Labour's 208. Under coalition this party balance remained largely unchanged. Hence the Labour opposition was significantly outnumbered in both chambers post-2010, though it could still defeat the government in the Lords if joined by sufficient Crossbenchers or other peers. Notably, in the distinctly less regulated—and less adversarial—environment of the Lords the official opposition enjoys fewer formal procedural privileges than in the Commons. There is no selection of amendments, or opposition days, and speaking time is shared out relatively proportionately among the different groups; nonetheless, conventions about opposition frontbench speeches at the opening and closing of each debate are similar in the two chambers. The 'usual channels' in the Lords are slightly more open to other groups beyond the main opposition party.

The second important consideration, in both Commons and Lords, is that the main opposition parties are not wholly homogenous blocs. It is the opposition frontbench which is most visible, and has most of the privileges (e.g. choosing topics for Commons opposition days). But just as on the government side, large opposition parties demonstrate some separation between front and backbench. Frontbenchers must stick to the collective party line, but backbenchers do not always do so. In this chapter we consider the contributions of opposition parties large and small, including both frontbenchers and backbenchers. But we primarily discuss the three largest parties that served in opposition during our period of study—Conservative, Labour, and Liberal Democrat—and the work of their frontbenchers. It is these groups who proposed by far the largest number of amendments to the case study bills.

Established Understanding of the Opposition

The classic adversarial view of Westminster is reflected in much of the academic literature. Within this setup, as explored in the previous chapter, the government is viewed as very much the dominant force. The traditional expectation in the Commons has been that a single, disciplined political party will form a majority government. Compared to other 'consensus' style legislatures (Lijphart 1999), where the party system is more fragmented and the norm is coalition or minority government, this makes it relatively difficult for other majorities against the government to form. Hence while the opposition traditionally has an important accountability role in getting the government to explain its policies on the record, it is generally not seen as having much policy power (e.g. Helms 2004, 2008, Kaiser 2008, Norton 2008, Uhr 2009). Anthony King's now classic account of 'modes of executive–legislative relations' in the UK, Germany, and France noted that the 'opposition mode' was 'the one in which the larger part of party politics in Britain takes place' (1976: 17) Yet this presented little real threat to the government or its legislation, since the 'Government fully expects the Opposition to make hostile speeches. It does not need, or want, the Opposition's moral support ... [or] votes' (ibid.: 18).

These arrangements are generally thought by academics not only to affect the opposition's policy influence, but also its behaviour and style. In a more pluralistic setting, where the opposition has more chance to negotiate policy changes, it will be motivated to do so. But in a majoritarian legislature such as Westminster—the argument goes—little such incentive exists, and the opposition's primary strategy will be office-seeking rather than policy-seeking. Consequently opposition politicians will prioritize presenting themselves as a credible alternative government and view parliament as 'merely a forum from which to influence the next election ... not an arena to influence public policy' (Andeweg 2013: 102). As Britain's longest-serving opposition leader of the twentieth century, Neil Kinnock, has put it, 'the only test of a good opposition is to stop being in opposition' (2011: 131).

The opposition's classic agenda-setting function in parliament may assist this process, by focusing attention on electorally salient issues which are awkward for government—though the extent of this power varies between different countries' legislatures, depending on how agenda control is distributed (Cox 2009). For example, Brunner (2012: 10), writing about bill sponsorship in several legislatures, notes how the opposition uses bills 'to signal [its] own policy positions and to show alternatives to government policies'. Since we use 'agenda setting' in a different sense in various places within the book, referring to the policy stage when issues reach the government's agenda (prior to their introduction to parliament in a bill), we instead adopt Seeberg's (2013) term 'issue politicisation'. He notes that this can be opposition politicians' most important policy tool, in deciding what gets discussed in parliament and drawing it to wider attention.

In terms of influence on the legislative process, all of the above implies that opposition parties may be relatively peripheral. Hence for example Greenberg's (2011) recent account, while structured by policy actor, devotes chapters to various government actors, and to the government's backbenchers in parliament, but gives no attention at all to the opposition.

Opposition politicians face various dilemmas. For example Johnson (1997: 498–9) notes that 'there is always a tension to be resolved between opposing government policies ... and "constructive opposition" which, if pursued too zealously, may take the edge off the competition for public support'. If the opposition is focused primarily on undermining the government, in order to replace it in office, it may even prefer to make government legislation worse rather than better. This was frankly expressed by Conservative backbencher Jacob Rees-Mogg when he admitted in respect of the Labour government's legislation to ban foxhunting that '[t]hose of us who were in favour of fox hunting wanted a bad Bill. We did not want an effective Bill'; hence 'you want to stymie your opponents, not help them' (Procedure Committee 2013: 16). Such an approach fits with Uhr's (2009: 67) characterization of the UK as 'a standout case of negative rather than constructive oppositional politics'.

This all points towards opposition proposals during the legislative process serving other functions beyond improving government bills—a dynamic acknowledged by various scholars studying the process. For example Griffith (1974: 38) noted that '[t]he purpose of many Opposition amendments is not to make the bill more generally acceptable but to make the Government less generally acceptable'. Likewise Herman (1972: 143) observed that '[s]ome of the amendments moved by the Opposition ... can be seen as propaganda exercises designed to attract the Government's and, it is hoped, the nation's, attention to what it perceives as flaws and inadequacies in the details of the Government's policies'. Studying the legislative process in the Scottish Parliament, Shephard and Cairney (2005: 307) observed that proposers of amendments may have 'masked motives' of 'numerous' kinds. Writing elsewhere, we have proposed a typology of such potential motivations (Russell et al. 2017); these are expanded below and in subsequent chapters.

But while the opposition may have many and conflicting motivations, it would be simplistic to assume that it has no immediate policy-seeking goals at all. Even Herman (1972: 143) noted that some opposition amendments 'represent sincere and relatively nonpartisan efforts to improve the legislation'. Griffith (1974) found that around 80 per cent of government report-stage amendments 'in response' picked up points from the opposition rather than government backbenchers—though many clearly dealt with minor points.

Crucially, of course, a good deal at Westminster has changed since these accounts were written. The old model of an adversarial, majoritarian Westminster could be seen as increasingly out of date, following the changes outlined in previous chapters. Select committees potentially make members more policy-focused, contributing to a culture where they are more prepared to think independently and work across party lines. The post-1999 House of Lords resembles a 'consensus' style parliament, where no party has an overall majority—making opposition parties what is sometimes referred to as 'pivotal voters' (Krehbiel 1998), able to determine voting outcomes. This applies to the Liberal Democrats in opposition, as well as the major parties (Russell 2013, Russell and Sciara 2007). Hence opposition parties may be able to extract policy concessions through the Lords, in ways that they rarely could in the Commons previously. We might expect this to result in more policy-focused behaviour, and consequently greater sensitivity to opposition policy concerns by government at earlier stages of policy formulation. As noted in Chapter 1, Manow and Burkhart (2007) have shown how, in Germany, the presence of a second chamber where the government lacks a majority results in 'legislative self-restraint'. Likewise Chapter 3 noted how in the UK anticipating the Lords' response has become important to government legislative preparation. To a significant degree this is about anticipating the response of the opposition.

Opposition Organization

In important respects opposition party organization mirrors that of the government. Larger parties when in opposition appoint a 'Shadow Cabinet' with similar collective decision-making authority to the Cabinet, and a team of more junior shadow ministers. Frontbenchers are appointed in both chambers, with the most senior concentrated in the Commons. These include whips, under the respective leadership of a Commons and a Lords Chief Whip. While the Conservatives and Labour selected a shadow team of roughly the same size as the government frontbench, the smaller Liberal Democrats when in opposition had fewer frontbenchers, often with wider portfolios (though a higher proportion of their parliamentarians were still frontbenchers compared to other parties). Where parties are even smaller (e.g. DUP, UUP, Plaid Cymru, Greens, and the SNP pre-2015) there is often no division at all between frontbench and backbench, with all members serving as frontbenchers, covering wide policy portfolios.

There are also many important differences between government and opposition. The most obvious is resources. While ministers have an entire civil service machine, including private offices, departmental policy specialists, government lawyers, and parliamentary counsel, opposition is a far more shoestring affair. Frontbenchers in the Commons rely on the staff paid for by their own parliamentary allowances (who also cover constituency work), alongside specific opposition funding known as 'Short money', and some limited support from party head office. The Short money (named after Commons Leader Ted Short, who introduced the scheme in the 1970s) was just over £6 million in 2011–12 for the Labour opposition as a whole, including roughly £700,000 for the leader's office.[1] This is significantly more generous than it used to be, but falls well short of the resources available to ministers.[2] In 2011–12 the second largest sum was £168,795, payable to the (then six-member) SNP. The equivalent system of 'Cranborne money' in the House of Lords is far more limited. In 2011–12 this provided Labour with £522,102, and there were no funds for smaller parties. When Labour was in government, both of these forms of funding were split primarily between the Conservatives and Liberal Democrats. Commenting on resources, one junior Commons frontbencher told us that 'it was basically me doing the research for this bill'—as the Shadow Secretary of State had only one researcher, working three days per week, and the Lords team had fewer resources still. Consequently, the opposition is often dependent on outside groups to support its legislative work (as discussed in Chapter 7), and benefits from the ability of impartial parliamentary clerks to help with drafting amendments, and parliamentary library staff for research.

In terms of opposition resources, and also seniority of frontbenchers, the Commons is very obviously the primary chamber. But, as indicated above, it is the Lords that offers opposition parties the most direct opportunity to influence legislation. This presents both organizational and political challenges, and on occasion results in significant intercameral tensions. On the government side, MPs and peers acting as ministers are supported by the same (sizeable) team of departmental officials. In opposition, intercameral connections between frontbenchers in the two chambers are far more fragmented, despite gradually having strengthened, from what one long-serving parliamentarian described as being 'almost-non-existent' in the 1980s. During Labour's period in office, when the Lords became substantially more important to both opposition parties, each party's frontbenchers came increasingly to meet on a bicameral basis, developing formal 'handover' processes for when bills passed from one chamber to the other. Labour bolstered such arrangements further when it entered opposition in 2010. Some peers began to gain support from relevant Commons researchers, with the two halves of the teams working more closely together, particularly when bills were in the Lords. Nonetheless, interviewees commented that good intercameral working still depends heavily on the personalities of individual frontbenchers concerned.

A key consideration for the legislative process is how opposition policy is set. Frontbenchers must respond publicly to detailed government proposals, and often propose alternatives through amendments. They do this within the constraints of a collective party policy line. The Shadow Cabinet will discuss high-level policy issues, but rarely focuses on the fine detail of bills. On important matters the leader's office will to some extent be involved, and the Shadow Chancellor's approval is likely to be required for decisions with significant spending implications. Here patterns again reflect the style of the individual protagonists involved, and the nature of the policy in question. One Conservative frontbencher said that it 'depends in opposition ... on whether the Leader of the Opposition wants to engage with it'; a Labour frontbencher post-2010 commented that (at least in his area of policy) the Shadow Chancellor 'has a pretty big role' whereas the leader 'dips in and out a bit more'. But opposition processes are generally far less formal than those in government. As one frontbencher put it, 'you live much more day-to-day with your colleagues in Shadow Cabinet, without any kind of mediation, as it were'; limited resources mean that you 'get to manage your own affairs' as a frontbencher to a considerable extent.

As in government, the frontbench must also act broadly in line with policy as approved by the wider party—including the annual party conference, and bodies such as Labour's National Policy Forum. Plus, there are parliamentary party organizations linking front and backbench, which vary slightly between the parties, and between how they organize in government and in opposition—as described more substantively in Chapter 5. For Labour the key body is the Parliamentary Labour Party (covering both chambers), and for the Conservatives the 1922 Committee in the Commons and the Association of Conservative Peers. These—and more focused policy subgroups within them—hold frontbenchers to account when the party is in government, and also to some extent in opposition. For the minor parties, clearly there are fewer parliamentary coordination problems. As one such member put it, 'there's only six of us so it's easy enough to wander down the corridor and speak to each other about things'. But for such parties, coordination with the party outside parliament—and its support in terms of policy development—features highly. Plus, there is a devolution dimension. For example, the SNP, is 'in government in Scotland ... so obviously we discuss with them and we take advice ... We're not going to take a stance down here that's going to be detrimental to the Scottish government'.

All of this indicates some of the pressures and challenges for opposition parties in the legislative process. They play a high-profile role, yet respond to complex policy with only limited resources compared to the government machine, and face various coordination challenges. The problems of negotiating a policy line between front and backbench, plus Lords and Commons, and of balancing established ideological positions with the demands of public opinion were all clearly visible on the 12 case study bills.

Opposition Responses to the Case Study Bills

In general, the position taken to a bill by opposition parties—particularly the official opposition—can be very important to the entire tone and content of parliamentary debates. Its power of issue politicization means that both the overall attention given to the bill (not least by the media), as well as the detailed topics discussed, may rest largely upon its response. Of course, where opposition parties do not strongly challenge a bill, government backbenchers or outside pressure groups (as discussed in subsequent chapters) may nonetheless do so. But the default frame for debate at Westminster remains one between government and opposition.

As indicated in previous chapters, some of the case study bills were significantly more controversial than others. Hence unsurprisingly the opposition's response varied a good deal bill by bill. But even some bills that were highly controversial were greeted cautiously by opposition parties, due to the need to balance the official opposition's role as primary scrutineer in parliament, the party's own policy and beliefs, and responsiveness to public opinion. It might therefore be said that there is not merely an 'opposition mode', to pick up King's (1976) phrase, but several alternative 'opposition modes' to suit different purposes. Not all of these are as adversarial as might be commonly assumed.

Some bills were genuinely uncontroversial in party political terms, and the opposition's response might even be described as fitting a 'consensual mode'. One example was Labour's Employment Bill, which introduced a range of relatively small measures, on which there was widespread agreement. Although there were some controversies on individual aspects, there was no in principle opposition to the objectives of the bill (as illustrated in Chapter 9), which helps to explain why it was introduced via the House of Lords. The same was true of many elements of Labour's Health Bill—while on the more controversial smoking aspects all parties faced internal divisions, meaning that the opposition as well as the government could maintain unity by supporting the principle of a Commons free vote. Neither of these bills offered much political capital to the opposition, and their scrutiny primarily explored—largely consensually and out of the media spotlight—whether implementation details could be improved.

Another of Labour's bills illustrated nicely how government and opposition can sometimes set out to work together. The Energy Bill passed through parliament in the final session before the 2010 general election, by which time it was widely expected that Labour would soon be out of office. For the kinds of measures included in the bill, such as incentives for carbon capture and storage at power plants or the pricing structure of household energy bills, political instability could create damaging market uncertainty. An opposition frontbencher on the bill explained in interview that 'quite a lot of the things which Labour was doing in this bill were things that we ... very much welcomed'. He recalled a discussion with a minister, who suggested that 'you can either play politics and you won't get investment, or you can be serious politicians and recognize you might be in government and to work constructively with us'. The opposition clearly took the latter approach on this bill. As the same interviewee put it, 'I was very keen indeed that we avoided divisions on a lot of this because I felt, from an investor's perspective, with an election coming up, the last thing they wanted to see was parliament divided'. As the bill went into 'wash-up' at the end of the 2005–10 parliament, the opposition's support was crucial—as further discussed below.

These were all examples of genuine political agreement; but at times lack of opposition complaints about government action is more tactical. This might be described as 'acquiescent mode'. Remaining with Labour's bills, such a dynamic applied to the Saving Gateway Accounts Bill, which established a system of savings accounts for those on certain benefits, incentivized through government contributions. At the bill's second reading, the Conservative spokesperson commented that '[w]e all share the Bill's laudable aims', suggesting that the accounts 'could be a valuable tool'.[3] An opposition interviewee explained that 'in opposition it's very hard to be against encouraging people to save more using taxpayers' money'; hence he sought 'to give a reasonable run through, test the government on some of the key issues, and that was really about it'. Another frontbencher recalled that 'at a time when there were huge tax incentives for the wealthy to save via pensions, it was difficult to say, "you shouldn't have a little experiment here that costs very little"'. But fundamentally, he suggested, 'I thought it was a pretty silly bill'. Notably, although there was little opposition at the time, the coalition abolished this scheme immediately upon taking office, through the Savings Accounts and Health in Pregnancy Grant Bill. The Corporate Manslaughter Bill was likewise seen as emotive and hence difficult to object to; one opposition frontbencher suggested that 'it was one of those bills where the view taken ... was that what the government was trying to achieve should not be opposed'. Although he had some doubts that the bill would be effective, its objective of aiding those affected by industrial accidents meant that 'politically we couldn't be seen to say no'.

Similar dynamics applied to several of the coalition's bills. Hence the Budget Responsibility and National Audit Bill came, in the words of one government source, 'as close ... in my experience ... to cross-party agreement as you could have'. The Labour Party had accepted the principle of establishing an Office for Budget Responsibility, and hence an opposition frontbencher said that 'there was a little element of going through the motions'. But there was an undercurrent of party politics beneath this apparent consensus. As one (government backbench) interviewee suggested, given the bill's introduction in the wake of the 2008–09 financial crisis, 'nobody was going to say "we really need the flexibility that Mr Brown had to fiddle the figures"'.

The pressure of public opinion created significant challenges for opposition parties on several other more high-profile and controversial bills; here they might be said to have responded in 'conflicted mode'. A key example was Labour's Identity Cards Bill, where the surrounding politics were extremely complex. As indicated in the previous chapter, government consultations on this policy had begun before the 1997 election. Indeed, Michael Howard, who was Conservative Party leader at the time of Labour's bill, had promoted the idea as Home Secretary in the previous Conservative government. This clearly somewhat compromised his party's ability to oppose the bill. Of course, in 1995, when Michael Howard's consultation paper was published, Labour was in opposition. Tony Blair, as party leader, had suggested that 'instead of wasting hundreds of millions of pounds on compulsory identity cards as the Tory right demand, let that money provide thousands of extra police officers on the beat'.[4] Unsurprisingly, these words were frequently quoted back at the Labour government. To further complicate matters, the Liberal Democrat Shadow Home Secretary at the time of the bill was Mark Oaten, who had voiced support for a 10-minute rule bill in favour of identity cards in 1998. As he records in his memoir, 'Home Secretary, David Blunkett, was quick to point [this] out when we had our first exchange over the issue on the floor of the House. It was embarrassing but I was able to point out that Tony Blair had voted against it' (Oaten 2009: 99–100). While the Liberal Democrat spokesperson might have been instinctively in favour of the cards, Conservative Shadow Home Secretary David Davis (in contrast to his leader), had libertarian instincts and was keenly against. At the bill's second reading he described the proposals as 'illiberal and impractical, excessive and expensive, unnecessary and unworkable'.[5] It was the only one of our seven case study bills under Labour that the opposition voted against outright at this stage.[6]

Another key difficulty facing the opposition was the apparent popularity of the identity card proposals, as demonstrated by public opinion polls. In April 2004 a MORI survey found 80 per cent of participants to be favour.[7] Opposing the bill head on could thus be electorally dangerous. Hence during the detailed Commons stages the opposition parties focused on various practical matters, such as how the scheme should be financed, the penalties for those failing to register and the kind of information to be printed on the cards. As Oaten (2009: 100) recalls:

By nature the [Liberal Democrats] wanted to focus on the civil liberties implications. I was less keen on this approach. It seemed to me that we needed to … try to persuade the 80 per cent who were in favour of ID cards that they were wrong.

The same MORI poll had indicated that only one in five people was prepared to pay the likely £35 cost of an identity card, so a focus on this issue could help to erode popularity. As one interviewee said, 'we managed to get, within a pretty quick period of time, the whole debate off civil liberties and onto cost … the cost issue overtook civil liberties'. In committee in the Commons, the opposition parties therefore chipped away with numerous amendments to tease out the scheme's costs and detailed operation. One official referred to this as a 'proxy war', to avoid outright opposition. When the bill reached the Lords this pressure was maintained, but the debate also shifted more squarely to civil liberties and the degree of compulsion in the scheme. Here, in the words of a Commons frontbencher, 'they were passionate about civil liberties issues, because that's the indulgence of the House of Lords. They didn't have to face the electorate.'

When the coalition later came to reverse this measure, via the Identity Documents Bill 2010–12, the mood had shifted, and Labour found itself in 'acquiescent mode'. This was, symbolically, the first bill introduced by the coalition—to indicate a clear change in direction. Labour frontbenchers concluded that there was little point opposing it, despite some of them having recently served as Home Office ministers responsible for implementing the policy. One such interviewee commented that 'it was the government's first triumph so they weren't going to be listening to us'. Like their predecessors, Labour frontbenchers focused partly on cost implications, but did not escalate this to any wider form of opposition.

In opposing the coalition's Welfare Reform Bill, Labour was instead in 'conflicted mode'. Like ID cards, many of the welfare reform measures—while undoubtedly controversial—were known to be popular with the public. In the context of 'austerity' the coalition was actively seeking to cut the benefits bill, which was loudly welcomed by parts of the media.[8] Labour frontbenchers, while troubled by the likely effects on benefit recipients, were also keen to rebuild the party's damaged reputation for fiscal prudence. Hence at Commons second reading Labour frontbencher Liam Byrne spoke of wanting 'to approach the vital question of welfare reform in the spirit of national consensus', which 'will be good for our country' and 'reduce the deficit'.[9] The opposition did not oppose the bill's second reading outright, though it did propose a lengthy 'reasoned amendment' indicating its shortcomings. Some aspects, such as the introduction of Universal Credit, were genuinely consensual. Nonetheless the bill presented Labour with difficult decisions, and caused significant tensions inside the party—most notably between the frontbench teams in the Commons and the Lords.

Finally, another coalition bill provides an example of something closer to outright 'adversarial mode' (which some might expect to be the default setting at Westminster). The Savings Accounts and Health in Pregnancy Grant Bill abolished 'asset-based welfare' schemes designed by Labour in earlier years. Its introduction offered Labour frontbenchers, still bruised by their ejection from government, an opportunity to challenge policy directly—partly because the overall costs of these schemes were relatively small (compared, for example, to the savings in the Welfare Reform Bill). At Commons second reading, Labour's David Hanson commented that the bill 'will hit children, women and families unfairly, it will hit the poorest in our society the hardest and it will undo the positive steps that the previous Labour Government took to tackle inequality'.[10] Labour MPs forced 19 divisions at the Commons committee stage, in full knowledge that they would lose—partly because, as one senior figure told us, they were 'feeling particularly bolshie just after the election'. In the eyes of the government, 'one of the hallmarks of this bill was the ability of the Labour frontbench to whip up a fuss about nothing'.[11]

Opposition Amendments and their Motivations

As shown in Table 4.1, the opposition parties were responsible for proposing the overwhelming majority of all amendments to the bills. Their 2,941 proposals outstripped those made without opposition support (by government, government backbenchers and non-party parliamentarians), by a factor of 2:1. Most opposition amendments came from the three main parties (i.e. Conservative and Liberal Democrat 2005–10, and Labour 2010–12)—and just 55 included a minor party signature. As shown in Table 4.2, in the 2005–10 parliament the Conservatives sponsored 993 amendments acting as a single party, and the Liberal Democrats 436. Joint action between these two opposition parties accounted for 113 amendments, and is discussed in more detail in Chapter 9. More than three-quarters of the 2,941 opposition amendments included a frontbencher among their signatories.

Table 4.1 illustrates how the number of amendments proposed by the opposition parties varies greatly by bill. In the 2005–10 parliament this ranged from 743 amendments on the Identity Cards Bill to 69 on the Energy Bill, clearly indicating the topics that the opposition sought to politicize. Those bills with the lowest number of amendments were described above as having been greeted in 'consensual mode'. Under coalition the number of opposition amendments per bill remained remarkably stable, despite the reduction from two main parties to one—an average of 237 in 2005–10 and 256 in 2010–12. Again in this period the number varied considerably by bill, largely in line with the 'modes' above. Notably the more adversarial response to the Savings Accounts and Health in Pregnancy Grant Bill is not reflected in amendments, since as a money bill there was no opportunity to table these in the Lords. In contrast, on several bills the number of opposition amendments in the Lords far outweighed that in the Commons.

At first glance these figures might suggest that opposition parties make great efforts to amend bills in parliament; and as we already know, few non-government amendments actually pass (for summary figures, see Table 4.2). Yet we also know that opposition amendments cannot necessarily be taken at face value. In line with the expectations from the literature, opposition frontbenchers were quite open with us that amendments have various purposes beyond changing the bill at hand. Hence

Table 4.1 Opposition amendments proposed by bill and chamber

	Commons			Lords			Total		
	Single party	With others	Total	Single party	With others	Total	Single party	With others	Total
2005–10 parliament									
Identity Cards	269	16	285	382	76	458	651	92	743
Health	126	18	144	78	58	136	204	76	280
Corporate Manslaughter	113	19	132	96	8	104	209	27	236
Further Education and Training	43	3	46	90	3	93	133	6	139
Employment	43	4	47	38	1	39	81	5	86
Saving Gateway Accounts	50	0	50	58	0	58	108	0	108
Energy	47	22	69	0	0	0	47	22	69
Total (2005–10)	691	82	773	742	146	888	1,433	228	1,661
2010–12 session									
Identity Documents	16	0	16	11	5	16	27	5	32
Savings Accounts	106	2	108	0	0	0	106	2	108
Budget Responsibility	43	0	43	38	2	40	81	2	83
Public Bodies	53	13	66	205	73	278	258	86	344
Welfare Reform	338	0	338	193	182	375	531	182	713
Total (2010–12)	556	15	571	447	262	709	1,003	277	1,280
Grand total	**1,247**	**97**	**1,344**	**1,189**	**408**	**1,597**	**2,436**	**505**	**2,941**

Note: These amendments do not distinguish between frontbench or backbench opposition. The 'with others' columns include cooperation between opposition parliamentarians from different parties as well as those sponsored jointly with non-opposition actors. All figures exclude amendments co-sponsored by the government.

Table 4.2 Opposition amendments proposed and success of opposition-initiated strands

	Amendments proposed by actor	Strands initiated by actor		% success of initiated	% of total successful strands in parliament
		Strands initiated	Of which successful		
2005–10 parliament					
Conservatives alone	993	577	34	6	20
Liberal Democrats alone	436	254	12	5	7
Minor opposition party alone	4	4	0	0	0
Conservatives and Liberal Democrats only	113	78	7	9	4
Other joint opposition only	10	3	1	33	1
Opposition with others	105	44	4	9	2
Total involving opposition	1,661	960	58	6	34
Total for all actors	2,389	1,161	169	15	100
2010–12 session					
Labour alone	996	551	42	8	32
Minor opposition party alone	7	3	0	0	0
Joint opposition only	6	1	0	0	0
Opposition with others	271	89	12	13	9
Total involving opposition	1,280	644	54	8	41
Total for all actors	1,972	889	131	15	100
Both parliaments					
Opposition party alone	2,436	1,389	88	6	29
Joint opposition only	129	82	8	10	3
Opposition with others	376	133	16	12	5
Total involving opposition	2,941	1,604	112	7	37
Total for all actors	4,361	2,050	300	15	100

Notes: The figures for opposition amendments exclude any co-sponsored with the government; all amendments with a ministerial sponsor are included within the 'total for all actors'. Within this table 'others' means parliamentary actors other than opposition. Of the 2,941 opposition amendments, 68 (2%) were agreed to, of which 12 (0.4% of the total) were neither subsequently overturned nor purely overturned an earlier amendment (as described in Chapter 3).

the number agreed or not agreed by parliament cannot straightaway be interpreted as a sign of 'success' or 'failure'. Whether such amendments succeed in their purpose depends, obviously, upon what that purpose was.

There is no perfect way of classifying the various motivations lying behind opposition party amendments. But we suggest that there are at least five, which we call 'information seeking', 'signalling', 'political gameplaying', 'procedural devices', and, finally, 'legislative change'. Notably, unlike in Griffith's (1974) day, we found little evidence of opposition 'tidying-up' amendments. The boundaries between our five categories blur to some extent, as we shall see; but they are sufficiently distinct to demonstrate the diversity that exists. As noted in subsequent chapters, other actors at Westminster can also pursue legislative amendments which are not wholly policy focused; but this phenomenon is particularly clear with respect to the opposition, so we treat it more fully here. We discuss each of the five opposition motivations in turn, using examples from the bills.

Information seeking

The first reason for opposition amendments is what we call 'information seeking'. As indicated in Chapter 2, the Westminster legislative process overwhelmingly structures debates around amendments. Hence what are commonly referred to as 'probing' amendments are often used to facilitate that debate. There are other means to tease out information from ministers during the legislative process, including evidence-taking sessions in Commons public bill committee. Nonetheless many amendments—particularly at the committee stage—are designed simply to draw out information about the government's intent.[12] Government backbenchers (and non-party parliamentarians in the House of Lords) do conduct some information seeking, but it is particularly central to the opposition parties' role. As one interviewee put it, 'an opposition's duty is to oppose', so:

You can resist what the government is doing simply to test to destruction what they are proposing, even if actually you think 'well there's not much of a problem with this', but if we just said 'oh there's not much of a problem with this, government do what you like', there'd be no point any of us being here.

A parliamentary official hence described probing amendments as essentially 'a form of question'. Another explained:

Quite often the role of those amendments is not to amend the bill at all, it's merely to provide a vehicle by which the government can explain what the bill means, or what it doesn't mean, or what it might mean, or what it could mean. So that whole category of probing amendments is designed to expose, in public, on the record, what the legislation is about.

The relatively less pressurized environment of the committee stage provides an opportunity for such discussion, without too much commitment on the part of the parliamentarian proposing the amendment—which helps to explain why committee stage amendments are so numerous. There is no expectation that probing amendments will be pushed to a vote, and proposers routinely withdraw them having heard the minister's response. For example at Commons committee stage on the Saving Gateway Accounts Bill, Conservative frontbencher Mark Hoban proposed an amendment to specify that the maximum amount payable into one of the new accounts within a month should be £25, stating that this had been tabled in a 'probing spirit'. He noted that the bill's explanatory notes suggested 'that the amount will be £25, and I suspect that that is in the regulations' (i.e. the secondary legislation to specify the detail of the scheme).[13] In response, the minister confirmed 'that the draft regulations set out savings of £25 a month'.[14] Hoban agreed that this was the right place to specify the figure, commenting that 'it might be decided in 10 years' time that £25 is not enough. It would be very tedious to have to introduce primary legislation to lift the limit from £25' (the possible effect, had his amendment been accepted).[15] Having received a satisfactory response, his amendment was therefore withdrawn.

A former opposition frontbencher emphasized that in such cases, 'you put down a probing amendment that you have no intention ever of pushing to a vote, that often is defective—so that if it was accepted into the bill it would make the bill make no sense, or it's very poorly drafted'. Indeed, as one of the officials above suggested, in such cases proposers 'definitely would be appalled if their amendments were accepted!'.

Information-seeking amendments may not create immediate pressure for legislative change; but they can nonetheless seriously challenge ministers and officials, by requiring them to defend the policy positions in the bill. Indeed, the minister's response in parliament can itself potentially have legal force, as mentioned in Chapter 3. This process greatly encourages the degree of government preparedness and pre-planning described in that chapter. Once an amendment has been tabled, civil servants will prepare briefing, which ministers must digest and be prepared to articulate. If the point has not previously been considered, this can prompt government rethinking. There is hence a blurry line between simply 'probing' and creating genuine pressure to change policy. A Commons frontbencher suggested that 'it's … about getting the minister to put things on the record that are helpful, seeing which ones they defend robustly and which bits they're a bit more ambivalent about'. An opposition peer likewise suggested, 'it's seeing, if I put pressure there, and I put pressure there, and I put pressure there, do any of those have any sign of somebody giving way a bit, or not?'. Probing amendments can thus have dual motives, and lead to more serious amendments later.

Signalling

The same can be said of amendments driven by the second opposition motivation. Signalling—of policy alternatives, and the fitness for office of the alternative government—is widely recognized in the literature as a core opposition activity. Amendments of this kind primarily enable the opposition to communicate with those outside parliament—who may include the media, interest groups of various kinds, or its own party activists—rather than to seek immediate change. Nonetheless, if these external messages are well received, they may contribute to serious pressure on the government to change direction.

There were numerous examples of this kind of activity by opposition parties on the case study bills, and the kinds of messages that they were seeking to communicate differed widely. For example, as already indicated, on Labour's Energy Bill the opposition parties were in 'consensual mode': keen to signal probity and future continuity to investors as the general election approached. One frontbencher also indicated their desire to signal the issues that Whitehall should be 'getting prepared to implement'. But relatively few amendments were proposed overall. More commonly signals—including through amendments—are actively targeted at the wider policy community in a subject area. Another opposition frontbencher pointed out that 'when there aren't bills going through parliament [interest groups] pretty much only engage with government'; so the legislative process provides an opportunity to think 'what are we going to do in relation to this bill that is going to strengthen our credibility as a potential future government?'.

Where there are deep differences between government and opposition policy positions, opposition amendments also provide an opportunity to communicate these to a wider public. As one interviewee explained, 'sometimes the massive, massive issue in the bill is something you know full well you're never going to win but it's a battle you still need to have'. Hence a frontbencher emphasized the need to propose amendments on issues that the party has:

an important political manifesto commitment on, and you feel a need to put down a marker that this is what you support, so that you can then push it to a vote and say you did actually solidly argue for that but sadly you were defeated and the wretched government steamrollered through this unjust piece of legislation.

Where the opposition's position is more conflicted on a bill, there may be serious dilemmas about what should be signalled to the wider world. As one opposition frontbencher told us, 'when you're in opposition you have to think quite carefully ... about where you pick the fights'. The Conservatives and Liberal Democrats grappled with these problems in opposing the Identity Cards Bill, as did Labour with the coalition's Welfare Reform Bill. In both cases these caused tensions between opposition frontbench teams in the two chambers, with the Commons more closely attuned to the likely electoral implications of its stances. A prime example on the latter bill was Labour's difficulties over an amendment proposed by a bishop in the Lords to soften the effect of the overall benefit cap—as described in more detail in Chapter 6.

Gameplaying

Information seeking and signalling probably account for the great majority of opposition amendments; but some also have other motivations, again not focused directly on changing the bill. One is straightforward 'political gameplaying', which is not so much about signalling the merits of the opposition but seeking to undermine or embarrass the government—as Griffith (1974: 38) suggested, to make the government 'less generally acceptable'. The most obvious way to do this is on substantive policy matters. For example, in the words of a Labour frontbencher, to force divisions simply 'to get the Tories to vote against something good and decent'. Under coalition, Labour put particular energy into seeking to embarrass the Liberal Democrats, and to drive wedges between them and their Conservative partners. Labour's strategy on the coalition's Savings Accounts and Health in Pregnancy

Grant Bill, where the opposition forced numerous divisions at the Commons committee stage, fits this model. Opposition members know that they have little chance of winning such divisions, but as one explained 'there's some times, even in committee, you'll want to push it to a vote just to get on the record ... [that] everyone else voted against you, because that can be politically important as well'. This kind of behaviour is much less common in the Lords, which receives relatively little media attention and (as further discussed in Chapter 6) has a culture of more rational, less partisan, debate.

The opposition can also seek to embarrass the government procedurally. It is a standard complaint that the government has not provided sufficient time for debating a bill, and is therefore seeking to avoid proper scrutiny. But for this case to be made convincingly the space provided for debate must be filled. So as one opposition frontbencher explained:

There's always this sort of slightly silly charade where [the government] suggest a certain number of committee sessions, we always ask for more, and then ... no matter how many you're allocated, you've got to be seen to be using up all those sessions ... [Hence] there are various tricks that you can use to string it out.

Filling up time may require the tabling of numerous amendments. Likewise, the same interviewee commented that 'we can't not bring amendments forward at report stage, because then it looks like either the government's doing something right or we're not interested'. This was in the context of a bill on which there was relatively little substantive disagreement, resulting in attempted shaming over the handling of the process instead.

Procedural devices

In addition, amendments are sometimes moved as 'procedural devices', essentially to manage the flow of debate. This might be done in support of other objectives—to ensure that a 'signalling' amendment is voted on in prime time, when the media may be paying greater attention, or that a policy-focused amendment is voted on when attendance in the chamber is high (particularly in the Lords, where numbers dwindle late in the evening). Important discussions can be brought on earlier by moving 'paving amendments', or pushed to later through what one interviewee referred to as 'filler amendments', which can be dropped as required.[16] By putting down numerous amendments the opposition (or indeed others) can thus speed up or slow down debate, and occasionally spring surprises on the government.

Policy change

The last motivation for opposition amendments is, of course, a sincere desire to change a bill. This blurs considerably with earlier motivations, as already seen. Probing amendments that uncover uncertainty, or signalling amendments that attract outside support, may encourage the government to change its position.

Opposition frontbenchers must clearly decide how to balance their strategy, and their amendments, between these different possible goals. Here the pattern differs by legislative stage, with a more scattergun approach at committee stage, where members propose amendments on all sorts of different matters in order to facilitate debate, without any implied commitment. As one frontbencher put it:

I may put down a lot of amendments and speak to them but there's obviously one or two that you will push and push and push because they are the important ones. Other ones if you lose in committee, okay you've lost in committee, move on, but let's take back to report stage the really important ones and try again.

It is often these more policy-motivated amendments from the opposition which will result in concessions, as further discussed below.

Evidence of Opposition Influence on the Case Study Bills

This leads to the question of the opposition's impact on legislative outcomes. Existing understandings would suggest little measurable change to policy, but perhaps more diffuse influence through determining what gets debated, and using the process to highlight weaknesses in the government's approach. In this section we start with the classic function of 'issue politicization' (i.e. shaping the parliamentary and wider political agenda), but then go on to explore the success of opposition amendments, followed by other more subtle influences on the process. We find that the opposition's classic functions remain important, but that its impact on immediate policy outcomes is also greater than traditional accounts suggest. Nonetheless this is subject to significant constraints.

Issue politicization

The case study bills offer clear illustrations of the opposition's power of issue politicization at work. This is employed from the point of the bill's second reading—in terms of the tone of speeches, and whether the bill's principles are pushed to the vote—and through all subsequent stages. Opposition amendments can be used to draw attention to particular issues, and to put the government under pressure; but the opposition can also use various other mechanisms at its disposal to increase this pressure further still.

We saw in Chapter 2 (Tables 2.4 and 2.5) how the debating time dedicated to bills varies widely. For example the coalition's Identity Documents Bill was subject to barely one-quarter the time spent on Labour's Identity Cards Bill in Commons committee, while its Lords committee stage was roughly one-tenth the duration. The opposition has some control over this matter through the 'usual channels' negotiations conducted in the Commons, particularly in discussions around the programme motion. In the Lords timetabling is more clearly determined by the number and distribution of amendments proposed. We have also seen that the overall number of such opposition amendments varies widely by bill

(Table 4.1)—the Identity Documents Bill attracted only 27 single-party opposition amendments, compared to the 651 on the Identity Cards Bill. Both formal timetabling and number of amendments are therefore very important in the amount of time and attention that government bills receive—in parliament itself and by the media and outside groups. Each is determined to a significant extent by the opposition.

Within individual bills, the clustering of amendments likewise indicates which topics the opposition chose to politicize. Hence the Identity Cards Bill as introduced in the Commons comprised 45 clauses and two schedules, but more than one-tenth of single-party opposition amendments were on the single clause which defined the national identity register. These included 40 such amendments at Lords committee stage alone, and a further 36 at other stages. We noted in Chapter 2 that Labour's Health Bill was arranged into five main 'parts', one of which related to smoking and attracted almost half of the amendments overall. A key reason for this was the distribution of opposition amendments; of 204 such single-party amendments, 97 concerned the smoking part, while 33 related to that on healthcare-associated infections, and just one to the part dealing with the NHS Appointments Commission. The lack of attention on the latter, in particular, implied opposition support for this element of the bill. One interviewee commented that 'it did slightly concern me that so much time ... was being spent on the smoke-free' part, whereas 'other bits later on in the legislation, I'm not sure how much scrutiny they got'. Likewise an official on another bill recalled spending 'days and months going into in enormous detail' on some issues, which then reached parliament and 'just passed through on the nod'. The opposition can hence in effect keep matters off the agenda, as well as drawing political attention towards them.

The opposition's ability to inflict defeat in the Lords can be seen as part of its issue politicization function—as this determines which potentially difficult issues are placed back on the Commons' agenda for reconsideration. During the period of Labour government, the two opposition parties combined could readily bring about Lords defeats. As discussed in Chapter 5, the 12 such defeats on the Identity Cards Bill presented ministers with some tricky political dilemmas in the Commons, and resulted in significant concessions. Under coalition this power was weakened however, as discussed below and in Chapter 6.

The opposition can also use other mechanisms to raise the profile of debate on bills. For example, under the coalition, Labour dedicated a Commons opposition day to debating controversial provisions in the Public Bodies Bill while it was still passing through the Lords. MPs were forced to vote on the proposition that 'the Government's intention in the Public Bodies Bill to sell off up to 100 per cent of England's public forestry estate is fundamentally unsound'.[17] Though this motion was defeated, the government announced 15 days later that the forestry clauses in the bill would be abandoned (as further discussed in Chapter 7). Similar tactics were successfully used with respect to proposals on Housing Benefit due to appear in the Welfare Reform Bill (as discussed further in Chapter 5).

Prime Minister's Questions (PMQs) is often seen as a mere 'pantomime', dominated by trivial party point scoring (Hansard Society 2014). But, as a very public forum, it provides another opportunity to boost opposition campaigns (and indeed potentially those of government backbenchers and others). For example PMQs played an important additional role in the politicization of forests.[18] Another interesting example was seen on the Savings Accounts and Health in Pregnancy Grant Bill, where an opposition backbencher—Labour's Paul Goggins—pressed for policy change. The bill abolished the Child Trust Fund, and at its second reading Goggins asked how children in (local authority, etc.) care, would be affected. Goggins was described by an interviewee as 'not a partisan figure', who 'spoke with authority', and worked with key charities such as Barnardo's on the issue. He went on to use PMQs as a highly visible platform to ask David Cameron for his support, 'in such a way that he'd have sounded very callous if he'd have said "no"', as another interviewee recalled.[19] A Conservative interviewee described this as a 'neat manoeuvre', which won Cameron's agreement. Change was not achieved through Commons amendments (which were proposed by both Goggins and the Labour frontbench). Lords amendments proved impossible, due to the unexpected certification of this as a money bill. But the Chancellor nonetheless announced three months after royal assent that a fresh scheme for looked-after children would be established.[20] In all of the cases above, opposition politicians ensured that controversial issues were aired and thoroughly debated, which encouraged government rethinking.

One specific circumstance in which the opposition's issue politicization power becomes very real is at the 'wash-up' which has traditionally occurred just before a general election. At this point any outstanding bills must either be rushed through or abandoned. In 2015 this process was less challenging as a result of the Fixed-term Parliaments Act, but it applied in its usual form in 2010. When the election was called Labour's Energy Bill had only recently reached the Lords from the Commons, and not yet had its committee stage. Its only hope of passage was hence cross-party agreement. But a government insider told us that they had the impression in advance 'that we're not going to have much trouble getting this through wash-up because [the opposition] pretty much accept most of it'. As discussed above the bill was uncontroversial, and it indeed completed its passage with only a handful of government amendments. In contrast other bills, such as the Constitutional Reform and Governance Bill, had key provisions removed during wash-up due to a failure to reach cross-party agreement (Newson and Kelly 2011). Hence at this point in the cycle, another government insider emphasized, 'you're dependent on what the opposition is going to agree'.

Opposition amendments and policy change

We have seen that opposition parties propose a very large number of amendments to government bills, and that one reason is the opposition's varied motivations, not all of them focused on changing the bill at hand. The classic expectation would be of an opposition using bills to showcase its credentials as an alternative government, with the present government nonetheless proceeding largely unimpeded. But developments at Westminster create greater potential for the opposition to achieve policy change than in the past. An examination of the ultimate outcome of opposition party amendments can demonstrate whether this potential is realized.

There are three primary obstacles to assessing impact of particular non-government actors in parliament through quantitative analysis of amendments.

- First, since many opposition amendments were never intended to bring about legislative change it would be misleading to interpret those non-agreed as an indicator of opposition 'failure'.[21] The extent to which these initiatives succeed obviously depends on their goal. We must therefore be cautious in interpreting opposition 'success rates'.

- Second, we know that even sincere non-government amendments are often withdrawn in favour of concessionary government amendments. Our creation of legislative 'strands' linking related amendments at different stages (as described in Chapter 2 and more fully in Appendix A), is designed to capture this. Table 4.2 therefore shows legislative strands which began with opposition amendments, as well as those amendments themselves.

- Third, even when considering strands, ideas often do not emanate from a single group. Individual amendments initiating a strand may be co-sponsored by opposition members with parliamentarians from other groups—which is captured in the 'with others' rows of the table. But additionally, strands may include separate amendments sponsored by actors from different groups; plus sometimes similar strands (which we call 'siblings'—see Appendix A) are sponsored by such groups. These other more subtle forms of cross-party sponsorship are not shown in Table 4.2, but reserved for Chapter 9. The table hence does not capture all initiatives to which the opposition contributed.

Unsurprisingly, very few opposition amendments were agreed to the bills. In total there were 68—all in the Lords, most of which were subsequently overturned in the Commons.[22] But the data on strands nonetheless shows that opposition actors had considerable success in triggering change to the bills. Across both parliaments, 112 of 1,604 strands initiated by opposition amendments (7 per cent of the total) resulted in some change that was made and not subsequently overturned. These accounted for almost four out of ten (37 per cent) of the distinct changes made to the bills. We already know from Chapter 3 that 55 per cent of successful strands were government-initiated—hence around four out of five of the remainder were opposition-initiated which, as indicated above, is a remarkably similar proportion to that found by Griffith (1974). The majority of these strands (88) began with amendments from a single opposition party. But there is some indication that the success rate of opposition party amendments was higher when more than one group—i.e. another opposition party, or non-opposition actor—was included as a sponsor (11 per cent versus 6 per cent overall). We do not seek to test these differences statistically at this stage, but they are explored further in Chapter 9.

We saw in Chapter 3 that the majority of government amendments lack policy substance, and that many strands initiated by government contain purely technical amendments. The same is not true of strands initiated by the opposition. Table 4.3

Table 4.3 Successful opposition-initiated strands by bill and degree of policy substance

	Policy substance	Procedure: regulations	Procedure: other	Technical	Total
2005–10 parliament					
Identity Cards	20	5	2	1	28
Health	7	1	0	2	10
Corporate Manslaughter	6	0	0	0	6
Further Education and Training	4	0	1	0	5
Employment	1	0	0	0	1
Saving Gateway Accounts	1	2	1	0	4
Energy	2	1	1	0	4
Total (2005–10)	41	9	5	3	58
2010–12 session					
Identity Documents	0	0	0	0	0
Savings Accounts	0	0	0	0	0
Budget Responsibility	5	0	0	0	5
Public Bodies	17	3	1	0	21
Welfare Reform	12	13	3	0	28
Total (2010–12)	34	16	4	0	54
Grand total	75	25	9	3	112

shows the 112 successful opposition-initiated strands broken down by extent of policy substance and bill. We see that three such strands were purely technical, while 75 had clear policy substance. In addition, 34 dealt with more procedural matters—mostly in terms of changes to ministers' ability to make regulations under the bill, but in some cases requiring other procedural change, such as ministers commissioning a report into a bill's implementation. The largest overall numbers of changes occurred on the Identity Cards Bill and the Welfare Reform Bill, while the largest number with clear policy substance were on the Identity Cards Bill and the Public Bodies Bill.

So the opposition appears to be an important initiator of policy change, but we do not yet know how the dynamics of this change process work. In the remainder of this section we hence discuss some successful opposition-initiated strands.

Various opposition proposals were accepted consensually, and in a handful of cases opposition party amendments were even agreed to bills without division. We have noted that minor drafting amendments from the opposition are unusual, but two were accepted on Labour's Health Bill, from Conservative frontbencher Earl (Freddie) Howe relating to duties to enforce the smoking ban.[23] Even these tiny changes were not incorporated immediately, but were withdrawn at the committee stage and accepted by the minister when proposed for a second time on report. But, as Chapter 3 indicated, changes of any kind are much more commonly made via government amendments responding to earlier non-government proposals. Other relatively consensual cases on the Health Bill in the Lords, for example to limit the types of person who could enter a private premises to inspect stocks of controlled drugs, followed this more typical pattern. Under the coalition, various opposition frontbench-sponsored amendments similarly succeeded consensually on the

Budget Responsibility and National Audit Bill, which started in the Lords. At committee stage Labour's Lord (John) Eatwell proposed a series of changes to bolster the independence of the new Office for Budget Responsibility and its oversight arrangements, which triggered government proposals on report.

Unsurprisingly, the number of concessions to the opposition is higher in the Lords than in the Commons—as discussed in Chapter 3 the government generally prefers to delay concessions until bills reach that chamber if it can. But consensual concessions to the opposition in the Commons do occasionally occur. For example on the Identity Cards Bill a government amendment at Commons report stage responded to a Conservative frontbench amendment in committee proposing that the offence of disclosing confidential information should apply explicitly to those manufacturing ID cards.

Of course concessions to the opposition are not always consensual, and even seemingly consensual changes can be a government tactic to deflect more adversarial approaches—particularly once bills reach the Lords. Where the opposition pushes its Lords amendments to division (or indeed supports amendments from other groups) the government will often be defeated. Such defeats played a part in some of the biggest changes to the case study bills in parliament. For example remaining with the Identity Cards Bill, the opposition's focus on costs culminated in a Lords defeat, which was ultimately met by a concession brokered by a government backbench MP (as described in Chapter 5). Questioning of the extent of compulsion in the scheme began with opposition amendments in Commons committee, and was resolved through a major climbdown when the bill returned from the Lords (also described in Chapter 5). A compromise over the timing of the cards' introduction, agreed only after lengthy ping-pong, ultimately helped kill off the scheme (as described in Chapter 6). On the Corporate Manslaughter Bill the highly contentious matter of the exclusion of deaths in police and prison custody was initially raised at Commons report stage in jointly sponsored amendments including Labour backbenchers and the Conservative frontbench; it subsequently became a central focus of debates in the Lords, and was likewise ultimately resolved by a government climbdown (as described in Chapter 6). In all of these cases opposition parties used their pivotal position in the Lords to force matters back onto the Commons' agenda, and significant concessions resulted.

After 2010, the Labour opposition was in a relatively weaker position in the Lords, and became more dependent on the support of nonparty parliamentarians—as indicated by the growth in amendments and strands 'with others' in Table 4.2. There were eight Lords defeats on the Welfare Reform Bill, but notably none of these were led by opposition peers.[24] Opposition frontbenchers adopted a deliberate strategy of remaining more in the background, and supporting proposals fronted by nonpartisan experts (as further discussed in Chapter 6). The government's increased numeric strength in the Lords, alongside the broader political context of 'austerity' (plus claims of financial privilege, further discussed below), all made it harder for the opposition to act assertively and extract concessions. On the Welfare Reform Bill opposition-initiated changes were therefore relatively low level. For example the bill proposed to limit the receipt of one form of Employment and Support

Allowance (ESA)—a benefit payable to those with limited capacity to work due to disability—to one year. Labour frontbench amendments in the Commons sought to extend this to at least two years, but were resisted by the government on the basis that there was a 'strong financial dimension' behind the limitation.[25] In the Lords Labour frontbenchers repeated their call, noting for example that those recovering from cancer would often not be able to return to work within a year. Concerns were expressed by the Joint Committee on Human Rights, and also by key Crossbenchers and Liberal Democrat backbenchers. The government was defeated on an amendment headed by Crossbench medic Lord (Narendra) Patel, which was overturned in the Commons. However, when the bill returned to the Lords a compromise was agreed with Labour frontbencher Lord (Bill) McKenzie of Luton, to retain the one-year limit but give ministers the discretion to extend it via secondary legislation. Proposing this from the Labour frontbench, Lord McKenzie commented that 'I am very grateful to the Minister for his acceptance of those amendments. He helped to draft them so he should accept them.'[26] Understandably given this agreement between the two main parties, this compromise was accepted by the Lords.

This was only a fairly small concession in response to the Labour opposition. In contrast, the coalition's Public Bodies Bill showed far greater opposition influence, again primarily wrought through the Lords (where the bill began). Labour pursued a two-pronged strategy, questioning individual decisions about bodies which the bill proposed to abolish or merge, and at the same time raising higher-level objections about the process being followed, including the adequacy of parliamentary scrutiny and government accountability for these decisions. With respect to the former, opposition frontbenchers and backbenchers (as well as other peers) proposed a coordinated set of individual amendments to exclude certain bodies—particularly from the highly controversial schedule 7 of the bill (which listed bodies that could potentially be abolished by future secondary legislation). At Lords committee stage more than 50 opposition amendments sought to delete individual bodies from schedule 7 alone; these could be seen as innocent 'probing' amendments to ensure adequate debate, but at the same time threatened to completely jam the process. Such pressure contributed significantly to the government's abandonment of schedule 7, as described in Chapter 9. The opposition also explicitly led the drive to insert a 'sunset clause' into the bill, so that it would cease to operate after five years. This was proposed in a Labour frontbench amendment (and also a related government backbench amendment) at Lords committee stage. The government initially rejected the proposal as disproportionate, but subsequently the minister added his name to an opposition-led amendment at report (presumably drafted by government), effectively to time-limit the bill to five years.[27] Speaking to the amendment, the minister, Lord (John) Taylor, said that 'I am delighted to have added my name to Amendment 72 ... [which] represents the outcome of genuine engagement and compromise on all sides of the House. I pay tribute to noble Lords who have assisted in presenting it to the House this evening.'[28] Although this language was consensual, the threat facing the government had it not conceded to the opposition's demands was clear.

We have presented just a few key examples of the 112 opposition-initiated changes to the bills. Overall, opposition parties were involved in some way in virtually every non-government initiative that successfully wrought legislative change—as further illustrated in later chapters. In one sense this is unsurprising, since it is usually impossible to garner a majority against the government without opposition support. Government backbenchers—as the next chapter explores—may be influential, but cannot actually defeat the government on their own. Opposition parliamentarians, likewise, cannot normally inflict defeat in either chamber without some kind of cross-party coalition. Not all concessions extracted from the government come through defeat, by any means, but the sense of threat created by a potentially winning coalition can greatly help to focus ministerial minds.

The opposition and anticipated reactions

Hence the opposition has a real ability to bring about policy change in today's Westminster—either consensually, or ultimately underwritten by the ability to inflict defeat in the Lords. The opportunity exists to force visible change through amendments, which is likely in turn to encourage government to second-guess the opposition's responses to some extent. That is, the opposition plays a clear part in parliament's power of anticipated reactions.

The previous chapter described the extent to which the government plans its legislation in order to avoid parliamentary confrontation, and prepares 'handling strategies' to ease its passage through both chambers. This is, to a significant extent, about managing relations with the opposition. Handling strategies first began with respect to the Lords rather than the Commons, at a time when the government could readily be defeated in that chamber by the two opposition parties combined. Although the Lords can ultimately be overridden by the Commons, confrontations hold various risks for government. At the very least, extended ping-pong takes up parliamentary time, and limits the ability to do other things (in particular, passing other legislation). Plus, if the opposition puts controversial matters onto the parliamentary agenda (using its power of 'issue politicization' and hostile amendments) these have always had potential to cause public embarrassment of reputational damage to ministers. Today, the greater threat of defeat in the Lords can ultimately result in difficult policy issues returning to the Commons for decision, drawing them to the attention of both the media and government backbenchers. This may be relatively unproblematic if ministers have solid backbench support, but can otherwise require ministerial climbdowns in a more risky public setting. For all of these reasons the government must think through the Lords' likely reactions carefully—and in doing so, consider the likely reactions of opposition parties.

These forces are most crucially at work in deciding which policies to place before parliament in the first place. But once bills have been introduced, the need to anticipate opposition responses, and to smooth over difficulties where possible, continues to exist. We have seen that part of parliamentary handling is policy negotiation, which involves meetings of various kinds between parliamentarians, ministers, and civil servants. Inclusion of government backbenchers in these kinds of meetings may appear natural and unsurprising, but opposition members are also often involved. Such consultation takes place in both chambers, but is naturally more prevalent in the Lords. Hence, under Labour, one Conservative frontbencher said that 'there was a concerted effort to engage with us in opposition, through formal meetings in the House of Lords, [and] one-to-one meetings in the department with officials present'. As a former frontbencher explained, 'a smart Lords minister will make an approach [to the opposition spokesperson] saying something like "I'm so pleased to hear that you are leading on this bill—can we have a chat?"'. Another Lords frontbencher explained that 'on the whole, government ministers will bend over backwards to help you and have meetings, because the last thing they want is a vote'. On occasion opposition members' opinions are sought in advance on the wording of government amendments. In the Commons these pressures are clearly not so great, but there is nonetheless some engagement with opposition frontbenchers, dependent to a significant extent on the personalities involved. For example as lead minister on the Energy Bill, Ed Miliband was described by an opposition frontbencher as 'very open to meetings with me and discussing possible amendments ... which actually left me rather well disposed towards him and more inclined to be a bit less combative in committee and on the floor of the House'. This comment illustrates how—at least on some bills—cordial relations between government and opposition can be advantageous to ministers.

The limits of opposition influence

Hence we see that the opposition has various important forms of influence. Traditional issue politicization, coupled with the government's lack of a majority in the Lords, can enable the opposition to win significant policy victories. In turn, this encourages ministers to think through and anticipate the opposition's responses in advance. But opposition parliamentarians of course do not always get their way. Even where they believe passionately that a government policy should be changed, this cannot be achieved unless at least some of those on the government side are prepared to support it. Any opposition party, in the end, holds only a minority of seats in the House of Commons.

The opposition therefore depends, to a large extent, on its leverage via the House of Lords—which, as the secondary chamber, brings clear limitations. As discussed in Chapter 2, the Lords is constrained by conventions of various kinds (for more detailed discussion, see Joint Committee on Conventions 2006). Its unelected nature raises concerns about legitimacy (Russell 2013), and it rarely challenges government legislation head-on. Hence votes to reject a bill at second and third reading are almost unheard of. Given the government's lack of a majority in the chamber, its legislative programme could be completely wrecked if the Lords didn't show restraint. But in practice this restraint goes far further. While opposition parliamentarians could cause major disruption by heavily amending bills, they are aware of the challenges to their legitimacy that would result, and largely respect House of Commons' primacy. They also realize that, while small changes might readily be negotiated, major policy reversals depend on the implicit or explicit support of

MPs—meaning, in practice, government backbenchers. If a bill is returned to the Commons with Lords amendments that do not command a majority among MPs, those amendments will simply be rejected. This is the primary limitation on the Lords, and hence on the opposition. Opposition frontbenchers in practice require both intercameral and interparty cooperation to achieve their goals.

The importance of the Lords to the opposition's policy influence is easily illustrated by some examples where the chamber's input into the case study bills was constrained. This occurs in particular on financial measures. Hence the certification of the Savings Accounts and Health in Pregnancy Grant Bill as a money bill greatly changed the dynamics on that piece of legislation. This was a bill greeted by the opposition in classic 'adversarial mode', and its more partisan amendments were largely ignored in the Commons. Paul Goggins's initiative on looked-after children did ultimately succeed, via a concession after the bill had passed, but other opposition attempts to limit or slow down the bill's effects entirely failed. However, some concessions might have been extracted had the bill not been subject to an expedited Lords passage. Its certification by the Commons Speaker clearly came as a surprise to the opposition. One Labour interviewee described going 'absolutely ballistic' when learning of the Speaker's ruling, because 'our campaign strategy around looked-after children was to return to the Lords'. Nonetheless we were told that government insiders had anticipated this outcome, and the bill had been drafted in the expectation that it would fall within the definition set out in the Parliament Act.[29]

Another key financial constraint on the Lords, which applies more frequently and forms part of the conventions, is the Commons' ability to claim financial privilege on individual Lords amendments—as briefly discussed in Chapter 2. This occurred most notably on the Welfare Reform Bill, where all of the Lords defeats were rejected with a claim of financial privilege—a development which proved controversial (Russell and Gover 2014), but further limited the opposition's chance of negotiating concessions.[30] This again emphasizes the centrality of the Lords to the opposition's ability to force change on the government.

Conclusions

In the classic view, the opposition at Westminster is relatively powerless, certainly over specific policy outcomes. It is not seen as policy-seeking, but as primarily using the platform of parliament to work towards its longer-term electoral goals. But this chapter suggests that the opposition's role is in fact more complex and multifaceted, and also that it is changing.

In responding to government bills, we have seen that opposition parties face many challenges. In contrast to government, the opposition is under-resourced, and—partly in consequence—can sometimes have difficulties coordinating its teams across the two parliamentary chambers. Fundamental conflicts between policy-seeking and vote-seeking also mean that opposition parties can sometimes find it difficult to devise policy responses to bills. While the classic culture of Westminster is said to be the 'opposition mode' (King 1976), there are in fact several different such modes discernible in reacting to government legislation. These include 'consensual mode', where there is genuine agreement about policy goals, 'acquiescent mode', where the opposition rather more reluctantly accepts government plans, 'conflicted mode', where there is a fine balance between the desire to support and oppose, and 'adversarial mode', where the opposition wholeheartedly rejects government proposals. Among our case study bills this last mode—which some people might expect to be the norm—was very much the exception.

One contributor to assumptions that the Westminster opposition is weak is the relative 'failure' of its amendments. Very, very few opposition amendments go on directly to be agreed—this applied to just 12 out of 2,941 (0.4 per cent) such amendments proposed to the case study bills (once those which were subsequently overturned have been excluded). But taking amendment figures at face value is problematic for two primary reasons. First, as explored in Chapter 3, the government always prefers to draft its own proposals in response to those from non-government parliamentarians rather than allowing the latter to reach the statute book. Second, most opposition amendments serve purposes other than seeking to change the bill at hand. Many are simply driven by the constitutional expectation that Her Majesty's Official Opposition will subject government proposals to rigorous scrutiny, and hold ministers publicly to account for their policies. A key mechanism for this is the tabling of 'probing' or 'information-seeking' amendments—which structure much of the debate during the Westminster legislative process, particularly during the committee stage—with no expectation that they will be agreed. Likewise, 'signalling' and 'gameplaying' opposition amendments conform to classic expectations that the opposition will use the legislative process to broadcast its own merits, and to embarrass the government where it can. In addition, some amendments are mere 'procedural devices' to facilitate discussion of more serious amendments.

But contrary to traditional expectations, we found plentiful evidence of opposition influence on legislative outcomes at Westminster. This operates partly through the amendment process, but becomes clearer once other forms of influence are taken into account. In total, we can identify at least four interrelated forms of opposition policy power in the process:

- The first is through the opposition's classic role of issue politicization, by putting controversial matters onto the public and parliamentary agenda—including determining which topics within a bill will receive greatest attention. As we have seen, this power can be exercised through amendments, debate contributions during the legislative process, and also the use of other parliamentary mechanisms such as questions and opposition day debates. Defeats in the House of Lords, which the opposition may force, also place matters prominently back onto the Commons agenda for decision. These interventions occur on the public record, and may attract media attention. Opposition politicians also clearly engage directly with the media, to influence the wider public agenda.

- Second, the opposition's numerous amendments serve not only to force change, but also to require that the government explains its policy decisions on the public record. 'Information seeking' or 'probing' amendments may generally fail to be agreed, as they were not intended for actual adoption into the legislation. But they provide clear incentives for government actors to prepare bills well and to be ready to defend their content.

- Third, where government explanations are unconvincing, or politicization of issues successfully influences the parliamentary and public mood, opposition amendments may result in legislative change. In total 112 distinct changes to the case study bills were initiated by opposition amendments, accounting for over 80 per cent of non-government initiated changes—an apparently similar pattern to that found by Griffith (1974). These covered both large and small matters, achieved in both relatively consensual and conflictual ways (though minor drafting changes from the opposition are now relatively rare). Change usually occurs through concessionary government amendments—offered by ministers in part to minimize such conflict. Notably, opposition parties' persuasive power was greatly enhanced by the 1999 reform of the House of Lords, which gave them 'pivotal' status in that chamber, and at the same time enhanced peers' confidence to use their powers. Though this ability was notably weakened during the period of coalition, it changed the incentives for the opposition, encouraging more policy-seeking behaviour.

- Finally, as a consequence of all of the above factors, the opposition plays a central role in parliament's power of anticipated reactions. It was the Lords' greater assertiveness post-1999 that provoked the adoption by government of increasingly elaborate 'handling strategies', as discussed in the previous chapter. This pre-planning by government may change the nature of bills introduced. Post-introduction, behind-the-scenes discussion between ministers and opposition parliamentarians (particularly frontbenchers) is extensive in the Lords, and also exists at a lower level in the Commons. This helps to facilitate agreement in response to at least some of the opposition's points.

Of course, there are clear limitations on opposition power. Opposition parties by definition lack a majority in the House of Commons, and while they can use the Lords to politicize issues, the unelected chamber exercises significant constraint and is limited on financial matters. Even where opposition parties promote change assertively through the Lords, this ultimately requires at least implicit support from other parliamentary actors to succeed. First and foremost, it depends on the key pivotal group in the Commons—government backbenchers. The next chapter focuses on this group.

Notes

1. The funds comprise a fixed amount for the Leader of the Opposition (i.e. the largest opposition party only), a general pot for each party based on seats and votes won, and a smaller travel allowance. The Leader of the Opposition and three opposition whips also receive a salary from public funds. All other opposition frontbenchers (unlike ministers) receive only their standard MP's salary or Lords allowance.
2. In 1998–9 the total Short money available to opposition parties was £1,696,131; by 2005–06 it was £5,350,509, and in 2014–15 it was £7,254,747. For a fuller discussion of Short and Cranborne money, see Kelly (2016).
3. Mark Hoban, House of Commons Hansard, 13 January 2009, columns 144–5.
4. Leader's speech to Labour Party conference 1995, available at http://www.britishpoliti-calspeech.org/speech-archive.htm?speech=201 [accessed 21 April 2016].
5. House of Commons Hansard, 28 June 2005, column 1181.
6. The Further Education and Training Bill was subject to a reasoned amendment from the Conservatives at its Commons second reading, to reject the bill for specified reasons, but they abstained on the second reading itself.
7. 'Public "Happy to Carry ID Cards"', *BBC News*, 22 April 2004, available at http://news.bbc.co.uk/1/hi/uk_politics/3648309.stm [accessed 28 August 2014].
8. For example on 18 February 2011 a *Daily Telegraph* editorial was headed 'Dependency Cannot Be a Lifestyle Choice' and suggested that '[t]he Coalition's Welfare Reform Bill, published yesterday, at long last confronts a wasteful and corrupt benefit system'. The editorial in *The Sun* on the same day proclaimed that '[t]he Sun has repeatedly called for welfare reform. Now it is happening. And it is likely to be the Coalition's greatest achievement', adding that '[t]here will be howls of rage from Lefties and their BBC mouthpieces. But this is good news for Britain. The Coalition is being brave and bold.'
9. House of Commons Hansard, 9 March 2011, column 934.
10. House of Commons Hansard, 26 October 2010, column 214.
11. On the Further Education and Training Bill the Conservative opposition seemed genuinely conflicted on whether it should adopt 'adversarial' mode or not. The bill began in the Lords, and at the end of its passage Conservative frontbencher Baroness Morris of Bolton commended peers for avoiding 'the trap of political point-scoring', and expressed 'considerable satisfaction at what we in this House have achieved' (House of Lords Hansard, 6 March 2007, columns 137–8). Yet, in the Commons, the Conservative leadership proposed a 'reasoned amendment' to defeat it at second reading. Liberal Democrat frontbencher Sarah Teather commented that she was 'baffled' by the Conservatives' 'sudden opposition to the Bill', which she interpreted as 'a grandstanding gesture' (House of Commons Hansard, 21 May 2007, column 1012).
12. Thompson (2015) explored whether the introduction of evidence-taking resulted in a reduction in probing amendments in Commons committee, which some had predicted would be an effect of the change. There was little to suggest any reduction.
13. Public Bill Committee (Saving Gateway Accounts Bill), 3 February 2009, column 76.
14. Ian Pearson, ibid., column 77.
15. Ibid.
16. For an example of a paving amendment, see the discussion of Lord Lester's amendment to the Public Bodies Bill in Chapter 5.
17. House of Commons Hansard, 2 February 2011, column 925.

18. House of Commons Hansard, 2 February 2011, column 860; 9 February 2011, column 298; 16 February 2011, column 952.
19. House of Commons Hansard, 27 October 2010, columns 310–11.
20. House of Commons Hansard, 22 March 2011, columns 834–5.
21. This question over interpreting failure is discussed more fully in Russell, Gover, and Wollter (2016).
22. This is a significant change since Griffith's (1974) study. As noted in earlier chapters, direct comparisons with his figures are difficult, but he found a small proportion (under 5 per cent) of opposition amendments to be agreed in the Commons. However, as already indicated, minor drafting amendments from the opposition also appear to have been far more common in this period, and to have accounted for the great majority of such amendments agreed.
23. These changed the words 'persons or descriptions of person specified in the regulations' to 'persons specified or persons of a description specified in the regulations'. As Howe argued, 'you cannot impose a duty on a description; you impose it on a person' (House of Lords Hansard, 9 May 2006, column GC381).
24. Six of these had a Labour co-sponsor, but in only two cases were they frontbenchers.
25. Chris Grayling, Public Bill Committee (Welfare Reform Bill), 3 May 2011, column 650.
26. House of Lords Hansard, 14 February 2012, column 739.
27. This amendment emptied the schedules listing bodies after five years, which would end the abolition threat. It was not actually agreed until the bill's third reading in the Lords, due to an unusual slip-up—whereby the opposition frontbench forgot to officially move it at report.
28. House of Lords Hansard, 28 March 2011, column 1074.
29. The Speaker certifies a bill in the form that it leaves the Commons, in order to allow for any Commons amendments which might change its status. But parliamentary counsel will consult at the drafting stage with the Commons Clerk of Legislation (who advises the Speaker) if hoping for such a certification.
30. Likewise, the Labour opposition failed to make any impact at all on the Identity Documents Bill—even through relatively small-scale amendments on issues such as allowing existing piloting of the cards to be evaluated, or securing refunds for the citizens who had already paid for cards (the latter of which also met claims of financial privilege).

5

The Role of Government Backbenchers

While the opposition parties may be the most visible non-government actors at Westminster, the most influential are often said to be government backbenchers. In the Commons the government must normally retain the support of this group in order to get its legislation agreed. But in recent years, scholars have noted that government backbenchers have become less willing to blindly follow the party line, and are more prone to question policy—including through casting 'rebellious' votes. These tendencies have been encouraged by changes highlighted earlier in the book, such as the growth in select committees and the broader parliamentary context created by a more assertive House of Lords. Hence while government backbenchers might always have had more persuasive power over ministers than the opposition, their power may also be growing.

In exploring who has influence on legislation at Westminster, we might therefore expect a large part of the answer to lie with government backbenchers. But such influence often operates in subtle ways. While opposition objections tend to be made openly and on the record, backbench influence frequently occurs behind the scenes. Consequently, it is difficult to measure, and some commentators suggest that it is more mythical than real.

This chapter explores the role of government backbenchers in the legislative process, using concrete examples from the case study bills. We examine backbench strategies, the nature of internal party relationships, and the extent to which backbench influence operates through visible channels on the public record (particularly amendments), versus less visible and more subtle means. The latter includes backbenchers' role in parliament's power of 'anticipated reactions', and in helping to determine the proposals that government puts forward. We examine how all of these dynamics differ between the two chambers, and highlight how backbenchers are key to resolving disputes between them. We also explore important differences in behaviour between the period of Labour single-party majority government and the Conservative/Liberal Democrat coalition.

This chapter has a similar structure to the previous two. We start by identifying who government backbenchers are, and how these groups were made up during our period of study. We then summarize what existing literature says about government backbenchers' role, both at Westminster and beyond. After this we review backbench organization, before turning to the attitudes of backbenchers to the case study bills. In the second half of the chapter we take a closer look at government backbench amendments proposed to the bills, including what motivated them and

Legislation at Westminster. First edition. Meg Russell and Daniel Gover. © Meg Russell and Daniel Gover 2017. Published 2017 by Oxford University Press.

their degree of policy success, and investigate less visible forms of backbench influence on the bills.

Government Backbenchers: Who Are They?

In both chambers of parliament the main political parties are divided into 'frontbench' and 'backbench'. Frontbenchers are those with collective policy responsibility on behalf of the party—that is, ministers and whips on the government benches and their shadows in opposition. In addition, Parliamentary Private Secretaries (PPSs) assist ministers and are likewise expected to follow the collective party policy line—that is, to vote reliably with the party or else to resign their position. Together these groups make up what is commonly (and rather inaccurately, given that PPSs receive no salary) referred to as the 'payroll vote'. This includes more than 120 members in the Commons on the government side, and a broadly equivalent number for the main opposition.[1] The payroll vote in the Lords is considerably smaller, as there are fewer ministers and no PPSs; in the 2010–12 session it amounted to roughly 30 members. Those parliamentarians not forming part of the payroll vote are classed as backbenchers.

In the 2005–10 parliament there were thus around 220 government backbenchers on the Labour side in the Commons. This was a large number for party managers to deal with (though considerably fewer than under the Blair governments of 1997 and 2001 when the party had over 400 MPs). Under coalition in the 2010 parliament the numbers in the Commons were similar but things became distinctly more complex, with government backbench MPs drawn from both sides of the coalition—Conservative and Liberal Democrat. There were hence two groups of backbenchers, potentially pulling in different directions, that government whips needed to keep onside. In the Lords, throughout the period 2005–12 the Labour and Conservative parties each had 180 or so backbenchers, while there were roughly 70 Liberal Democrat backbench peers.

Established Understanding of Government Backbenchers

As indicated in the previous chapter, the classic working arrangement at Westminster is what Anthony King termed the 'opposition mode'. King did not consider the opposition particularly influential—seeing it as generating more heat than light. Instead, he suggested that it was the 'intraparty mode'—that is, relations between ministers and their own backbenchers—that had greatest potential to influence policy. While indicating that ministers could largely ignore opposition concerns, he emphasized that 'ministers have needs of Government backbenchers. They need their moral support. They need them not to cause rows and to make hostile speeches that will attract publicity. They need, above all, their votes' (King 1976: 15). This dynamic was captured by the claim of former cabinet minister Tony Crosland in the 1970s that 'the British Cabinet's concern today is not for its majority over the

Opposition, because that is almost automatic, but for its majority inside its own Party' (quoted in Norton 1978: 31).

The rudimentary (but nonetheless profound) formal modelling of the House of Commons in King's analysis has been followed by more mathematically sophisticated equivalents in other settings. Notably Krehbiel (1998) has characterized legislatures in terms of 'pivotal voters' whose support is required in order to get policy agreed.[2] In parliamentary systems, where the government relies on maintaining the confidence of the lower house, these pivotal voters are in a potentially powerful position. Under majority government, such as usually applies at Westminster, the key pivotal voters in the House of Commons will be parliamentarians from the governing party (or parties). If enough of them side with the opposition in a division, the government will lose. While individual rebellions need not threaten the government's survival (as most divisions are not 'confidence votes'), rebellious voting potentially threatens government legislation. Plus, if cohesion became persistently poor, more serious dangers could arise. Thus even governments with comfortable majorities will seek to maintain backbench MPs' goodwill.

In the House of Lords a rather different dynamic applies. The confidence vote does not apply, while various groups—including non-party parliamentarians and Liberal Democrats—can potentially act as pivotal voters. As explored in Chapter 4, this gives significant leverage to the opposition. But the government will nonetheless always want to maximize support among its own backbench peers. Indeed analysis shows that ministers are more likely to give in to Lords defeats when such peers join with the opposition (Russell 2013). This is in large part because a Lords defeat pushes a question back onto the agenda of the Commons, where dissent in the party is a serious danger for ministers.

Rebellious votes are the most obvious means for government backbenchers in either chamber to express dissatisfaction. Here the standard expectation in most modern parliamentary systems (though presidential systems may operate differently) is a very high level of party cohesion (Olson 2003, Sieberer 2006). The UK is often seen as having prototypically cohesive parties, but British scholars have shown this assumption to be increasingly inaccurate. In the period 1945–70 Norton (1975: 609) found rebel votes to be 'more prevalent than has been generally realised'. Dissent then rose in the 1970–74 parliament, and has continued to grow. Contributing factors include more highly educated MPs, with better access to resources and research support, as well as the large majorities of the early Blair years, which made rebellion less risky. More recently Cowley and Stuart (2012) note that by the 2005–10 parliament rebellious votes were being cast in 28 per cent of Commons divisions—a post-war record—and reached 44 per cent of divisions in the 2010–12 session under the coalition. Of course there were then two parties whose members could potentially rebel—Conservative backbenchers cast dissenting votes in 28 per cent of divisions, and Liberal Democrats in 24 per cent. In the Lords, members more often absent themselves from votes rather than voting against the party line. Nonetheless rebel votes were cast in 29 per cent of divisions under Labour 1999–2010, and an impressive 56 per cent under the coalition 2010–12 (Russell 2013).

A good deal of recent scholarly attention has focused on patterns of rebellion. Rather less has examined the extent to which backbench dissent indicates, or leads to, policy influence. If governing MPs rebel, but not in sufficient numbers to cost the government its majority, their long-term effect could be nil. Indeed Dunleavy suggests that 'Westminster-model authors focusing on Parliament have always talked up the importance of majority-party dissidents in influencing the policy process. In fact it took eight years for the Blair government to suffer a *single actual defeat* in the Commons' (2006: 325, emphasis in original). Likewise Greenberg (2011) suggests that backbenchers are likely only to wield real influence in unwhipped 'free' votes. Yet scholars have long emphasized how backbench influence at the decision stage may be exercised primarily not through votes, but through behind-the-scenes contact, with government proposals altered if necessary to reduce visible public conflict (e.g. Brand 1992, Butt 1969, Lynskey 1970). Both party and parliamentary channels provide ample opportunities for such discussion between backbenchers and ministers. In all parliaments, including Britain, the parliamentary party group (PPG) is an important form of internal organization and of leadership accountability (Heidar and Koole 2000, Norton 2000). Hence specialist scholars have long noted that 'voting against one's party in the division lobby represents only the tip of an iceberg', and rebellions 'will normally constitute an admission of failure on the part of dissenting Members to have influenced policy … at an earlier stage' (Norton 1975: ix, 611). In terms of change in parliament, government 'retreats' can be far more important than defeats (Russell and Cowley 2016: 125–6).

Even more importantly, however, backbenchers potentially have what Dorey (2014: 141) refers to as 'latent power', in terms of ministers consulting them before bills are introduced. Ministers and backbenchers after all are normally drawn from the same political party, and stand on the same party manifesto, so will share similar policy preferences. Both are accountable to the same party bodies outside parliament. Plus of course ministers depend on backbenchers for their survival. Hence in terms of parliament's 'power of anticipated reactions' it is backbenchers' reactions that they will probably be most keen to anticipate. Indeed, backbenchers' desires are also likely to be internalized, and to shape government's own policy preferences—in line with what Lukes (1974) dubbed the third face of power (summarized in Chapter 1). Consequently, a focus only on visible influence at the decision-making stage will significantly underestimate backbench influence, because this also occurs—less visibly—at the agenda setting and policy formulation stages.

Given the history of single-party government at Westminster, and the figures on dissenting votes above, an interesting question is what happened to patterns of backbench influence under the coalition post-2010. With two parties in government the natural incentives to appear cohesive may have declined, and indeed new and opposing incentives have been created. Scholars noted the Liberal Democrats' 'serious problem … [of] signalling to the public their distinctive contribution in [the Conservative-led] government' (Yong 2012: 115), which may have resulted in more public disagreement but with unpredictable policy effect. Studies of coalition elsewhere suggest that parliament can provide an important forum to signal policy differences between the partners (e.g. Martin and Vanberg 2008, 2011), with the smaller partner(s) often focused on 'policing the bargain' reached on policy in coalition agreements. Hence a key question for this chapter is not only how and to what extent government backbenchers exercise influence in the legislative process, but how these dynamics changed under coalition—and how this affected parliament's influence overall.

Government Backbench Organization

Formal organizational arrangements vary slightly both between the parties and the two chambers. The parliamentary party has its own internal structure, and performs important linkage functions between frontbenchers and the world beyond Westminster—via MPs' relationships with their constituents, and outside groups, as well as party members and activists. Nonetheless, as with so much in parliament, while formal structures clearly matter, it is informal channels that are often more important.

Chapter 4 briefly touched on the basic parliamentary party organization in the three main parties. For Labour the key organ is the Parliamentary Labour Party (PLP), which includes all MPs, plus peers on a non-voting basis, and meets weekly. Labour peers also have a separate weekly meeting. The equivalent organizations for the Conservatives are the 1922 Committee in the Commons and the Association of Conservative Peers, both of which are in contrast backbench-only organizations. These all-group meetings are primarily reporting forums for frontbenchers, used mostly for announcements and general discussion, rather than making decisions. At least as important are the regular private meetings that take place between the officers of the parliamentary group and the party's frontbench leadership. While serious discontent may be aired in plenary meetings—where, in the words of one interviewee, 'sometimes ministers have had a bit of a rough ride'—concerns fed in privately via these smaller sessions are likely to be taken more seriously. In addition the Conservatives have a set of backbench committees which shadow government departments, and can serve as an important communication mechanism with individual ministers. Labour has similar groups, but these are considered relatively less important.

Liberal Democrat backbench arrangements changed significantly when the party entered coalition (Yong 2012). Traditionally, the smaller Lib Dems did not make a clear distinction between front and backbenchers, with all meeting together. But on joining the government there was pressure for greater backbench separation. This resulted in a new set of backbench policy committees organized bicamerally, with one 'co-chair' drawn from each of the Commons and the Lords. Although officially backbenchers, the co-chairs developed a novel position somewhere between the standard front and backbench roles. As most ministers were Conservatives, one co-chair explained that 'we found that we would be silent on vast swathes of government if we didn't have something akin to a shadow spokesman system'. Another such member described himself as 'the official spokesman for the Lib Dems outside government', in contrast to the minister, who was 'the official spokesman of the coalition'. The co-chairs hence provided a means for Lib Dem dissent to be expressed. They were routinely placed on relevant public bill committees in the Commons, and proposed backbench amendments on behalf of the party. Although Conservative backbenchers also wanted a distinct voice, there was general appreciation that their party was far more dominant in the coalition.

Beyond these kinds of formal party structures there are numerous other groupings that bring backbenchers together and provide forums for fermenting policy ideas. Within the parties these include interest groupings such as regional groups, groups of women parliamentarians, the trade union group of Labour MPs, and factions of a formal or less formal nature. Many of these connect to party organizations or pressure groups outside parliament. In addition the select committees, plus numerous All-Party Parliamentary Groups (APPGs) including both Lords and Commons members, bring backbenchers into contact with each other across party lines (as further described in Chapters 7 and 9).

With respect to formal parliamentary bodies dealing with legislation, the selection of backbench members to serve on public bill committees remains somewhat controversial (Russell, Morris, and Larkin 2013). While select committee membership was reformed in 2010 to require members to be elected inside their party groups, appointments to public bill committees continue to be controlled by party whips (see Chapter 2). This results in frequent accusations that committee membership is manipulated in order to avoid questioning of government policy by its backbenchers. As a senior backbencher put it:

The whips' duty and mission is to get the government's business. They are not interested in policy, they just want a piece of legislation through, the faster the better and with least demur. And so their job is shutting down debate, shutting down discussion, and keeping rebellions to a minimum.

This characterization may be slightly unfair; some whips are instinctively more pluralist, and all must listen to backbench concerns and feed those upwards to the leadership, as well as communicating downwards from the leadership to backbenchers. But serious disruption on a public bill committee could become problematic for ministers. Hence one MP (and former minister) commented that, while members with a policy interest may seek positions on public bill committees, sometimes it is possible to be 'too much of an expert'. Notoriously, Conservative backbencher and former GP Sarah Wollaston was denied a place on the public bill committee for the coalition's Health and Social Care Bill in 2010–12, having expressed a desire to propose amendments to improve the bill.[3] But input in public bill committee is not as meaningless as sometimes assumed—as earlier chapters have already begun to indicate (see also Thompson 2013, 2015)—and participation has opened up since the time when Brand (1992: 26) reported a 'generally accepted rule that government backbenchers will not speak'. Some Labour interviewees indicated that practice became more open during their party's time in government, from what one interviewee described as 'the kind of robot, don't question the leadership era' immediately after 1997, when 'in some committees they were leaned on not to speak, never mind put down an amendment'. Another said that 'over recent years, one of the features has been the emergence of backbenchers on bills who actually do know what they're talking about'. A clear example among our case studies was the Energy Bill, where Labour backbench members included Alan Whitehead and Alan Simpson, both independent-minded MPs with a strong track record on the topic. However, this was a relatively technical and low-profile bill. Membership of more controversial or publicly salient bills is still generally more controlled.[4]

Throughout the passage of most bills, ministers will maintain regular contact with their backbenchers. Major bills are discussed at all-group meetings, plus meetings of policy committees, and ministers will stay in touch with backbench members on the public bill committee and may meet with them privately. Amendments put down by backbench members will often have been discussed through such party channels before being formally debated. Whips, special advisers, and PPSs all provide alternative and well-used routes of communication. The extent of these contacts is further indicated later in the chapter.

Finally, as well as these party channels, and informal means of organization, there are various other formal parliamentary mechanisms that government backbenchers can use to try to influence the legislative process. These are available to all parliamentarians, but may be particularly key to this group (and, in turn, involvement of this group is often particularly key to their success). Mechanisms include House of Commons early day motions (EDMs) and private members' bills of various kinds. These are often dismissed as unimportant, but can help backbenchers to apply pressure on frontbenchers. EDMs are not debated or voted upon, but allow MPs to gather signatures for a proposition (usually from backbenchers only) and are both printed and published online. They are sometimes dismissed as 'parliamentary graffiti', but can have an indirect policy effect. As one member explained, 'if you can get one that's got 100, 200 signatures, then they really make the government sit up and think, and particularly if you can get a lot of government members to sign something that is against government policy'. Private members' bills exist in both chambers, and in the Commons include both ballot bills—which are discussed on Fridays—and 10-minute rule bills, whose debate is scheduled during 'prime time', including immediately after Prime Minister's questions. While most such bills are never passed (indeed 10-minute rule bills are often not even printed), they can act as effective vehicles for keeping up pressure on government.

Government Backbench Responses to the Case Study Bills

The starting assumption is that government backbenchers will support government legislation. Ministers and backbenchers in their party share broad policy preferences; they wish to maintain the party's reputation (including for unity), and its electoral support. Hence the default setting—at least traditionally, in a context of single-party government—is for backbenchers to back, and indeed broadly to welcome, government bills. Nonetheless, as indicated above, it has become increasingly common in recent years for at least some backbenchers to openly express dissent. Post-2010 the coming together of two parties in coalition—which had stood on two distinct manifestos—created additional strains.

The general pattern was for most backbenchers to be supportive of the central principles of most of the case study bills. For example, Labour's Corporate Manslaughter and Corporate Homicide Bill met a long-standing commitment by the party, and indeed—as discussed further below—had long been pressed on ministers by backbenchers. Its Employment Bill included welcome provisions to tighten up regulation of the minimum wage, and its Health Bill implemented the smoking ban promised in the 2005 manifesto, alongside various other less controversial measures. The Saving Gateway Accounts Bill extended saving opportunities to those on lower incomes, and the Energy Bill contained relatively uncontroversial 'green' measures. Under coalition, several of the 2010–12 bills implemented key general election promises, including the scrapping of ID cards and creation of a statutory Office for Budget Responsibility.

One of the first opportunities to publicly gauge backbenchers' response to a bill is the second reading debate, at which point bills might be expected to receive general plaudits. But frequently second reading also enables those backbenchers with concerns to signal their discomfort. On some of the case study bills this discontent was voiced loudly and strongly, on central aspects of the legislation, indicating trouble ahead. The prime example under Labour was the Identity Cards Bill, which was the only case study bill to face a Commons backbench rebellion (of 20 MPs) on its second reading, which was followed by 17 subsequent such rebellions (see Cowley and Stuart 2006). Identity cards were a divisive issue in the party, and some backbenchers opposed them on principle. Even prior to second reading one backbencher had proposed an EDM stating that 'a convincing case … has not been made' for the cards and that 'the risks involved far outweigh any discernible benefit'.[5] During the debate Labour backbencher Lynne Jones described the bill as 'not only dumb, but very dangerous', suggesting that '[t]his Bill should be killed at birth'.[6] David Winnick, a Labour member of the Home Affairs Select Committee (which had carried out an investigation into the draft bill) commented that 'I always knew that I could not vote in favour of the Bill. Given the strong views that I have long held on this issue since the idea of ID cards was first introduced, that would be a form of political prostitution on my part.'[7] Backbenchers' concerns were numerous, including the civil liberty implications of the national identity register, and the costs of the scheme. But central among them was the degree of compulsion associated with having an identity card. Labour's 2005 manifesto had explicitly stated that '[w]e will introduce ID cards including biometric data like fingerprints, backed up by a national register and rolling out *initially on a voluntary basis* as people renew their passports' (Labour Party 2005: 52–3, emphasis added). In fact, the published bill made entry onto the national identity register automatic on application for a passport. This meant, as a government insider conceded in interview, that the scheme was 'completely voluntary unless you happen to go abroad!'. This conflict between the party's election promise and the bill's wording came up repeatedly during parliamentary debates. In the House of Lords, which by convention does not reject policy appearing in government manifestos, resistance by opposition peers was fuelled by claims that they were actually seeking to hold the government to its manifesto.

Even on bills that were broadly welcomed, Labour backbenchers raised some significant concerns about the detail of provisions included—or sometimes excluded. The Corporate Manslaughter and Corporate Homicide Bill was a key example. Here, Andrew Dismore—who had previously campaigned for its introduction and was chair of parliament's Joint Committee on Human Rights—used the bill's second reading to highlight what he saw as several significant weaknesses. He noted that unincorporated bodies were excluded, and while welcoming the fact that there would not be blanket Crown immunity, he suggested that exclusions applied 'in precisely those contexts in which the positive obligation ... is at its strongest, and in which a criminal prosecution should be brought: [including] the use of lethal force by the police or army [and] deaths in custody'.[8] Likewise on the Employment Bill, Labour left-winger John McDonnell MP (who went on to become Shadow Chancellor after Jeremy Corbyn's surprise election as Labour leader in 2015) used his second reading speech to highlight 'those areas in which some of us will seek to amend the Bill in Committee and on Report'.[9] These included the right to strike and requirements for strike balloting arrangements—on which action did indeed follow, as further discussed below.

Under coalition, with two distinct sets of backbenchers to appeal to, the dynamic changed. As seen in previous chapters, there were particular tensions between the two parties over the Welfare Reform Bill. While the Conservatives had fought the election on a strong commitment to cut the benefit bill, many Liberal Democrats were distinctly uneasy. As one backbencher active on the bill explained in interview, this was an area where some parliamentarians agonized, given that 'we are talking about people's lives being very, very affected'. Such misgivings became very clear at Commons second reading. Liberal Democrat co-chair for work and pensions Jenny Willott welcomed certain aspects of the bill, 'especially the introduction of the universal credit system' (which also had in principle Labour support), but expressed concerns about a number of other elements.[10] These included proposals to time-limit contributory Employment and Support Allowance (ESA—as was discussed in Chapter 4), and to require individuals to have been limited by their disability for six months before being eligible for the new Personal Independence Payment (PIP), as well as the potential implications of the new household benefit cap. Willott's Liberal Democrat colleague John Leech also raised concerns about the 'under-occupancy penalty' (aka 'bedroom tax'), which were echoed by the other Liberal Democrat co-chair, Lord (Mike) German, during the bill's second reading in the House of Lords.

Objections from the smaller coalition party signalled difficulties ahead for the government, but these were mild compared to the strongly expressed criticism of the Public Bodies Bill on its second reading in the Lords—including from backbenchers on both sides of the coalition. Conservative Lord (Philip) Norton of Louth, a member (and former chair) of the Constitution Committee, declared that he had 'no problem with the declared ends of this Bill, but I have a fundamental objection to the means'.[11] Likewise senior Liberal Democrat lawyer and member of the Joint Committee on Human Rights Lord (Anthony) Lester of Herne Hill emphasized that:

Legitimate ends do not justify unconstitutional or disproportionate means, especially where they erode Ministers' accountability to Parliament and put at risk aspects of the rule of law and fundamental rights and freedoms, whereas the Bill as it stands ... contains inadequate safeguards against the misuse of Ministers' delegated powers.[12]

While approving of the bill's broad principle to streamline quangos, government backbenchers were thus very concerned by the proposed mode in which this was to be done. As Liberal Democrat Lord (Tony) Greaves put it, 'I support the Bill's aims in many cases. I am not a fan of quangos ... But the way in which this Bill proposes to deal with quangos is undemocratic and entirely unacceptable'.[13] Backbenchers also expressed concern about the treatment of many different individual bodies— Greaves, for example, raised serious objections about national parks and forestry. At the end of the second reading debate he and one other Liberal Democrat (alongside 29 Crossbenchers and three others) voted for a proposal by the opposition to refer the bill to a special select committee for consideration before it could proceed to its next stage. Opposition frontbenchers probably hoped for more government rebels, but in their absence this bid failed, and the bill proceeded to its committee stage in the usual way.

Government Backbench Amendments and their Motivations

As shown in Table 5.1, government backbenchers proposed over 500 amendments to the case study bills. This is a substantial number, though well short of the nearly 3,000 from opposition members. We see that joint sponsorship between government backbenchers and other groups is in general relatively common, and across the period accounts for almost half of such amendments proposed. Amendments were targeted at all but one of the bills, and the numbers varied substantially between them. Under Labour, the largest numbers were proposed to the Corporate Manslaughter and Corporate Homicide Bill and the Employment Bill—both of which covered classic trade union issues. Actually relatively few were proposed to the controversial Identity Cards Bill. Under coalition the overall number of government backbench amendments increased, with the Public Bodies Bill and Welfare Reform Bill both attracting particularly large numbers.

Comparing the periods pre- and post-2010, we see some other very clear differences. During the period 2005–10, Labour backbenchers in the Commons tabled almost double the number of amendments as in the Lords. During the period 2010–12, in contrast, almost nine out of 10 government backbench amendments were tabled by peers, and the proportion of these co-sponsored with other groups increased substantially—to more than half. Table 5.2 breaks this amendment data down further by party group, showing that a disproportionate number of government backbench proposals under the coalition came from

Table 5.1 Government backbench amendments proposed by bill and chamber

	Commons			Lords			Total		
	Single party	With others	Total	Single party	With others	Total	Single party	With others	Total
2005–10 parliament*									
Identity Cards	22	0	22	3	0	3	25	0	25
Health	4	17	21	2	18	20	6	35	41
Corporate Manslaughter	39	14	53	15	5	20	54	19	73
Further Education and Training	23	1	24	3	2	5	26	3	29
Employment	9	7	16	29	1	30	38	8	46
Saving Gateway Accounts	4	0	4	2	0	2	6	0	6
Energy	5	8	13	0	0	0	5	8	13
Total (2005–10)	106	47	153	54	26	80	160	73	233
2010–12 session									
Identity Documents	0	0	0	4	8	12	4	8	12
Savings Accounts	0	0	0	0	0	0	0	0	0
Budget Responsibility	0	0	0	9	2	11	9	2	11
Public Bodies	7	12	19	69	60	129	76	72	148
Welfare Reform	16	0	16	59	76	135	75	76	151
Total (2010–12)	23	12	35	141	146	287	164	158	322
Grand total	129	59	188	195	172	367	324	231	555

* During the 2005–10 parliament we classify MPs representing Labour's sister party in Northern Ireland, the SDLP, as government backbenchers, as it would be less accurate to consider them opposition members. They sponsored only seven amendments to the 2005–10 case study bills, all jointly with Labour MPs.

Note: All figures exclude amendments co-sponsored by the government.

Table 5.2 Government backbench amendments proposed and success of government backbench-initiated strands

	Amendments proposed by actor	Strands initiated by actor			% of total successful strands in parliament
		Strands initiated	Of which successful	% success of initiated	
2005–10 parliament					
Labour backbench alone	160	80	7	9	4
Labour backbench with others	73	29	6	21	4
Total involving government backbench	233	109	13	12	8
Total for all actors	2,389	1,161	169	15	100
2010–12 session					
Conservative backbench alone	46	22	4	18	3
Liberal Democrat backbench alone	118	84	7	8	5
Conservative & Lib Dem backbench only	0	0	0	n/a	0
Conservative & Lib Dem backbench with others	5	3	2	67	2
Conservative backbench with others	17	10	1	10	1
Lib Dem backbench with others	136	76	9	12	7
Total involving government backbench	322	195	23	12	18
Total for all actors	1,972	889	131	15	100
Both parliaments					
Government backbench alone	324	186	18	10	6
Government backbench with others	231	118	18	15	6
Total involving government backbench	555	304	36	12	12
Total for all actors	4,361	2,050	300	15	100

Note: The figures for government backbench amendments exclude any co-sponsored with the government; all amendments with a ministerial sponsor are included within the 'total for all actors'. Within this table 'others' means parliamentary actors other than government backbenchers. Of the 555 government backbench amendments, 25 (5%) were agreed to, of which eight (1% of the total) were neither subsequently overturned nor purely overturned an earlier amendment (as described in Chapter 3).

Liberal Democrat backbenchers. They sponsored 259 amendments (118 as a single party, and 141 with other groups such as Labour), compared to Conservative backbenchers' 68 (made up respectively of 46 plus 22). This is counterintuitive, given the relative size of the two parties. Once this is taken into account, Liberal Democrats were 14 times more likely to propose amendments than were Conservatives. Another striking feature seen in Table 5.2 is that not a single amendment under coalition was tabled by only Liberal Democrat and Conservative backbenchers acting jointly.

The most obvious reading of these 555 amendments is that there were fairly concerted efforts by government backbenchers to change some bills, under both governments—but particularly by Liberal Democrats under coalition. However, we saw in the previous chapter that legislative amendments are not always sincere attempts at policy change. A good starting point is therefore to ask what moves government backbenchers to propose amendments.

With respect to the opposition, we identified five relatively distinct motivations for proposing legislative amendments: information seeking (probing), signalling, gameplaying, procedural devices, and pursuing immediate policy changes. Unsurprisingly, not all of these apply in equal measure to government backbenchers—which helps to explain the major discrepancy in numbers of amendments proposed by these two groups. In particular political gameplaying (which seeks to embarrass or shame the government) is unlikely to be pursued among members on its own side. Signalling alternative policy positions might also seem unlikely, but as we shall see does exist—and particularly applied under coalition. The other three previously identified motivations can also all be seen to some extent.

Backbench information seeking

Government backbenchers do use probing amendments, whose purpose is to tease out questions and structure debate rather than to actually be added to the bill. But the primary responsibility for getting the government to explain itself on the record is taken by the opposition. Opposition frontbenchers are better resourced than government backbenchers, and also generally willing to ask sharper and more critical questions. They also lack the privileged behind-the-scenes access to ministers that government backbenchers enjoy through party channels. Nonetheless, backbenchers may sometimes want reassurance on the record that the government's policy has been adequately thought through, and in particular that it is consistent with party policy or ideology—under either single-party or coalition government this can be seen as a means of 'policing the bargain'. The great majority of government backbench amendments are proposed at the committee stage, and many of these are probing amendments. Backbenchers spoke to us about this mechanism in very similar terms to opposition frontbenchers (see examples in Chapter 4), and it is relatively easy to find such examples on the bills.[14]

Backbench signalling

Signalling amendments, in the context of the opposition, are those which communicate the party's policy agenda to those outside parliament—including the media, interest groups, and the wider public. It might be assumed that such activity is unnecessary on the government's own side, which is relatively united. But while the motivations may be slightly different, there was clear evidence on the case study bills of some government backbench amendments intended to have a signalling effect.

When Labour was in power, there were few incentives for backbenchers to signal publicly their difference from the leadership. But all of the major parties are to some extent 'broad churches', drawing together members with slightly differing politics and ideologies, so internal factions will sometimes want to get their voices heard. The clearest example of this occurred on the Employment Bill, on the intervention that John McDonnell had promised at the bill's second reading (see 'responses' section above). No progress on the matters he raised was made during the committee stage (McDonnell not being a member of the committee), but they were returned to at report.[15] McDonnell proposed five new clauses on different aspects of workers' rights.[16] His key concern was employer support for strike balloting, which he had previously pursued unsuccessfully in the 2006–07 session via a private member's bill (the Trade Union Rights and Freedoms Bill), and an EDM supported by 133 (mostly Labour) MPs.[17] In debate McDonnell claimed that his new clauses were supported by a wide range of trade unions, and by the Trades Union Congress (TUC). Although these matters were quite far from the other topics in the bill, he and his allies clearly saw an opportunity to 'piggyback' upon it. The government had anticipated such attempts; an official told us that 'we worked very hard on the [bill's] long title, so as to try and keep out of scope the whole raft of potential nightmares that could have been inserted around employment law'; but while other amendments might have been ruled out of order, McDonnell's managed to get through.

These amendments were jointly sponsored by a group of over 35 Labour MPs, mostly from the left or with strong links to the trade unions. McDonnell made clear at the outset that he was only actually seeking a decision on one of them, saying:

> I hope that the Government will think seriously about balloting procedures, so I will want to test the will of the House on new clause 2. On new clauses 1 and 3, I would welcome a statement from the Minister that there are issues to be addressed and that the Government will look into how to address them.[18]

In this respect, some of his proposals could be seen as a kind of probing—to gain the minister's on-the-record response. But their tabling for discussion on the floor of the House also sent a clear signal to the trade unions, and to others on the Labour left. Their sponsors' expectation of success must have been minimal, as both the government and the Conservative opposition were hostile to the proposals—so the government won the division on strike balloting arrangements by 408 votes to 53. But McDonnell's amendment was supported by 45 Labour MPs, making this the largest

Labour rebellion of Gordon Brown's premiership (Cowley and Stuart 2014)—and could have caused a defeat had sufficient opposition MPs voted for it. A government insider expressed frustration that the bill's report stage had in practice been hijacked by discussion of McDonnell's amendments, suggesting that the focus on matters which 'were really well beyond the intention of the bill' was 'taking attention away from good measures to toughen up enforcement of the minimum wage, to deal with the situation around tips and the minimum wage'. Debate on the bill (which had started in the Lords) thus culminated by focusing on the government's alleged failings, rather than its achievements.

This case has similarities to the signalling conducted by opposition parties. In both cases the proposers of such amendments probably support them sincerely; in a sense they take on a 'signalling' character only once it is clear that they have no real chance of success. It becomes clearer that this is a fine distinction when looking at amendments from the government's own side. Nonetheless, under coalition, public signalling by government backbenchers—particularly Liberal Democrats—became far more prevalent, helping to explain the sharp increase in government backbench proposals post-2010. Amendments offered Liberal Democrat members an opportunity to distance themselves from their Conservative partners, and to try to demonstrate to the world outside parliament that the party had a distinctive voice. Indeed, one of the key rationales behind the Liberal Democrats' establishment of backbench co-chairs was to ensure that such a voice was heard.

This was very clear during the passage of the Welfare Reform Bill, which attracted the highest number of government backbench amendments overall. For example, the relevant co-chair in the Commons, Jenny Willott, tabled numerous amendments, including to soften the effects of time limits on ESA, and to extend eligibility to the new Personal Independence Payment. Points raised often concerned policy areas that Liberal Democrat supporters were known to find uncomfortable; indeed, in these two cases Labour frontbenchers could refer in debate to motions passed by the Liberal Democrat party conference that criticized the government's positions.[19] So while some of these amendments may have been partly 'information seeking' (and some even helped encourage changes to the legislation), they also served to publicly record distance between the party and the government's position. Some Labour interviewees were quite critical of this kind of behaviour by the junior coalition partner, and saw such signalling as hollow—since these amendments were almost universally withdrawn, rather than pressed to a vote. As one put it, 'what they wanted was to be seen to be making a fuss, but they weren't prepared to push it to its logical conclusion' by voting to defeat the government.

Non-legislative policy change

Although government backbenchers may table amendments for other purposes, the proportion of their proposals which are sincere attempts at policy change is clearly higher than that for the opposition. Government backbenchers generally approach bills relatively constructively, and wish to see them improved—rather than, as the opposition may sometimes hope, undermined. But sometimes the concessions sought by backbenchers are sufficiently small that they do not require legislative change, and there is therefore again no real intention that the amendments should pass. We have already discussed in Chapter 3 how parliamentarians with genuine policy concerns can be satisfied by non-legislative concessions. A simple statement of the government's intent, and particularly one that may influence future judicial interpretation, can be valuable. Likewise, a promise about phrasing of guidance to officials, or future regulations to implement the detail in the bill, may satisfy members. On occasion, guidance or regulations are even circulated during the bill's passage to give reassurance, and some redrafting may be negotiated. For example, on the Budget Responsibility and National Audit Bill, the Charter for Budget Responsibility which set out the remit of the new Office for Budget Responsibility (OBR) was published in draft alongside the government's bill. At the bill's committee stage in the Lords the minister, Lord (James) Sassoon, promised to 'listen carefully' to points raised—including by Liberal Democrat backbencher Lord (Matthew) Oakeshott of Seagrove Bay—and potentially to 'improve the drafting'.[20] These kinds of changes are very much at the level of detail, affecting policy implementation rather than bigger principles. They are more likely to satisfy backbenchers—whose policy demands will often be more modest—than the opposition.

Markers for the future

Debates on a bill can be seen as part of an ongoing dialogue between frontbenchers and backbenchers within a party, meaning that some government backbench amendments are focused on the longer-term future. Backbenchers are often keen to nudge the government in new policy directions, and can use the legislative process to do so—without any serious expectation of immediate gains. Proposing an amendment brings a policy question to the minister's attention, and importantly also requires their officials to engage with it. Officials will need to prepare briefing for the minister, and either or both may meet with the backbencher concerned. If the proposal is debated, the minister must also make a statement on the public record, even if the amendment is ultimately withdrawn. Having engaged the minister's attention, discussions may then continue after the bill has passed—through both government and party channels. Hence one backbencher who had tabled amendments told us that 'I wasn't planning to try and seriously get any amendments to the bill', but rather making proposals for 'things I wanted ministers to think about'. One example might be a series of amendments from backbencher Roberta Blackman-Woods on the Further Education and Training Bill, concerning support for those entering post-16 education or training. After the amendments had been debated in committee, Blackman-Woods withdrew them, urging the minister 'to ensure that these issues are high up the agenda' when making future policy.[21]

Hence while government backbench amendments may be more often sincere than those from the opposition, they are not always focused on achieving immediate policy change. But of course backbenchers do often engage with ministers and others in serious discussions about such change. The extent to which this pressure succeeds is discussed in the next section, alongside backbenchers' wider influence on the process.

Evidence of Government Backbench Influence on the Case Study Bills

As in the opposition chapter, we begin our discussion of government backbench influence by considering forms of influence most classically associated with this group: that is, backbenchers' role in policy development and parliamentary anticipated reactions. We then go on to discuss backbench amendments and support for amendments, before examining backbenchers' pivotal role in other conflicts, and the importance of their support for the government.

Agenda setting, policy formulation, and anticipated reactions

Through various party channels, and private meetings, ministers clearly have plentiful opportunities to engage with backbenchers. Such discussion takes place during the formal legislative process, but is almost certainly more important before it actually begins—and may strongly influence policy outcomes. Since policy is developed in consultation with parliamentarians and the wider party, and ministers themselves are drawn from among party parliamentarians, it is somewhat artificial to attempt to separate the preferences of front and backbenchers on the government side. Yet if these relationships lead to relative harmony between the government and its backbenchers, the visible result is no different to what it would be if backbenchers were purely acquiescent to ministers—that is, public agreement between the two. This encourages sceptical comments about backbench influence, such as that from Dunleavy (2006) above.

It may be impossible by definition to find evidence of Lukes's (1974) elusive third face of power at work between government and its backbenchers, because it operates at a subconscious level which even those involved in the process may not recognize or articulate. But there were some very clear examples of the power of anticipated reactions with respect to government backbenchers on the case study bills. This is traceable in terms of changes prior to introduction, which is what we discuss here, as well as afterwards (as further discussed below). It is seen both through legislative provisions held back, and those brought forward due to pressure from the party. It was visible both during the period of Labour government and under the coalition.

Under Labour the clearest example was the Corporate Manslaughter and Corporate Homicide Bill, where backbenchers worked hard to keep the topic on the parliamentary and wider political agenda, maintaining pressure that ministers found hard to resist. As indicated in Chapters 2 and 3, this measure had been advocated for many years prior to its introduction by the trade unions and others. Yet following the announcement of in principle support by Home Secretary Jack

Straw in 1997, and a subsequent manifesto pledge that '[l]aw reform is necessary to make provisions against corporate manslaughter', little progress was made (Labour Party 2001: 33). Three years later, with no sign of a bill, the so-called 'Warwick agreement' emerged from a meeting of Labour's National Policy Forum. This was widely seen as an accommodation between the party leadership and trade unions, and stated that 'we are fully committed to reforming the law on corporate manslaughter and will publish full proposals in a draft bill before the end of the current Parliamentary session' (Labour Party 2004: 42). This bill, it was promised, would 'include provisions that extend to include the Crown' (i.e. bodies under the direct control of government departments). Even then it was another year before a draft bill was produced, and two years before it was formally introduced to parliament.

We have seen that there are various parliamentary mechanisms that government backbenchers can use to force issues onto the policy agenda and maintain pressure on ministers. As mentioned in Chapter 3, Conservative backbenchers used private members' bills to press for introduction of ID cards prior to 1997.[22] Labour backbenchers did the same with respect to the smoking ban—including years before the party entered power.[23] Parliamentary mechanisms such as these are classically dismissed as weak, and even pointless, but do require civil servants to focus on an issue and prepare briefing, which ministers must read in order to respond on the public record. They also potentially change the mood among parliamentarians and the wider public. This can all lead to policy reflection and sometimes action.

Similar pressure was very evident with respect to corporate manslaughter, in order to keep the issue on the government's agenda, and hence to 'police the bargain' between ministers and the wider party. As early as 2000 Andrew Dismore—who had worked as a lawyer on cases such as the Zeebrugge disaster and King's Cross fire, and had close connections to the TUC—proposed a 10-minute rule bill urging the government to act on Jack Straw's promise.[24] Like most such bills this made no formal progress, but highlighted the issue in prime parliamentary time. After the 2001 general election the proposal was raised repeatedly by backbenchers in PLP meetings, including when the Leader of the House consulted on priorities for the government's legislative programme. Various EDMs were also initiated by Labour backbenchers calling on the government to legislate, including one by Dismore which attracted 120 Labour signatures.[25] In May 2003 Dismore tried a new approach, proposing an amendment to the government's Criminal Justice Bill, with supporting signatures from 67 other Labour backbenchers.[26] This was not selected for debate, but Home Secretary David Blunkett nonetheless responded by promising a draft bill.[27]

This degree of delay in implementing a party policy was unusual. Our interviews made clear that ministers were facing significant pressure from the private sector, but there was also significant resistance to the policy from inside government itself. A former minister told us that officials thought it 'went too far', and were 'nervous' about the implications of the bill for public bodies. As a senior official put it, 'it was the Crown application that was agitating all round Whitehall', and 'there were lots of departments who said "how is it going to affect us?"—they didn't like it'. Indeed, one person close to the policy inside government suggested that there was 'a massive internal Whitehall operation to kind of kill it'. Concerned departments naturally included the Department of Trade and Industry, but also the Department of Health, Ministry of Defence, and the Home Office, due to deaths in prison and police custody.

Consequently, some ministers were resistant, and we were told that this resistance extended to Prime Minister Tony Blair himself. A source close to him recalled that 'TB didn't want corporate manslaughter legislation, for a variety of reasons'. But, the interviewee explained, the government 'came under quite a lot of pressure' on the issue from its own side. Despite the executive's supposed strength in the Westminster system, it is not always possible to resist such pressure; because the government relies on backbenchers for its majority, it must also listen to them. Summarizing the relationship, this same interviewee concluded that 'you have to reach a sort of modus vivendi with them and that has to have some policy agreement on some issues that they think are important'. But once the bill was introduced to parliament, in a weaker form than some proponents had wanted, the government could not wholly control the process. As one senior interviewee said, 'it took on a life of its own ... because the government was hesitant about it in the first place and hadn't really thought through where they wanted to end up'. When the government came under further pressure from Labour members to strengthen certain provisions, concessions had to be made. Most obviously, backbenchers played a key role in the battle over extending the offence to deaths in custody.

Backbenchers' power of anticipated reactions can also play a crucial role in policies *not* being introduced, or being revised post-introduction—in these cases the fear of backbench hostility is greater, as the ultimate price could be defeat.[28] Under the coalition, the dividing lines within the government were clearer than under a typical single-party majority government, and ministers from one party were not automatically attuned to views held by backbenchers of the other, which made these pressures unusually visible. The coalition agreement had laid down the key policy compromises, but in terms of implementation, and of policy not mentioned in the agreements, the two coalition partners often pulled in different directions. Consequently some policies were withdrawn in anticipation of parliament's response.[29] An example frequently mentioned by interviewees in connection with the Welfare Reform Bill was the proposed cut in Housing Benefit for those who had been claiming Jobseeker's Allowance for over a year. This proposal—which did not appear in a coalition agreement—was announced by Chancellor George Osborne in the June 2010 Budget, and was set to save £110 million per year (HM Treasury 2010: 40). One Liberal Democrat backbencher described it as a 'completely crazy' policy, and explained that the party 'work[ed] very hard behind the scenes making sure that it didn't get into the final legislation'. The initial announcement had been facilitated by the fact that new policies in the budget are subject to far less prior consultation than others; but subsequently there was significant lobbying for change. This occurred privately, but also on the record in parliament. For example, Liberal Democrat co-chair Jenny Willott co-sponsored an EDM which called for the policy to be reversed, which was supported by 77 MPs, including 10 other Liberal Democrats.[30] Labour encouraged pressure by staging an opposition day debate on the policy, during which Willott made a speech claiming that it '[made] no sense'.[31]

Consequently, despite initial expectations, the Welfare Reform Bill omitted this measure. At the bill's Commons second reading Willott warmly welcomed the change, commenting:

> I am glad that a couple of earlier proposals have already been reconsidered . . . I am delighted that the Government listened to Liberal Democrats, the Select Committee and others throughout the United Kingdom who called for the proposal for a 10% cut in housing benefit for those who have received jobseeker's allowance for a year to be dropped, because it was unfair. It is very good news that the proposal has indeed been dropped.[32]

Aside from this intervention, and a few others like it, one senior Liberal Democrat noted in interview that 'there was no legislative trace' of this as a concession.[33] The fact that such changes occurred behind the scenes, and had little visibility with voters, was a source of considerable frustration to Liberal Democrats—who had traditionally attracted considerable centre-left support, and went on to pay a heavy electoral price in May 2015 for their time in coalition with the Conservatives.

　Thinking through backbench concerns clearly begins early in the policy process, but continues to form a crucial component of government 'handling' once bills are introduced. Ministers remain attentive to backbench concerns, and may negotiate changes in order to head off rebellions. As a former cabinet minister explained in interview, 'generically your own backbenchers are the ones you worry about the most because . . . even if it's a small rebellion you're still losing goodwill on your own side, you're depleting your majority'. Another former minister commented that 'you'd be barmy' if you didn't listen to government backbenchers, whereas with respect to concerns raised by the opposition you can if necessary 'just plough on'.

Government backbench amendments and policy change

The most obvious and visible means for backbenchers to influence legislation post-introduction is through amendments. But we know that the commonest means for such initiatives to succeed is for ministers to propose concessionary amendments in response. Table 5.2 therefore shows both government backbench amendments, broken down by party grouping, and legislative 'strands' initiated by such amendments alongside their levels of success.[34] We see that while the number of back-bench amendments actually agreed to was tiny there are further successes traceable through legislative strands. But the numbers are still small: just 36 government backbench-initiated strands resulted in change across the 12 bills.[35] This suggests that government backbenchers' success rate may exceed that of opposition parliamentarians (see Table 4.2)—12 per cent of backbench-initiated strands succeeded, compared to the opposition's 7 per cent. A chi-squared test shows this to be a statistically significant difference (with probability <0.01 of occurring by chance). But the total number of successful opposition-initiated strands was nonetheless far higher, at 112. As already noted in Chapter 4, this is in line with the balance of responsiveness found by Griffith (1974).

　As already discussed in that chapter, any such figures need to be treated with great caution. First, we know that both opposition members and government backbenchers propose amendments for reasons other than achieving immediate legislative change. This means that 'success rates' may have little value. Second, backbenchers clearly have other forms of influence. As well as behind-the-scenes influence, as just discussed, this crucially includes lending their support to initiatives from other non-government parliamentarians. Chapter 4 discussed how opposition members have an important 'issue politicization' function, and this group is responsible for initiating by far the greatest number of strands. A key means by which government backbenchers may have influence is thus through showing their support for such initiatives. Sometimes this occurs publicly through their own amendments later in a strand, which is not captured in the table, but discussed later in this chapter and further in Chapter 9. Less visibly, backbenchers may respond to opposition amendments by expressing concerns to ministers, which may encourage concessions.

Ministers' dependence on government backbenchers means that amendments initiated by this group are likely to be taken particularly seriously. As Cowley (2002: 181) notes, this applies less to 'constant whingers', who are unlikely to gain widespread support for their political views. But it imbues some backbenchers with particular importance. As one of our interviewees put it:

In a way, the significant people are the mainstream backbenchers, because I think governments ... know the usual suspects who rebel on just about everything, and they anticipate determined campaigns by oppositions, but it's the moment there starts to be that peeling off of mainstream, otherwise reliable and reasonably loyal MPs from the government benches, that you start to think 'oh, okay, if we pushed this we might not win it'. And so I think it is those kinds of MPs who are probably the most influential.

John McDonnell, cited earlier, could at the time readily be dismissed by ministers as a 'usual suspect', and he took an unusually adversarial approach.[36] Most proponents of successful backbench initiatives could not be so easily dismissed, and many changes were agreed relatively consensually. Under Labour, for example, former care minister Stephen Ladyman proposed that the scheme introduced by the Saving Gateway Accounts Bill should be extended to recipients of Carer's Allowance (the scheme as originally proposed applied only to recipients of other benefits and allowances, such as Working Tax Credit). He tabled an amendment at Commons committee stage, but withdrew it when the minister promised to 'reflect further'.[37] At report stage no government amendment was forthcoming, but under continued pressure from Ladyman the minister claimed to be 'certainly minded to table an amendment for consideration in the [House of Lords] that would ensure that people of working age in receipt of carer's allowance should be able to qualify'.[38] As promised, two such government amendments were proposed and agreed.

Ladyman's approach was nonconfrontational; he worked closely with external pressure group Carers UK and attended private meetings with ministers (though he had also taken the precaution of contacting peers who might press the proposal in the Lords had the government not acted). A government insider said that Ladyman 'did exactly what you would expect of a government backbencher'. That is, he 'made his case privately' and 'made his case in parliament in a very reasonable way', rather than 'forcing divisions and all those kinds of things that annoy ministers'.

Similar consensual concessions were made to the Health Bill, in response to proposals from Jeff Ennis MP—a former PPS at the Department of Health—that the minimum age at which a person could be sold tobacco products should be raised from 16 to 18. The minister, Caroline Flint, resisted the amendments in committee, promising 'to return to the issue on Report to give an indication of what I intend to do'.[39] We were told that the bill team had not anticipated this proposal, which may help to explain why the government did not fully concede. Instead a government report stage amendment was offered allowing ministers to alter the age limit via future secondary legislation. This was welcomed by Ennis (and the Conservative frontbench, which had proposed a similar amendment), and agreed. The increase to 18 was subsequently implemented in October 2007.[40] Likewise, concessions were made in the Lords on Labour's Employment Bill in response to Labour backbenchers Lord (Bill) Wedderburn of Charlton and Baroness (Muriel) Turner of Camden, who were seen as experts in the field—described by one government insider as 'very formidable opponents ... they knew what they were talking about'. Baroness Turner similarly secured 'naming and shaming' of organizations convicted under the Corporate Manslaughter and Corporate Homicide Bill (ultimately adding her name to a government amendment), and a small change to the Further Education and Training Bill.[41]

Respected backbenchers do sometimes engage in more adversarial behaviour, which can succeed. Under Labour a key example was the initiative to extend the provisions in the Corporate Manslaughter and Corporate Homicide Bill to deaths in custody. The first amendments on this were proposed at the bill's report stage in the Commons, with two separate initiatives sponsored respectively by Andrew Dismore, who was by then chairing the parliamentary Joint Committee on Human Rights, and by former Home Office minister John Denham, who chaired the special select committee which had considered the bill in draft (see Chapter 8). Both amendments were jointly sponsored with Conservatives. Home Secretary John Reid dismissed the proposals, and Denham withdrew his amendment, perhaps hoping to leave the matter to the Lords. But Dismore's approach was more confrontational, and he pushed his to a vote—which was won comfortably by the government, with just five Labour rebels. Reid seemed positively to encourage Dismore to do this, in order that the Commons could 'express an opinion' on the matter.[42] He presumably hoped that this would discourage subsequent Lords resistance. But as seen in Chapter 6, this did not prove successful, and the matter was ultimately resolved in Dismore's favour.

There were also some quite adversarial clashes between the government and its backbenchers during the coalition period, including several that resulted in defeat. One of these on the Welfare Reform Bill occurred on an amendment sponsored by highly regarded former Lord Chancellor Lord (James) Mackay of Clashfern. This concerned new proposals to charge parents making an application for child maintenance, a system which Mackay had been closely involved in introducing under the Child Support Act 1991. The government's consultation document had suggested that such a fee might be as high as £100, but following the defeat ministers announced that it would be capped at £20. On the Public Bodies Bill, two highly unusual defeats occurred on Conservative backbench amendments in Commons committee. These were sponsored by Charlie Elphicke, the MP for Dover, and concerned the future of the Dover Harbour Board. In response to a local campaign to promote community ownership rather than privatization of the body, Elphicke's amendments inserted a provision to allow (but not compel) this. They were supported by the Labour opposition but initially resisted by ministers (who tabled report stage amendments to overturn them). Ultimately the rebel amendments were accepted, when ministers took the rare step of choosing not to move their own.

Another example from the Public Bodies Bill demonstrates the perils for backbenchers in taking the lead on hostile amendments, rather than leaving this 'issue politicization' to the opposition. On the first day of the bill's Lords committee stage Lord Lester of Herne Hill (whose concerns at second reading were noted above) proposed an amendment to limit ministers' powers to abolish bodies, particularly those with judicial or other similar functions. This was an ingeniously worded 'paving amendment', which inserted a reference in line 3 of the bill to a new clause entitled 'Restrictions on ministerial powers'. The purpose of paving amendments is to get an early debate on an issue, and Lester had hoped that the government would accept the principle of his amendment and come back with such a clause in time for debate on the later parts of the bill. If not immediately successful, he intended to follow the common practice of withdrawing the amendment in a relatively consensual manner, having generated discussion. But concerns in the Lords were high and many peers had attended the committee determined to force the government to concede. The minister proposed some immediate government amendments at this stage, thanked Lester for being 'constructive in his approach and [for] his work with my officials to help make improvements', adding that 'I want to continue working in a collaborative way and will reflect further ... I ask my noble friend to withdraw his amendment'.[43] Lester expressed a willingness to do so, stating that:

> I am trying to consider how best to persuade the coalition Government, whom I support, to make these changes. I believe that we will have more influence by not dividing the Committee. Having said what I have said, I hope that noble Lords ... will hold off for now so that we can come back quite strongly ... I think it is much better that we stay united and that the Government listen to the Committee as a whole rather than that we play games at this time.[44]

However, once an amendment has been moved, it becomes the property of the committee (or whole house, at other stages), rather than its sponsor, and other peers were unimpressed with the government's response. Crossbench co-signatory to the amendment Lord (David) Pannick chose to press it to a vote, which resulted in in a government defeat. There were no government rebels, and Lester—having pledged not to 'play games'—felt compelled to vote against his own amendment. Some other Liberal Democrats also found themselves falling into similar traps on other bills.[45] Notably, this kind of behaviour was reported by Griffith (1974: 86, 95–6), so is not new—but creates a clear disincentive for government backbenchers to propose serious amendments. Liberal Democrat interviewees complained about such tactics, one suggesting that 'the Labour Party were complete bastards so I stopped tabling amendments'. In the Lords, the party's members became supportive of bills being sent to grand committee, where divisions cannot occur, in order that their amendments could be discussed more freely. Nonetheless, despite any initial discomfort,

Lester's amendment to the Public Bodies Bill proved influential. Following intense discussions behind the scenes, involving Lester, various ministers and officials and other peers, a version of his proposed clause was tabled later in the committee stage and co-sponsored by the government. This was agreed without division.

These last examples all included confrontation, but both ministers and backbenchers will generally prefer to avoid this where they can. Changing legislation in response to the government's own side is usually relatively collaborative, and indeed can sometimes even involve a degree of collusion—in the face of resistance from civil servants, or from ministers in other departments. Hence as one backbencher explained, 'ministers often say "put pressure on, because then we can put pressure on the Treasury"'. Likewise a former minister said that 'if you're presenting a bill you will know the areas of controversy or weakness, or the areas where you yourself would wish to be pushed forward', while a civil servant commented that 'if you don't manage to achieve something you want by negotiating [inside government] ... sometimes ministers can try and get issues raised on the floor'. We found examples of this under Labour, but they became more obvious with respect to the Liberal Democrats under coalition. A senior backbencher active on the Welfare Reform Bill described being taken aside by a minister and told 'you must do everything that you can to kibosh this benefit cap'. As he went on, '[t]his was a minister of the Crown saying to me, as a backbench Lib Dem, "you must do your damnedest to confront the government policy, because it will strengthen Nick [Clegg]'s hand in getting some kind of alternative"'. Hence negotiation over policy sometimes became quite intense under the coalition, and while activism by Liberal Democrat backbenchers in proposing amendments was widespread, there were some complex games going on. Despite the new more formal division between the two, frontbenchers and backbenchers continued to work quite cohesively together to put pressure on the larger coalition party. In turn, there may have been more attempts inside government to manufacture concessions in order to enable Liberal Democrats to claim victory.

When controversies arise on legislation, those with ministerial experience indicated that they preferred if possible to give concessions to their own backbenchers rather than to the opposition. As one commented, 'if there's an opportunity to use that concession to build up a bit of credit with your own side, then that's worth doing'. There is also some ministerial resistance to allowing the other side to be seen to win. Talking about the source of amendments, another interviewee suggested that 'you just hope it's not a Conservative or a Lib Dem if you're a Labour minister, and if it is a Conservative or a Lib Dem you have to figure out how the hell am I going to make it look like it's all my work'. Hence, as this interviewee explained, sometimes:

You get your own backbenchers to start lobbying for it, you get them to put the amendments down, then you ultimately say, 'well I'm persuaded by my honourable friends'. Sometimes you will acknowledge that the Conservatives are on the same page, or the Lib Dems are on the same page, you just won't give them the credit of saying they were there before you.

This demonstrates again the challenges of seeking to assess parliamentary influence, and the difficulty of fully separating contributions from the different actors involved.

Government backbenchers as pivotal

One reason that ministers are keen to be responsive to their backbenchers is this group's pivotal role in deciding outcomes in the House of Commons. Ultimately the government depends on backbenchers and their goodwill. Such members can hence often be central to resolving policy conflicts over bills. Indeed, it is hard to imagine ministers giving ground on any major issue if the change had no support from their own backbenchers—this kind of behaviour could be politically danger-ous, and even make it hard for the government to build a Commons majority for the change. Government backbenchers played some part in resolving many of the biggest conflicts on the case study bills (as illustrated further in several later chap-ters). But even where this occurs relatively visibly, through government backbench amendments, these often appear not in backbench-initiated strands, but at the later stages of legislative strands initiated by others.

Under coalition, many of the concessions given in response to the multitude of Liberal Democrat backbench amendments were very small. One example of a more substantive policy success concerned the eligibility criteria for the new Personal Independence Payment for disabled people. This was to be payable only after six months living with a condition, compared to the three-month qualification period that applied to Disability Living Allowance (which the new benefit replaced). Amendments in Commons committee by the Labour frontbench to reduce the required period to three months were resisted. In the Lords, Liberal Democrat back-bencher Baroness (Celia) Thomas of Winchester made similar proposals at com-mittee stage, supported by several Crossbenchers. She re-tabled her amendments at report, with a cross-party list of supporters, at which point the minister added his name as a sponsor and they were agreed. A Liberal Democrat interviewee told us that 'it was known' that the government was going to reconsider this point following the Commons debate. Indeed, some saw this as little more than a 'manufactured' concession; another Liberal Democrat interviewee close to the process said 'I didn't regard that [change] as much of a victory', claiming that 'as soon as I saw that in the draft bill I thought this was ludicrous, it must be three months not six'.

Under Labour there were some clear examples of government backbenchers using their pivotal role to resolve more major conflicts, particularly in the govern-ment's handling of House of Lords defeats. As indicated above, earlier studies show that such defeats are more likely to be accepted by ministers when there is evidence of backbench dissent. The previous chapter pointed out how the ability to inflict Lords defeats is an important form of 'issue politicization' exercised by the oppos-ition. If the Commons has already seen a bill, a Lords defeat throws the issue back to MPs to consider very publicly on the floor of the House. In some cases, the issue in question will not previously have received detailed scrutiny there. If peers press for change, and backbench MPs have some sympathy with the Lords' position, the government may prefer to concede rather than risk a rebellion and possible Commons defeat. An example of miscalculation occurred (beyond our case studies) on Labour's Racial and Religious Hatred Bill 2005–06, where rebel votes resulted in the government being defeated when seeking to overturn Lords amendments

(Russell 2013). Ministers would clearly always prefer to avoid such situations. Peers are quite well attuned to backbench MPs' opinions, and knowledge of dissent on the Commons backbenches will encourage them to press their cases. Hence the Commons' anticipated reactions help to drive behaviour by both the government and the Lords. A more recent example of such dynamics was seen in the Lords defeat of the Conservative government's tax credits proposals in October 2015 (see Chapter 3), where Conservative backbenchers in the Commons had previously expressed both public and private doubts. Following the defeat, the government chose to drop the policy rather than ask MPs to overturn the Lords' position.

Similar interactions were visible on two issues in the Identity Cards Bill. The first of these was compulsion. As originally introduced, the bill included a clause allowing ministers to initiate the transition from a voluntary identity card scheme to a fully compulsory one for the whole population via future secondary legislation.[46] During the initial Commons stages opposition parties proposed amendments to delete the relevant provisions from the bill, but they were not agreed to. In the Lords, however, a similar package of amendments was passed following a defeat at report stage—one of several Lords defeats on the bill. All of these posed challenges given its controversy on the Commons backbenches, leaving the government facing difficult questions about which they should seek to overturn. To reverse this particular defeat ministers would have needed to ask MPs to vote explicitly to reintroduce compulsion—a risky move politically given known backbench disquiet, and the words in the manifesto. Having argued strongly against the proposal in the Lords, the government hence made no attempt to reverse it.[47] The lack of visible conflict on this matter could make it appear less important than the other very public showdown that occurred between the chambers over compulsion, concerning initial requirements on those applying for a passport (as discussed in Chapter 6). But one opposition frontbencher described the passport issue as 'minor' compared to this reversal, which was largely unnoticed outside parliament.

Another example on this bill demonstrated the capacity of Commons backbenchers to broker deals with the Lords more explicitly. This occurred on the matter of costs, which was hotly debated during the bill's entire parliamentary passage (as further discussed in Chapters 4 and 7). Here the government had faced no major threat in the Commons, but was heavily defeated at Lords report stage on an amendment jointly sponsored by the Conservative and Liberal Democrat frontbench, which was supported by some Labour peers. This sought to delay introduction of the national identity register until there had been a full report on the scheme's costs and benefits. On the bill's return to the Commons, Labour backbencher (and former minister) Frank Dobson proposed a compromise amendment to require regular six-monthly reporting. The minister indicated the government's preparedness to support this, and MPs rejected the Lords amendment in favour of Dobson's proposal. This neutralized the cost issue, in both the Commons and the Lords. But the compromise was clearly more than window dressing; we were told by officials that it was 'a very clever amendment that had a great deal of impact on how the scheme then worked going forward'.

Support for the government

It may seem banal to say that backbenchers tend to support the government. As already indicated, this is their default setting. If they did not do so, ministers would be unable to legislate, or indeed ultimately to survive in office. But as a final comment on backbench influence it is important to note that this default setting cannot automatically be dismissed as a lack of power. In the relatively (and increasingly) independent environment of Westminster, backbenchers who support the government do so by active choice. Ministers and whips actually have relatively few means to impose discipline on backbenchers, beyond persuasion. In some other legislatures the party and its whips control not only access to seats on committees, but also speaking time in the chamber, the allocation of questions, and even the funds for parliamentarians to employ staff (Bowler, Farrell, and Katz 1999, Heidar and Koole 2000). At Westminster none of these apply. In addition, the whips' pre-existing power has been gradually eroded, through changes such as the greater availability of office space, and the 2010 Wright committee reforms. In the Lords the 'carrots and sticks' possessed by the whips have always been relatively limited (Norton 2003, Russell 2014).

Hence backbenchers clearly have agency, and can decide whether or not to support ministers on specific policies. Where they offer cohesive support the government generally gets its way. It is within this framework of mutual consent that the backbencher's role, much of the time, is to defend government policy against proposals from others in parliament. In Chapter 7 we note the concept of 'counteractive lobbying', which has been used to emphasize that pressure group power can be manifested not only through challenging government policy but also through supporting it against opposing claims from other groups (Austen-Smith and Wright 1994, Dür 2008). The dynamic of parliamentary parties follows a very similar logic. Opposition parties have the primary responsibility for 'politicizing' issues and can use various mechanisms to put them onto the parliamentary agenda. The test of whether such initiatives succeed—as opposition parliamentarians know very well—is often whether or not they can attract government backbench support.

Government backbench influence should therefore be conceived not only in terms of what changed on the bills, but also what didn't. On many issues the government was simply supported by its backbenchers. In some cases this was because the policy issues were uncontroversial, with little attempt by the opposition or others to 'politicize' them (as illustrated in Chapter 4). But on other occasions opposition parliamentarians sought to press the government, and made little progress because backbench opinion was solid. This applied for example to Labour's protests about the coalition's Savings Accounts and Health in Pregnancy Grant Bill, and its attempts to complete the pilot study on ID cards, or to negotiate refunds for those who had already purchased the cards. In all three cases ministers could hence proceed unimpeded. In contrast, in the case of John McDonnell's proposed amendments to Labour's Employment Bill, it was the opposition that applied counteractive pressure, alongside more mainstream backbenchers.

During coalition the distinction between the two partners made the possibility of dividing the government more obvious and, as again noted in Chapter 4, Labour sometimes specifically sought to do so with its amendments. Maintaining the support, or at least acquiescence, of Liberal Democrat backbenchers was crucial to securing the government's programme. On occasion these members expressed their displeasure by abstaining in divisions, rather than actively rebelling. Hence on the Welfare Reform Bill a Labour peer said of the Liberal Democrats that 'all I asked was not to vote with us but to simply come in and listen to the debate' (since government backbenchers often just arrive at the sound of the division bell and pass through whichever lobby their whips advise). Abstentions (as well as rebellious votes) contributed to several defeats on the bill in the Lords. But in no case were these sufficient to deny the government its majority in the Commons. This period illustrates clearly the fine line that ministers must sometimes walk in order to maintain their parliamentary majority, and the latent power of government backbenchers.

Conclusions

This chapter has explored the role of government backbenchers in the legislative process. They are the group that classic accounts (most obviously King 1976) suggest are the most influential at Westminster. We have seen that much backbench influence operates in subtle, and even largely invisible, ways. Notably, our analysis shows that relatively few changes to the case study bills were initiated by amendments from this group. Nonetheless, taking a broader perspective, much of our evidence strongly underlines their importance.

In comparison to other parliamentarians, backbenchers clearly have fairly ready access to ministers. They also, understandably, often support the government's policy priorities. Ministers and backbenchers are drawn from the same party (or parties, under coalition) and share both ideological goals and an interest in maintaining the party's reputation. Nonetheless, increasingly independent backbench behaviour—including in terms of voting—is well documented (e.g. Cowley 2002, 2005). As shown in the 'responses' section above, backbenchers sometimes speak out in strong disagreement to points in government bills. They also frequently propose amendments, though such amendments are far less numerous than those from the opposition. Like opposition members, backbenchers have various motivations for proposing amendments, but many are sincere. There are few incentives for 'game-playing', and 'signalling' is normally relatively rare. However, during the period of coalition, when ministers from one party did not automatically understand—or even sympathize with—the policy demands of backbenchers from the other, the number of government backbench amendments rose sharply, particularly from the junior partner, the Liberal Democrats. This indicated greater signalling, in order to publicly distance Liberal Democrat backbenchers from the government's line. Other government backbench amendments are 'markers for the future', as part of an ongoing dialogue with frontbenchers regarding the development of policy. Some are 'information seeking', to tease out ministers' intentions on the record. Once again, therefore, the relatively low 'success' rate for government backbench amendments (or the legislative strands which they initiate) should not necessarily be read as a measure of failure. But more importantly, this group has other important means to influence government legislation.

The analysis in this chapter has demonstrated at least five interconnected forms of power exercised by government backbenchers:

- First, influencing the content of bills before they are introduced. Backbenchers' role in the formulation of government policy is a consequence of the British parliamentary system and what it rests upon. Not only do ministers and backbenchers share a party allegiance, but the former ultimately depend on the latter to remain in office. In the words of an interviewee who formerly held several cabinet positions, 'the government is only the government rather than the opposition because it commands the confidence of the House of Commons'; hence it would be erroneous to assume 'that government is not related to the majority of MPs in parliament. It is'. Ministers work with the party, including its MPs, in developing policy, and are naturally attentive to backbench policy demands. This dynamic was seen particularly clearly on the Corporate Manslaughter and Corporate Homicide Bill, promised publicly in the party's manifesto, but delayed and resisted inside government. Backbench pressure in parliament helped to keep the issue on the agenda and ensure that a bill was introduced despite scepticism, and even outright resistance, inside government. Once published, backbenchers maintained pressure to further strengthen the bill. Both on this bill and the smoking provisions in the Health Bill, backbenchers used various parliamentary mechanisms to put policy issues onto the agenda and ensure that they received ministerial attention. This agenda-setting power has received little academic attention, and would be worthy of more systematic study. It runs counter to commonly held assumptions about the legislative process, that 'parliament is rarely involved prior to the formal introduction' of government bills (Norton 2013: 71).

- Second, once a bill has been introduced backbenchers can obviously pursue changes through amendments. In total, on our case studies 36 changes resulted from government backbench-initiated strands. The government will be particularly responsive to senior backbenchers (e.g. former ministers, or select committee chairs) who cannot be dismissed as serial rebels or 'usual suspects'. We have seen that ministers will prefer, where possible, to give concessions to their own backbenchers than to opposition parliamentarians, and a degree of collusion may even be involved in bringing this about. In addition, ministers will sometimes work covertly with backbenchers in parliament in order to resolve prior policy differences inside government. During the coalition period there was particularly strong evidence of such contact between frontbench and backbench Liberal Democrats, though often with little policy effect.

- Third, and connectedly, as parliament's key pivotal voters, backbenchers are often the ultimate arbiters in policy disputes instigated by others—most commonly the opposition. Backbenchers were involved in many of the largest changes to the bills, albeit usually not at the forefront of calling for change. The typical dynamic is that backbenchers will voice their concerns privately, with more public objections being raised by other groups. Hence, as another interviewee said, backbenchers are 'the ones that the opposition and anyone is seeking to seduce'. This means that it is often impossible to disentangle the influence of different groups; if backbenchers join policy initiatives at later stages they may or may not already have been pressing these matters behind the scenes. The Lords offers the opposition its greatest opportunity to extract change through amendments, and although government backbenchers are less obviously pivotal there than in the Commons, they can play a central role in resolving disputes between the chambers (as seen for example in the Dobson amendments on the Identity Cards Bill). Previous research has shown that ministers are more likely to give in following Lords defeats where there is support for their opponents' position among government backbench peers—which may indicate wider dissent within the governing party (Russell 2013). In effect the Lords—often fuelled by the opposition—can perform an 'issue politicization' function by putting matters back on the Commons agenda for decision, giving government backbenchers the ultimate deciding role. This means that the influence of the two chambers cannot be fully separated either.

- Fourth, underpinning all of this is perhaps backbenchers' greatest power, exercised through 'anticipated reactions', or even more subtly through ministers internalizing backbenchers' desires—in line with what Lukes (1974) called the third face of power. When devising proposals ministers will routinely consult backbenchers, and think carefully about their views. They may well choose to abandon proposals that cannot command adequate backbench support, and there was clear evidence of this on the bills. When thinking through 'handling strategies' in advance of bills being introduced, the likely views of senior backbenchers will be given close attention. After bills have been introduced, further backbench concerns may be privately resolved. In this context, public conflict with backbenchers during the passage of a bill generally indicates that internal party channels of communication have not resolved matters adequately.

- Finally, and in line with this, backbenchers' ability to support the government and its legislation can also be seen as a form of power. In an environment where backbenchers are able to speak out relatively freely against the government, and where dissenting votes are increasingly commonplace, support for government bills must be seen as an active choice. The government relies on the exercise of this backbench power (on all but the rarest of occasions) to get its legislation agreed.

As already indicated, the coalition period offers a particularly interesting illustration of some of these dynamics. Unlike under 'normal' periods of single-party government, the divisions within government were very clear. At the same time, ministers were less inclined than previously to be responsive to backbenchers' demands. While the number of Conservative backbench amendments was relatively small, concessions to the numerous Liberal Democrat amendments were fairly limited. The literature on coalition suggests that the junior partner will often take responsibility for 'policing the bargain'—that is, holding the senior partner to its previous policy agreements (Martin and Vanberg 2008, 2011). In contrast on our case study bills—particularly the Welfare Reform Bill—Liberal Democrat backbenchers sought not simply to hold the Conservatives to the coalition agreements, but to moderate the proposals that they contained—with limited success. This was in part an indication that the party had not negotiated these agreements particularly well, as various commentators have noted (Bale 2012, Fox 2010, Hayton 2014). Meanwhile, despite the term 'policing the bargain' being coined to describe coalition dynamics, it was arguably Labour backbenchers in the previous period who worked most successfully to such ends—in terms of holding ministers to the promises previously made to the party and its supporters. The Corporate Manslaughter and Corporate Homicide Bill offered a particularly clear example.

Hence backbenchers exercise significant, but often subtle, power in the legislative process. Because this is well hidden it is often not recognized, including among backbenchers themselves. Members of this group can sometimes be unaware of the degree to which their views are taken into account during government planning. A former backbencher who built strong relationships with the Brown administration described to us how it was 'quite surprising how much attention they paid to us which we did not have knowledge of'. Indeed he suggested that 'the amount of attention paid to what happened in the Commons was quite staggering to me, who'd been in the Commons feeling I was completely impotent. There wasn't a movement or a current in the Commons that No. 10 weren't aware of.' Previously this interviewee suggested that much parliamentary work had 'felt like a display of impotence, and you used to rage about it, but actually we were doing far more than we realized', adding 'we hadn't understood the significance of what happens in the Commons'.

Notes

1. Under the 2010 coalition this number reached a peak of over 140 members (Parry and Kelly 2012).
2. This bears some resemblance to the 'veto players' theory of Tsebelis (2002). But we use the term 'pivotal voters' throughout the book, partly because Tsebelis's theory assumed that political parties acted as cohesive blocks—which is clearly not the case when considering rebellious backbenchers.
3. See Abbott (2011), Russell, Morris, and Larkin (2013). Ironically, Wollaston was later elected by the whole house to chair the Health Select Committee.
4. Russell and Paun (2007) analysed bill membership for the 10 bills with the largest government backbench rebellions at second reading during the period 1997–2007, eight of which had their committee stage 'off the floor'. In six of the eight cases rebels were underrepresented, and in four cases the bill committee included no rebels at all. Among our case study bills only the Identity Cards Bill was subjected to a rebellion at Commons second reading, and none of these rebels were selected to serve on the bill committee.
5. EDM 263 of session 2005–06, sponsored by Neil Gerrard.
6. House of Commons Hansard, 28 June 2005, columns 1198–1200.
7. Ibid., column 1184.

8. House of Commons Hansard, 10 October 2006, column 218.
9. House of Commons Hansard, 14 July 2008, column 55.
10. House of Commons Hansard, 9 March 2011, column 953.
11. House of Lords Hansard, 9 November 2010, column 152.
12. Ibid., column 99.
13. Ibid., column 156.
14. For example Liberal Democrat peer Baroness (Sally) Hamwee described one of her amendments to the Identity Documents Bill as 'probing' and intended to allow peers 'to hear a little more about, and to get on the record, the Government's thinking' (House of Lords Hansard, 3 November 2010, column GC49).
15. It would have been possible for McDonnell to table amendments for discussion at committee stage, despite not being a member of the committee, though a committee member would have needed to move them. The fact that he chose not to pursue this route, but to reserve them for report stage, is perhaps further indication that these were more about publicity-seeking than achieving legislative change.
16. These related respectively to preventing dismissal of employees engaging in industrial action, requiring employers to cooperate in supporting strike ballots, preventing employers using agency staff in place of existing employees during industrial action, guaranteeing time off for workplace environmental representatives, and repealing certain exemptions from the national minimum wage.
17. EDM 532 of session 2006–07.
18. House of Commons Hansard, 4 November 2008, column 166.
19. For example, Public Bill Committee (Welfare Reform Bill), 10 May 2011, columns 861–2; House of Commons Hansard, 1 February 2012, column 834.
20. House of Lords Hansard, 29 November 2010, column GC86.
21. Public Bill Committee (Further Education and Training Bill), 14 June 2007, column 163.
22. These included Anthony Favell's British Identity Card Bill (1987–78), Ralph Howell's National Identity Card Bill (1988–89), David Amess's Voluntary Personal Security Cards Bill (1992–93), and Harold Elletson's Identity Cards Bill (1993–94).
23. Including George Foulkes's Tobacco Smoking (Public Places) Bill (1985–86), Joe Ashton's No-Smoking Areas in Public Houses Bill (1985–86), Tessa Jowell's Tobacco Smoking (Public Places) Bill (1994–95), Gareth Thomas's Smoking (Restaurants) Bill (2002–03), Lord Faulkner of Worcester's Tobacco Smoking (Public Places and Workplaces) Bill (2003–04), and Julie Morgan's Smoking in Public Places (Wales) Bill (2004–05).
24. See House of Commons Hansard 18 April 2000, column 831. Dismore's Corporate Homicide Bill is available at http://www.parliament.the-stationery-office.co.uk/pa/cm199900/cmbills/114/2000114.htm [accessed 3 June 2015].
25. EDM 793 of session 2002–03. See also EDM 561 of session 1999–2000 (42 signatures, 36 Labour) sponsored by George Galloway calling for a review of the law, EDM 1270 of 2001–02 (88 signatures, 73 Labour) sponsored by Roger Berry welcoming government proposals, EDM 1447 of 2001–02 (51 signatures, 46 Labour) sponsored by John Cryer calling for a bill to be in the Queen's Speech, EDM 1086 of 2002–03 (116 signatures, 105 Labour) sponsored by Tom Cox and pressing the government to act and EDM 1155 of 2002–03 (47 signatures, 38 Labour) sponsored by Dismore and calling for the government to act 'without further delay'.
26. Available at http://www.publications.parliament.uk/pa/cm200203/cmbills/063/amend/30401a07.htm [accessed 11 June 2016].

27. 'Blunkett Confirms Plan for Corporate Killing Law', *Guardian*, 20 May 2003 http://
    www.theguardian.com/politics/2003/may/20/immigrationpolicy.ukcrime   [accessed
    21/07/2016].

28. For further discussion of this dynamic under Labour, see Cowley (2002, 2005).

29. The most obvious was the House of Lords Reform Bill, withdrawn by the government
    after its second reading in 2012 (Russell 2013).

30. EDM 1182 of session 2010–12.

31. House of Commons Hansard, 9 November 2010, column 183.

32. House of Commons Hansard, 9 March 2011, column 954.

33. The change of heart was also explicitly indicated in the government's response to the
    select committee report referred to in Willott's comment, which stated that '[s]ubsequent
    to the Budget decision, the Government has ... decided not to introduce this particular
    change to Housing Benefit' (Work and Pensions Committee 2011: 17).

34. Strands were introduced in Chapter 2 and are fully discussed in Appendix A.

35. Table 4.3 showed the distribution of successful opposition-initiated strands by bill
    and degree of policy substance. In comparison, there were 13 successful government
    backbench-initiated strands fairly evenly distributed between Labour's bills: all but
    one being subject to between one and three such changes; under coalition there was
    one change to the Budget Responsibility and National Audit Bill, seven to the Welfare
    Reform Bill and 15 to the Public Bodies Bill. In total, 27 of the 36 had clear policy sub-
    stance, eight dealt with regulations and one with other procedure.

36. During the 2001–05 parliament McDonnell had been the second most rebellious
    Labour MP, after Jeremy Corbyn (Cowley 2005: 53).

37. Ian Pearson, Public Bill Committee (Saving Gateway Accounts Bill), 3 February 2009,
    column 68.

38. Ian Pearson, House of Commons Hansard, 25 February 2009, column 296.

39. Caroline Flint, House of Commons, Standing Committee E (Health Bill), 15 December
    2015: column 256

40. 'Higher Tobacco Age Limit in Force', *BBC News*, 1 October 2007, http://news.bbc.
    co.uk/1/hi/uk/7021320.stm [accessed 23 December 2015].

41. This made establishment of a body to review and formulate strategies for the Greater
    London Learning and Skills Council mandatory (simply changing the words in the bill
    from 'may' to 'shall'): see House of Lords Hansard, 23 January 2007, column GC352.

42. House of Commons Hansard, 4 December 2006, column 109.

43. House of Lords Hansard, 23 November 2010, column 1035.

44. Ibid., columns 1038–9.

45. For example Labour MPs pushed two of Jenny Willott's amendments on the Welfare
    Reform Bill to a division (Public Bill Committee, 10 May 2011, columns 819, 822–3).

46. Clause 6 of the bill provided that this should be done via the 'super-affirmative'
    procedure—requiring more parliamentary oversight than most secondary legislation,
    but well short of that for primary legislation, as discussed in Chapter 8. Distinct from
    the case indicated below, this clause concerned compulsory inclusion within the scheme
    of those who had not applied for a passport.

47. This was also an example of the power of select committees—three of which had com-
    mented adversely on the clause, as described in Chapter 8.

6

The Role of Non-Party Parliamentarians

The previous chapters have focused on well-known groups of parliamentary actors: the government, opposition parties, and backbench members of governing parties. In this chapter we analyse the contribution of parliamentarians who are far less often discussed, and less well understood—that is, members who do not take a party whip. In the House of Commons such members are unusual, but in the House of Lords they are very numerous. Since Lords reform in 1999 such peers have had significant potential to influence the legislative process.

A greater voice for independent parliamentarians could be seen as fitting, given the public mood towards party politics. Both electoral support and membership of the two main parties have shown long-term decline (e.g. Fisher 2008). In recent decades there has been growing support for other parties—first the Liberal Democrats, followed by the SNP and UKIP post-2010. Importantly, the proportion of people expressing 'very strong' support for *any* political party declined sharply from 43 per cent in 1966 to just 13 per cent in 2010.[1] Many people might thus welcome a significant independent voice in parliament.[2] But because most non-party parliamentarians sit in the unelected chamber, whose activities are relatively little reported in the media, they have low visibility and only rarely come into public view. Nonetheless a book about parliamentary actors and government legislation would clearly be incomplete without consideration of this group. As we will see, non-party parliamentarians played an important role in several of the case study bills; during the period 2010–15 in particular their votes could be seen as 'pivotal' in the Lords.

In line with other chapters, we begin by introducing the various types of non-party parliamentarian. We then review what little has been written about the contribution of these groups. After this we describe how non-party parliamentarians—particularly the Crossbenchers and bishops in the Lords—organize themselves, in the absence of whips and an external party machine. In the second part of the chapter we turn more specifically to the contribution of these groups to the case study bills—how non-party parliamentarians responded to the bills, the amendments that they proposed and what motivates these amendments, and finally their overall influence on the process.

Non-Party Parliamentarians: Who Are They?

In the House of Commons independent members are a rarity. In 2005 just two independent MPs were elected—Peter Law and Richard Taylor.[3] The former was the more

Legislation at Westminster. First edition. Meg Russell and Daniel Gover. © Meg Russell and Daniel Gover 2017. Published 2017 by Oxford University Press.

typical, having taken this status after splitting from his party. Law had been a Labour member of the National Assembly for Wales, but ran as an independent in the 2005 general election, having been denied the right to contest his seat due to an all-women shortlist. He died shortly afterwards, and was replaced by another independent, Dai Davies, but neither contributed significantly to the case study bills. The 2005 parliament also included a small number of other members who served as independents for part of the period, having split from their parties while sitting as MPs.[4] Richard Taylor was more unusual, having had no previous party connections. He won his Wyre Forest seat in 2001 on a campaign to reinstate the Accident and Emergency department at Kidderminster Hospital, where he had previously been a consultant doctor. Taylor held the seat until 2010, became a member of the Health Select Committee, and played some part in debates on the Health Bill 2005–06. In 2010 just one independent member was elected—Lady Sylvia Hermon, who had previously represented the Ulster Unionist Party. She played only a very small role on the case study bills.

In the House of Lords there are many more non-party parliamentarians, who fall into three distinct groups. The largest comprises the Crossbenchers, who numbered almost 200 throughout the period 2005–12 (see Table 2.1 in Chapter 2). Today Crossbenchers are parliamentarians who explicitly take a non-party independent stance.[5] The main route onto these benches is via the House of Lords Appointments Commission, established in 2000 to select independent peers. It invites applications from people 'with a record of significant achievement', interviews candidates, and provides nominations to the Prime Minister on request.[6] The Prime Minister may also appoint such members directly, and this route is often used to reward retiring senior public officials, for example, the head of the civil service (Cabinet Secretary) and head of the armed forces (Chief of the Defence Staff). Crossbenchers selected by the House of Lords Appointments Commission are more diverse, and mostly comprise people who have reached senior positions across a range of professions, including academia, the law, business, and the voluntary sector. Consequently, many of the valued 'experts' in the Lords sit on the Crossbenches.

The second long-established non-partisan group in the chamber comprises the Church of England bishops.[7] They hold 26 seats, five of which go to particular officeholders (the Archbishops of Canterbury and York, and Bishops of London, Durham, and Winchester). The remainder are allocated to English diocesan bishops according to seniority (i.e. length of service) in the church.[8] Unlike other members of the Lords, bishops retire at age 70 when they give up their full-time positions.

Beyond these two groups, the Lords generally includes a small number of other members who do not take a party whip. They are more akin to independents in the House of Commons, many having represented political parties in the past.

Established Understanding of Non-Party Parliamentarians

To date, relatively little academic attention has been paid to independent members at Westminster. Since the Crossbenchers in the Lords are by far the largest independent grouping in any of the world's legislatures, analysis of such members in other settings has also been very limited.[9] In advanced democracies independents generally struggle to win seats in elections dominated by political parties. The House of Lords, as an unelected chamber, is hence a quite unusual exception.[10] Some studies in other settings have sought to classify the types of independents that exist, for example distinguishing those who are 'fully independent' from those with vestigial party links (e.g. Copus, Clark, and Bottom 2008, Weeks 2009). Others have explored to some extent these members' parliamentary contributions (e.g. Chubb 1957, Costar and Curtin 2004, Hansen 2010, Sharman 1999). But the most detailed such work has been on the UK.

Historical texts on the House of Lords shed some light on the development of independent parliamentarians in that chamber (e.g. Bromhead 1958, Walters 2003). Presence of such members did not result from conscious design, but grew from the late nineteenth century onwards—as a result of changed appointment processes which rewarded more public servants and celebrity figures, coupled with the long-standing fact that many of those born into hereditary membership arrived with no party allegiance (Russell 2013). The Crossbench group took on its own organization only in the post-war period, with the emergence of a 'convener' (emphatically not a 'leader'), who by 1964 was circulating a 'non-whip' to 125 members (Morgan 1975: 25). But as a group that had relatively little influence in the Conservative-dominated and largely timid pre-1999 chamber, the Crossbenchers attracted relatively little academic interest. Shell (1992: 91) did note that under the Conservatives in 1983–84, members of the group 'cast more than twice as many votes with the Government as against it'. Writing on the period after 1999, Russell and Sciara (2009: 38)—in the most detailed study to date—found that many Labour members remained suspicious of the Crossbenchers, considering them 'Tories in disguise'. Surveyed in 2005, 93 per cent of Conservative peers thought the Crossbenchers 'genuinely independent', while just 45 per cent of Labour peers agreed.

But the 1999 reform fundamentally changed the nature of the Crossbench group, with the departure of its hereditary members and establishment of the House of Lords Appointments Commission. Russell and Sciara (2009) found Crossbenchers in 2007 to be on average centrist on a left–right scale. Although 62 per cent of their votes 1999–2007 were cast against the government, Crossbenchers were more motivated to vote when government policy was seen as weak, and the group's turnout in divisions averaged only 12 per cent. Partly as a consequence, although the Crossbenchers were sufficiently numerous potentially to dictate the outcome of most Lords divisions, they rarely did so. In a separate analysis, Russell and Sciara (2007) showed that low turnout and generally split votes meant that Crossbenchers determined the outcome of just 50 out of 806 government-whipped divisions during the period 1999–2005. Across the longer period 1999–2010 the group proved pivotal in only 7 per cent of divisions overall, and in 19 per cent of government defeats (Russell 2013). With respect to the Commons, Cowley and Stuart (2009) likewise found that independent MPs had a relatively low voting turnout. Unsurprisingly, given their low numbers, these members have little chance of influencing the outcome of divisions.

The bishops' presence in the House of Lords is also highly unusual in comparative terms, Steven (2011: 75) judging it as 'unique among all advanced democracies in Western Europe and North America'.[11] The 'Lords Spiritual' are among the most long-standing members of the Westminster parliament, though their importance has greatly declined, due both to reduction in their numbers and declining activism (Bromhead 1958, Russell 2013). Studies of the bishops' behaviour in the 1980s found that they attended and voted relatively infrequently, although when they did vote this was largely against the government (Bown 1994, Partington 2006). These studies also demonstrated some engagement by bishops in legislative scrutiny, but with most influence limited to specific policy areas. Despite some increase in activism post-1999 (Partington and Bickley 2007), Russell (2013) found that the average bishop turnout in divisions during the period 1999–2010 was less than one member, and that their votes affected outcomes in under 1 per cent of divisions. But, as various authors note, the primary influence of the bishops is likely to be not through their own votes but through their capacity to sway the opinions of other peers.

Indeed, studies of both chambers emphasize that independent members' most important influence comes not through voting, but through private conversations with ministers, persuasion of other members, and affecting the overall culture of debate. In the Lords, Russell and Sciara (2009) emphasize that these members play a major part in maintaining the chamber's relatively nonpartisan culture, that they effectively sit in judgement of the quality of arguments made by party frontbenchers, and they can potentially broker agreements between government and opposition. In the Australian Senate, Sharman (1999: 359) similarly notes that independent members have contributed significantly to creating a culture of 'detailed and independent scrutiny of legislation'.

Authors both in the UK and elsewhere also emphasize the significant pressure that nonpartisan members face, including in deciding how (and indeed whether) to vote. In Australia, individual independents in potentially pivotal positions have been subject to substantial media and public attention.[12] In the Lords it has been noted that non-party members are less inclined to escalate their policy concerns to the point of confrontation than are party members—recognizing their lack of elected mandate (Russell 2013, Russell and Sciara 2009). In Australia, Bach (2008) suggests something similar, as independent senators—despite being elected—may face very personal criticism, and lack the security of a party group or support of a party machine.

In 2010, when the Liberal Democrats entered government with the Conservatives, non-party peers potentially became much more important political actors. As seen in Chapter 4, the Lib Dems had previously been pivotal in deciding the outcome of most Lords divisions. Now that they were expected to vote with the government, the Crossbenchers largely took on this role. In the 2010–12 session, Russell (2013) found their votes to be decisive in 81 per cent of Lords defeats. This placed the group in a far more sensitive position than previously, and could cause its interventions to become more controversial and contested. Nonetheless, as she notes, such a central role for nonpartisan experts could be seen as in keeping with other recent developments—including trends towards 'depoliticization' (e.g. Flinders 2012, Hay 2007) and the so-called 'rise of the unelected' (Vibert 2007).

Non-Party Organization

Several of the authors above emphasize that organizing in parliament without the support of a political party is challenging. Parliamentarians who represent parties, and particularly the larger parties, have well-established machines to support them. Party organizations—inside and outside parliament—provide two key things that sustain the work of their MPs and peers. The most obvious is resources, including party staff and activists. These facilitate campaigning for election, as well as policy development and research. But parties also crucially organize collective decision-making. Once party policy is decided—be it by activists outside parliament, or by the parliamentary leadership—its representatives are generally expected to follow a collective line. This is communicated to parliamentarians through the whip system, meaning that members do not usually need to take active policy decisions; the default position is to follow their whip. Non-party parliamentarians in contrast have no whip, and no collective line to follow. They also have few resources.

The Crossbenchers and bishops in the House of Lords do have well-developed organizational structures, though these differ in important ways from those of a political party. Other non-party members in both chambers operate more straight-forwardly as individuals, with no infrastructure to support them at all, aside from the staff of parliament.

Starting with the Crossbenchers, this group's organization has become increasingly sophisticated, with the main coordination point remaining the 'convener'. When former Speaker of the House of Commons Lord (Bernard) Weatherill took up this role in 1995 he sought gradually to develop the group's organization. Crucial to this was negotiating that the Crossbenchers should have some share of the 'Cranborne money' that supports non-government peers. The initial sum secured in 1999–2000 was just £10,000 per year, contributing to the employment of a part-time secretary. By 2011–12 the figure had reached £67,063 (Kelly 2016), enough to employ at most two or three staff. This was less than one-eighth of the sum payable to the opposition Labour Party (see Chapter 4), with a broadly similar number of peers. Indeed even the far smaller Liberal Democrats received £237,136 in the year immediately before they entered government. Crucially, of course, unlike the parties, the Crossbenchers have no extra-parliamentary organization upon which they can rely for additional support.

The staff funded by the Cranborne money work in the office of the Crossbench convener. They circulate information to members about forthcoming business in the chamber (and committees), and prepare research briefings to support Crossbenchers' work. When the House is sitting, there is a weekly meeting to which all such peers are invited, chaired by the convener. This is similar to a party group meeting, inasmuch as it is a forum for the exchange of information and discussion of forthcoming business, and often has an external speaker. But it is also dissimilar, in that the group does not seek to reach a collective view. Indeed some Crossbenchers resist being considered a 'group' at all. As one member put it, 'the only thing that we have in common is that we're Crossbenchers'—that is, a diverse group of independent individuals who make up their minds on an issue-by-issue basis. Given most Crossbenchers' achievements outside politics, another interviewee described them as 'a collective of expertise, not of ideology or viewpoint'. Hence if a Crossbench member is sponsoring an amendment to a bill, they may raise this for information at the weekly meeting, but it would be controversial even to lobby other members for support. As another Crossbencher explained, more acceptable language would be 'I do hope you'll be able to get along to hear the debate', which he considered code for 'I hope you'll come and vote for my blooming amendment!'.

While resolutely not adopting a collective line, Crossbench organization has taken on some increasingly party-like features. In the past, Crossbenchers, in the absence of a whip, were often unaware of when key votes were likely to take place. Enhanced organization, and technology, now enable the convener's office to alert peers by text message or e-mail to important business. Members are never advised how to vote, just that they might wish to be present. Such communication has been facilitated by closer integration of the Crossbench convener into the 'usual channels'—that is, behind-the-scenes discussions between party whips. In the past, the Crossbenchers were seen as relatively peripheral; their low turnout in divisions and tendency to split their votes made whips reluctant to engage with the convener, as he or she had no votes to trade. But the close party balance in the Lords after 1999 encouraged all parties to build up goodwill with the Crossbenchers, and ministers even began to address Crossbench meetings to provide information about their bills. Post-2010 the focus on the Crossbenchers increased further, as did their level of responsibility as the key 'pivotal' group, and they expanded their organization. This included appointing 'liaison peers' for individual government departments, who would be expected to aid communication between ministers and the wider Crossbench group. While it used to be Labour who were suspicious of the group, these developments—and Crossbenchers' ability to combine with Labour to defeat the government—raised suspicions on the coalition side. Thus one senior Conservative interviewee suggested that 'the Crossbenchers have always been in danger of creating the Crossbench party'.

Crossbench organization demonstrates the challenges of maintaining an independent presence in parliament which is also well informed and effective. Individual Crossbenchers, who (like other peers) receive no defined staffing allowance at all, must choose which policy issues to pursue and how to vote on bills with relatively little support or guidance. Some benefit from personnel based in external organizations with which they are involved (e.g. businesses or universities), some use their own resources to pay for such support, and others are wholly dependent on briefing from pressure groups. Many Crossbenchers are active in All-Party Parliamentary Groups (APPGs, discussed further in Chapters 7 and 9), which are often supported by these kinds of outside bodies.

Hence Crossbenchers have significant freedom compared to party parliamentarians, but also face distinct challenges. As one such member put it, 'the best and the worst thing is that nobody tells us how to vote'. Another explained:

When a division is called, people flood into the House, and if they're government benches or opposition they just go through the lobby, while if it's Crossbenchers we all huddle round and try to work out what it's about, asking someone who's been there what is the nature of the issue.

Though non-party peers will ultimately make up their own minds, the views of expert members can hence be persuasive.

The bishops share similarities with the Crossbenchers, but are also different in important ways. They likewise take no collective line, and each member makes decisions according to their own beliefs; but they do clearly have a kind of collective ethos that the Crossbenchers lack. Importantly, of course, all bishops have full-time paid positions outside parliament, in many cases based far outside London, making them very part-time members. But these positions also give them the support of an extra-parliamentary organization, including dedicated policy specialists at Church House (where most of the Church of England's central administration is based). In justifying their presence in the Lords the bishops are keen to emphasize that they provide 'a voice for all people of faith, not just Christians', and some degree of inter-faith dialogue occurs.[13]

Unlike the Crossbenchers, the bishops organize on a rota, so that there is always a 'duty bishop' in the Lords. Others may also attend, but their roles outside parliament mean that participation tends to be low. Like the Crossbenchers, the group has a convener, and bishops do hold semi-formal policy portfolios (often linked to responsibilities that they have on Church of England committees or other bodies). Presence of speakers in the chamber is coordinated, and positions on bills are discussed between members, but each is free to make up their own mind. There is no regular bishops' meeting in the Lords—as most are usually absent—but the duty bishop often attends the Crossbench meeting.

Non-Party Responses to the Case Study Bills

Non-party parliamentarians clearly do not speak with one voice, so it is not possible to discern a collective response from them to the case study bills. But individual non-party parliamentarians frequently spoke out strongly—both in support and opposition to the government's policy. These actors' stated positions were often rooted in professional expertise—making them potentially formidable opponents, or useful allies.

On some bills, non-party parliamentarians voiced clear opposition from an early stage. For example at second reading of the Further Education and Training Bill respected Crossbencher Lord (Ron) Dearing, who had coordinated a major report into the future of higher education a decade earlier (National Committee of Inquiry into Higher Education 1997), expressed concerns about the proposal to grant degree-awarding powers to further education colleges. He pursued these at subsequent stages, as discussed below. Opposition to key elements of the Corporate Manslaughter and Corporate Homicide Bill was likewise expressed by several Crossbench peers when the bill reached the Lords. Particularly notable was Lord (David) Ramsbotham, who had been Chief Inspector of Prisons for England and Wales 1995–2001. He used his second reading speech to quote from a government review that he had led into self-harm and suicide in prisons (HM Inspectorate of Prisons 1999), and to strongly support complaints from other Crossbenchers about the exclusion of deaths in police and prison custody from the bill. Among other critics, Baroness (Frances) D'Souza—a human rights specialist who later became Lord Speaker—referred to the exclusions as 'neither logical nor acceptable'.[14] Baroness (Vivien) Stern—a former director of the National Association for the Care and Resettlement of Offenders, and member of the Joint Committee on Human Rights—likewise dedicated her second reading speech to this point.

Particularly strong criticism was voiced by a number of non-party peers towards the coalition's Public Bodies Bill. For example Lord (Harry) Woolf, a former Lord Chief Justice, described the bill as 'a matter of grave concern to the judiciary', and expressed particular concerns about the threats to numerous judicial bodies (subsequently pursued by Liberal Democrat backbencher Lord (Anthony) Lester of Herne Hill, as described in Chapter 5).[15] Various peers expressed concerns about Schedule 7—which gave ministers substantial discretion over the future of certain public bodies, and was ultimately dropped from the bill, as discussed in Chapter 9. Objections from Baroness (Ilora) Finlay of Llandaff, a professor of palliative care and former President of the Royal Society of Medicine, about plans to abolish the Chief Coroner were taken up at subsequent stages, as discussed in Chapter 7. At the end of second reading 29 Crossbenchers supported the unsuccessful attempt to refer the bill to a select committee, with only five voting against.

On other occasions, non-party peers offered the government valuable support. For example at second reading of the Identity Cards Bill Lord (John) Stevens of Kirkwhelpington, a former Metropolitan Police Commissioner, suggested that there was an 'overwhelming case for identity cards', and that 'the police and others in the security services are absolutely certain that there is a need for a certainty of identification'.[16] Likewise the Bishop of Oxford declared himself to 'strongly support the idea of identity cards'.[17] As discussed later in the chapter, the coalition government also benefited from supportive remarks by key Crossbench experts on its Budget Responsibility and National Audit Bill.

Yet, given their independent nature, non-party parliamentarians can clearly also take opposing positions, as was evident on some bills. For example at the second reading of the Welfare Reform Bill, Crossbencher and businessman Lord (Karan) Bilimoria commented that 'in the area of welfare the Government are doing absolutely the right thing'.[18] But numerous other such peers were very concerned. The Bishop of Leicester questioned whether the 'reforms measure[d] up to a national moral responsibility to ensure the well-being of the most vulnerable', raising in particular the effect on children.[19] Lord (Richard) Best, a former Director of the National Federation of Housing Associations and Joseph Rowntree Housing Trust, drew attention to the impact on tenants; Lord (Narendra) Patel, former President of the Royal College of Obstetricians and Gynaecologists, warned about the potential consequences for cancer patients; and Lord (Colin) Low, Vice-President of the Royal National Institute of Blind People (RNIB), raised issues concerning disability and Employment and Support Allowance.

Proposals for the smoking ban in Labour's Health Bill also drew some mixed comments, though specialist opinion was very much on the government's side— or indeed sought to push ministers further. In the Commons, independent MP Richard Taylor argued that moving to a comprehensive ban on smoking in public places would be 'the one most important thing to improve the prevention of cancer'.[20] By the time the bill reached the Lords, MPs had voted in favour of this position, and several peers with medical expertise commended the new drafting. For example Lord Patel suggested that 'the Government have made a greater contribution to public health and health gain than any government in decades'.[21] Nonetheless some other non-aligned peers expressed concerns—for example the academic Lord (Robert) Skidelsky condemned the provisions as an 'assault on freedom', and became one of a small group who sought unsuccessfully to overturn or weaken the ban.[22]

Non-Party Amendments and their Motivations

Compared to opposition parties, non-party parliamentarians propose relatively few legislative amendments. But, as shown in Table 6.1, their contribution to the case study bills was nonetheless substantial. Indeed, across our whole period of study the number of non-party amendments proposed was very similar to that from government backbenchers (see Table 5.1 in Chapter 5), and these were distributed in a very similar way. The number varied significantly by bill, with some of the biggest and most controversial bills—Health, Corporate Manslaughter, Public Bodies, and Welfare Reform—unsurprisingly attracting the largest numbers. Almost all of the 'single group' amendments on the Corporate Manslaughter Bill resulted from the determined initiative by Lord Ramsbotham on deaths in custody, further described below. On the Health Bill there were many co-sponsored amendments which mostly came from a small group, including Lord Skidelsky, opposing the smoking ban. Under coalition the number of non-party amendments increased sharply, and there was a particular rise in those co-sponsored with party peers (though notably co-sponsored amendments made up a majority in both parliaments). The non-party amendments in 2010–12 were concentrated on the Public Bodies Bill and, particularly, on the Welfare Reform Bill, which jointly accounted for around two thirds of the total across all 12 bills.

Of course, in contrast to party amendments, almost all (97 per cent) of those shown in Table 6.1 were proposed in the Lords—where the great majority of non-party parliamentarians hold their seats. In the Commons there were just four amendments co-sponsored by Richard Taylor on the Health Bill, and a small handful by members on other bills. In the Lords, the great majority of amendments (as

Table 6.1 Non-party amendments proposed by bill and chamber

	Commons			Lords			Total		
	Single group	With others	Total	Single group	With others	Total	Single group	With others	Total
2005–10 parliament									
Identity Cards	0	0	0	11	1	12	11	1	12
Health	0	4	4	8	57	65	8	61	69
Corporate Manslaughter	0	0	0	36	9	45	36	9	45
Further Education and Training	0	0	0	4	3	7	4	3	7
Employment	0	3	3	0	0	0	0	3	3
Saving Gateway Accounts	0	0	0	0	0	0	0	0	0
Energy	0	5	5	0	0	0	0	5	5
Total (2005–10)	0	12	12	59	70	129	59	82	141
2010–12 session									
Identity Documents	1	0	1	0	9	9	1	9	10
Savings Accounts	0	2	2	0	0	0	0	2	2
Budget Responsibility	0	0	0	0	0	0	0	0	0
Public Bodies	0	0	0	6	49	55	6	49	55
Welfare	0	0	0	94	175	269	94	175	269
Total (2010–12)	1	2	3	100	233	333	101	235	336
Grand total	1	14	15	159	303	462	160	317	477

Note: A non-party 'group' refers here to one of the following three categories: Crossbench, bishop, other non-party. The 'with others' columns include cooperation between parliamentarians from different non-party groups as well as those sponsored jointly with party actors. All figures exclude amendments co-sponsored by the government.

shown in Table 6.2) were sponsored by Crossbenchers, with far fewer involving bishops and other groups. Just two bishop-only amendments were proposed (on the Further Education and Training Bill and the Welfare Reform Bill respectively), and in the 2005 parliament there was only one amendment co-sponsored by a bishop. But in 2010–12 the number of such co-sponsored amendments significantly rose, to 23.

In previous chapters we have asked what drives amendments from different groups of parliamentarians, and have concluded that multiple motivations exist. Opposition frontbenchers move many amendments that are simply 'information seeking' (i.e. 'probing'), while others are used to 'signal' to those outside parliament, or as part of 'gameplaying' by shaming or embarrassing the government. None of these are immediately focused on changing policy in the bill. While government backbenchers also engage in information seeking, and some signalling (which increased under the coalition), a higher proportion of their amendments are sincere attempts at policy change. Non-party parliamentarians are not motivated to play games or embarrass the government, and they have limited incentives to 'signal' to those outside parliament (not least because most of them are unelected), though some signalling to outside groups may occur. Particularly given their lack of policy support, they do use probing amendments to understand better the policy provisions in a bill, and to get ministers to explain their proposals on the record. Otherwise non-party amendments largely represent straightforward attempts at policy change.

To understand these policy-focused motivations better it is useful to consider more broadly what non-party parliamentarians seek to achieve through their work in parliament. Clearly the small number of non-party MPs elected have constituency interests to represent, and may also have particular policy areas to defend—the obvious example being Richard Taylor on health policy. In the Lords the motivations of bishops and Crossbenchers are rather different from each other—and wide-ranging, given the diversity of members within these groups.

The bishops are the only members of the Lords with any formal sense of geographic representation, through their diocese. They also clearly see themselves as representing faith interests—in quite a broad sense—and bringing a moral dimension to debates. Their presence is particularly felt on 'conscience' issues such as assisted dying or embryo research. Nonetheless most major Lords debates will include a contribution from a bishop—whether on issues where the church has a clear and direct interest (e.g. education) or not. Where the church does have a clear interest, bishops may feel moved to propose amendments—for example, those on the Further Education and Training Bill concerned the role of the Learning and Skills Council in supporting students' spiritual and moral needs. But more generally, the Lords is considered better able than the Commons to resist 'populist' policies, and to protect the interest of vulnerable minorities—such as asylum seekers, prisoners, or benefit claimants. The bishops see themselves as having a particular role in this regard. As one interviewee suggested, 'I think you will find ... where the bishops have intervened, that quite a lot of that will be in terms of particular groups within society that ... don't have enough of a say themselves'.

Table 6.2 Non-party amendments proposed and success of non-party-initiated strands

	Amendments proposed by actor	Strands initiated by actor			% of total successful strands in parliament
		Strands initiated	Of which successful	% success of initiated	
2005–10 parliament					
Crossbench alone	56	11	1	9	1
Bishops alone	1	0	0	n/a	0
Other non-party alone	2	0	0	n/a	0
Joint non-party	3	1	0	0	0
Non-party with party	79	38	3	8	2
Total involving non-party	141	50	4	8	2
Total for all actors	2,389	1,161	169	15	100
2010–12 session					
Crossbench alone	99	31	0	0	0
Bishops alone	1	1	0	0	0
Other non-party alone	1	0	0	n/a	0
Joint non-party	1	0	0	n/a	0
Crossbench with party	210	64	8	13	6
Bishops with party	11	5	0	0	0
Crossbench and bishops with party	11	4	0	0	0
Other non-party with party	2	0	0	n/a	0
Total involving non-party	336	105	8	8	6
Total for all actors	1,972	889	131	15	100
Both parliaments					
Non-party group alone	160	43	1	2	0
Joint non-party	4	1	0	0	0
Non-party with party	313	111	11	10	4
Total involving non-party	477	155	12	8	4
Total for all actors	4,361	2,050	300	15	100

Note: The figures for non-party amendments exclude any co-sponsored with the government; all amendments with a ministerial sponsor are included within the 'total for all actors'. Of the 477 non-party amendments, 66 (14%) were agreed to, of which 4 (0.8% of the total) were neither subsequently overturned nor purely overturned an earlier amendment (as described in Chapter 3).

The role of the Crossbenchers is different, and necessarily—given the group's larger size—also more varied. This group is seen as the main repository of expertise in the Lords (although there are also numerous acknowledged experts on the party benches). Many of its members remain well networked within their professions, bringing specialist knowledge in science, the law, the arts, business, and so on. The various former civil servants and diplomats can be seen as experts in the practice of government itself. Hence Crossbenchers seek to inject a greater degree of rational, evidence-based policy-making, drawing on their own and others' expertise. Like the bishops, in some cases this expertise involves working with the vulnerable—for example through the medical professions, or voluntary organizations. Such Crossbench interests were particularly visible through interventions on the Welfare Reform Bill. A fairly small group of Crossbenchers, often working jointly, were responsible for most of the large number of non-party amendments on this bill. Disability campaigners Baroness (Tanni) Grey-Thompson, a former Paralympic athlete, and Baroness (Jane) Campbell of Surbiton, herself severely disabled, each sponsored over 100 amendments. Lord Low sponsored 45 amendments (though only one as lead—described below), while Lord Best sponsored 31. In total, the 269 proposals on the bill involved 22 Crossbenchers.

As already indicated, the environment in which the Crossbenchers operated changed significantly post-2010. Their increase in proposed amendments coincided with a new status as the key 'pivotal' voters in the Lords, showing recognition both inside and outside the group of their new importance. One Labour interviewee suggested that 'Crossbenchers didn't throw their weight about too much against a [Labour] government which could be sufficiently well challenged by the political forces in the Lords', but under coalition 'several of them think that there is a greater duty upon them to challenge the government'. This could be seen as reflecting an enhanced Crossbench motivation to ensure that government was held to account. Under Labour, amendments from this group were relatively few, and often on fairly small, relatively uncontroversial matters. They rarely resulted in government defeats—Lord Ramsbotham's amendments being very much an exception. But under the coalition one Lords interviewee even suggested that 'the only votes that count here are [those of] the Crossbenchers', because the government had sufficient peers to override solely Labour opposition.

This new situation altered Lords dynamics substantially. Compared to the previous period, subtler opposition tactics were needed if the government was to be defeated, or persuaded to back down, due to a long-standing resistance by Crossbenchers to taking sides in party disputes. As a Labour interviewee said of the group under coalition, 'if I'd put down, as a frontbencher now, an amendment, they really can't vote for it ... so it's quite important that either a Crossbencher puts their name to it, or at least a Labour backbencher'. Hence a good deal of Labour's energy went into working with individual non-party peers (particularly Crossbench experts, but sometimes also bishops), and encouraging them to propose amendments, in order to maximize support across the House. Another interviewee said of opposition strategy in this period that 'if they're scoring political points they want it to be "Labour has defeated the government", but if they actually want to change something then a Crossbencher's much more likely to win over the government'. Part of this is also about attracting government backbench support. As a senior Conservative described with respect to the previous period of Labour government:

If you're going to get Labour peers to rebel it is much easier to do it if they feel that they're participating in a cross-bench (in the wider sense) initiative, than if they're being 'suckered' into rebelling to support the opposition. So historically getting amendments tabled in the Lords by Crossbenchers is a very good device for precipitating good-quality debate and indeed rebellion on the government benches.

This does open up a risk that Crossbenchers get drawn into opposition party 'signalling' or 'gameplaying', though most will take care to avoid such risks. Post-2010 some on the coalition side claimed that the new political situation had 'politicized the Crossbenchers', or that they were 'being totally used by Labour'. From the Crossbenchers' point of view, their amendments (or signatures to amendments) demonstrated that there was sincere and serious concern on an issue. Rather than the group becoming politicized, many members saw this as seeking to depoliticize key arguments and bring expert judgement to bear.

Evidence of Non-Party Influence on the Case Study Bills

Earlier chapters have emphasized the extent to which legislative influence cannot be measured solely through success of amendments. We have seen how the opposition classically has a function of 'issue politicization', in terms of determining which topics get parliamentary time and media attention, and forces government to explain its policy on the record. Government backbenchers meanwhile play a large part in parliament's 'power of anticipated reactions', and also contribute through something akin to Lukes's (1974) elusive third face of power (as introduced in Chapter 1), by ministers internalizing their desires. In addition, government backbenchers, and more occasionally opposition members, can exercise influence through the policies that they choose *not* to oppose. That is, by providing counteractive pressure against others who might seek to challenge the government. Some of these same patterns are seen with respect to non-party parliamentarians. However, they have other more unique contributions as well—most notably depoliticizing debates, bringing expertise to bear, and brokering compromises.

Encouraging informed debate

As already indicated, previous work has emphasized the role of non-party parliamentarians in affecting the overall tone and content of debate, not just specific decisions. Because such members must individually make up their minds how (and whether) to vote based on of the facts presented and quality of argument, debates in the Lords are less partisan and more evidence-based than they would otherwise be. The need to appeal to—or at least not to offend—Crossbenchers and other non-party peers contributes greatly to the difference in tone between it and the House of Commons. This influence is wholly unquantifiable, but very important.

Non-party parliamentarians influence debate not only through listening, and assessing the evidence, but also by actively contributing. The views expressed by authoritative non-party figures can influence the views of others, both inside and outside parliament. For example a former Cabinet Secretary commented to us that 'if you have been what I was, and if you speak fairly rarely in the House, when you do stand up and speak people listen, because they think you've got something to say'. Another Crossbencher explained that 'if you prove your expertise in the chamber, then people remember that and it carries a lot of weight'. If members of this kind suggest that the government's case is weak, this will be taken seriously. As an outside group representative put it, 'if you manage to persuade Crossbenchers that your argument is legitimate, I think that helps persuade other people'.

The bishops are widely seen in this way, despite their own votes only very rarely affecting outcomes. One peer suggested that in terms of debates (here with particular reference to the Welfare Reform Bill) the bishops:

have various kinds of importance. One is that, obviously, they have some moral authority and if it's a matter of morality, and quite a lot of this treatment of poor people is an issue of morality, they're more authoritative than a layperson. But also because they will influence some Crossbenchers, they demonstrate the respectability of the argument, and . . . there would be some feeling within government that churchgoing people up and down the land might respect what the bishops [say].

Echoing these sentiments, another peer said of the bishops that 'if they can stand up and say, "it is immoral to do this to the poorest people in society", that's powerful'.

Individual non-party peers can thus contribute to an 'issue politicization' function, in terms of bringing particular issues to attention—but unlike with respect to the opposition, this is clearly politicization strictly with a small 'p'. These members serve to take the party politics out of issues, rather than inject it. Indeed, more broadly, the bishops and Crossbenchers are the primary guardians of the House of Lords' well-known 'less partisan' culture when compared to the Commons, and encourage rational, evidence-based debate.

Non-party amendments and policy change

We have already seen that non-party parliamentarians proposed a relatively small number of amendments to the case study bills in the 2005–10 parliament, and substantially more in 2010–12. Table 6.2 shows these figures broken down by type of non-party parliamentarian, alongside the number of distinct legislative 'strands' initiated by such amendments, and their degree of policy success.[23] In line with figures in earlier chapters, the number of amendments that were actually agreed is very small—particularly once those overturned at later stages are excluded. But we get a fuller picture by looking at legislative strands.

Notably, while the number of amendments proposed by non-party parliamentarians was broadly similar to that of government backbenchers, the number of strands that these initiated (155) was only around half as great, and just 12 such strands resulted in change to the bills.[24] One reason for the small number of non-party-initiated strands is obvious: because most such parliamentarians sit in the Lords, while most bills start in the Commons, they often by necessity join initiatives started by others. But even in the Lords, non-party parliamentarians sometimes step in to strands initiated by others (particularly the opposition) only at the later stages. This was particularly the case under Labour. Some examples of both patterns are provided below. Hence, like government backbenchers, non-party parliamentarians' success in achieving change through their amendments is not fully captured by looking at the strands that they initiated. They often play an important part in cross-party pressure for change (as discussed in Chapter 9).

In 2005–10 there were just 50 non-party-initiated strands, of which four succeeded. Two followed Lord Dearing's intervention on the Further Education and Training Bill, which resulted in significant government concessions. Under existing rules only higher education institutions had degree-awarding powers, although they could 'franchize' these to further education (FE) colleges offering two-year 'foundation degrees', from which many students progressed to complete their final year at the university. This bill sought to give FE colleges power to award their own degrees. But there had been little consultation on this proposal, which several interviewees described as having come 'out of the blue'.

The bill began in the Lords, and at committee stage Dearing tabled an amendment to restrict the provision, in particular to prevent such institutions from themselves 'franchizing' to others, and to guarantee that students studying for foundation degrees could still progress to university. Concern on such points was widespread, with similar amendments tabled by the Conservative frontbench, the Liberal Democrat frontbench, and Labour backbencher Baroness (Diana) Warwick of Undercliffe—then Chief Executive of Universities UK, an umbrella group representing the university sector. Dearing's intervention further underlined that these concerns were not party political, and that they had expert backing. His amendment was the widest-ranging of those tabled, and he went on to press the points at two subsequent stages.

The initial committee stage amendment was not passed, but was proposed again at report stage, with the other three groups (who largely abandoned their own amendments) indicating their support. Ministers clearly realized that their policy was at risk, and brought forward concessionary amendments, to (as Dearing had proposed) conduct a review within four years, and to enable franchising power to be withheld. Draft guidance was also circulated on the operation of the policy to peers. Dearing declared himself only partly satisfied, but again held fire on his amendment. By third reading revised guidance had been circulated, specifying that only FE colleges with a six-year record of delivering their own foundation degrees would be eligible for franchizing powers—which Lord Dearing described as 'extremely helpful' (this provides a clear example of a policy concession not written into the bill itself).[25] The final sticking point was whether students would be guaranteed the ability to progress to a higher education institution. Here a third reading amendment from Dearing elicited a ministerial promise of a government amendment in the House of Commons. Dearing responded by 'assur[ing] the Minister that we will give him every possible help in drafting the amendment that he promised us', and at Commons committee stage a change was indeed agreed to make progression arrangements compulsory.[26]

This case is notable in several ways. Most obviously, it illustrates the power of a non-party peer who is an established expert to negotiate change, and visibly to unite the parties. Second, it provides an example of agreeing substantive change by outward consensus—there having been no defeats, or even divisions, on Dearing's amendments. Because the changes occurred relatively non-confrontationally, through intervention by a widely respected Crossbench expert, the government avoided being seen to give in to opposition parties. As one opposition frontbencher who chose to drop amendments in favour of these ones put it, 'undoubtedly we knew that the government would usually listen to Ron Dearing'.

Non-party peers were distinctly cautious in challenging government policies under Labour. The opposition—and particularly the Liberal Democrats, given their view that they were unfairly disadvantaged by the Commons electoral system— clearly considered it legitimate to use the Lords to sometimes exert quite strong policy pressure. But because Crossbenchers have no elected representation at all, and members operate very much as individuals, they have greater concerns about triggering confrontation. Hence one interviewee described the Crossbenchers as a distinctly 'soft opposition'. Many other non-party interventions in this period were more low-level, and less successful. For example on the Health Bill the large number of interventions seeking to limit the smoking ban were not proposed with any particular expectation of success, given that MPs had spoken clearly in a free vote. On the same bill Crossbencher Lord (Adrian) Palmer proposed an amendment that prescription drugs should be labelled with their actual cost to the NHS, to improve public transparency. This was pressed at two subsequent stages, but found relatively little support. At report stage the minister referred to the 'very considerable practical problems and costs' that could result, while at third reading Baroness Finlay of Llandaff used her medical expertise to question the policy.[27] Although Lord Palmer's proposal attracted some sympathy, he spoke from no particular position of professional expertise and could not succeed in gathering a coalition of support for his idea. These examples indicate how non-party parliamentarians working as isolated individuals—unlike Lord Dearing—will tend not to gain much traction.

A notably assertive and successful Crossbench initiative during Labour's time in office was Lord Ramsbotham's expert intervention on the exclusion of deaths in police and prison custody from the Corporate Manslaughter and Corporate Homicide Bill. Ramsbotham was not alone in these concerns, as indicated above and in earlier chapters. Two senior Labour backbenchers proposed amendments at Commons report stage to remove the exemption from the bill (both MPs being chairs of key committees that had expressed concerns, as further discussed in Chapter 8). Their amendments were supported by the opposition, but rejected by ministers. Conservative frontbencher Dominic Grieve subsequently declared himself 'convinced that the Minister will have to revisit the matter when the Bill comes back from another place [i.e. the House of Lords]'.[28] These predictions proved correct, and during the bill's Lords passage the matter of deaths in custody became a major controversy.

At committee stage Lord Ramsbotham jointly sponsored an amendment with the Conservative frontbench to extend the new offence to deaths in custody. This was resisted by the minister. Ramsbotham's proposals were withdrawn, but he returned to the issue at report, with both opposition frontbenches, and some Labour backbenchers, in support of his amendments. The government was defeated, with the size of the defeat (223 votes to 127) aided by 36 Crossbenchers choosing to follow Ramsbotham's lead, while only one voted against. But the government urged MPs to overturn the amendments, and they did so.[29]

In the majority of intercameral disputes this would have been the end of the matter, but Ramsbotham went on to propose the amendments again at repeated rounds of ping-pong, in a stand-off between the chambers which ran from February to July 2007.[30] Initially the government offered minor concessions, to enable the Secretary of State to impose a duty of care over deaths in custody by future secondary legislation—which did not satisfy the Lords, as there was no guarantee that such a power would be used. Ultimately personnel changes in government seemed crucial to resolving the issue in the Lords' favour. The bill was initially handled by the Home Office, under Tony Blair's Home Secretary John Reid; but when Gordon Brown became Prime Minister in June 2007, Jack Straw was made Secretary of State for Justice, with responsibility for the policy.[31] He privately suggested a deal, and subsequently proposed Commons amendments which wrote deaths in custody into the bill itself. These were welcomed by MPs (including the opposition, and movers of the original Labour backbench amendments), who questioned only whether the change would come into effect quickly enough. On the bill's final return to the Lords Ramsbotham initially proposed a maximum delay of three years, but following ministerial assurances concluded that 'it would be churlish to press for more'.[32] The Lords hence agreed the bill, which came into force in 2008. The extension to deaths in custody occurred in 2011.[33]

This was an unusually assertive stance for a Crossbencher, as acknowledged publicly by Ramsbotham himself.[34] Interviewees told us that concerns were expressed privately by 'a number of elderly distinguished Crossbenchers'. But others clearly welcomed Ramsbotham's determination. Interviews suggested that some in government were privately happy to see these changes, but that ministers had faced considerable pressure from the police and prison service to resist them. This hence provides another example of conflicts over legislation inside government (as discussed in Chapter 3) ultimately being resolved through its public scrutiny in parliament, and of a nonpartisan expert boosting the legitimacy of a call for a change in policy.

We have seen that non-party parliamentarians took on a potentially pivotal role under coalition. But because the coalition was numerically far stronger in the Lords than Labour had been, it had fewer imperatives to compromise. Labour sought to maximize the chances of achieving policy change by encouraging non-party peers more often to take a lead, and the number of such initiatives greatly increased. Nonetheless this group initiated very few successful strands. Table 6.1 showed that there were large numbers of non-party amendments on both the Public Bodies Bill and particularly the Welfare Reform Bill. All eight successful non-party initiated strands were on the former and several of these are illustrated in other chapters.[35] On the Welfare Reform Bill such members had less evident success. Here we discuss one example of a non-party peer playing a key role in bringing about change to the bill. Further less successful examples are discussed in the 'limits of non-party influence' section below.

The intervention by disability rights campaigner Lord Low (whose concerns at second reading were noted above) followed a classic pattern of a Crossbencher bringing convincing expertise to bear. The bill replaced the previous Disability Living Allowance (DLA), payable to disabled people, with a new Personal Independence Payment (PIP). Under the new benefit, the 'mobility' component would be removed from care home residents. Concerns were raised from the early stages of the bill, and an amendment from the Labour frontbench at Commons committee to reinstate eligibility was defeated. In a separate move, Lord Low was commissioned by disability charities to chair an independent review into the change. Its report, published during the Lords committee stage, concluded that the eligibility should be retained (Independent Review of Personal Mobility in State Funded Residential Care 2011). Having taken evidence from key stakeholders, and produced a lengthy analysis, this had weight. In response to a further Labour amendment in Lords committee the minister indicated that the Low report was being considered. At report stage Low himself co-sponsored Labour's amendment to reinstate the benefit, and the government responded by tabling its own amendments to this effect. Introducing these, the minister explained that the government had 'considered in detail the excellent report produced by the noble Lord, Lord Low'.[36] Again in this example a significant concession was won by a Crossbench expert, allowing the government to climb down in the face of evidence—without a single defeat having taken place. Again, because Lord Low picked up a policy proposal begun in the House of Commons, this influence is not visible in Table 6.2 as a Crossbench-initiated strand.

Non-party parliamentarians as brokers

Non-party parliamentarians in the Lords are at times numerically pivotal, but we have also seen that they can help to take the heat out of arguments and to negotiate compromises between party groups.

One even more explicit example of a Crossbencher acting as an 'honest broker' between government and opposition concerned the central controversy on Labour's Identity Cards Bill, on the degree of compulsion in obtaining an ID card when applying for a passport. Argument on the topic went to an unusually drawn out five rounds of ping-pong, on repeated opposition amendments headed by the Liberal Democrat frontbench, with some Labour backbench support—whose goal was to prevent individuals who applied from having to be entered onto the national identity register. These amendments were overturned by the Commons four times. When the bill returned to the Lords for the fifth time former Cabinet Secretary Lord (Robert) Armstrong of Ilminster (who prior to that was Permanent Secretary in the Home Office) intervened, despite having played no part in previous debates. He proposed a compromise amendment, whereby individuals applying for a passport would be able actively to opt out. This was initially rejected by the minister, and became the subject of another government defeat.[37] But when the bill returned to the Lords yet again ministers accepted an alternative compromise from Armstrong, which allowed an opt out to individuals applying before 1 January 2010—in effect delaying the wholesale introduction of ID cards until after the general election. This compromise gained the support of opposition frontbenchers and allowed all sides to claim a victory. As one key protagonist put it, 'everybody saw that accepting an amendment from a Crossbencher was a way of not climbing down: a way out for both the government and the opposition'; thus government was 'accepting arbitration, if you like'. Subsequently, of course, the identity cards scheme was scrapped by the incoming coalition government.

Although this Crossbench intervention was essential to resolving the dispute, it is once again not visible from Table 6.2, since Armstrong joined the legislative strand only at a late stage of ping-pong. Like other examples above, including those of Lord Ramsbotham and Lord Low, this demonstrates that the relatively low success rate for Crossbench-initiated strands downplays this group's important contribution.

The limits of non-party influence

Returning to the highly contentious Welfare Reform Bill, it is notable that not a single opposition-led amendment was agreed on division in the Lords. But there were nonetheless eight Lords defeats. Seven of these were led by non-party peers, and (as discussed in Chapter 5) the eighth by a government backbencher. Hence the bill demonstrates a high point in non-party assertiveness. But this assertiveness was not matched by policy success. A key characteristic of the bill was the extent to which the Labour opposition took a back seat in challenging the government, seeking instead to encourage non-party peers to do so. This was partly because non-party peers had a better chance than the opposition of gathering a winning majority in the chamber (given their pivotal position, and Crossbenchers' reluctance to join overtly partisan initiatives). But this tactic was also an indicator of the Labour opposition being in 'conflicted mode' (as discussed in Chapter 4). The events on this bill demonstrate that non-party parliamentarians' ability to press policy change has clear limits.

There were six Crossbench-led defeats on the bill, headed by three different members. Following his concerns expressed at second reading, Lord Patel sponsored two initiatives on time restrictions for Employment and Support Allowance. As described in Chapter 4 one of these, which had previously been rejected in the Commons, came to be resolved by a fairly small concession negotiated with Labour frontbencher Lord (Bill) McKenzie; the other explicitly sought to exclude cancer patients from the time limits, and elicited no more than a ministerial promise to keep thinking about the issue. Two further initiatives from Baroness (Molly) Meacher focused on the bill's effects on children and young people, both picking up proposals previously made by the Labour frontbench in the Commons. One concerned rates of Universal Credit payable to those with responsibility for disabled children, while the other concerned access by severely disabled young people to Employment and Support Allowance. Like Lord Patel's amendments these were both rejected by the Commons, citing financial privilege; on return to the Lords both elicited only a fairly vague ministerial promise to keep matters under review.

There was marginally more movement on proposals pursued by Lord Best to limit the effects of the so-called 'bedroom tax', which would remove benefit from social housing tenants judged to have a 'spare room'. The initial heavy defeat (by 258 votes to 190) took place at report stage, on an amendment co-sponsored by a bishop, plus Labour and Liberal Democrat backbenchers with strong welfare credentials. Its intent was to prevent the restriction applying to those with no more than one extra room, which went further than the opposition's Commons amendments— these having focused more narrowly on the impact on certain groups. When the bill returned to the Commons Best's amendment was overturned, with financial privilege once more invoked. However, the minister did announce £30m of funding for discretionary housing payments by local authorities.[38] As this fell well short of Lord Best's proposal he provoked a second defeat during Lords consideration of Commons amendments, on a narrower amendment exempting groups such as war widows and foster carers. But this was also subsequently overturned, again with nothing more than the promise of a government review.

Lord Best's inability to attain further concessions on this contentious policy illustrates important dynamics about the bicameral relationship, particularly under coalition—though with clear resonance in examples under Labour above. Like all non-government parliamentarians, Crossbenchers need support from others for policy success. While being pivotal in the Lords, Crossbench amendments ultimately require Commons approval, which depends (as discussed at greater length in the previous chapter) on the government backbenchers who are pivotal in that chamber. Some of those closely involved in Best's initiative had hoped that it would elicit Liberal Democrat backbench support, given the junior opposition party's clear discomfort with the policy. But in the words of one, 'a sufficient rebellion did not occur'. On this bill even Labour was in a difficult position given the overall context of 'austerity' and public support for benefit cuts. Without wholehearted support from party groupings, there were clear constraints on what expert Crossbenchers could achieve.[39]

The final non-party defeat on this bill demonstrated sharply the controversy that can be generated if non-party peers (or potentially unelected peers in general) challenge populist government policies. This concerned the benefit cap, with the key amendment led by the Bishop of Ripon and Leeds. It provides an even clearer example of non-party parliamentarians taking a stand on policy matters considered 'too hot to handle' by the parties. Although such concerns applied throughout the bill, the benefit cap in particular was known to be publicly popular.[40] During the initial Commons passage the Shadow Work and Pensions Secretary made clear that Labour in principle 'support[ed] a cap on benefits'.[41] The opposition frontbench tabled a series of amendments to modify the cap, but pressed only one to a division. In the Lords it sought to maintain this discipline. But the day before the Lords debated the policy in committee a letter appeared in the *Observer* newspaper signed by 17 bishops, protesting that the benefit cap 'could push some of the most vulnerable children in the country into severe poverty'.[42] The first bishop-led amendment was then debated in committee, to exclude Child Benefit from the calculation of the cap—maintaining the emphasis on children previously made by the Bishop of Leicester at the bill's second reading, referred to above. This was one of the issues that the Labour frontbench had raised in the Commons, but chosen not to press.

Proposing the amendment the bishop pointed to research by the Children's Society, an organization with close Church of England connections, which suggested that over 200,000 children would be affected by the cap, compared to just 70,000 adults. It was greeted sympathetically by both the Labour frontbench and the relevant Liberal Democrat co-chair, but rejected by the minister on cost grounds, and because 'work should always pay more than out-of-work benefits'.[43] The amendment was withdrawn at this stage but pressed to a division at report stage, requiring Labour to decide how to instruct its peers to vote. A Labour frontbencher told us that this led to 'some particularly intense discussion' between representatives in the two chambers. In the event, the party whipped in favour of the bishop's amendment, and thus contributed to a narrow defeat.[44] This led the minister to accuse Labour of 'extraordinary ... flip-flopping' when the bill returned to the Commons, at which point MPs overturned the defeat.[45]

The bishop's intervention hence largely failed, with the government simply promising some transitional support for those affected. Nonetheless, an interviewee from an outside group suggested that it mattered, 'in terms of what it represented, in a sense—[demonstrating that] this wasn't a party political issue, this was a moral issue'. Yet in the process the bishops, alongside the Labour opposition, suffered significant public criticism. A week after the vote the *Sun* newspaper carried a front-page story entitled 'Red Revs out of Touch with Britain Today', suggesting that 'the Church of England has long lost its moral compass' and that the bishops should be removed from the Lords.[46] This kind of response further helps to explain why non-party peers usually exercise significant caution.

Non-party parliamentarians and anticipated reactions

We have seen that a good deal of effort by both government and opposition peers now goes into appealing to Crossbenchers in particular. One interviewee described such members as 'the seducible group in the Lords', while another commented that 'everyone is wooing them hard, all the time'. This is partly about numbers, and Crossbenchers' potential as pivotal voters. As a third interviewee put it, if the government's argument is weak, the Crossbenchers will 'sniff it out and vote with [the opposition]'. But the parties' interest is also about trying to attract the support of key respected individuals, whose voices can be influential over how others choose to vote. Hence ministers seek to maximize non-party parliamentarians' assent to their policies, and in turn to minimize their dissent—in terms of amendments, speeches, and in the division lobbies.

This means that non-party parliamentarians play a significant role in parliament's power of anticipated reactions, and can be quite crucial when devising parliamentary 'handling strategies'. In addition to considering the responses of opposition politicians and government backbenchers, ministers and civil servants will think carefully about the likely attitudes of high-profile or particularly expert non-party peers. At times such members may be contacted individually and asked their views before legislation is introduced.

Post-introduction, non-party parliamentarians continue to have relatively ready access to ministers. During Labour's time in office the weekly Crossbench meeting became a target for ministerial attention, with senior ministers often offering to speak and answer questions about their legislation. This practice continued under coalition. In addition, the open meetings held in the Lords as a part of government handling strategies, to which all peers are invited, are particularly well used by non-party parliamentarians (because many others will prefer to be briefed on policies in their party meetings). Non-party peers also frequently engage in smaller private meetings with ministers and their officials to discuss concerns on bills.

All of this forethought, and consultative activity, takes place 'in the shadow' of possible defeat in the Lords should a prominent Crossbencher choose to propose an amendment, or sufficient non-party peers side with the opposition. As one Crossbench peer explained, 'there is the implied threat in the [public] discussions you have, but all the real business is face-to-face with ministers, that's what achieves the change'. Indeed he suggested that:

The exchanges on the floor of the House have value as rehearsals for meetings outside the House, they have value in mustering votes if you've got to that critical stage, but you can't negotiate really very successfully on the floor of the House.

Hence behind-the-scenes meetings with this group, like those with opposition frontbenchers and government backbenchers, can be important to ministers in easing the passage of their bills and often encourage government amendments.

Support for the government

When considering the policy impact of parliament, it is important to emphasize that parliamentarians' influence comes not only through their challenge to government policy, but also how the government benefits from their support. This is obvious with respect to government backbenchers, as was discussed in Chapter 5. But it also applies to other groups, including 'expert' non-party parliamentarians. In 'handling', ministers and civil servants are therefore hoping not only to neutralize non-party opposition, but where possible to garner non-party support.

A good example of such support occurred on the coalition's Budget Responsibility and National Audit Bill. This bill was largely consensual, though there were some challenges from the opposition frontbench following its introduction into the Lords (resulting in minor concessions, as described in Chapter 4). We will see in Chapter 8 that the government was keen to emphasize the legitimacy of the proposals by citing the support of the Commons Treasury Committee. Likewise, in arguing for the proposals as they stood, ministers pointed to the support of prominent Crossbenchers. These included in particular two former senior civil servants: Lord (Andrew) Turnbull, who was Cabinet Secretary 2002–05 and before that Treasury Permanent Secretary, and Lord (Terry) Burns, who had also held the latter post. Both peers spoke in support of the bill at its second reading—Turnbull describing the OBR as 'an idea whose time has come' and Burns offering 'wholehearte[d] support'.[47] Members of the bill team kept in close and regular contact with them during the bill's passage through the Lords, and the minister, Lord (James) Sassoon, cited their views in support of the government's position several times during the parliamentary debates.[48] Hence while challenges of the kind made by Lord Dearing or Lord Ramsbotham can prove uncomfortable for government, and result in policy reversals, the endorsement of policy by prominent non-party parliamentarians can also be important to government success.

Conclusions

The most visible actors at Westminster are government and opposition, and sometimes government backbenchers; but non-party parliamentarians also play an important role—largely out of the public eye, through the House of Lords. Indeed these members have the potential to be pivotal in Lords divisions, and hence to determine which issues are sent back to the Commons for decision.

Non-party parliamentarians have relatively little support, in terms of staffing and other resources, and face the challenge (unlike party members, who can generally rely on their whips) of personally deciding how to vote on each piece of legislation. Nonetheless, the Crossbenchers and bishops both have well-developed forms of organization in the Lords. Collectively members of these groups table similar numbers of amendments to government backbenchers, and their proposals are likewise largely sincere—though they also make some use of 'information seeking' (probing) amendments to force ministers to explain their policies on the record. Non-party parliamentarians vote far less often than others, and never as a cohesive bloc, which introduces significant uncertainty to the process of agreeing legislation. Their contributions once again demonstrate how legislative influence can take many forms, from visible and on the record—through changes to bills—to more invisible and immeasurable effects.

This chapter has demonstrated at least six interrelated forms of power exercised by non-party parliamentarians in the legislative process:

- First, they have a crucial role in encouraging rational and well-informed debate. These members are to a large extent the keepers of the 'less partisan' culture of the Lords, not only through their own behaviour but the effect that their presence has on the wider nature of debate. Many bring specific expertise, which can be influential on the views of others, and few will be impressed by partisan point-scoring. Non-party peers hence help to ensure that government proposals are subjected to challenging scrutiny, and that ministers are held to account and required to provide convincing explanations. This is connected not only to such members' expertise, but also their ability to be pivotal in the Lords. As a former opposition frontbencher explained in interview, 'when you're putting an amendment forward, you gauge the sort of feeling you're getting around the House', and a frontbencher will know that they are 'on to something' if they are 'getting lots of nods from the Crossbenchers'. In contrast, if Crossbenchers are 'sitting there stony-faced' this offers distinctly less comfort. As Russell and Sciara (2009) noted, the Crossbenchers both change the tone of debate and serve as a kind of political jury in assessing the arguments made in the Lords.

- Second, non-party parliamentarians can occasionally play an 'issue politicization' function, bringing topics in bills to wider attention. However, while opposition members 'politicize' issues in the party sense, non-party parliamentarians act to take the party politics out of issues—which can make their arguments challenging for ministers to rebut.

- Third, and connectedly, non-party parliamentarians have an impact through amendments. On occasion they lead the call for changes to bills. This kind of expert intervention occurred, for example, when Lord Dearing negotiated concessions on key points in the Further Education and Training Bill, and Lord Low proposed changes to the Welfare Reform Bill. Both of these peers were respected, and seen as strictly nonpartisan, and their interventions succeeded in defusing partisan arguments, without a single government defeat. It is more risky and unusual for non-party peers to push hard in confronting government policy. The clearest example under Labour was Lord Ramsbotham's determined intervention—which also ultimately succeeded—on deaths in police and prison custody on the Corporate Manslaughter and Corporate Homicide Bill. Here he had support not only from opposition parties, but key government backbenchers. This kind of assertive intervention by non-party peers became more common under the coalition, when the Labour opposition actively sought to work with such members to achieve its policy goals, and their amendments triggered more government defeats. But the 2010 government was numerically stronger in the Lords, and few of these nitiatives succeeded.

- Fourth, non-party peers can sometimes act explicitly as 'brokers' in resolving policy disputes. The potential for nonpartisan and expert 'arbitration' was particularly clear in the case of Lord Armstrong's intervention on the central issue of compulsion on the Identity Cards Bill, where government and opposition in the two chambers had been at loggerheads. Non-party amendments, like those of government backbenchers, hence sometimes resolve rather than spark legislative disagreements.

- Fifth, as a consequence of these other potential means of influence, non-party parliamentarians also play an important part in parliament's power of anticipated reactions. As non-aligned voters, the government will seek to avoid their criticism and encourage their support. Hence second-guessing the views of this group is very important to government 'handling' of legislation. Significant effort goes into managing the government's relationship with Crossbenchers—through open meetings, ministerial attendance at the group's meetings and numerous private conversations.

- Finally, like government backbenchers, non-party parliamentarians may exercise their power not just by choosing to oppose the government, but also by choosing to support it. Ministers realize that if Crossbench experts can be convinced to speak up for their policies this will be persuasive on the views of others. Given that such members are completely free to decide what they say, and when and how they vote, their endorsement can be important to the success of government policy.

Despite all of the above, there are of course clear limitations on the influence of non-party parliamentarians. They rely on the ability to build alliances with others to achieve their policy goals, and members without proven expertise (such as Lord Palmer on the Health Bill) may well fail to do so. Ultimately, Labour's efforts to enlist the support of nonpartisan experts on the coalition's Welfare Reform Bill tested the limits of non-party activism. While Crossbenchers and bishops were able to tackle some sensitive issues that were awkward for the opposition, the legitimacy of unelected peers seeking to block policies of an elected government could readily be questioned, particularly on policies popular in the country. Without adequate support from government backbenchers (and with even the opposition behaving cautiously), what non-party parliamentarians could achieve was limited.

This period illustrates a conundrum. As one such member put it in interview, 'the Crossbenchers are in a very difficult position because our *raison d'être* is that we're not politicians ... the more you are seen to be operating in a political manner, the more you undermine any effectiveness you have as a Crossbencher'. Many non-party peers are respected figures, whose most important contribution is perhaps through changing the minds of others. They seek to take a principled stand based on expertise and (particularly in the case of the bishops) morality; but if they can be painted as oppositionalist this risks raising awkward questions about their own role, and indeed about the House of Lords as a whole.

Notes

1. Figures from the British Election Study, as cited in Denver, Carman, and Johns (2012).
2. There is little polling evidence on attitudes to independent members of parliament, but in a 2007 survey 83 per cent of respondents felt that 'presence of numerous independent members' was important to 'how legitimate the House of Lords is as a chamber of parliament' (Russell 2013: 248).

3. In addition, the House of Commons Speaker traditionally runs as a non-party candidate, and sits independent of party. But while the Speaker presides over legislative proceedings, s/he by convention does not propose amendments and does not normally vote.

4. This is the commonest model of independent MP at Westminster (Cowley and Stuart 2009), but the numbers were higher than usual in 2005–10 due to the expenses scandal. Non-expenses-related departures from the parties included Clare Short (Labour) and Lady Sylvia Hermon (UUP).

5. Previously this term had a broader meaning, also encompassing members of minor parties and those who had chosen temporarily not to take a party whip.

6. 'Criteria Guiding the Assessment of Nominations for Non-Party Political Life Peers', House of Lords Appointments Commission, http://lordsappointments.independent. gov.uk/selection-criteria.aspx [accessed 20 June 2016].

7. The bishops are also not formally 'peers'; however, we use this term to refer to all members of the Lords.

8. Although the Lords Spiritual (Women) Act 2015, passed following the Church of England's decision in 2014 to allow women to be appointed as bishops, established a 10-year period during which female bishops are to be fast-tracked into the Lords ahead of their more senior male colleagues.

9. Russell and Sciara (2009) surveyed membership of national parliaments around the world in 2006 using the Inter-Parliamentary Union database, and found only five other parliaments claiming to include more than 30 independent members: in Iran, Malawi, Russia, Syria, and Uganda. However, the status and definition of such members will clearly differ widely.

10. Russell (2013) also includes a survey of the compositional methods of second chambers around the world based on the Inter-Parliamentary Union database in 2011. Of 74 second chambers, just 16 included no elected members. While a further 20 second chambers included some appointed members, in most cases these were the minority.

11. Though one bishop does sit in the Manx parliament.

12. See particularly discussion of Senator Brian Harradine in Costar and Curtin (2004), Russell (2000), and Sharman (1999).

13. 'The Lords Spiritual', Church of England, https://www.churchofengland.org/our-views/the-church-in-parliament/bishops-in-the-house-of-lords.aspx [accessed 22 December 2015].

14. House of Lords Hansard, 19 December 2006, column 1907.

15. House of Lords Hansard, 9 November 2010, column 75.

16. House of Lords Hansard, 31 October 2005, columns 28–9.

17. Ibid., column 34.

18. House of Lords Hansard, 13 September 2011, column 673.

19. Ibid., column 643.

20. House of Commons Hansard, 29 November 2005, column 219.

21. House of Lords Hansard, 1 March 2006, column 294.

22. Ibid., column 307.

23. Strands were introduced in Chapter 2 and are fully discussed in Appendix A.

24. Eight of these were on the Public Bodies Bill, two on the Further Education and Training Bill (as discussed immediately below), one on the Health Bill and one on the Energy Bill; 10 of the 12 explicitly changed policy, while two dealt with more procedural matters.

25. House of Lords Hansard, 6 March 2007, column 138.

26. Ibid., column 145.
27. Lord Warner, House of Lords Hansard, 26 June 2006, column 1057; ibid., 4 July 2006, column 150.
28. House of Commons Hansard, 4 December 2006, column 118.
29. While there had been a handful of rebels when the Commons voted on Andrew Dismore's amendment at report stage, there were no rebels during consideration of Lords amendments. In a speech at the first round of consideration, Dismore described himself as still 'concerned'; he also pointed out that the minor concessions offered by the government at this stage might have been sufficient to satisfy the Commons, but it would probably need to do more in order to satisfy the Lords (House of Commons Hansard, 16 May 2007, columns 676–8). This seemed to indicate that government rebels were not opposed to further Lords intervention, despite voting against the Lords amendments.
30. His amendments during this process account for 33 of the 66 non-party amendments agreed to the bills, all of which were overturned during consecutive stages of the ping-pong process.
31. It is an interesting quirk of these case studies that John Reid held two cabinet posts that gave him initial responsibility for the policy in a bill, which subsequently passed to a successor who negotiated a change of policy. The other example is the Health Bill, as described in Chapters 3 and 8.
32. House of Lords Hansard, 23 July 2007, column 558.
33. '"Deaths in Custody" Corporate Manslaughter Crime Created', *BBC News*, 1 September 2011, http://www.bbc.co.uk/news/uk-14739854 [accessed 22 December 2015].
34. He stated that 'I am aware that some noble Lords are understandably ... cautious that in proposing [the amendments] again [at repeated rounds of ping-pong] I am entering into dangerous constitutional waters' (House of Lords Hansard, 25 June 2007, columns 450–1).
35. Examples of non-party participation in successful strands on the Public Bodies Bill include the involvement by Lord (David) Pannick in the initiative to protect judicial bodies, described in Chapter 5, the intervention by Baroness Finlay on the Chief Coroner, described in Chapter 7, the proposal by Lord Ramsbotham on the Youth Justice Board, described in Chapter 8, and the removal of schedule 7, described in Chapter 9.
36. Lord Freud, House of Lords Hansard, 17 January 2012, column 560.
37. There was a completely equal split among the non-party peers on this division: 27 Crossbenchers and three bishops voted for the amendment, and 29 Crossbenchers and one bishop against.
38. House of Commons Hansard, 1 February 2012, column 919. Although not written into the bill, we were assured by one housing specialist that it was 'definitely a concession'.
39. Of course, the claims of Commons financial privilege on Lords defeats on this bill also weakened the chamber's bargaining power—but these bigger political factors mattered substantially more.
40. A poll in January 2012 found that 71 per cent supported the principle of a benefit cap, compared to 14 per cent who disagreed. See 'A £26,000 Welfare Benefits Cap?' Survation Survey Checks Public Opinion (Daily Star Sunday)', available at http://survation.com/a-26000-welfare-benefits-cap-survation-survey-checks-public-opinion-daily-star-sunday/ [accessed 18 March 2016].
41. Liam Byrne, House of Commons Hansard, 15 June 2011, column 885.

42. 'A Bishop's Duty is to Speak out Against the Benefits Cap', 20 November 2011.

43. Lord Freud, House of Lords Hansard, 21 November 2011, column GC345.

44. By 252 votes to 237, with five bishops voting in favour and none against.

45. Chris Grayling, House of Commons Hansard, 1 February 2012, column 871.

46. Trevor Kavanagh, 30 January 2012.

47. House of Lords Hansard, 8 November 2010, columns 22 and 37.

48. For example, House of Lords Hansard, 8 November 2010, column 46; 1 December 2010, column GC199; 31 January 2011, column 1192.

7

The Role of Outside Pressure Groups

All previous chapters have focused on actors that are part of parliament itself and, in the case of ministers, the civil servants that support them in nearby Whitehall. Yet parliament clearly does not exist in a vacuum. Bills debated there are often the product of wider discussions involving various external actors, particularly a diversity of so-called 'pressure groups'.

Academic studies of the role of such groups in the policy process, particularly in Britain, have tended to focus on their contact with government. In contrast public policy scholars have often downplayed groups' relations with parliament, and even parliament's role overall. But such impressions can be misleading. Outside groups play a hugely important role in informing legislative debates in parliament today. Lobbying parliament can be an important means for such groups to either press for policy change, or to defend policies previously negotiated successfully in Whitehall. The input of groups can be essential for non-government parliamentarians, who lack the specialist support to scrutinize government policy alone. For government, the lobbying of parliament by outside groups can hence be key to determining how their legislation is received. To understand the ways in which parliament influences government legislation it is thus necessary to pay proper attention to the contributions of outside groups.

In this chapter we use evidence from the case study bills to illustrate some of the diverse roles that outside pressure groups play in the Westminster legislative process. As in other chapters, we begin by identifying what we mean by 'pressure groups'. These bodies are very diverse, and their cataloguing and classification has been the focus of much academic attention. Having established the basics, we go on to review what the existing academic literature suggests about the parliamentary role of such groups. Next we touch very briefly on how these groups organize themselves, particularly with respect to engagement with parliament. Then we look at group attitudes to the 12 case study bills, and consider pressure group strategies in seeking to influence legislation. In the final main section, as in other chapters, we consider patterns of parliamentary influence—in this case in terms of how they are facilitated by outside groups, using some examples on the case study bills for illustration.

Pressure Groups: Who Are They?

Pressure groups are both extremely numerous and very diverse. Grant (2000: 7–8) defines them as 'groups that seek to influence public policy', describing them as

Legislation at Westminster. First edition. Meg Russell and Daniel Gover. © Meg Russell and Daniel Gover 2017. Published 2017 by Oxford University Press.

'organised entities that have characteristics such as a defined membership, stated objectives in relation to public policy and, often, a paid staff working to attain those objectives'. This wide definition can encompass anything from individual private sector organizations to industry-wide groups, trade unions, voluntary organizations, and public sector bodies. Jordan and Maloney (2007) estimate that there are many thousands of such bodies in the UK, or perhaps even hundreds of thousands if those at the local level are included. Not all engage directly with parliament but, when it is considering legislation of immediate interest, many do. There is also a blurry line between pressure groups and other forms of external bodies that engage with parliament, such as commercial 'lobbyists' (who may work *for* pressure groups), think tanks and other research organizations, and media bodies (such as campaigning newspapers). We primarily focus on pressure groups in the classic sense, but some other external actors are also mentioned in our discussion.

Given the diversity of pressure groups, they can be classified into various different types. At the most basic level, they are clearly drawn from different sectors: private, voluntary, or public. Another term frequently used to describe such groups is 'NGO'—or non-governmental organization—though some are better described as 'quangos' (i.e. quasi non-governmental organizations, such as regulators, and various publicly funded bodies). The relevance of the coalition's Public Bodies Bill to the latter groups should be obvious from earlier chapters. Another very simple form of variation is between large and small organizations; a pressure group may range from a tiny core of volunteers to a large transnational company, or a well-funded charity with hundreds of members of staff. Some of the largest organizations are so-called 'umbrella groups', representing a number of others across a sector. Classic examples include the Trades Union Congress (TUC), whose member organizations are individual trade unions, and the Confederation of British Industry (CBI), representing businesses.

Beyond this, much academic energy has gone into classifying groups into different, more complex types. These debates can become very involved, but some of the divisions used are helpful in understanding external influences on parliament. One distinction scholars make is between 'primary' and 'secondary' pressure groups, based on whether or not the group's primary purpose is to represent interests to policy-makers. Thinking about the 12 case study bills, it is easy to identify examples of both. For example the group NO2ID was established specifically to oppose the Labour government's identity card scheme, and is thus a primary group. Other primary groups active on this bill included Liberty (founded as the National Council for Civil Liberties in 1934), and Justice (a campaign group specializing in law reform and human rights). Likewise the groups Action on Smoking and Health (ASH) and the Freedom Organisation for the Right to Enjoy Smoking Tobacco (Forest), took opposing positions on the provisions on smoking in the Health Bill, and Greenpeace sought to influence debates on the Energy Bill. On these same bills, examples of 'secondary' groups would include professional organizations such as the Law Society and British Medical Association (BMA), the energy regulator Ofcom and individual energy companies.

A final well-known distinction which is useful when considering group activity is that between 'insider' and 'outsider' groups (Grant 2000, Page 2002). This boundary is again somewhat blurry and disputed, but nonetheless captures something useful about group tactics. Insider groups are those that are well connected with policy-makers, and often operate behind the scenes, in particular through exercising influence privately in Whitehall. Outsider groups do not enjoy such good access, and may instead seek to influence policy-makers' thinking indirectly—via routes such as petitions, demonstrations and the mass media. In any policy field there may be a range of groups, from well-connected insiders to noisy, outspoken outsider protest groups. As an official but very public forum, parliament can be targeted by groups from across this spectrum.

Established Understanding of Pressure Groups and Parliament

There is a very large body of literature about pressure groups and their policy role, both in the UK and internationally. As noted in previous chapters, the public policy literature has often given a central place to such groups (e.g. Baumgartner and Jones 1993, Rhodes and Marsh 1992, Sabatier and Jenkins-Smith 1993). Some scholars in this field have hence downplayed the role of parliaments in policy-making, instead seeing the key relationships as those between ministers and civil servants on the one hand, and outside groups on the other. A particularly striking example was Richardson and Jordan's (1979) study describing Britain as a 'post-parliamentary democracy'. The claim here was that de facto control over agreeing policy had largely shifted to 'policy networks' comprising pressure groups and government actors. As Richardson (1993: 88) later argued, 'policies are peace treaties between government and the affected interests. Like all peace treaties which have been difficult to negotiate, there is a marked reluctance to renegotiate them once they have been agreed.' This implied that, policy having been carefully negotiated in Whitehall, there was little space left for parliament to intervene.

Richardson and Jordan's book provoked a minor backlash by scholars in legislative studies. In a volume edited by Rush (1990), various members of the Study of Parliament Group specifically explored the relationships between parliament and pressure groups, drawing on a 1986 survey of 253 such organizations. In some regards the survey results seemed to back up the assumption of parliament's relative lack of status for groups. For example, when asked to rank which bodies were important to influence on policy, respondents placed parliament fourth, behind civil servants, ministers, and the media. But the study also found clear evidence of groups targeting parliament. For example with respect to legislation, Norton (1990b) noted that almost half the groups surveyed had contacted MPs to propose amendments, and nearly three-quarters had contacted members of the House of Lords. Of course this study is now relatively dated, and no similar survey has since been conducted.

The volume by Judge (1993) was designed specifically as a riposte to Richardson and Jordan. He argued that any deals struck between groups and Whitehall insiders over legislation were necessarily framed by the subsequent need to get parliamentary approval (i.e. anticipated reactions)—hence it would be wrong to assume that parliament was weak. Judge also provided evidence of groups themselves using parliament to attain influence, and drew attention to further subtleties in these relationships. For example, parliament may provide access for those—perhaps typically 'outsider'—groups who were not party to Whitehall discussions, or who failed to convince the government of their case. In line with this, today's public policy scholars note that '[w]hen groups are excluded at one level, they "venue shop", or seek influential audiences in other venues' (Cairney 2012: 13). In addition, even Richardson and Jordan (1979: 135) had noted that parliament may act as an 'insurance policy for groups', to defend previous gains, otherwise new groups opposed to the initial deal may successfully lobby parliament to reverse the policy. A key term used by pressure groups scholars is 'counteractive lobbying', which communicates how group intervention is often required specifically to prevent influence by opposing groups (Austen-Smith and Wright 1994). This makes the legislature a potentially important battleground.

It is fairly obvious that groups pursue these activities as a means of gaining policy influence. Meanwhile for parliamentarians, groups can provide essential support. This relationship is now commonly modelled as one of resource exchange, whereby groups provide parliamentarians with expertise, research, public profile, and even financial resources, in return for the influence that may be achieved (e.g. Binderkrantz, Christiansen, and Pedersen 2015). Since non-government parliamentarians lack the kind of expert resources available to the government through the civil service, they can find these relationships very useful. The Hansard Society's study of the legislative process noted that outside groups 'provided valuable expertise to the government and Parliament alike', and were particularly important in more technical policy areas (Brazier, Kalitowski, and Rosenblatt 2008: 41). Interventions by groups were noted as important to building cross-party alliances, either around amendments or in support of the government's plans.

The comparative volume which sought explicitly to link public policy and legislative studies approaches suggested that group interaction with parliaments will vary across policy fields—being more likely on issues where groups either disagree with the government or disagree with each other (Mezey 1991, Olson and Mezey 1991). These authors also noted that group activity will encourage parliamentary engagement with policy. Other comparativists highlight international variation. Binderkrantz (2014: 527) comments that, while 'Congress has always been central for American interest groups, parliaments have traditionally been rather neglected by European groups'. But she suggests that this has changed, and that groups now see 'parliamentary contacts … as a crucial part of the action repertoire' (ibid.: 530). Although the area remains underresearched, there are various reasons to believe that relationships between groups and parliament have strengthened in the UK since Richardson and Jordan's (1979) work was published. Authors have previously pointed to changes likely to encourage this, including a growth in groups and group resources, a reluctance by governments in the 1980s to engage with such groups, growing backbench independence, and establishment of the select committees (Grant 2000, Norton 1999). More recent changes include evidence-taking by Commons public bill committees (Thompson 2015) and the reform of the House of Lords (Russell 2013). The Lords in fact was always seen as particularly useful to groups, as a less party-controlled chamber than the Commons, where many peers work part-time and maintain direct relationships with outside bodies of various kinds (Baldwin 1990). The more assertive 'no overall control' chamber that developed after 1999 offered clear opportunities for groups.

The question of pressure group influence on policy is a thorny one, which has been much discussed by scholars. For example Olson (1965) classically expressed concerns about how small and well-organized groups (e.g. those representing business) may have significant advantages over larger and less organized ones (e.g. the low paid or unemployed). Hence there may be particular concerns about 'insider' groups and relatively closed 'policy networks'. Some may fear that such groups have unfair access to parliament; but it can clearly also open the process up to 'outsider' groups. Recent research suggests that UK parliamentarians in fact pay significantly more attention, for example, to charities than to business interests (Parvin 2007). More generally, it is very tricky to assess how much influence groups gain by access to parliament, or indeed other venues—just as it is difficult to assess parliament's impact on policy overall. Academics focusing on pressure group influence note three key problems: that groups use various public and private channels to seek influence; that they do so at various stages of the policy process; and that groups' most important achievement may be using counteractive lobbying against the claims of other rival groups (Dür 2008, Dür and De Bièvre 2007). The last of these means that influence may be largely invisible if the net result is continuation of the status quo.

There are hence many interesting questions about pressure groups' relationships to Westminster, not all of which can be addressed in one short chapter. This topic was not the central focus of our study, and is ripe for fresh research. Here we focus on a fairly narrow subset of questions about interactions between parliament and pressure groups on legislation, as demonstrated by our case study bills. In particular, we consider how groups facilitate work by the various parliamentary actors that were discussed in previous chapters, and how they contribute to the different forms of parliamentary influence that those chapters identified. We also touch on some normative questions about the benefits and risks of group interaction with parliament, and the extent to which group and parliamentary influence can actually be separated.

Pressure Group Organization

Before turning to outside group engagement with the 12 case study bills, some basic indication of how groups organize themselves, and their contact with parliament, may be useful. As might be expected given the diversity of groups, this varies considerably.

Some groups have both a high degree of interest in public policy and the resources to engage with it thoroughly, which is reflected in their internal organization. One such example is the TUC, representing around 50 trade unions. It has a large research capacity, with several of its internal departments structured around particular areas of public policy: for example economic and social affairs, equality and employment rights, and EU/international policy. It also has a dedicated campaigns and communications department, including a parliamentary officer whose entire purpose is engagement with MPs and peers. Arrangements at the umbrella industry group the CBI are similar. Large groups such as these which are strongly geared towards public policy clearly have greater capacity than others to engage with parliament. As one representative of such a group told us, having substantial resources meant they could keep a 'hawk eye' on developments and quickly identify relevant bills.

In contrast, many groups have much smaller teams responsible for policy work, while others have no dedicated staff at all, making their ability to engage with legislation limited. 'Secondary' groups often preserve their resources largely for service delivery; more radical campaign groups, in turn, may depend only on a small pool of voluntary labour. One interviewee told us of his experience working for a relatively small pressure group, which had struggled merely to gather the e-mail addresses of key parliamentarians in order to send them briefing material on a bill. Even a representative of a group with moderate capacity for political work explained that 'bill work is incredibly intensive', and that consequently the organization had decided not to get involved with a highly contentious bill that might otherwise have been of interest.

The work conducted by parliamentary officers and campaign staff in outside groups can take various forms—from behind the scenes to very visible, from highly targeted to relatively scattergun, as discussed further below. Some groups contact parliamentarians directly, while some will encourage their members and supporters to do so. This 'lobbying' has moved gradually from face-to-face contact (i.e. literally seeking to meet a member in the parliamentary lobby) to letter writing and post-card campaigns, and today to electronic contacts of various kinds. In addition some outside bodies work with interested parliamentarians collectively through providing the secretariat for All-Party Parliamentary Groups (APPGs—further touched upon in Chapter 9).[1] For example the APPG on Carers is supported by the charity Carers UK, and the APPG on the Chemical Industry by the Chemical Industries Association.

Recent years have seen new forms of group organization. For example pressure groups now often collaborate, sometimes building relatively formal and outward-facing coalitions in order to achieve shared policy goals. Work on the Welfare Reform Bill was coordinated by a Disability Benefits Consortium—comprising around 50 organizations such as the Royal National Institute for Blind People and charities Mencap (which supports those with learning disabilities) and Age UK (supporting older people). Likewise a coalition in support of the smoking ban in the Health Bill included campaign group ASH, charities such as Cancer Research UK, British Heart Foundation, and Asthma UK, and professional bodies such as the BMA and Royal College of Physicians. Such coordination not only helps to minimize duplication of resources by groups, but also to avoid those with similar goals being played off against each other by opposing groups of parliamentarians. Another important development is online organizing, which allows some pressure groups to mobilize wide networks with relatively few resources. Notably there was significant public pressure on the Public Bodies Bill organized by very new groups. These included the general internet campaign platform 38 Degrees, and hastily formed bodies such as Save Our Woods, on the forestry provisions in particular. This is further discussed below.

Pressure Group Responses to the Case Study Bills

As already seen in previous chapters, some of the case study bills were far more controversial than others, and in many respects this was reflected in the attitudes of outside groups to the bills. Indeed, in line with Olson and Mezey's (1991) observations, often bills were contentious inside parliament precisely because they were so heavily contested by groups outside. In several cases policy changes made in parliament indicated one set of groups winning out over another.

Chapter 3 discussed how there is often extensive consultation before bills are introduced to parliament. Such consultations during the policy formulation stage are designed in large part to test the views of external groups. In addition, established 'insider' groups often have more informal interaction with civil servants at this stage. Hence one interviewee, very much echoing the comments of Richardson (1993) above, suggested that 'parliament gets the consequences of departmental discussions with pressure groups'. Policy-makers value group input at the early stages partly because such groups bring expertise, but also because they have the capacity to mobilize opinion—through their members, supporters, and the media—and hence can play an important role in legitimating policy decisions. Conversely, if policy is devised against the wishes of key groups this can create difficulties for government, which are often played out in parliament.

Where there was consultation on the case study bills, many relevant groups had hence already fed in their views. For example Labour's Employment Bill had been preceded by the Gibbons review, which achieved near consensus between trade unions and employers on key aspects. A government insider told us that 'everybody was sort of agreed that we wanted dispute resolution which is not too expensive, shouldn't be too formal, and the more that this can be done before we get to tribunals the better'. Consequently these parts of the bill proved uncontentious in parliament.[2]

Some bills were more obviously controversial. For example the Corporate Manslaughter and Corporate Homicide Bill had been pushed by the trade unions, but business groups were resistant. The government initially set out its proposals in a consultation paper, which received over 150 responses from bodies as diverse as the TUC, British Retail Consortium, Construction Industry Council, and Victim

Support (Home Office 2000a, 2000b). Subsequently the Home Affairs and Work and Pensions Committees (2005), reported jointly on the draft bill, having collected oral and written evidence from a similar range of groups. Those representing victims (e.g. the Marchioness Contact Group and Disaster Action) strongly welcomed the proposals, while employers' groups (e.g. the CBI) were more cautious. On the contentious question of whether the offence should apply to deaths in police custody, there was conflict between the Association of Chief Police Officers (ACPO), which supported the government's intention to exempt such deaths, and others such as the Prison Reform Trust and Inquest (a small charity supporting families of those who have died in custody and detention), which lobbied against the exemption. The exemption remained in the government's bill as introduced, but pressure from the latter groups contributed significantly to a parliamentary reversal (as described in Chapter 6).

Some similar patterns were seen on the Health Bill. Provisions on healthcare-associated infections, the management of controlled drugs, and the supervision of pharmacies were relatively uncontentious—attracting attention from groups like the Royal College of Nursing, and Royal Pharmaceutical Society primarily during the policy formulation stage. In contrast on the smoking ban there was fierce competition between groups on opposing sides. A consultation on these provisions attracted over 57,000 responses, including pro-forma letters instigated by the BMA and Cancer Research UK (Department of Health 2005). Once the bill reached parliament the anti-smoking coalition argued that the government's proposals for a partial ban did not go far enough, and pushed for a comprehensive ban. By contrast, Forest, alongside the tobacco manufacturers, sought to limit the ban.

Sometimes bills are highly contentious and political, but outside groups more united. A good example among the case studies was the Welfare Reform Bill—which, like other coalition bills, had necessarily been subject to relatively little prior consultation. One of the central policies in the bill, of introducing Universal Credit, had been inspired by think tank the Centre for Social Justice (2009)—established by Iain Duncan Smith, who later became the Secretary of State responsible for the legislation. This proposal itself was not particularly controversial, but there was concern from a wide array of groups representing different sections of society about its implementation, and about other proposals, such as the new Personal Independence Payment for disabled people and changes to the child maintenance system. Somewhat contrary to Olson's (1965) classic claim of imbalance in favour of more privileged groups, very few outside organizations had a direct interest in presenting the opposing view. Nonetheless an interviewee from one charitable organization did tell us that they faced dilemmas—not lobbying as hard as they would have liked against benefit cuts, which were seen to be publicly popular, for fear of losing support and donations.

Some bills attracted relatively little parliamentary attention from outside groups because there were few clear interests at stake. The Budget Responsibility and National Audit Bill was uncontroversial and affected few outside interests directly, though groups such as the Institute for Fiscal Studies and UK Statistics Authority provided evidence to the prior select committee inquiry (Treasury Committee

2010). There was also relatively little visible lobbying on the Savings Accounts and Health in Pregnancy Grant Bill, though the charity Barnardo's supported Paul Goggins's attempt to protect looked-after children from the abolition of the Child Trust Fund (see Chapter 4). The previous Saving Gateway Accounts Bill had attracted attention from groups such as the British Bankers' Association and Building Societies Association, who sought to make the planned savings scheme more favourable for their members to operate. Others, most notably Carers UK (which worked successfully with Stephen Ladyman—see Chapter 5), sought to ensure that particular types of individual were entitled to open accounts. But when the scheme was subsequently abolished even those groups that had supported it recognized that outside pressure was likely to fail, due to the government's determination to cut spending.

Finally the Public Bodies Bill illustrates how certain types of group can fail to lobby, even where they are significantly affected. This bill implemented the so-called 'bonfire of the quangos', making it a direct threat to many publicly funded outside groups. In some respects it was therefore a natural candidate for significant group activity. But bodies threatened with abolition clearly felt constrained to raise their voices. One non-government parliamentarian commented that 'people working for these organizations did not have the courage to speak to people in the House of Lords or their elected representatives' and were 'frightened'; another claimed that the groups affected 'were under very strict instructions not to communicate with us'. Meanwhile, interviewees claimed, some voluntary sector groups were silent because they stood potentially to gain from the bill. This left much of the initiative with parliamentarians themselves, with fairly isolated pressure on some issues from outside groups—including 38 Degrees on forestry, and the Royal British Legion on the threat to abolish the Chief Coroner (both discussed below).

Pressure Group Strategies During the Legislative Process

Unlike parliamentarians, outside groups clearly cannot directly table amendments to legislation. They can, however, enlist parliamentarians in furthering their goals. Those groups which are happy with the government's position will wish to defend the policy in a bill against amendment. Others that were not listened to at the earlier stages (because they were excluded, deliberately ignored, or simply didn't engage) may use parliament to seek a change in the government's position. In this section we review briefly some of the lobbying strategies used by outside pressure groups, before turning in the next section to some of their more specific interventions on the case study bills.

We have seen that pressure groups often engage with policy well before bills are introduced into parliament, and many seek to do so afterwards. When groups devise their strategies, the question of engaging with government or parliament is not a simple 'either/or'. In line with long-established assumptions, a former minister told us that 'all serious lobbyists, and the organizations seriously affected by legislation, are relating to the civil service long before the bill comes anywhere near parliament'. Likewise, a group representative commented that 'we saw working with officials as more the way to get things through'. Nonetheless, groups viewed parliament as an important route to influence, where other politicians (as well as the media, and public opinion) could be mobilized in support of their view. One group representative suggested that parliament can be used 'where there has been a failure process beforehand'. Another commented that he would go to the government and say 'we like these bits [of a policy] and will support you on that; we don't like those bits and we're going to talk to the opposition'. This indicates how groups can play off one set of politicians against the other, and seek to win gains both privately and publicly.

Once a bill has been introduced to parliament some groups operate very openly, and are frequently acknowledged on the record, while others continue to operate largely behind the scenes. This kind of divide can be seen in some of the cases already discussed. For example the anti-smoking group ASH was mentioned 40 times during the parliamentary debates on the Health Bill, compared to just eight mentions of the pro-smoking group Forest and four of the Tobacco Manufacturers' Association. Nonetheless we were told that tobacco company representatives were often present in the room at committee stage, and they were assumed to be working with the group of peers who sought to limit the ban (as mentioned in Chapter 6). This could be seen as a classic insider/outsider split. But the defenders of smoking no longer had safe 'insider' status, and it was their opponents who won the day. Likewise on deaths in custody in the Corporate Manslaughter and Corporate Homicide Bill, victims' groups won out over the more obvious 'insider' interests. And on the highly contentious Identity Cards Bill (and the subsequent Identity Documents Bill) a number of mostly civil liberties groups very publicly opposed the introduction of the scheme and then supported its abolition, while bodies favouring the cards—such as the police and security services—tended to communicate with ministers behind the scenes. Again outsiders used parliament to successfully argue against insiders.

In general, in line with Parvin's study (2007), we found that parliamentarians were rather suspicious of industry groupings. Speaking about the Energy Bill, one interviewee suggested that 'I would reasonably trust Friends of the Earth not to be pursuing any kind of vested interest, because their only goal in life is to pursue a greener and more environmentally friendly society', whereas even with respect to 'green' industry organizations such as the Renewable Energy Association 'I would just want to stop and think ... actually, is this too much about their own members' vested interests?'. Likewise a senior Conservative commented that he would 'beware of those groups that either have an obvious commercial axe to grind, like the tobacco companies, or who really don't represent anyone very much at all'. Some groups will hence have difficulty finding parliamentary proponents. If they manage to strike deals privately with government, but these do not stand up to scrutiny in the public forum of parliament, any such agreements may prove fragile.

A key question for outside groups in deciding their parliamentary lobbying strategy is who to target. Under-resourced or inexperienced groups may struggle with these choices, but those well established in lobbying will tend to have networks of parliamentarians that they know well, and with whom they work on a regular basis. These include, for example, members of relevant select committees, frontbenchers with related portfolios, and backbenchers with a keen interest in the topic. Who groups choose to approach depends to a large extent on what they are trying to achieve. Several interviewees commented that it can be most sensible to work behind the scenes with those on the government side—to get 'respected, authoritative [backbenchers] to speak to the ministers involved'. Yet if a group wants policy change, backbenchers may be more hesitant than the opposition to engage on contentious issues or press amendments to a division. In the Lords, many peers have professional connections to outside groups, and there is much respected professional expertise (particularly on the Crossbenches). Links in that chamber are therefore strong. In choosing between the chambers, groups familiar with the lobbying process recognize that the Commons may be useful for raising the profile of an issue, but the Lords is often where government concessions can be won.

Of course as well as contacting parliamentarians directly, groups often use external campaigns to increase pressure. Hence, for example, in its staunch opposition to the Identity Cards Bill NO2ID guided grass-roots activists on lobbying politicians, writing to the local media, and organizing protests. On the Welfare Reform Bill the single-parent charity Gingerbread coordinated a letter-writing campaign involving over 1,000 supporters. On the Public Bodies Bill 38 Degrees encouraged thousands of opponents of the forestry provisions to e-mail peers. Such approaches can become quite overwhelming for parliamentarians. Speaking about two distinct policy topics, interviewees commented that on 'most of the bills in this area you get very, very extensive lobbying from all sorts of organizations' and 'on any bill like this, you will get hundreds of e-mails and letters pushing various things'. MPs have full-time staff who can help them filter such communications, but most members of the House of Lords do not. In addition, as another interviewee pointed out 'because people don't have constituencies, anybody in the country can lobby any peer'. One interviewee suggested that the new online campaign methods of groups such as 38 Degrees represented a 'paradigmal shift' in lobbying, which a peer described as having a 'really ... profound' effect, that presents quite major challenges for parliament.

Pressure Groups and Parliamentary Influence on the Case Study Bills

Given this book's focus on parliament's influence in the legislative process, a key question here is how outside groups contribute. Previous chapters have considered the contributions of different groups of actors inside parliament, and identified various kinds of parliamentary influence, from visible to relatively less visible. In this section we indicate how outside groups facilitate some of these different actors and forms of influence, illustrated with examples from the case study bills.

Agenda setting and issue politicization

We have seen in previous chapters how parliamentarians can play a role in putting issues onto the policy agenda, and how specific groups in parliament (particularly the opposition) can be important in 'politicizing' issues within a bill. Outside groups are often centrally involved in both types of activity.

The role of groups in getting issues onto the policy agenda is well established in the public policy literature. Examples on the case study bills included the work of the trade unions in arguing for the new offence of corporate manslaughter, and the years of research and campaigning by key outside groups prior to Labour's decision to introduce a smoking ban. We saw in Chapter 5 how government backbenchers used various parliamentary mechanisms to force these matters onto the policy agenda and gain ministerial attention. As well as pressing government directly, or running public campaigns, outside groups frequently support initiatives such as these. For example with respect to the smoking ban, when proposing a private member's bill to control smoking in restaurants in 2003, government backbench MP Gareth Thomas cited research provided by groups such as the BMA and ASH.[3] When sponsoring a Westminster Hall debate on smoking in public places, fellow Labour backbencher Linda Perham thanked the British Heart Foundation and Smoke Free London for providing support.[4] With respect to corporate manslaughter, the trade unions and other outside groups supported Labour backbenchers like Andrew Dismore in using early day motions and parliamentary questions to maintain pressure on government to introduce a bill. As already noted, these kinds of mechanisms are classically seen as weak, but can help to change the parliamentary and public mood, and most also require a public ministerial response. When backbenchers pursue such initiatives, they are more often than not relying on behind-the-scenes support from some kind of outside group.

Once a government bill has been introduced, outside groups have a similarly important role in determining which issues within the bill get 'politicized'. As a civil servant put it, 'it depends whether there are outside lobby groups ... If there is nothing being supplied by a third party organization you don't generally get a lot of action in the Commons chamber'. The response from specialist outside organizations can be particularly important as to how the opposition receives a bill; lack of external pressure for change helps explain why some bills are greeted in 'consensual mode' (as described in Chapter 4). Where groups raise legitimate objections, on the other hand, these will often be pursued by opposition frontbenchers.

Hence while groups recognize the importance of working with influential government backbenchers, they can also form important alliances with opposition frontbenchers in generating doubt about government proposals, and in drawing wider attention towards them. Pressure groups (particularly 'outsiders') and opposition parliamentarians can be outspoken in their criticisms, using the parliamentary arena to try and change the public mood and—connectedly—to raise doubts among government backbenchers. Here one group representative explained to us that the opposition can be 'incredibly important' in achieving changes to government policy:

if you really want to get something debated where the government has taken a particular view then you go to the opposition first and start to get them to put the issue on the table, ask questions, request meetings ... table amendments to pieces of legislation. So that's how you start to create an environment in which you can't be ignored any more, and that creates an opportunity for you to talk to the ministers again and maybe get a slightly more receptive hearing ... all of a sudden you've created a problem for the civil servants who are briefing ministers, because they have to respond ... and then that creates an opening for you to go and have a much more constructive conversation at official level as well.

Examples from earlier in the book include the work of groups such as Inquest and the Prison Reform Trust in highlighting the issue of deaths in custody (Chapters 5 and 6), and the support of Barnardo's for Paul Goggins's high-profile intervention at Prime Minister's Questions on looked-after children (see Chapter 4). Another example of issue politicization by outside groups not previously discussed was the work on the forestry provisions in the Public Bodies Bill by 38 Degrees and others. This case illustrates how the opposition can both be spurred to action by outside groups in politicizing issues in parliament, and greatly benefit from their subsequent support.

When this bill was introduced to the Lords, it included relatively vague provisions to enable the Secretary of State to modify functions in the Forestry Act 1967 and the role of the Forestry Commissioners. There were press rumours that ministers were preparing for 'a massive sell-off of Britain's Government-owned forests' in order to save public funds.[5] At the Lords second reading in November 2010 Labour frontbencher Baroness (Jan) Royall of Blaisdon was one of many peers to express concerns, commenting that '[i]t is hard to conceive why Ministers want such draconian powers, unless it is the Government's intention to dispose of much or all of the Forestry Commission's land'.[6] By early 2011, various bodies had been formed—including both the overarching Save Our Woods, and numerous local groups such as Save the Sherwood Forest and Save Haldon Forest—with much of the coordination conducted by 38 Degrees. This campaign received considerable media attention, and one rally against the plans held at the Forest of Dean was reportedly attended by 3,000 people.[7]

In late January 2011 the government published a formal consultation, which outlined proposals for a new 'mixed-model approach' to forestry management, including for 'commercial operators to take on long-term leases for the large-scale commercially valuable forests' (Forestry Commission England and Department for Environment 2011: 7). By then a 38 Degrees petition opposing the sale of forests had collected over a quarter of a million online signatures, and polling commissioned by the group revealed overwhelming popular opposition.[8] It was in this context that Labour used an opposition day to force a debate on the proposals, and applied further Commons pressure through Prime Minister's Questions (see Chapter 4). By mid February the online petition had reached around half a million signatures, and numerous amendments to the provisions had been tabled for the committee stage in the Lords.[9] At this point the government backtracked—announcing that its consultation was being withdrawn and that the provisions in the bill would be dropped.[10] The Lords minister added his name to the non-government amendments to remove the relevant clauses, and these were passed.

Facilitating informed debate

The previous example was a dramatic one, of external group pressure helping to ensure that a specific topic in a bill reached wide attention, including in parliament. More routinely, diverse groups are essential in ensuring that non-government parliamentarians are well briefed in preparation for parliamentary debates on bills and are aware of any key voices—and important evidence—either in support of or opposition to the government's proposals. Well-resourced groups sometimes provide extensive briefing—one interviewee spoke of doing so on 'every clause at every stage, and every amendment that was tabled, absolutely everything', though admitted that this was an 'extreme case'. Others with less capacity may circulate limited material to just a few interested members. Some groups organize open meetings where parliamentarians are invited to hear the arguments, some hold smaller bilateral briefings, and others work through bodies such as APPGs.

An important means by which outside groups seek to inform parliament on legislation is through evidence to relevant committees. Commons public bill committees accept written evidence on most government bills (which is published online), and where bills begin in the Commons oral evidence sessions are usually also held. For example the public bill committee examining the Energy Bill heard oral evidence from representatives of 17 separate outside groups—including energy companies, environmental groups, and the energy regulator. Although less common, groups can also contribute evidence to relevant select committee inquiries during the formal parliamentary passage of a bill. As further discussed in Chapter 8, the Commons Health Select Committee held a rapid inquiry into the smoking provisions in the Health Bill—which heard oral evidence from various external groups including Imperial Tobacco UK, the Royal College of Nursing and the British Beer and Pub Association. Committee hearings enable groups to present their arguments, and MPs to question them directly. As Thompson (2015) notes, they often lead to parliamentarians quoting group evidence later in the process, to strengthen their case. When debating amendments to the Energy Bill, for example, opposition MPs quoted public bill committee evidence given by groups such as Scottish and Southern Energy and Consumer Focus.[11]

Pressure groups were particularly active on the Welfare Reform Bill, which provides many illustrations of group expertise informing parliamentary deliberations. A search of the parliamentary record found over 100 groups referred to in debate by MPs and peers. Those mentioned particularly frequently were mostly the better resourced groups—including the Citizens' Advice Bureau, well-respected economic think tank the Institute for Fiscal Studies, campaign organization the Child Poverty Action Group, and various charities such as Macmillan (which works with cancer sufferers), Shelter (which focuses on housing issues), and the Children's Society. Although outside groups were referred to for various reasons, one of the most important was referencing expertise and information that they provided, which parliamentarians then used to bolster their arguments.

Looking at these debates, pressure groups were sometimes cited as expert authorities. For example discussing the provisions about the Social Fund (which offered support to people facing hardship), Labour's Baroness (Dianne) Hayter of Kentish Town commented that 'various charities, which know a thing or two about vulnerable people, have ... contacted us about this', going on to quote from briefing materials provided by the charities Crisis, Family Action, Barnardo's, and Scope.[12] Specific facts and figures from outside groups were used by parliamentarians to challenge the government's positions—as for example when MP Karen Buck referred to findings of 'Cambridge university research that was commissioned by Shelter'.[13] Labour backbencher Frank Roy used such information to challenge the minister directly on changes to child maintenance, asking, 'Does she agree with what Gingerbread has said—that 72 per cent of single parents would not be able to come to an agreement and that 50 per cent of those parents would not be able to afford the application fees?'[14] Case studies supplied by outside groups of those likely to be affected were also frequently quoted. Responding to proposals to limit receipt of Employment and Support Allowance, for instance, opposition frontbencher Stephen Timms read from a briefing provided by Macmillan, including the case of 'Chris from Worcester, who was diagnosed with lung cancer' who was quoted as saying: 'It'd really hurt if I lost this money, I'd be in the mire.'[15]

Notably, all of these interventions came from opposition politicians, who—given their heavy responsibility for scrutiny and relative lack of resources—find outside group input particularly valuable. As another Labour frontbencher on the Welfare Reform Bill, Margaret Curran, publicly stated, '[t]he Opposition do not enjoy the same level of support as the Minister does from her officials, so those briefings are greatly appreciated'.[16] An interviewee who had served as a Conservative frontbencher likewise noted how in opposition 'you don't have access to civil service machines so you pick up your ideas from talking to outside groups'. When the smaller Liberal Democrats were in opposition they had even fewer resources, and one former party frontbencher recalled 'sitting in the bill not knowing what I was doing half the time' while 'the ministers all had civil servants handing them notes'. His response was to work with key outside organizations, which 'handed me what to say before I went into the chamber'. Hence outside group support can be very influential in driving frontbench opposition thinking, with these politicians actually dependent to an extent on groups. Nonetheless some interviewees saw this close relationship as positive—one frontbencher commenting that 'part of your job ... in opposition is to be a mouthpiece for legitimate outside organizations'.

Of course, government backbenchers and non-party parliamentarians also work closely with outside groups and use their briefing material. For example a Crossbencher told us that briefing from outside groups on the Welfare Reform Bill 'was really helpful', because some aspects of the bill were 'so complicated'. In summary, a former minister observed:

If you're in government you see, by and large, that the parliamentarians who are raising issues on a bill are actually getting most of their lines from external sources—you know, from NGOs, from industry, from business, from private associations of various kinds ... the world of the lobbyists tends to supply a lot of the information to parliamentarians who are not part of the government.

Furthermore, the government may already be familiar with some of this material, having already weighed up the arguments presented by different groups behind the scenes. But if such groups can provide parliamentarians with evidence that cannot be adequately refuted by government, this may be key to forcing policy change.

A particularly noteworthy example of change driven by external briefing was seen on the Identity Cards Bill, where one of the issues dominating parliamentary debate concerned the cost of the scheme and whether the government's own assessment was accurate. As discussed in Chapter 5, following a Lords defeat calling for a review of costs and benefits, the government accepted a compromise amendment by Labour backbench MP Frank Dobson. Throughout the bill's passage there was a great deal of focus on its cost implications, in part because (as outlined in Chapter 4) it was tricky for the opposition to tackle the principle of identity cards head on, particularly in the Commons. But the widespread parliamentary concern on costs was also greatly fuelled by a report from a cross-departmental group of academics at the London School of Economics (LSE). This estimated the cost of the scheme over 10 years as 'between £10.6 billion and £19.2 billion' (LSE 2005: 5), while the government's own estimate was significantly lower, at no more than £584 million per year.[17] These discrepancies offered considerable ammunition to other outside groups such as Liberty and NO2ID campaigning against the bill. They cited the LSE figures prominently in briefing materials, as did non-government parliamentarians during the debates.

In total the LSE was named 160 times in debates (which is twice as many times as any pressure group found in debates on the Welfare Reform Bill). Such references started when Shadow Home Secretary David Davis claimed at Commons second reading that the LSE estimates 'could raise the average cost of each card ... to £230 a person'.[18] In the Lords, Liberal Democrat frontbencher Lord (Andrew) Phillips of Sudbury commented that 'the only figures that give a convincing indication of what is involved are those estimated by the LSE'.[19] References to the research continued right up to the Commons consideration of Lords amendments stage, when the government concession on costs was agreed.[20] This provision of information from external experts was clearly decisive in strengthening the case of the bill's opponents, both inside and outside parliament. As well as fuelling this specific amendment, it helped to undermine the wider case for the identity cards scheme.[21]

Supporting amendments

Previous chapters have shown that amendments proposed by non-government parliamentarians are often important in driving policy change. The promotion of such amendments is another key activity pursued by outside groups. The survey by Rush (1990) shows that this work has been commonplace for many years. One opposition interviewee even claimed that 'the vast majority of amendments will have been promoted by some outside interest group', while a parliamentary official suggested that non-government amendments are sometimes submitted 'almost on headed notepaper from an external organization'. A group representative suggested that 'there's no point telling people what is wrong with it unless you're offering a solution, so you would always have ready-drafted amendments for people who you thought might be interested'. Not all outside groups do this, as it requires both resources and technical expertise, but they may nonetheless provide briefing and speaking notes in support of amendments that have been tabled.

Parliamentarians clearly differ in their attitudes towards using outside group amendments. One opposition frontbencher described it as 'very rare' that she would adopt such an amendment verbatim, but others commented that when working with trusted groups they would 'usually adopt their wording'. A Liberal Democrat interviewee suggested that 'NGOs have enormous resources to research amendments, to draft amendments for you, to produce stuff and put it forward'.

Sometimes group support in preparing amendments is obvious from the public record. For example in introducing an amendment to the Employment Bill, which would have extended the national minimum wage to employees on ships that were UK-registered or in UK territorial waters, Labour backbencher Baroness (Muriel) Turner of Camden commented that it had been 'drafted by legal advisers at the RMT' (National Union of Rail, Maritime, and Transport Workers).[22] On the Welfare Reform Bill, amendment sponsors likewise referenced 'the Child Poverty Action Group, which suggested both amendments', and 'Shelter, Homeless Link and the National Housing Federation, which have formulated a series of amendments here'.[23] At other times group input was fairly clear from interviews. For example we were told that the Children's Society drafted the bishop's amendment on the benefit cap which led to a Lords defeat on this bill, as well as coordinating the letter by bishops to the *Observer* newspaper (as discussed in Chapter 6). Similarly, Gingerbread worked with Lord (James) Mackay of Clashfern on amendments on the child maintenance provisions (described in Chapter 5). On the Further Education and Training Bill both opposition parties proposed Lords amendments to remove clauses giving the Learning and Skills Council (LSC) new powers to intervene in 'failing' further education colleges, which resulted in a defeat and ultimately significant concessions. We were told that this work was closely supported by the umbrella organization representing the sector, the Association of Colleges.

Often proposers emphasize outside group support for amendments during debate in order to lend greater weight to their arguments. For example on the Health Bill, Liberal Democrat Commons frontbencher Steve Webb commented that one of his amendments, which sought to redefine healthcare acquired infections, 'relates to worries expressed by the Royal College of Nursing [RCN] about the definition'; likewise Conservative Lords frontbencher Earl (Freddie) Howe proposed an amendment to the definition, describing it as 'designed to flag up a concern originally raised by the Royal College of Nursing'.[24] At the same point the government proposed its own Lords amendments, again acknowledging the input of the RCN, which were accepted into the bill with support from both opposition parties.

This example illustrates something else important about the role of outside groups, and particularly their amendments—in terms of their ability to join up initiatives by different parties inside parliament, and between the two chambers. Outside group briefing and support for amendments is in fact often crucial to the very existence of legislative 'strands' as analysed throughout the book. Very similar amendments may be moved by parliamentarians from different groups at different stages, creating the appearance of significant coordination. But sometimes connections exist only indirectly, through the work of outside groups. This was made very clear by some interviewees. For example one peer commented that 'I really struggled to follow the bill through the Commons', and yet despite not having 'any communication whatsoever with anybody in the Commons', she pursued amendments that had begun in that chamber. As another peer said of outside groups, 'if they lose an issue in the Commons then they'll come with the same issue to the Lords'. Such groups therefore play a large part in both bicameral and interparty coordination. They can also sometimes serve as intermediaries between government and opposition, as indicated below.

A final example from the Public Bodies Bill demonstrates how well-respected outside groups can be particularly successful in changing both parliamentary and public opinion. This concerned the challenge led by Crossbench medical expert Baroness (Ilora) Finlay to proposals to abolish the post of Chief Coroner. This post had been created in the previous government's Coroners and Justice Bill 2008–09, and the new government now threatened to abolish it without any prior consultation. Work outside parliament involved campaign groups such as Inquest and Justice (both mentioned above); but the key member of the external coalition was the Royal British Legion, which supports armed forces families—due to its concerns about the effects on military inquests. While some other groups might have been seen as 'outsiders', the RBL was normally very much an 'insider', which is both moderate and highly regarded—including within the Conservative Party.

Finlay expressed her concerns at second reading, and then proposed an amendment at committee stage deleting the Chief Coroner from the scope of the bill. When the minister resisted, she pressed it to a division, resulting in a heavy government defeat (by 277 votes to 165).[25] Subsequently there were numerous private meetings on the issue. The RBL worked closely with parliamentarians behind the scenes, as well as making public statements in support of Finlay's position, and mobilizing supporters to write to their local MPs. In total, the organization was mentioned nearly 50 times during Commons debates. Its campaign attracted significant attention in the traditional media; for example on the day before the Commons second reading the right-leaning *Daily Telegraph* carried a critical article written by the organization's Director General.[26] Nonetheless the Ministry of

Justice was very resistant and a government amendment in Commons committee brought the Chief Coroner back within the scope of the bill. At report stage Conservative backbench MP Andrew Percy proposed an amendment to overturn this, whose rejection generated further press criticism of the government.[27] On the bill's return to the Lords Finlay re-tabled her amendment, making a second defeat very likely. At this point the government proposed its own amendment to reverse the Commons position. Justice Secretary Ken Clarke commented that he had listened to concerns from groups 'including the Royal British Legion', and the group was also cited by the Lords minister.[28] An opposition interviewee on the bill judged the group to have been 'instrumental', while a government insider commented that going 'head to head with the Royal British Legion' could have been a 'PR disaster'. Hence parliament, external media and grass-roots pressure combined to force the government to concede.

Counteractive lobbying and support for the government

All of these examples concern groups seeking to use parliament to change government policy. But we have seen that groups often push in different directions, presenting parliamentarians with competing arguments—which ministers will often have already adjudicated between. Hence group success cannot always be measured in terms of amendments made; an unamended bill is often precisely what some groups want.

A good example of conflicting pressures occurred on the proposals in the Further Education and Training Bill to give degree-awarding powers to further education institutions (discussed in Chapter 6), on which there had been little prior consultation. During the debates, Liberal Democrat frontbencher Baroness (Joan) Walmsley noted that peers had 'been lobbied by both Universities UK and the Association of Colleges, which take diametrically opposed positions'.[29] The Association of Colleges briefed that it was 'delighted' by the proposals, which represented 'a revolution in higher education'.[30] But Universities UK, representing higher education institutions, strongly opposed the move. Whereas the ideal scenario of the Association of Colleges was for the policy to be fully enacted, Universities UK wanted the provision to be dropped.

The universities were in a particularly strong position to lobby because of the number of peers with formal connections to such bodies. Describing the bill's second reading in the Lords (where it was introduced) one interviewee joked that 'every chancellor of every university put their name down to speak'.[31] Government backbencher Baroness (Diana) Warwick of Undercliffe, who was then Chief Executive of Universities UK, was among those who tabled amendments to restrict further education colleges' degree-awarding powers. The government made significant concessions before the bill left the Lords, and watered down the new powers even further in the Commons. In one sense Universities UK was the most successful of the opposing forces, because the bill was significantly amended. Yet the Association of Colleges also viewed the outcome, in the words of one on that side of the argument, as 'a major success'. Although it had previously encouraged ministers to make the change set out in the bill, and would have preferred the policy to remain unchanged, it had also feared a total policy reversal.

In other cases parliament was presented with a much more settled position, where key groups sought to maintain agreements previously reached behind the scenes. This was notably the case with respect to the trade unions and provisions in Labour's Corporate Manslaughter and Corporate Homicide Bill. One interviewee described this bill as having taken 'years and years and years' to reach parliament, under significant union pressure. Having finally got what they had long campaigned for, the imperative for the unions was to see the bill pass. Another interviewee noted that following the bill's introduction to parliament, 'the business bodies were lining up against it', claiming that it would 'stop innovation, stop people taking risks' (see also Gobert 2005). Hence the trade union side engaged in 'counteractive lobbying', briefing strongly in favour of the bill to protect their gains against possible dilution. Indeed, following the Lords defeat on deaths in custody the TUC was so fearful about losing the bill that it circulated material—contrary to pressure from other groups such as Inquest and the Prison Reform Trust—urging peers to allow the government's position to prevail. Nonetheless we were told that some individual trade unions 'weren't good at recognizing that you've got to keep on going for what you've already got', thinking that 'once you've got what you want in the bill that was it, and all the other opposition would melt away like snow'. This is clearly not the case, and lobbying *for* central provisions in this bill may have been important to them remaining intact.

On occasion, support from outside groups can be very important to government in bolstering its case in parliament. It is easy to find examples on the record of ministers using respected groups to legitimize their policy positions, as for example when Baroness Royall commented on the Health Bill that the 'important point is that … the Royal Pharmaceutical Society … is content with the provisions in the Bill'.[32] At times there is even behind-the-scenes contact between government and groups to try and encourage wider support. One pressure group representative recalled, in the context of a government amendment, 'the bill team manager ringing saying, "we're going to put this in, can you brief the opposition to say you support it?" '. Hence groups can be influential in discouraging, as well as encouraging, pressure from non-government parliamentarians. Indeed, reflecting on the Identity Cards Bill, which was heavily amended in parliament following fierce public resistance from some outside groups, but subject to little visible support from others supporting the scheme, a government insider reflected that 'that's the political lesson; there had been a silence and this vacuum got filled'.

Pressure groups and anticipated reactions

Finally, we have emphasized throughout the book that parliament's power of anticipated reactions is an important dimension of its policy influence. That is, government actors carefully think through their bills prior to legislative introduction, to ensure that they will not face resistance—which could result in time-consuming conflicts and possible defeats. Although this is a power held by parliamentarians, their close and interconnected relationships with outside groups—as emphasized throughout this chapter—mean that such groups are key to the government's calculations. The risk of groups encouraging and supporting parliamentary resistance is an important reason for ministers and civil servants to consult with them at the earlier policy formulation stages. Hence one former senior government whip told us that he urged bill teams to speak with outside groups early on to 'cut the flow of amendments off upstream'. In other words, far from indicating parliament's weakness, government contact with groups at this pre-legislative stage is at least partly driven by fears that such groups will feed subsequent parliamentary opposition.

Conclusions

The academic public policy literature has typically assumed that links between pressure groups and the Westminster parliament are fairly weak. In the words of Grant (2000: 15), 'pressure groups tend to cluster where the power is, which in Britain ... is principally at the executive branch of government'. Indeed strong connections between pressure groups and the executive have sometimes been presented as sidelining parliament (e.g. Richardson and Jordan 1979). The relationship between pressure groups and parliament has been distinctly under-researched in recent years, but real-world developments highlighted throughout the book seem likely to have made it stronger. These include the increasing importance of select committees, the establishment of Commons public bill committees, declining party cohesion, and a more assertive 'no overall control' House of Lords which offers real opportunities for policy change.

This chapter has shown that connections between pressure groups and parliament are indeed very extensive when it comes to scrutiny of government legislation. Although such groups engage directly with government at the policy formulation stage—through official consultations, behind-the-scenes meetings, and public campaigns—lobbying parliament is an extremely important complement. Groups whose views were not initially listened to use parliament routinely to press for changes in government bills. In turn, this means that groups which are more supportive of bills must often lobby parliament to ensure that policy *doesn't* change. In addition, parliament plays an important role in pressure group strategies at the early stages. Seemingly weak mechanisms such as parliamentary questions, private members' bills, and non-legislative debates can all be important in getting issues onto the policy agenda and pressing government to act. Hence from the very beginning of the policy process, and subsequently, groups of all kinds prioritize working with parliamentarians to achieve their goals. In turn, as resource-exchange models suggest (Binderkrantz, Christiansen, and Pedersen 2015), non-government parliamentarians rely on support of various kinds from external groups in order to carry out their scrutiny role.

Examples in the chapter demonstrate how integral outside groups are to parliament's work. The bills that it receives are often a result of negotiations by government with groups, which may have competing interests and demands. Ministers and civil servants must navigate between these competing interests. When bills reach parliament, groups will present many of the same arguments in the public arena. Outside group responses are so central to 'issue politicization' that issues such groups consider uncontentious will often—in line with Olson and Mezey's (1991) predictions—receive relatively little parliamentary attention. Groups help to inform parliamentary debate, and many even draft legislative amendments. Hence parliamentarians must judge not only the merits of government policy proposals, but the counterclaims of outside groups. On occasions when the government's arguments do not stand up well to this public scrutiny, groups that lost out in private negotiations may persuade parliamentarians to overturn government decisions, and help them to do so. In contrast, where there has been little prior consultation, arguments between groups will be played out more directly in parliament. If respected groups support the government, ministers will be keen to cite them in debate in order to legitimize their policy (just as the government's opponents will be keen to cite groups in support of policy change). Because government insiders want the support of outside groups, and have reasons to fear the possible effects of their mobilizing against bills in parliament, pressure groups also contribute centrally to parliament's power of anticipated reactions.

The interwoven nature of pressure group and parliamentary scrutiny raises some tricky questions of both a normative and a methodological kind. Normatively, we have seen that non-government parliamentarians—and the opposition in particular—are very dependent on ideas and support from pressure groups. Yet not all groups have the resources to work closely alongside parliamentarians in constructing arguments and drafting amendments. This could fuel concerns about unequal access, and about whether certain privileged groups (classically well-resourced industry groups) have undue influence. In fact, contrary to Olson (1965), and in line with Parvin's (2007) more recent research, our interviews suggested that parliamentarians were more open to arguments from NGOs and charities than from industry bodies—though we have noted that large, well-resourced charities do have far more substantial access than smaller groups. On the case studies, it was actually often 'outsiders' who won in parliamentary arguments over 'insiders'. This occurred, for example, on identity cards (through campaigns by Liberty, NO2ID, and others) and deaths in custody (through the work of Inquest, Justice and the Prison Reform Trust). In these cases establishment voices (such as the police and prison officers) found few advocates in the public forum of parliament. In a similar way groups such as ASH, various professional medical bodies and trade unions won out against the tobacco companies on the Health Bill.

Methodologically, we have seen that pressure group influence is to some extent responsible for the links between parliamentarians of different parties and across the two chambers. We have emphasized throughout the book the challenges of disentangling the influence of different groups of parliamentarians, arguing that policy pressure often comes from different interconnected groups (as will be further discussed in Chapters 9 and 10). But these connections do not happen spontaneously, or purely due to parliamentarians' own relationships across boundaries; to a large extent they too are facilitated by outside groups.

This leads to an obvious question, of the extent to which influence on legislation is really being exercised by parliament, as opposed to by pressure from external groups. But this distinction is fundamentally a false one to draw. The pressure group literature emphasizes the complexity, and indeed intractability, of tracing policy influence to different actors—not only due to 'counteractive lobbying', but because influence occurs in different ways at different stages of the policy process, and its channels are often hidden (Austen-Smith and Wright 1994, Dür and De Bièvre 2007). Such insights inform not just this chapter but the whole of the book. As various interviewees emphasized, it is impossible ultimately to separate the influence of parliament and outside groups, and the two are not in competition with each other. Parliament provides a public forum where the arguments between these groups are played out, but where the input of parliamentarians themselves is also essential.

A nice illustration of this dynamic comes from the campaign on forestry in the Public Bodies Bill, discussed above. This provides a prime example of how external group interaction with parliament has changed, and deserves further study—the campaign methods of 38 Degrees and other groups risked overwhelming parliamentarians (particularly peers). But the outcome was a significant success for proponents of change. When the government announced its policy reversal Labour peer and former chair of the Forestry Commission Lord (David) Clark of Windermere, who had co-sponsored key amendments, joked to the minister that:

I am not sure whether it was my arguments that persuaded him to move his position or whether it might have been the half-million people who signed the 38 Degrees [petition], or the 82 per cent of their own supporters who opposed their initiative, or the 86 per cent of the general public who opposed the Government's proposals.[33]

In reality, as is often the case, it was a combination of all of the above. Although much of the campaign activity occurred outside, parliament was key to its success. Because the bill required parliamentary approval supporters could contact parliamentarians with concrete demands, and ministers were forced to respond to these on the public record. As many of those who signed up to new groups hastily created to defend the forests were, in the words of one interviewee, 'natural Tory supporters', ministers must have realized that a Lords defeat would be very difficult to ask Conservative MPs overturn. Equally importantly, however, the strength of external pressure helped convince the opposition to prioritize the issue. It was thus an inextricable combination of external groups and parliamentary actors that forced the government climbdown. As one MP put it, it 'was clearly an external campaign from 38 Degrees that did exactly what it was supposed to do', but this 'was implemented ... by parliamentarians'.

Notes

1. These kinds of relationships have raised some propriety concerns and are subject to significant regulation (Gay 2016, Kelly and Yousaf 2014).
2. See quotations in Chapter 9. The government's proposed response to the *ASLEF v. UK* case proved more contentious, as illustrated there and in Chapter 8.
3. The Smoking (Restaurants) Bill—see House of Commons Hansard, 14 April 2003, columns 647–50.
4. House of Commons Hansard, 14 October 2003, columns 1WH–22WH.
5. 'Ministers Plan Huge Sell-off of Britain's Forests', *Telegraph*, 23 October 2010.
6. House of Lords Hansard, 9 November 2010, column 70.
7. 'Forest of Dean Protesters Fight Big Woodland Selloff', *Guardian*, 3 January 2011.
8. 'Rally to Save Cumbria's Forests', *38 Degrees*, 26 January 2011 https://home.38degrees.org.uk/2011/01/26/rally-to-save-cumbrias-forests; 'Poll 84% of Public Say Forests Should Stay in Public Hands', *38 Degrees*, 22 January 2011 https://home.38degrees.org.uk/2011/01/22/poll-75-of-public-are-against-the-forest-sell-off/ [both accessed 6 May 2016].
9. 'Good News But We Need to Keep Going', *38 Degrees*, 11 February 2011 https://home.38degrees.org.uk/2011/02/11/good-news-but-we-need-to-keep-going/ [accessed 6 May 2016].
10. House of Commons Hansard, 17 February 2011, columns 1155–6.
11. Public Bill Committee (Energy Bill), 12 January 2010, column 130; ibid., 14 January 2010, column 261.
12. House of Lords Hansard, 11 January 2012, column 212.
13. House of Commons Hansard, 13 June 2011, column 589.
14. Ibid., 1 February 2012, column 912.
15. Public Bill Committee (Welfare Reform Bill), 3 May 2011, column 634.
16. Ibid., 10 May 2011, column 851.
17. This figure was very much disputed, but was provided in the Regulatory Impact Assessment for the bill, as covering the scheme for issuing both passports and ID cards (Ward 2005).
18. House of Commons Hansard, 28 June 2005, column 1177.
19. House of Lords Hansard, 16 January 2006, columns 433–4. Other examples include Conservative frontbencher Baroness Noakes, House of Lords Hansard 16 January 2006, column 430; Conservative frontbencher Edward Garnier, House of Commons Hansard 13 March 2006, Column 1253.
20. For example, House of Commons Hansard, 13 February 2006, columns 1204–5.
21. For an account of this interaction from the academics concerned, see Whitley et al. (2007).
22. House of Lords Hansard, 13 March 2008, column GC271.
23. Stephen Timms, Public Bill Committee (Welfare Reform Bill), 29 March 2011, column 191; Lord Best, House of Lords Hansard, 21 November 2011, column GC333.
24. Public Bill Committee (Health Bill), 20 December 2005, column 319; House of Lords Hansard, 15 May 2006, column GC33.
25. Notably, Crossbench votes were cast overwhelmingly against the government: 84:3.
26. Chris Simpkins, 'Bereaved Forces Families Deserve Better', *Telegraph*, 11 July 2011.

27. See 'Yet Again Our Military Men and Women Are Betrayed by the Government', *Daily Mail*, 26 October 2011; also 'Kenneth Clarke Faces Commons Revolt over Armed Forces Inquiries', *Telegraph*, 24 October 2011.
28. 'Ken Clarke Ditches Plan to Scrap Chief Coroner', *Guardian*, 23 November 2011; House of Lords Hansard, 23 November 2011, column 1106.
29. House of Lords Hansard, 13 December 2006, column 1603.
30. Quoted in 'More Colleges to Award their Own Degrees', *Daily Mail*, 15 November 2006 http://www.dailymail.co.uk/news/article-416648/More-colleges-award-degrees.html [accessed 17 June 2016].
31. This was clearly an exaggeration, but speakers included Lord Sawyer (Chancellor of University of Teesside), Baroness Blackstone (Vice-Chancellor of University of Greenwich), Lord Plumb (Chancellor of Coventry University), Baroness Morris of Yardley (Pro-Vice-Chancellor of the University of Sunderland), Baroness Murphy (Chair of Council at St George's University of London), Lord Sutherland of Houndwood (Vice Chancellor of the University of London).
32. House of Lords Hansard, 22 May 2006, column GC90.
33. Ibid., 28 February 2011, column 813.

8

The Role of Select Committees

Few might expect to find an entire chapter on the role of select committees in a book analysing the legislative process. One of the procedural features that distinguishes Westminster from many other legislatures (including those throughout most of Europe, and the US Congress) is that its permanent, specialist committees do not formally consider the 'committee stage' of legislation. As outlined in previous chapters, this stage is instead usually taken in temporary 'public bill committees' in the House of Commons, convened individually for each bill, and either on the floor or in grand committee in the House of Lords. Select committees have largely focused instead on executive oversight and investigations. Nonetheless, there are numerous ways in which Westminster select committees—directly or indirectly—can interact with legislation.

The House of Commons' system of specialist committees was only established in its modern form after 1979, therefore postdating Griffith's (1974) landmark study of the legislative process.[1] Since then the Commons committees have gained considerably in profile, resources, and reputation, while the select committee system in the House of Lords has also gradually grown. Although few select committees have a formalized role in the legislative process, and none can normally amend bills, changes such as the publication of more draft bills for pre-legislative scrutiny have drawn the committees closer into the process. Nonetheless the full extent of select committee interaction detailed in this chapter may surprise some readers familiar with Westminster. Little attention has previously focused on the connections between select committees and legislation, and our study shows these to be extensive. Its findings thus contribute to the small but growing literature on select committee influence, as well as to understanding parliament's impact on legislation.

The remainder of the chapter proceeds as follows. First, we provide a brief outline of the select committee systems in the Commons and the Lords, indicating how the committees are structured and who their members are. Next we summarize previous studies of select committees and their policy contribution. We then outline how the committees work, and the various ways in which they can now interact with the legislative process, before summarizing their main links to the case study bills. After this we move on to focus on the discernible effects that these committees had on development of the 12 case study bills, including through their initial framing, debates about them in parliament, and actual statutory changes achieved via

Legislation at Westminster. First edition. Meg Russell and Daniel Gover. © Meg Russell and Daniel Gover 2017. Published 2017 by Oxford University Press.

amendments. Taking all of these into account—alongside other forms of influence such as anticipated reactions—we conclude that the select committees make a very considerable contribution to the legislative process, despite their lack of formal powers.

Select Committees: Who Are They?

Permanent specialist committees came relatively late to the Westminster parliament. Although various kinds of committees had existed previously, it was not until the 1960s that pressure mounted for a complete set of committees to shadow government departments. A small number of specialist committees were established in the Commons on a trial basis in the late 1960s, and the move to a more generalized system followed in 1979 (Kelso 2009, Seaward and Silk 2003). Initially, reformers had proposed that departmentally focused committees should handle the formal committee stage of bills (Crick 1964, Walkland 1979); but the new specialist committees were given more limited powers—primarily focused on conducting investigations ('inquiries') and scrutinizing the work of government. This remains largely the case today, as further discussed below.

Since the 1970s the Commons select committees have become increasingly well-established, and gradually acquired greater resources and reputation. There are normally around 20 departmental select committees (under standing order no. 152), with the exact number and remit varying as necessary in response to the changing competencies of different government departments.[2] As shown in Table 8.1, the Commons also has various other specialist policy committees with more cross-cutting roles. The prestigious Public Accounts Committee always has an opposition chair, while chairs of other committees are allocated roughly proportionately according to party strengths in the chamber. Committee members, who on most Commons committees number 11, are also proportionally allocated. Unlike public bill committees, all members of select committees (in both chambers) are normally backbenchers.[3]

Until 2010 the system for choosing members of Commons select committees was similar to that for public bill committees, that is, essentially, selection by party whips. Once members were chosen, the committees then elected their own chairs. But this patronage system was controversial, and was changed in 2010 to one where chairs of the main committees are now elected by all MPs on a cross-party basis, and their members are subsequently elected within the parties.[4] Another key difference between these committees and the public bill committees is that their members are not whipped, and divisions (i.e. recorded votes) are rare. Their work is conducted in a largely non-partisan manner, with reports almost invariably published on a unanimous cross-party basis.

Committees in the Lords have both notable similarities and dissimilarities to those in the Commons. There are no departmental committees, and all instead are cross-cutting. The first committee established was the European Union Committee in 1974, and several newer committees have broadly constitutional interests (Russell

Table 8.1 Key select committees in the 2010–12 session, and number of members

House of Commons departmental committees		Other House of Commons committees	
Business, Innovation and Skills	11	Environmental Audit	16
Communities and Local Government	11	European Scrutiny	16
Culture, Media and Sport	11	Procedure	12
Defence	12	Public Accounts	14
Education	11	Public Administration	11
Energy and Climate Change	11	Political and Constitutional Reform**	11
Environment, Food and Rural Affairs	11	Statutory Instruments	6
Foreign Affairs	11		
Health	11	**House of Lords committees**	
Home Affairs	11	Communications	12
International Development	11	Constitution	12
Justice	12	Delegated Powers & Regulatory Reform (DPRRC)	10
Northern Ireland Affairs	14	Economic Affairs	13
Science and Technology*	11	European Union	19
Scottish Affairs	11	Science and Technology	14
Transport	11	Merits of Statutory Instruments	11
Treasury	13		
Welsh Affairs	12	**Joint committees**	
Work and Pensions	11	Human Rights (JCHR)	12
		Statutory Instruments	13

* The Commons Science and Technology Committee is unusual, being formally constituted as a departmental committee but instead shadowing the semi-autonomous Government Office for Science.
** The Political and Constitutional Reform Committee was not formally constituted as a departmental committee but was in practice very similar to one, shadowing the work of Deputy Prime Minister Nick Clegg during the 2010–15 parliament.

2013, Torrance 2012). These include the Delegated Powers and Regulatory Reform Committee (DPRRC, established 1992) and Constitution Committee (established 2001).[5] The Lords now also establishes four temporary 'ad hoc' select committees per session, and in 2016 created a new committee on International Relations. In addition, members of both chambers contribute to joint committees—most notably the Joint Committee on Human Rights (JCHR, also established 2001). As further discussed below, the DPRRC, JCHR, and Constitution Committee do routinely consider government bills, but do not have the power to amend them. Members of Lords committees continue to be chosen by party whips (or conveners, in the case of Crossbenchers and bishops), in a similar manner to the old Commons system. Like the Commons committees, they operate in a non-partisan manner and usually publish unanimous reports.

Established Understanding of Select Committees

Conventionally, British parliamentary committees are viewed by academics as relatively weak. This is in part because of their late development. King's (1976) analysis of executive–legislative relations lamented the lack of a 'cross-party' or 'non-party' mode of parliamentary activity at Westminster which might have been facilitated by specialist committees like those found in his comparator countries, Germany and France. For Polsby (1975), the lack of such committees was a key factor in classifying Westminster as an 'arena' legislature. The House of Commons select committee system developed in its present form only after these analyses. But even in later years, many scholars have largely disregarded the select committees, with some using their lack of formal role in the legislative process to treat Westminster essentially as though it had no specialist committees at all (e.g. Andeweg and Nijzink 1995, Mattson and Strøm 2004). Strøm suggests that committee oversight at Westminster 'is almost entirely absent' (2003: 73), while Saalfeld—despite acknowledging the select committees—suggests that they 'have had little impact on specific government policy' (2003: 635).

Generally, specialist committees are considered central to the 'institutionalisation' of legislatures: that is, to their ability to develop an independent and distinct identity from the executive (Norton 1998a). Such committees enable parliamentarians to develop expertise, and can bring more evidence into the parliamentary policy-making process. In addition, through drawing members together in smaller groups, committees may help to break down partisan animosities and even develop a 'cohesion' to rival that of parties (Arter 2003). Indeed some legislative studies scholars have viewed committees and parties as 'contradictory and even mutually exclusive means of internal organization' in legislatures (Olson, quoted in Shaw 1998: 228). As King (1976) emphasized, committees may change how members perceive their roles, so that they prioritize nonpartisan scrutiny over party loyalties. His concern was that this system was both underdeveloped and weak at Westminster.

Since the establishment of the Commons select committees they have attracted a fair amount of interest by British scholars. Contributing to the very first such study Giddings (1985: 372) noted that the committees had adopted a largely consensual style, and that MPs' self perceptions might indeed be changing—so that 'the experience of inter-party cooperation and agreement may encourage the habit of dissent'. He pointed out that committee evidence sessions provided an important forum for external pressure groups to be heard, while the requirement on ministers and civil servants to 'answer to Parliament, to explain, justify, defend, and to do so (largely) in public and on the record' had been greatly enhanced (ibid.: 376). More than a decade later Norton (1998b) detected 'nascent institutionalisation', commenting that the Commons select committees had made parliament more powerful and effective, and its members better informed—though there were clear limitations, as the committee stage of bills continued to be taken in ad hoc temporary committees.

Such observations raise obvious questions about how committee effectiveness can be assessed. In general, comparative scholars associate effectiveness with factors such as committees' size, stability of membership, degree of specialization and ability to set their own agendas (Shaw 1979, 1998)—dimensions on which the select committees score relatively well. But the standard measure of influence is the number of committee amendments made to legislation, which clearly does not apply. An alternative measure in the British case is the number of recommendations in committee reports that are adopted by government. Studies using this approach include Hawes's (1992, 1993) work on the Commons committees and environmental policy, Klug and Wildbore's (2007) work on the JCHR, and Hindmoor, Larkin, and Kennon's (2009) study of the Commons Education Committee. In the most recent example, Russell and Benton's (2011) study of seven Commons committees 1997–2010 found that around 40 per cent of recommendations targeted at central government were implemented. Yet even the very first study of the Commons committees noted that '[a]ttempts to measure in any precise way the impact of select committees upon government are bedevilled from the outset by problems of causality' (Drewry 1985a: 6). For example pressure group demands, committee recommendations and government action may all influence each other.

Given their lack of direct involvement in the legislative process, the impact of select committees on government bills might be expected to be small. Russell and Benton (2011), in examining 2,865 recommendations from Commons departmental committee reports, found that only 4 per cent called explicitly for legislative change. Hindmoor, Larkin, and Kennon (2009) approached the question from the opposite direction, examining policies in government education bills for signs of influence by the Education Committee, and finding that of 93 government proposals, 20 showed close similarity to previous committee proposals. This indicates some possible committee influence on the framing of government legislation, but the evidence is clearly limited.

In any case, committees can clearly have many different effects, some of them relatively immeasurable. Hawes (1992, 1993) noted various subtle forms of committee influence, including raising the profile of a policy topic and acting as a 'spur to action', sometimes years later (which he termed the 'delayed drop' effect). Benton and Russell (2012: 772) concluded, in line with earlier authors, that 'counting successful recommendations is a poor proxy for committee influence overall', suggesting seven further means of committee influence on policy. These comprised spotlighting issues, providing evidence, influencing debate, brokering agreements, and acting as forums of accountability and public exposure, plus perhaps most importantly 'generating fear'—that is, anticipated reactions—inside government, with ministers and civil servants thinking through their policies more carefully in order to avoid committee criticism. Likewise some scholars have suggested that the greatest influence of the JCHR has been preventative, through helping create a 'culture of rights' in Whitehall (Hiebert 2006). This committee's influence through informing parliamentary debates was also explored by Hunt, Hooper, and Yowell (2012), who found over 1,000 mentions of the JCHR in Hansard during the period 2005–10.

A specific means by which select committees can influence legislation is clearly through consideration of draft bills published for pre-legislative scrutiny— though, as indicated in Chapter 3, this applies to only a small minority of bills (Kelly 2011, 2015b). Such scrutiny has been subject to relatively little study. One interesting exception is an analysis by Smookler (2006) of two bills published in draft. In both cases the government incorporated some of the committee's recommendations into the final version of the bill, while others were rejected. However, the author noted that these committee reports can inform parliament, as well as government, and she found various examples of parliamentarians taking up committee proposals at subsequent stages and persuading ministers to rethink. Likewise Mulley and Kinghorn (2016: 57) emphasize that committees' 'evidence, considered observations and conclusions' on draft bills influence both government and parliament.

As the select committees cannot amend bills directly, we clearly need to take a more holistic approach to their influence on the process. This is consistent with the rest of the book, which has emphasized how parliamentary power takes different forms, only one of which is making amendments to bills. In the remains of the chapter we consider the various ways that the select committees inform and shape legislation, illustrated by examples from the case study bills. We find evidence of various forms of committee influence, throughout the legislative process.

Select Committee Organization

The select committees in both chambers carry out an increasingly wide range of functions. House of Commons standing order no. 152 states that the role of the departmental committees is 'to examine the expenditure, administration and policy of the principal government departments ... and associated public bodies'. The bulk of these committees' time is spent on inquiries into specific policy topics, which committee members themselves decide. Such inquiries usually involve gathering of written evidence, oral hearings with external witnesses, ministers and civil servants, and later publication of a report—to which the government is expected to provide a written response within two months. The Commons committees also scrutinize departmental annual reports, conduct one-off evidence sessions with ministers, and hold hearings with senior appointees to public bodies. All of these duties fall within a set of 'core tasks', which are determined and monitored by the Liaison Committee—which is made up of select committee chairs.[6] Most committees meet weekly (typically for sessions of two to three hours) to carry out these various tasks.

We have seen that the Commons select committees do not routinely deal with legislation. The obvious exception is the occasional opportunity to examine government bills when these are published in early draft form for pre-legislative scrutiny—which is included within the core tasks. Additionally, committees can choose to issue reports on bills during their formal passage, but this happens only very rarely. In either of these scenarios committee reports are purely advisory, containing recommendations for the government and/or parliamentarians to consider. Russell and Benton's (2011) study of the departmental committees found that just 5 per cent of reports related to pre-legislative scrutiny. Among standard inquiry reports, the majority responded to government policy that had already been agreed and was being implemented, compared to 22 per cent which responded to new policy proposals, and only 8 per cent which were judged 'agenda setting'. This indicates that committees have potential influence throughout the policy-making process, with some scope for influencing the forward legislative agenda, but with most reports focused on the implementation and evaluation stages.

While most of the cross-cutting committees in the House of Lords likewise consider legislation only rarely, both the Constitution Committee and the DPRRC have terms of reference which explicitly include reporting on any relevant facets of bills during their parliamentary passage in order to inform parliamentary debates.[7] Both also have the ability to conduct general inquiries, but the balance between these two types of work differs significantly between them. For example in the 2010–12 session the two committees each produced 25 reports. All of those from the DPRRC related to legislation, covering 39 bills in total. A key source of information for this committee is the delegated powers memorandum prepared by the government alongside each bill, which it scrutinizes with the bill itself in order to report on the appropriateness of any powers delegated to ministers to make secondary legislation. For example the committee frequently recommends that order-making powers in a bill should be subject to the 'affirmative' rather than 'negative' procedure—thus requiring greater parliamentary oversight of future ministerial decisions (see Chapter 3). The Constitution Committee only considers bills with significant constitutional implications, and its recommendations tend to be on wider matters. Of its 25 reports in 2010–12 just 13 commented on government bills. The JCHR, made up of MPs and peers, operates in a similar way by considering the human rights implications of bills and reporting selectively on those which might raise concerns. In the 2010–12 session the committee produced 24 reports in total, 13 of which reported on bills.

None of these three committees has the power directly to amend legislation, though they may explicitly suggest changes (sometimes including words that might be taken up as amendments) for consideration during the process. All three seek to report as quickly as possible—with the two Lords committees invariably doing so before the bill has reached its committee stage in that chamber. This maximizes opportunities for ministers or non-government parliamentarians to respond to any recommendations made. All three committees have respected memberships, and the Constitution Committee and JCHR in particular often include senior subject experts. Like select committees in general, all three produce balanced non-partisan reports. These factors all enhance the likelihood that their recommendations will be taken seriously.

Very occasionally a proposal is made in the Lords at the end of second reading to refer a bill to a specially convened select committee for detailed consideration. For example the government was defeated on such a motion on the Constitutional Reform Bill (which established the Supreme Court) in 2004 and the Trade Union Bill in 2016. In both cases these committees took evidence and proposed amendments, which resulted in policy change. Nonetheless, use of this mechanism is rare. As mentioned in Chapter 4, the opposition made such a proposal on the Public Bodies Bill, but it failed to be agreed.

Select Committee Links to the Case Study Bills

Other chapters have focused on the 'responses' from different groups to the case study bills. While this question clearly applies to the select committees—most notably the DPRRC, JCHR, and Constitution Committee—select committee engagement with the bills can go far wider. For example, if committees have informed government thinking before bills are introduced, looking only at their subsequent responses will mask that influence. In addition, we cannot look in the same places for select committee 'responses' as we can for other groups. Previous sections have for example used speeches from second reading debates to discern the positions of different groups; but committees do not contribute collectively to such debates. In this section we hence discuss committee links to the bills more broadly.

Table 8.2 shows some of the most obvious connections between the case study bills and reports produced by both chambers' select committees. This is not intended to be exhaustive, but shows the main reports specifically responding to the bill, and various others which touched on key policy matters within bills (as further discussed below). We see that the three constitutional committees frequently issued reports—the DPRRC routinely does so on all bills, and sometimes also on new amendments. For some bills (e.g. the Employment Bill and Budget Responsibility and National Audit Bill) the committee found nothing that it wished to draw to parliamentarians' attention, but on several others it did raise concerns. Most strikingly, it published no fewer than four separate reports into the Public Bodies Bill. The Constitution Committee also reported on this bill and on the Identity Cards Bill, while the JCHR reported on seven of the bills.

Some of the other connections shown in the table are already clear from previous chapters. Most obviously, two of the bills were considered in draft form by select committees. The Identity Cards Bill received pre-legislative scrutiny in the 2003–04 session from the House of Commons Home Affairs Committee, while the Corporate Manslaughter and Corporate Homicide Bill was considered in draft during the 2004–05 session by a specially convened committee combining members of the Commons Home Affairs and Work and Pensions committees.

Beyond this, there are several other reports from Commons committees of relevance to the bills. In most cases under Labour the relevant reports pre-date the session in which the bill was introduced. For example the Further Education and Training Bill followed a review of the sector carried out for the government by Sir Andrew Foster (2005). In July of the following year the Commons Education and Skills Committee (2006) reported on Foster's findings, and the government's bill to implement some of his proposals was introduced four months later. An interesting counterexample to this usual pattern was the report by the Commons Health Committee (2005a) on the Health Bill, regarding the proposed partial ban on smoking in public places. After the bill appeared in the Queen's Speech, the committee announced a short, focused inquiry into the smoking proposals, whose report was published during the bill's Commons committee stage. This criticized the government's position and—as discussed below—proved very influential in encouraging change.

Under the coalition the most obviously relevant select committee reports were produced within the same session as the bills that we studied, though of course this was an unusually long session, lasting two years. Some of these are unsurprising—for example the involvement on policy related to the Welfare Reform Bill of the Work and Pensions Committee, which shadowed the responsible government department. One interesting example concerned the Budget Responsibility and National Audit Bill, which as we have seen legislated for a new Office for Budget Responsibility—as proposed by the Conservatives before the 2010 election. The Office for Budget Responsibility had been established on a non-statutory basis straight after the election, with legislation to follow. In response the Treasury Committee began an inquiry in July 2010 into what the permanent arrangements should be. This reported in September (Treasury Committee 2010), with the government's bill published in October. The committee's report again proved to be influential on debates, as discussed below.

Evidence of Select Committee Influence on the Case Study Bills

These very few examples already indicate how committees may influence bills at different stages of the policy process, and in different ways. In some cases reports published before the legislation is introduced can be important. At other times—and particularly with regard to the three key constitutional committees—committee thinking can be important post-introduction. The views of committees may influence the whole tone of debate on bills, and be used to support non-government parliamentarians' positions against the government, or alternatively the government's position against its opponents. We consider all of these different forms of committee influence here, with illustrations from the case study bills.

Agenda setting and policy formulation

As discussed in previous chapters, the first policy stage recognized by scholars is 'agenda setting': that is, getting a policy proposal onto the government's agenda for future action. Select committees may contribute at this stage by making proposals in policy fields that government has given little previous consideration. We have seen that Russell and Benton (2011) classified few House of Commons departmental select committee reports as agenda setting; but individual recommendations in other reports can also have an agenda setting role. As one former select committee chair put it in interview, 'the select committee, if it works well, acts as a reservoir of fresh ideas' and can help 'make sure there is a culture of interest' in a particular topic. In some parliaments, committees would be able to promote these ideas through their own 'committee bills'. At Westminster no such formal mechanism exists (though at least one Commons committee has published a bill and successfully persuaded the government to adopt its content).[8] More commonly, therefore, recommendations in committee reports will be incorporated into government bills.

The Role of Select Committees

Table 8.2 Main select committee reports relevant to the case study bills

	Commons committees	Lords and joint committees
2005–10 parliament		
Identity Cards	• Home Affairs (2003–04): *Identity Cards**	• Constitution Committee x2 (2004–05, 2005–06) • DPRRC (2005–06) • JCHR x3 (2004–05 x2, 2005–06)
Health	• Health (2002–03): *The Control of Entry Regulations and Retail Pharmacy Services in the UK* • Health (2005–06): *Smoking in Public Places* • Public Administration (2002–03): *Government by Appointment: Opening up the Patronage State*	• DPRRC x2 (2005–06) • JCHR x2 (2005–06)
Corporate Manslaughter	• Home Affairs and Work and Pensions (2005–06): *Draft Corporate Manslaughter Bill**	• DPRRC x3 (2006–07) • JCHR x2 (2005–06, 2006–07)
Further Education	• Education and Skills (2005–06): *Further Education*	• DPRRC (2006–07)
Employment		• DPRRC x2 (2007–08) • JCHR (2007–08)
Saving Gateway Accounts	• Treasury (2006–07): *Financial Inclusion Follow-up: Saving for All and Shorter Term Saving Products*	• DPRRC (2008–09)
Energy	• Business and Enterprise (2007–08): *Energy Prices, Fuel Poverty and Ofgem* • Environment, Food and Rural Affairs (2008–09): *Energy Efficiency and Fuel Poverty* • Science and Technology (2005–06): *Meeting UK Energy and Climate Needs: The Role of Carbon Capture and Storage*	• DPRRC (2009–10)
2010–12 session		
Identity Documents		• DPRRC (2010–12) • JCHR (2010–12)
Savings Accounts		
Budget Responsibility	• Treasury (2010–12): *Office for Budget Responsibility*	• DPRRC (2010–12)
Public Bodies	• Justice (2010–12): *The Proposed Abolition of the Youth Justice Board* • Public Accounts (2010–12): *The Youth Justice System in England and Wales: Reducing Offending by Young People* • Public Administration (2010–12): *Smaller Government: Shrinking the Quango State*	• Constitution Committee (2010–12) • DPRRC x4 (2010–12) • JCHR (2010–12)

Table 8.2 *Continued*

	Commons committees	Lords and joint committees
Welfare Reform	• Communities and Local Government (2010–12): *Localisation Issues in Welfare Reform* • Work and Pensions (2010–12): *Changes to Housing Benefit Announced in the June 2010 Budget* • Work and Pensions (2010–12): *The Government's Proposed Child Maintenance Reforms*	• DPRRC (2010–12) • JCHR (2010–12)

* Formal pre-legislative scrutiny on draft bill.

Abbreviations: DPRRC = Delegated Powers and Regulatory Reform Committee; JCHR = Joint Committee on Human Rights.

Some of the case study bills showed clear evidence of committee influence at the agenda setting stage. For example Labour's Health Bill contained a wide range of provisions, some of which had previously been brought to the government's attention by select committees. Part 5 of the bill replaced the NHS Appointments Commission with a new, slightly more general Appointments Commission, in direct response to proposals from the House of Commons Public Administration Select Committee (PASC). The bill's explanatory notes made explicit that this part of the bill:

is in line with the Government's response to the Public Administration Select Committee … which indicated that some Departments could benefit from using the services of the NHS Appointments Commission to support their sponsor teams in making appointments but that statutory authority would be needed to achieve this.

These proposals had appeared in a wide-ranging committee report entitled *Government by Appointment*, which sought to improve accountability for public appointments (Public Administration Select Committee 2003). PASC had originally hoped that the Commission's remit would be widened to include all government departments. The government's response indicated that it did not wish to go that far, but it conceded that some smaller departments could benefit from using the Commission, promising to 'look at how this might be achieved, subject to Parliamentary time being made available' (Cabinet Office 2003: 11). During debate on the bill, Secretary of State for Health Patricia Hewitt acknowledged that this part 'respond[ed] to the Public Administration Committee's report on government by appointment'.[9] Perhaps partly thanks to PASC's support, the proposals proved uncontroversial in parliament.

Once an issue has reached the government's agenda, select committees may also influence government thinking at the policy formulation stage. This can occur when a policy is under general discussion, including sometimes during formal government consultations, or in the minority of cases where the bill is published in draft form.

The former dynamic occurred on another topic in the Health Bill—the regulation of pharmacists. Here a report from the Office of Fair Trading (OFT) (2003) had

proposed that such regulations should be relaxed. But while its conclusions were welcomed by supermarket chains, they were criticized by many community pharmacists.
The House of Commons Health Committee subsequently reported on the topic,
agreeing that the pre-existing system was 'overly inflexible and in need of reform' but
concluding that the OFT proposals had 'the potential to make certain pharmacies
unviable, potentially leaving some of the most vulnerable communities … without
any local pharmacy provision' (Health Committee 2003: 18). In its formal response
(Department of Health 2003), the government agreed with the committee's analysis
over that of the OFT, and the bill introduced more limited deregulation.

Under the coalition, select committee input into policy formulation—even in the
absence of a formal government consultation—was also quite visible. One example
was the government's proposed policy to cut Housing Benefit by 10 per cent for those
who had spent more than a year on Jobseeker's Allowance. As discussed in Chapter
5, this change was announced in the June 2010 Budget, and had been expected
to appear in the Welfare Reform Bill. The Work and Pensions Select Committee
(2010) conducted a rapid inquiry into these proposals, concluding that the change
would be problematic, and the government's response to the committee indicated
that it had decided not to proceed, partly due to its intervention (Work and Pensions
Committee 2011). As Chapter 5 notes, pressure from the Liberal Democrat side of
the coalition was also key in bringing about this reversal. Parliamentarians opposed
to the policy were able to use the select committee's report to bolster their case.

Where select committees consider draft bills, they obviously hope to shape the
final bill as introduced. There was some evidence of this with respect to both the
Identity Cards Bill and the Corporate Manslaughter and Corporate Homicide Bill.
A full analysis of the differences between the draft and final versions of the bill was
outside the scope of our study, but the committees' reports had clearly had some
impact pre-introduction, at least at the level of detail. At the second reading of the
Corporate Manslaughter and Corporate Homicide Bill, referring to the joint work
by the two select committees on the draft bill, Home Secretary John Reid proudly
claimed that the government had 'adopted a number of the Committees' recommendations', though he admitted that this had been 'not in every particular'.[10] At
the second reading of the Identity Cards Bill Home Affairs Committee chair John
Denham (who coincidentally chaired the committee inquiries into both draft bills)
complained that, with reference to the committee's detailed concerns, '[a]lthough
the Government have responded to some criticisms, they have not responded to
many'.[11] Hence a straightforward analysis of recommendations accepted by the
government pre-introduction might suggest that these committees had limited
success. But their reports clearly informed parliamentarians at the subsequent
stages. As an official on one of these bills stated, parliamentarians 'were much more
honed in their points because of the pre-legislative scrutiny'. We return to this
dynamic below.

Informing debates

Once a bill has been introduced, select committee work of various kinds can be
influential on debates—at all stages, and in both chambers. In order to investigate

this, we searched the Hansard record for all mentions of select committees during debate on the bills. This analysis found 1,723 explicit references—perhaps a surprisingly high number—representing an average of over 140 mentions per bill.[12]

Each mention of a committee was coded for chamber and committee(s) referred to, with results summarized in Table 8.3. This shows considerable variation by bill, which is in part a product of their size and level of controversy, and therefore the

Table 8.3 Mentions of select committees in debates on the case study bills

	Number of committee mentions	% Commons: Lords	Main committees mentioned (and as % of total mentions on that bill)
2005–10 parliament			
Identity Cards	256	32:68	HC Home Affairs (29); HL Delegated Powers and Regulatory Reform (DPRRC) (26); HL Constitution (19); Joint Committee on Human Rights (JCHR) (6)
Health	133	56:44	HC Health (50); HL Economic Affairs (19); HL DPRRC (13)
Corporate Manslaughter	201	70:30	HC Home Affairs and Work and Pensions (47); JCHR (43)
Further Education	48	90:10	HC Welsh Affairs (56); HC Education and Skills (27)
Employment	26	77:23	JCHR (92)
Saving Gateway Accounts	21	38:62	HL DPRRC (43); HC Treasury (29); HC Public Accounts (10)
Energy	78	87:13	HC Energy and Climate Change (35); HC Science and Technology (15); HC Environment Food & Rural Affairs (14); HL DPRRC (14)
2010–12 session			
Identity Documents	37	68:32	HC Home Affairs (51); JCHR (32)
Savings Accounts	10	60:40	HC Treasury (50); HC Work and Pensions (40)
Budget Responsibility	290	55:45	HC Treasury (72); HC Public Accounts (11); HL Economic Affairs (8)
Public Bodies	434	18:82	HL DPRRC (21); HL Constitution (18); HC Public Administration (7); HC Welsh Affairs (7); HC Justice (5)
Welfare Reform	189	52:48	HC Work and Pensions (51); HC Public Accounts (12); HL DPRRC (8); JCHR (6); HC Communities and Local Government (6)
Total	1,723	47:53	**HC Treasury (13); HL DPRRC (13); JCHR (10); HL Constitution (7); HC Work and Pensions (6); HC Home Affairs (6)**

Abbreviations: DPRRC = Delegated Powers and Regulatory Reform Committee; JCHR = Joint Committee on Human Rights; HC = House of Commons; HL = House of Lords.

overall time dedicated to debate. But there were also other factors at play.[13] Notably the Budget Responsibility and National Audit Bill was relatively uncontroversial and faced little parliamentary opposition, but had the second highest number of select committee mentions—210 of which were to the Treasury Committee (contributing to it being the most commonly mentioned committee overall). Unsurprisingly, in this and several other cases the committees mentioned most frequently were those that had specifically issued reports on the bills. The three main constitutional committees were mentioned numerous times, and collectively account for around one-third of comments made. They proved particularly prominent in debates on some bills—particularly the Public Bodies Bill. As we already know from Table 8.2, the three committees between them produced six reports focused on this bill; it accounted for the highest number of references to committees in our sample.

We see that the total number of references to select committee was very balanced between debates in the House of Commons and House of Lords, but for several individual bills it was strongly skewed. This reflects on both the chamber into which the bill was first introduced and the nature of the committees mentioned. For example the Public Bodies Bill was introduced in the Lords, and the main reports came from Lords committees—hence four out of five mentions occurred in that chamber. The Identity Cards Bill was introduced in the Commons, but much of the controversy was again in the Lords and the DPRRC's report was frequently referred to. In contrast the Corporate Manslaughter and Corporate Homicide Bill, likewise introduced in the Commons, saw much discussion of Commons committees—in particular the committees that had jointly considered the draft bill. Strikingly, 72 per cent of mentions of Commons committees occurred in the Commons, while an overwhelming 96 per cent of mentions of Lords committees occurred in the Lords. References to joint committees were almost equally split between the chambers.

We also coded mentions of select committees according to the content of the reference, and these results are summarized in Table 8.4. The majority of references concerned the select committees' previous policy contributions—including reports, recommendations, evidence, or other stated policy positions (various examples are given below). These together accounted for 60 per cent of mentions, with general reference to a report being the largest category. Another kind of reference was that conferring status on members—for example mentioning that a previous speaker had authority due to being a select committee chair. For example debating the Energy Bill, Simon Hughes referred to fellow Liberal Democrat MP Phil Willis as 'a much respected Chairman of the Science and Technology Committee'.[14] There were also a substantial number of references to possible future committee work—for example, suggesting that a committee should keep the policy under review during implementation. For example discussing the Corporate Manslaughter Bill, Edward Garnier MP noted that 'there are issues that the Select Committees dealing with the work of the Department for Work and Pensions and the Home Office ... might wish to consider once the Bill becomes law'.[15] Collectively these categories accounted for nine out of ten select committee mentions overall.

In understanding committee influence on debate it is important also to explore who is doing the speaking. The 1,723 references were divided remarkably equally

Table 8.4 Select committee mentions in debate by type of reference and chamber

Type of reference*	Commons	Lords	Total	% of total
1. Mention of committee recommendation	73	112	185	11
2. Mention of committee report	168	360	528	31
3. Mention of committee evidence	159	37	196	11
4. Mention of committee policy position (other)	58	66	124	7
5. Status of member(s)	126	91	217	13
6. Future committee work	127	157	284	16
7. Other	92	97	189	11
Total	**803**	**920**	**1,723**	**100**

* Where more than one code could apply, the highest ranked code in the table was assigned.

between government frontbench (23 per cent), opposition frontbench (24 per cent), government backbench (27 per cent), and other backbench (25 per cent).[16] This suggests that committees are used almost equally to defend and to question the government's position. For example on the Identity Cards Bill, government minister Baroness (Patricia) Scotland of Asthal stated that '[t]hese statutory purposes have been expressed in an explicit manner following the recommendations of the Home Affairs Committee'—thereby using the committee to confer legitimacy on the government's stance.[17] On the Corporate Manslaughter and Corporate Homicide Bill, Conservative frontbencher Ed Davey noted 'that the Joint Committee on Human Rights expressed concern on that point, so I hope that the Minister can give us assurances', clearly using the committee's position to raise doubts about the government's policy.[18] These opportunities to use committee findings either to challenge the government, or in support of the government, are further explored below.

Changes through amendments

We have seen in previous chapters that 752 amendments were agreed to the case study bills (excluding those which merely overturned earlier amendments, or were overturned themselves), which contributed to 300 agreed legislative strands.[19] Although the great majority of agreed amendments were proposed in the name of ministers, many represented concessions to points previously raised in amendments from non-government parliamentarians of different kinds—that is, opposition members and government backbenchers in both chambers, and non-party parliamentarians. In Chapter 7 we saw that pressure groups often play a significant part in supporting such amendments. Our interest in this chapter is clearly the role of the select committees. Despite such committees' inability to formally propose amendments, our analysis found many examples of changes made to the 12 bills which could be traced—at least in part—to previous select committee proposals.

Tracing agreed amendments to similar select committee proposals is not as straightforward as tracing them to previous amendments on a bill. At times there is explicit on-the-record acknowledgement by parliamentarians of select committee influence on amendments. But sometimes amendments are proposed which are partly inspired by ideas from select committees, without any mention of these committees. Indeed, even where committees are mentioned, such references might sometimes be spurious. To trace links between amendments and select committee recommendations we therefore took a two-pronged approach. First, we reviewed all reports from the committee(s) shadowing the department(s) sponsoring each bill, and any other obviously relevant reports including those from the three main constitutional committees, which were published during the session(s) when the bill was considered. Amendments were counted as responding to a recommendation if they made a related change to the same specific policy or provision. Second, we followed up on-the-record mentions of any other committee reports during debate on amendments by reading the relevant reports (including those from previous sessions) to verify connections claimed. This exercise was necessarily imperfect: in particular, some amendments may have been made which were influenced by reports that were published in preceding sessions but not mentioned in debate. On balance any shortcomings in our approach are likely to underestimate rather than overestimate committee influence.

There are three means by which a select committee recommendation can influence an agreed legislative strand. First, the government itself may volunteer one or more amendments responding directly to the committee. This is most likely to happen, of course, with respect to recommendations made after the bill was published (otherwise the government could have included the relevant proposals in the bill as introduced). Second, the government can come under pressure from non-government parliamentarians, who table amendments which would implement committee recommendations. If the government offers concessionary amendments, these can be seen as indirectly influenced by the committee. Third, and only rarely, a non-government amendment pressing a committee's case will find its way directly into a bill. In the latter two cases any affected strands will already have appeared in the tables in earlier chapters showing influence from the proposers of the non-government amendments concerned. In contrast the first category contains influence unique to this chapter.

These three routes are reflected in Table 8.5, which shows that at least 50 of the 300 agreed strands (one in six) involved some kind of committee influence. There were signs of committee influence on 122 agreed amendments in total. We see significant variation between the bills, with the most numerous examples of select committee influence evident on the Identity Cards Bill and the Public Bodies Bill, whether counted by strands or amendments. There were also a large number of such amendments made to the Corporate Manslaughter and Corporate Homicide Bill, though these contributed to only five distinct legislative strands.

There were 12 government-initiated strands which nonetheless directly implemented select committee recommendations, without any non-government amendments involved (which included 34 agreed government amendments).[20] Most of these (10 strands and 27 amendments) responded to the DPRRC. Notably the government's own *Guide to Making Legislation* dedicates a whole chapter to handling

Table 8.5 Strands (and amendments made) traceable to select committee recommendations

	Total strands agreed	Strands containing successful amtds* responding to SC				Total successful amdts resp to SC*	% of successful strands on bill resp to SC
		Govt amdts resp only to SC	Govt amdts resp to NG amdt & SC	Non-govt amdts resp to SC	Total strands		
2005–10 parliament							
Identity Cards	40	6	6	2	14	32	35
Health	45	0	3	0	3	11	7
Corporate Manslaughter	27	2	3	0	5	25	19
Further Education	20	1	1	0	2	3	10
Employment	13	0	1	0	1	4	8
Saving Gateway	7	0	0	0	0	0	0
Energy	17	2	1	0	3	8	18
Total (2005–10)	169	11	15	2	28	83	17
2010–12 session							
Identity Documents	2	0	0	0	0	0	0
Savings Accounts	0	0	0	0	0	0	n/a
Budget Responsibility	7	0	0	0	0	0	0
Public Bodies	50	1	11	1	13	28	26
Welfare Reform	72	0	8	1	9	11	13
Total (2010–12)	131	1	19	2	22	39	17
Grand total	**300**	**12**	**34**	**4**	**50**	**122**	**17**

* These figures include only agreed amendments that were neither subsequently overturned nor purely overturned an earlier amendment (as described in Chapter 3).

this committee, and indicates that '[i]t is usual for the Government to accept most, if not all, of the DPRRC's recommendations' (Cabinet Office 2015: 124). Minor amendments from the committee indeed often directly trigger government amendments. For example on the Energy Bill one government amendment changed a power to create secondary legislation using the negative procedure to instead require the affirmative procedure in several sections of the bill. Others in response to DPRRC recommendations limited the Secretary of State's power to determine whether certain fuel poverty scheme requirements applied. Likewise, several changes to the Identity Cards Bill introduced the affirmative procedure, while others tightened up definitions and restricted ministerial discretion in other ways, on the recommendation of the committee.

Despite the words in the Cabinet Office guide, and comments from government interviewees that acceptance of DPRRC proposals is 'always the default position', there is often further pressure from non-government amendments. Responses to the DPRRC also contributed to 25 of the 34 strands responding both to a committee and to non-government amendments. Indeed, of the 122 agreed amendments traceable to select committee recommendations overall, 68 (i.e. more than half) were at least in part traceable to the DPRRC.

Sometimes these changes can make non-government amendments look more influential than they really are—or at least offer alternative explanations for government acceptance of the principles in such amendments. For example on the Energy Bill, Liberal Democrat frontbencher Simon Hughes raised concerns at Commons committee stage over the lack of definition of 'fuel poverty' on the face of the bill, and the Secretary of State's potential to alter its interpretation. No amendment was made, but the DPRRC raised similar points, and several government amendments addressing them were made in the Lords.[21] Notably Hughes's intervention occurred in January 2010, and the committee reported only in March. Ministers will often explicitly reject amendments on such matters until the DPRRC has reported, effectively deferring to its position as arbiter. For example responding to non-government amendments on regulations around smoking in the Health Bill the Commons minister commented that 'I will listen to the views of the Delegated Powers and Regulatory Reform Committee ... when it comes to scrutinise the Bill. On that basis, I cannot support the amendment but remain of an open mind and open to persuasion.'[22] Subsequently some of these points were conceded when backed by the committee.

On small matters responses to the DPRRC can raise suspicions of 'manufactured' concessions. One government interviewee suggested that on regulation powers 'I think we probably ... [if] the precedent suggests we could go either way, we would go for negative on the grounds that you could then move to positive and it was a kind of costless concession'. On one bill he suggested that such an amendment 'genuinely created a sense of goodwill: the government had made a concession and actually it didn't really matter to the government'. This impression can be enhanced where there are non-government amendments proposed on the topic. For example, several Liberal Democrat backbench amendments on the Welfare Reform Bill proposed switching regulations from the negative to the affirmative procedure, following a DPRRC report. The government's positive response allowed backbenchers to claim a victory; but the change might well have happened anyway, even had they not intervened.

Nonetheless, government does often initially resist proposals for change from select committees, including more major proposals from the DPRRC—meaning that pressure from non-government amendments becomes essential to achieving change. Responses of this kind to recommendations from the three main constitutional committees played a part in some of the most important policy reversals on the bills.

The bill probably most changed as a result of select committee intervention was the coalition's Public Bodies Bill. We have seen that this attracted the largest number of select committee mentions in debate, and 13 strands (and 28 successful amendments) were traceable to select committee proposals—of which only one was immediately volunteered by the government. These included responses to the DPRRC, whose four reports during the bill's passage were highly critical. The bill delegated very substantial power to government to merge, reconfigure or abolish numerous public bodies without future primary legislation, which this committee argued would 'grant to Ministers unacceptable discretion to rewrite the statute book' (Delegated Powers and Regulatory Reform Committee 2010b: 3). The committee called for various changes to the bill, including addition of a sunset clause in order that its provisions would expire after a given period of time. Equally critical reports from the Constitution Committee, the JCHR and the Commons Public Administration Committee approached the bill from slightly different angles, but raised many overlapping points. The Constitution Committee (2010: 3) concluded that the bill threatened a 'fundamental principle of the constitution that parliamentary scrutiny of legislation is allowed to be effective'. The JCHR was particularly concerned about bodies with quasi-judicial functions (Joint Committee on Human Rights 2011). The Public Administration Select Committee (2011) supported the call for a sunset clause. In addition, both the Justice Committee (2011) and the Public Accounts Committee (2011) in the Commons expressed concern about the likely effects of the proposed abolition of the Youth Justice Board.

As described in other chapters numerous major government concessions to the bill were made in response to amendments from opposition members, government backbenchers and non-party peers (both separately and jointly). These included the sunset clause (discussed in Chapter 4), greater protection for judicial bodies (discussed in Chapter 5), and the removal of the list of 150 bodies for possible abolition in schedule 7 (discussed in Chapter 9), all of which had been highlighted in these committee reports. As one government interviewee put it, 'a lot of the concessions had started because of strength of feeling of those committees', adding that their high reputation meant that 'if a chair or member of a committee stood up and said "we think that x", that was kind of it'. As an opposition frontbencher explained, once the committees had reported 'we were able to then use those reports that are respected by all peers to win the arguments and to put pressure on ministers, and they had to fold'. These were major parliamentary victories, clearly underpinned by proposals from select committees. Following amendments from Crossbench peer and former Chief Inspector of Prisons Lord (David) Ramsbotham, the government also removed the Youth Justice Board from the bill.[23]

Significant changes influenced by the constitutional committees also affected several other bills. One such case was the intervention by senior Liberal Democrat backbencher Lord (Anthony) Lester of Herne Hill regarding the response to the *ASLEF v. UK* case in the Employment Bill. This concerned the ability of trade unions to expel members of extremist political parties, following a European Court of Human Rights ruling, on which the government's proposals aroused significant cross-party concern (as documented in Chapter 9). The ruling had upheld the union's right to expel a BNP member, despite UK law previously disallowing discrimination on grounds of party membership. Hence the government sought to bring the law into line with the ruling, using clause 17 of this bill. Its preferred means of achieving this—by giving trade unions significant freedom to expel members for their party affiliations—concerned Lester, a prominent human rights lawyer and JCHR member. He consequently proposed amendments to include safeguards, in line with the alternative option that the government had previously consulted upon. Subsequently the JCHR reported on the bill, suggesting that the government's wording could breach an individual's right to freedom of association, and explicitly proposing an amendment very similar to Lester's. His proposal gained support from both the Liberal Democrat and Conservative frontbench, and a government amendment was ultimately agreed accepting his formulation. In proposing this, the minister acknowledged that the government had been 'mindful of the views of the Joint Committee on Human Rights'.[24]

The Joint Committee on Human Rights (2006) similarly expressed concerns about the government's exclusion of deaths in police and prison custody from the scope of the Corporate Manslaughter Bill. Notably, the same point had previously been made by the committee considering the draft bill (Home Affairs and Work and Pensions Committees 2005). All of this helped to fuel the long parliamentary conflict over the matter, which began with unsuccessful amendments proposed by the Labour chairs of these two committees at Commons report stage (see Chapter 5), and ended with a government climbdown following repeated Lords defeats proposed by Lord Ramsbotham (as discussed in Chapter 6). In line with Smookler's (2006) findings, this was a clear example of a delayed victory by the pre-legislative scrutiny committee; though it was only achieved following the support of other committees and determined objections by non-government parliamentarians. Some other recommendations from the committee on the draft bill were likewise not initially incorporated by the government but were conceded after its introduction. For example the committee had argued, in line with the earlier recommendations of the Law Commission, that a test requiring clear liability by senior managers in order for a body to be convicted of the offence would make such convictions more difficult to secure. The government initially ignored this objection, but subsequently proposed amendments at Commons committee stage to remove the test. Again there were dual pressures operating: the minister had faced joint proposals from the Conservative frontbench and Labour backbenchers on similar points, which were withdrawn when the government offered its own amendments. In fact, all 25 committee-inspired amendments to the bill reflected changes recommended by the pre-legislative scrutiny committee.

Some similar dynamics were seen on the Identity Cards Bill, which was likewise initially scrutinized in draft form. This bill was subject to the largest number of amendments traceable to select committees, 26 of which responded to the DPRRC, due to the extensive delegated powers which it contained. In its original form one of the most notable of these was the provision allowing ministers to move to a compulsory scheme using delegated legislation, albeit subject to the 'super-affirmative' procedure.[25] The Home Affairs Committee (2004: 61), in its consideration of the draft bill, had concluded that '[t]he move to compulsion is a step of such importance that it should only be taken after the scrutiny afforded by primary legislation', describing the super-affirmative procedure as 'not adequate' and suggesting that the government was open to accusations of 'proceeding by stealth'. Ministers initially ignored this objection and left the provision in the published bill. The DPRRC did not actually speak out against it, but the Lords Constitution Committee (2005: 8) agreed that the bill 'should be amended to secure that the extension of the scheme to the entire population would require further primary legislation'. As discussed in Chapter 5 the government suffered a defeat on the matter in the Lords, which it chose to accept rather than risk asking MPs to overturn. In addition to sitting uncomfortably with the party's manifesto commitment, the objections from these committees clearly provided strong ammunition to the bill's opponents. Despite the government's initial resistance, when responding to the Lords amendments the Commons minister acknowledged the Home Affairs Committee's desire for this change, stating that 'we have now succumbed to that will'.[26] The chair of the committee, John Denham, welcomed this reversal.[27]

Almost all of the changes to the bills traceable to pressure from select committees (roughly 110 of 122 amendments) related at least in part to proposals from the three constitutional committees, and/or a committee that had considered the bill in draft. But there were also some clear examples of other forms of responsiveness to Commons departmental committees. The most important concerned the Health Select Committee's intervention over the smoking provisions in the Health Bill. As indicated in Chapter 2, the published bill reflected Labour's manifesto, which had promised a ban with limited exemptions—for pubs that did not serve food and for private members' clubs. These exemptions were controversial among health professionals, as well as trade unions with members in the hospitality industry; by taking the unusual step of holding an inquiry during the bill's passage, the committee allowed such concerns to be publicly aired. The new chair of the committee, Kevin Barron, was a Labour backbencher with a long-standing interest in smoking and health, who used his new position to agitate on the issue—and to exploit the known divisions in government (see Chapter 3).[28] The inquiry took evidence from various groups (see Chapter 7) and key figures. Among them was the government's Chief Medical Officer, who described the compromise in the bill as 'unsatisfactory' and suggested that 'the case for widening the present proposals to all enclosed public places and workplaces is ... very strong' (Health Committee 2005b: 59). The committee's report concluded that the exemptions were 'unfair, unjust, inefficient and unworkable', and that 'a comprehensive ban would achieve the Government's stated aims in a much more satisfactory fashion' (Health Committee 2005a: 48).

While there were undoubtedly also other factors at play, this report greatly increased the parliamentary pressure for a comprehensive ban, lending support to those in government who wanted this outcome. Particularly given Labour's manifesto commitment, committee members pressed behind the scenes for ministers to allow Labour MPs a 'free' (unwhipped) vote on the subject at Commons report stage. An early day motion (EDM) calling for this was also signed by 104 members, including Conservative Shadow Secretary of State Andrew Lansley and 71 Labour backbenchers.[29] Kevin Barron tabled an amendment calling for a total ban, whose signatories included all but one of the members of his committee. This degree of pressure made a government defeat look possible; ministers thus conceded the free vote, tabling a menu of options to be voted upon (enabling Barron to withdraw his proposal in favour of a similar government proposal). In the vote, the committee's preferred position easily prevailed.[30] Many members paid tribute to its contribution, with the Secretary of State claiming to be 'particularly grateful to the Select Committee on Health',[31] while a senior Conservative backbencher described the committee's role as 'courageous' concluding that:

The role of the Select Committee has been decisive in this debate and it is a model of what Select Committees should do. It detected an argument that had unsound foundations, exposed it, then produced a clear, unambiguous, unanimous report that has been of enormous assistance to the House.[32]

Kevin Barron commented that it was 'a good day for Parliament' and 'a good day for the Select Committee system'.[33] Government interviewees privately acknowledged the centrality of the committee's role, with one saying it had a 'very strong influence on where the legislation went'. But this committee influence received little media attention.[34]

Support for the government

These examples have so far focused on select committees' input into challenging and changing government legislation. But the conclusions of a select committee can also be used in parliament by the government to legitimate its policy. As we have seen, around one-quarter of mentions of select committees in debate are made by ministers themselves—often in order to indicate to members that a policy is in line with what a committee recommended, or evidence that a committee has heard. We have seen in particular that the DPRRC is used by ministers to fend off proposed amendments to the power delegated in bills. Where the committee does not recommend a change, ministers will cite this as evidence that the government has got it right. For example on some aspects of the Health Bill the Lords minister defended the original wording in the bill, by arguing that 'the Delegated Powers and Regulatory Reform Committee was content with the approach we were adopting'.[35]

Committee support on the bigger policy issues in a bill is of course even more important. We have seen that the Budget Responsibility and National Audit Bill had a high number of select committee mentions in debate, mostly due to Treasury Committee's inquiry into the setting up of the Office for Budget Responsibility which reported the month before the bill was published. The committee's chair, Andrew Tyrie, was an independent-minded Conservative, and studies show that it receives more media coverage than any other select committee (Kubala 2011, Russell and Benton 2011). This made it a daunting potential opponent. Ultimately, the government's bill closely resembled what the committee had recommended—which helped contribute to its relatively easy passage through parliament. As one government insider explained, 'if you held it up against the bill you would struggle to come up with more than three substantive differences', whereas 'if the two had looked very different we would have had a very difficult parliamentary passage'. Many of the mentions of the Treasury Committee referred to its position on points in the bill. For example the minister, Justine Greening, pointed out at the opening of Commons committee stage that the bill had 'benefited from the inquiry undertaken by the Treasury Committee. I am pleased to say that the Bill is very much in line with the recommendations in that Committee's report'.[36] Despite the numerous mentions of the Treasury Committee, Table 8.5 showed no amendments made to this bill to implement committee recommendations. Such changes were not necessary, because the government had already taken the committee's concerns on board. This illustrates nicely how the support from a select committee for the government's position can be as important to the passage of a bill as the ammunition which it can provide for the bill's opponents.

Select committees and anticipated reactions

Finally, and clearly connectedly, the government is likely to think carefully during the preparation of its legislation about any likely objections from the well-respected select committees. In some cases this planning is very explicit. The chapter in the government's *Guide to Making Legislation* dedicated to the DPRRC notes that '[t]here is ... benefit in departments anticipating the views of the DPRRC when drafting the bill to avoid the need for amendments', and that the committee's 'advisers are willing to be consulted informally before introduction' (Cabinet Office 2015: 124). The same document also advises officials to 'be aware of the Constitution Committee's role and consult the Government Whips' Office in the Lords if they think the Committee will take an interest in the bill' (ibid.: 230). In the period immediately before introducing legislation, therefore, the constitutional committees are clearly (and understandably) considered important to government 'handling'.

But concern about objections from select committees is likely to go far wider. Russell and Benton (2011: 89) found that those inside government give significant attention to the likely responses of select committees when thinking through policy options—quoting an official and a minister respectively reporting that 'you've always got to think, how would I explain that to the committee?', and 'from a policy point of view, you would always bear [the committee] in mind'. This is connected to the committees' 'exposure' function, because both ministers and senior officials can face public questioning by select committees (creating what another interviewee described as 'the fear of having to appear in front of them'), alongside committees' ability to collect evidence and publish critical reports that can stoke parliamentary opposition. Select committees need to be taken particularly seriously because their cross-party nature, and the high regard in which they are held, may unite other parliamentarians across party lines in support of what they propose. This risks sparking the most dangerous kind of opposition from ministers' point of view (as further discussed in Chapter 9). We saw clear examples above on the Public Bodies Bill, and the smoking ban in the Health Bill.

When thinking through legislation in advance, both ministers and civil servants are therefore likely to take careful account of the potential reactions of select committees. Conscious planning may involve behind-the-scenes consultation with those from key committees before bills are published. Discussions at the official level between civil servants and those working for the constitutional committees are clearly relatively commonplace. We were told that similar discussions went on with respect to the Budget Responsibility and National Audit Bill and the Treasury Committee. In addition, there is much informal contact at the political level. Sensible ministers will seek to maintain friendly contact with relevant select committee chairs and members shadowing their departments—albeit usually at arms' length to maintain propriety. As one minister told us, 'you have regard to the chair of the select committee or members of the select committee because, bluntly, they can make your life difficult if they want to'. Another talked of the importance of 'conversations in the tearoom', and how when preparing a policy they might approach the chair of the committee asking 'have you got any thoughts, any views, any issues around it?'. All of these informal mechanisms can provide an early warning system with respect to possible parliamentary resistance.

Conclusions

Despite their formally weak position in the legislative process, this chapter has demonstrated a strong link between the work of select committees and the parliamentary passage of government bills, suggesting that these committees have a perhaps surprising degree of influence on the policy that results. This influence applies throughout the entire policy process, from the very first to the final stages. Where relevant select committees have endorsed the government's position, this may greatly ease the passage of a bill; where they voice criticisms, this may cause significant difficulties in parliament.

We have seen that the various interconnected, and often subtle, forms of power exercised by select committees throughout the legislative process include the following:

- First, like government backbenchers, the committees have a potential agenda-setting role. As Russell and Benton (2011) indicated, and as other authors have similarly acknowledged, they can 'spotlight issues' and draw them to governmental and wider public attention. By gathering evidence and reflecting on it on a cross-party basis, they put issues into the public domain that ministers may well choose to consider. The fact that government must respond to all select committee reports encourages such reflection. We saw several examples on the bills of government implementing changes that had previously been proposed by committees.

- Second, select committees can be influential during the policy formulation stage. This most obviously applies where they conduct pre-legislative scrutiny of government bills in draft. Most bills are not subject pre-legislative scrutiny, and the government does not necessarily adopt the recommendations of committees when such scrutiny occurs (though see below). Nonetheless the evidence gathered and recommendations made through this process can help to shape bills before they are formally introduced. In addition, committees can make other interventions at the pre-legislative stage. For example the short, targeted inquiry conducted by the Work and Pensions Committee on the coalition's proposed cuts to Housing Benefit helped ensure that this policy was omitted from the Welfare Reform Bill.

- Third, the work of committees can be very influential on the content of debate once bills have been introduced. Where the government is legislating in line with previous recommendations from a select committee, ministers will be keen to emphasize this to legitimize their policy. Where previous recommendations have been ignored (including from pre-legislative scrutiny) this may well result in difficult questioning and pressure for policy change. Reports, evidence, and recommendations from prior inquiries are frequently used by parliamentarians when considering the merits of government proposals. Reports published during the passage of a bill, including by the three key constitutional committees—the House of Lords Constitution Committee and Delegated Powers and Regulatory Reform Committee (DPRRC) and the Joint Committee on Human Rights (JCHR)—are particularly likely to inform debate. On occasion, other committees also choose to intervene and report on bills at this stage. As seen with respect to the Health Select Committee's intervention on smoking, this can have significant effect.

- Fourth, recommendations from committees can consequently result in amendments to bills. We saw that of the 300 agreed legislative strands across the 12 bills, at least 50 showed some sign of this kind of select committee influence. The constitutional committees were particularly important here, with the DPRRC alone playing a part in around half of committee-related amendments made. Many of these amendments were on relatively small matters, but various other changes wrought by the constitutional committees were more major. In addition there was a 'delayed drop' effect from select committees conducting pre-legislative scrutiny, with important changes made to both the Identity Cards Bill and Corporate Manslaughter and Corporate Homicide Bill in line with prior committee recommendations that the government had rejected. Most such changes were facilitated by non-government parliamentarians taking up committee proposals and pressing them through their own amendments. This same dynamic applied to the important change to the Health Bill, where an amendment proposed in the name of Health Select Committee members helped to force a Commons free vote and the reversal of a government manifesto policy—with the most vocal critic being the government backbencher who chaired the committee.

- Fifth, as a consequence of all of the above, the select committees play a key role in parliament's 'power of anticipated reactions'. Civil servants and ministers privately confess to carefully thinking about how the committees will react when preparing policy. One interviewee thus suggested that their primary impact on the process was 'not actually on the legislation but on the way ministers think, which would translate obviously into the legislation'. Ministers know that where they go against the wishes of cross-party committees they may ultimately face amendments from non-government parliamentarians that prove difficult to resist. As a ministerial interviewee put it, committees comprise 'parliamentarians looking at things from a parliamentary point of view, so it has an authority' and they have no 'axe to grind' like outside groups. Endorsement by a select committee therefore suggests that a criticism of government policy is not just partisan sniping or special pleading.

- Sixth, the flip side of this threat is the potential benefit of committee endorsement. This is a form of committee influence not previously noted by others such as Russell and Benton (2011). Just as committee recommendations can legitimize the arguments of non-government parliamentarians in questioning policy, they can also legitimize ministers' arguments, and make it significantly easier to negotiate the parliamentary passage of their bills.

- Finally, and beyond the scope of our study, committee influence continues after the formal decision-making stage, to include evaluation of policy once it is in place. As noted above, Russell and Benton (2011) found that the majority of select committee reports responded to government policy that was already being implemented. This activity may in turn prove agenda setting for the future.[37]

Hence we see that the views of select committees permeate the whole legislative process, shaping the positions of both government and non-government parliamentarians. The changes encouraged by select committees through legislative amendments can to some extent be quantified, but their other effects are far more difficult to capture. Indeed, as scholars have frequently pointed out, specialist committees' most important influence can be their diffuse general impact on the policy environment both inside and outside parliament. Select committees provide crucial contact points between outside groups and parliamentarians; they take evidence in public, and are frequently reported in the media, which influences wider debate. They expose parliamentarians to evidence, discourage slavish loyalty to party lines, and enable members to build up expertise. One interviewee hence told us that she felt far more confident moving amendments as an opposition frontbencher having served time on the relevant departmental select committee. These effects are all immeasurable, but important.

Committees hence have significant potential strength in the legislative process, but this remains to some extent unrealized. Amendments proposed collectively by select committee members are potent, but rare. One government interviewee talking about an amendment proposed by committee members said that this forced ministers to think 'this is not just a maverick MP, this is a bunch of serious people who think about these things, who've done reports, who've listened to evidence'. There has recently been some discussion in the Commons of formalizing select committees' ability to propose amendments, and prioritizing such amendments for debating time (Liaison Committee 2010, Procedure Committee 2009). No change has occurred, but this could significantly boost committee strength. However, the initiative by the Health Select Committee shows what committees can already achieve within existing procedures. Ultimately, this perhaps demonstrates how committee influence could be even greater if Westminster adopted structures more similar to those in many other parliaments, where permanent specialist committees routinely consider government bills (Russell, Morris, and Larkin 2013).

Notes

1. Griffith therefore barely mentions select committees, though he does discuss the possibilities for greater use of such committees to scope future legislation, or even to handle the committee stage in future.
2. For example the Energy and Climate Change Committee was created in January 2009 to shadow the newly created Department for Energy and Climate Change. Later that year the committee on Business, Enterprise and Regulatory Reform became the Business, Innovation and Skills committee, to reflect changes in the government department.
3. This is a strict rule on the government side, and for all groups in the Lords. In the Commons there is occasionally more latitude for opposition frontbenchers, especially in the smaller parties.
4. For a discussion of the pre-2010 controversy, see Kelso (2009); for a discussion of the 2010 reform, see Russell (2011).
5. Note that several of the committees mentioned in this paragraph have changed their names over time, and the names given are those in current use.
6. Other core tasks include scrutinizing EU legislative proposals and petitions, plus public outreach.
7. As set out in the *Companion to the Standing Orders*, the Constitution Committee is required to 'examine the constitutional implications of all public bills coming before the House', and the DPRRC to report on 'whether the provisions of any bill inappropriately delegate legislative power, or whether they subject the exercise of delegated power to an inappropriate degree of parliamentary scrutiny' (House of Lords 2015: 227).
8. This was the Public Administration Committee's proposal to put the core civil service values (integrity, honesty, objectivity, and impartiality) on a statutory footing, which

was implemented through Labour's Constitutional Reform and Governance Act 2010. Notably, Russell and Benton (2011) found that this committee produced an unusually high percentage of 'agenda setting' reports (18 per cent, against an average of 8 per cent). It influenced the Health Bill, as indicated below.

9. House of Commons Hansard, 14 February 2006, column 1377.
10. Ibid., 10 October 2006, column 196.
11. Ibid., 28 June 2005, column 1205.
12. We searched all stages (including public bill committee proceedings) for mentions of the term 'committee', excluding those which were irrelevant (such as mentions of public bill committees themselves, or committees external to parliament) and focusing on mentions of select committees. We coded at the level of Hansard paragraphs, and created a separate entry for mention of each committee. Hence there were slightly fewer than 1,723 unique paragraphs, as a small number referred to more than one committee. On the other hand, where a single committee was referred to several times within a paragraph this reference is counted only once.
13. One of the less obvious committees indicated in the table is the Welsh Affairs Committee on the Further Education and Training Bill. This committee had recently reported on the new procedures for Legislative Competence Orders for Wales, under the enhanced devolved powers in the Government of Wales Act 2006 (Welsh Affairs Committee 2007). Some members raised the procedure with respect to policies in the bill, causing this report to be frequently mentioned.
14. Public Bill Committee (Energy Bill), 12 January 2010, column 133.
15. House of Commons Hansard, 10 October 2006, column 262.
16. Around one-quarter (27 per cent) of mentions came from a member of the committee concerned.
17. House of Lords Hansard, 23 November 2005, column 1667.
18. Standing Committee B (Corporate Manslaughter and Corporate Homicide Bill), 26 October 2006, column 137.
19. Legislative strands were introduced in Chapter 2 and are fully discussed in Appendix A.
20. As indicated in Appendix A, strands are defined as collections of amendments, and since these strands began with a government amendment they are treated in other chapters as government-initiated strands. However, these amendments were included as responsive to parliament in the 'amendments' section of Table 3.6.
21. As acknowledged by the minister, Lord Hunt of Kings Heath: House of Lords Hansard, 7 April 2010, column 1572.
22. Caroline Flint, House of Commons Hansard, 14 February 2006, column 1375.
23. This followed an initial defeat at Lords report stage which was jointly sponsored with Labour and Conservative backbenchers. The defeat was overturned in the Commons, but Ramsbotham's proposal to reinstate it during LCCA won support from the minister. This agreement was reached on the same day that the Justice Committee's report was published.
24. Lord Jones of Birmingham, House of Lords Hansard, 2 June 2008, column 15.
25. The super-affirmative procedure provides more safeguards than the usual 'affirmative' procedure: in this case not only approval by both chambers of parliament, but also a requirement for prior parliamentary approval of a report setting out the terms, to be tabled by the Secretary of State.
26. Tony McNulty, House of Commons Hansard, 13 February 2006, columns 1145; 1150.
27. Ibid., column 1159.

28. Among other things, Barron had introduced the Tobacco Advertising Bill (to ban advertising) as a private member's bill in the 1993–94 session.
29. EDM 888 of session 2005–06.
30. An initial vote to remove the exclusion for licensed premises was won by 453 votes to 125, and a subsequent vote to exclude private members' clubs was won by 384 to 184 (with the great majority of Labour members voting in favour of both).
31. Patricia Hewitt, House of Commons Hansard, 14 February 2006, column 1293.
32. Sir George Young, ibid., column 1325.
33. Ibid., column 1316.
34. See for example 'Smoking Ban in All Pubs and Clubs', *BBC News*, 14 February 2006, http://news.bbc.co.uk/1/hi/uk_politics/4709258.stm [accessed 9 May 2016]; 'MPs to Vote on Smoking Ban', *Guardian*, 14 February 2006.
35. Lord Warner, House of Lords Hansard, 9 May 2006, column GC383.
36. Public Bill Committee (Budget Responsibility and National Audit Bill), 1 March 2011, columns 3–4.
37. While we did not study this in detail with respect to the case study bills, there are clear examples of committee follow-up in some cases. For example with respect to the Welfare Reform Bill, both the Public Accounts Committee (2013) and Work and Pensions Committee (2014) issued critical reports on the introduction of Universal Credit, and the former likewise reported on the Personal Independence Payment (Public Accounts Committee 2014). Implementation of both policies proved problematic and controversial.

9

The Role of Cross-Party Working

The earlier chapters of this book have focused on relatively discrete sets of actors, and their engagement with the parliamentary legislative process. In particular, the initial chapters concentrated on partisan groupings in parliament—the government, opposition parties, government backbenchers and then those who explicitly define themselves by independence from the parties. But as has been seen repeatedly, these groups do not operate in isolation. Instead, parliament provides a forum for them to come together and debate and negotiate policy. Particularly when considering policy influence, and government changing its plans in response to parliament, some degree of cross-party work is generally involved.

Conventional views of Westminster have presented cross-party connections as weak, particularly as compared to other legislatures. The dominant actor has been seen as the single governing party. But various changes, as discussed throughout the book, have helped to erode single-party dominance. They include the growth of specialist select committees (as explored in the previous chapter), declining party cohesion (discussed in Chapter 5), the reform of the House of Lords into a chamber where no party has a clear majority and, most recently, the 2010 coalition. Such changes have fed other dynamics, such as the increasing engagement by outside groups with parliament (as discussed in Chapter 7). This all encourages greater pluralism at Westminster, whereby parliamentarians seek to work together across party lines. Since any single group will struggle to get the government to change course (notably, even backbenchers offer no immediate threat unless their position is likely to find support from others), there are clear incentives for cross-party cooperation.

This final group-related chapter hence concentrates on cross-party working at Westminster, and the impact that cross-party coalitions—broadly defined—can have on the legislative process. As in other chapters, we preface our analysis by briefly reviewing existing academic assumptions. Next we outline the different mechanisms for cross-party working, which range from the formal and explicitly organized to the informal and accidental. After this, we turn to evidence from the case studies. We partly echo previous chapters by considering cross-party attitudes to the bills, then reviewing the number of legislative amendments that can be ascribed to cross-party groups and what motivates such amendments. In turning to the influence of cross-party work we move on to take a slightly different approach. We consider the success rates of cross-party amendments, and of legislative strands that in some way show cross-party support, demonstrating that such initiatives enjoy a significantly higher likelihood of success than those supported by single

Legislation at Westminster. First edition. Meg Russell and Daniel Gover. © Meg Russell and Daniel Gover 2017. Published 2017 by Oxford University Press.

groups. We then illustrate with some brief examples of cross-party initiatives, most of which were discussed more fully earlier in the book. The analysis in this chapter then leads naturally into a more general discussion of the impact of Westminster on government legislation, which is the subject of the next and final chapter.

Established Understanding of Cross-Party Working

Unlike the distinct groups discussed in previous chapters, there is very little literature devoted to the question of cross-party working at Westminster. Indeed, the impression given by scholars is often that such work is weak to non-existent. This claim was particularly explicit in King's classic analysis, which emphasized the importance to the Westminster parliament of the 'opposition mode' and the 'intraparty mode', as discussed in Chapters 4 and 5. We saw in Chapter 8 that King considered the 'cross-party' or 'non-party' mode to be unimportant, given the underdeveloped nature of specialist committees. In Germany he found the cross-party mode to be more prevalent, due both to the presence of strong committees, and the fact that '[c]ross-voting [was] common'. In contrast he remarked that 'alliances between Conservatives and Labour backbenchers in Britain, although by no means unknown, have always been fairly rare' (King 1976: 31).

The obvious observation is that much has since changed at Westminster. As discussed at greater length in previous chapters, specialist committees are now much better developed, parties are less cohesive, and so on. Committees in particular are seen by specialist scholars as key to breaking down blind party loyalty and encouraging more policy-focused work. In addition, the rise of third and minor parties means that the opportunities for cross-party work go far beyond the single relationship envisaged by King. Yet the academic literature—particularly when presenting Britain from a comparative perspective—has been very slow to adjust. For example even the latest edition of Lijphart's (1999, 2012) widely cited analysis continues to present Britain as fundamentally majoritarian: characterized by single-party domination, centralized decision-making, and a second chamber that is weak. More specifically, a revisiting of King's analysis in the 1990s—by when specialist committees, cross-voting and third party representation were all well established—concluded that the cross-party mode remained almost entirely absent. The authors presented this as a distinguishing feature of the British parliament, as compared to all other parliaments in Western Europe. Instead, the interparty mode was judged to be 'almost overwhelming' at Westminster (Andeweg and Nijzink 1995: 174).

Some authors writing in the UK context do of course acknowledge opportunities for cross-party collaboration. There are plentiful suggestions that Lijphart's majoritarian stereotype no longer applies (e.g. Bevir 2008, Flinders and Curry 2008, Hazell 2008, Russell 2013, Schleiter and Belu 2016). As seen in earlier chapters, there is also widespread acknowledgement of the importance of cross-voting (e.g. Cowley 2002, 2005, 2015) and of select committees (e.g. Benton and Russell 2012, Norton 1998b, 2013, White 2015), as well as clear recognition of the role of pivotal voters in the House of Lords that go beyond the two main parties (Cowley

2006, King 2007, Russell 2013, Russell and Sciara 2007, Shell 2007). All of this provides indications of the increasing importance of cross-party work in policy development, and in bringing about policy change. The Hansard Society study of the legislative process specifically commented on the importance of cross-party support for amendments during the period of Labour government, claiming that 'when the two opposition parties worked together, particularly with backbenchers of the governing party, the government was far more likely to make amendments or grant concessions' (Brazier, Kalitowski, and Rosenblatt 2008: 93). Such claims are very plausible, but have as yet not been tested statistically.[1]

Cross-Party Organization

Previous chapters have looked at the organization of fairly distinct and well-defined groups at Westminster. In considering cross-party working the focus needs to be rather different. Instead of formal organization which exists for the purpose, much contact across party lines takes place on an ad hoc and informal basis. There are clearly numerous such relationships that can be developed. For example members of opposition parties may work together, at either frontbench or backbench level (particularly under Labour when there were two major opposition parties); such members may link up with government backbenchers; likewise any of these groups may work with non-party parliamentarians. Hence—particularly when minor parties are added to the mix—a very complex web of connections can exist between different groupings, at different levels and across the two chambers.

Some cross-party relationships are clearly relatively formalized, while others are far more informal or even accidental. An indication of the range of such relationships is given in Figure 9.1. The most obvious formal venues are the select committees, which bring members in both chambers together across party lines, involving them in joint enterprises based around some collective expertise. As discussed in Chapter 8, which considers the contribution of the committees in greater detail, this can help to break down partisan barriers, particularly given the strong convention of producing unanimous cross-party reports. The relationships fostered in the committees can then help to build more informal networks, as discussed below. The Commons public bill committees of course also bring members together across party lines, and have the ability to amend legislation. But since they are temporary and non-specialist, disbanding after a bill has completed its committee stage, these committees are less likely to be cohesive, or to foster lasting relationships. This has led to criticism, with a particular complaint being their lack of overlap with the membership of relevant specialist select committees (see Russell, Morris, and Larkin 2013). However, such overlap does occasionally occur. An illustration among our case studies was Labour's relatively uncontroversial Energy Bill, whose public bill committee included seven members of the Energy and Climate Change select committee, and the chair of the Commons Science and Technology committee.[2] These MPs hence not only had a long-standing interest in the topics in the bill, but were also members of an established cross-party network. It is relatively

	Mechanism	Possible results
Formal	Select committees	Evidence, reports
	Public bill committees	Evidence, amendments
	All-Party Parliamentary Groups (APPGs)	Evidence, reports, amendments
	Frontbench collaboration	Amendments, support in debate, coordinated whipping
Informal	Organized backbench networks	EDMs, PMBs, Backbench Business Committee debates, amendments, support in debate, joint voting
	Uncoordinated joint action (front/backbench)	Support in debate, joint voting

Figure 9.1 Mechanisms for cross-party working, from formal to informal

cohesive groupings such as these that proponents of public bill committee reform would like to foster. This committee's make-up was consistent with Thompson's (2015) observation that public bill committees on energy and environmental matters often enjoy a more expert and less partisan membership.

A slightly less formalized mechanism for bringing backbenchers together across party lines is the All-Party Parliamentary Group (APPG). As indicated in Chapter 7, these bodies are often—though not always—coordinated by an external pressure group of some kind. Propriety concerns have led the parliamentary authorities to set down quite specific rules for their recognition, including the requirement to join a register (indicating any external support), to be open to all members of both chambers, and to have a cross-party group of officers.[3] At the start of the 2010 parliament there were around 600 registered APPGs, and clearly some operate a good deal more effectively than others. One interviewee on the Health Bill complained about how approximately 80 APPGs existed in that field alone, which limited their impact. Nonetheless through meetings involving external specialist speakers, for example, such bodies can be a useful source of specialist knowledge for parliamentarians, helping them to build up expertise. They can also be used to plan cross-party strategies on bills. One interviewee active in moving amendments recalled that 'it was at some of the all-party group meetings that I met people who then offered me a lot of support'. Examples active on the bills included the APPG on Disability (supported by the pressure group Disability Rights UK) on the Welfare Reform Bill, and the APPG on Smoking and Health (supported by ASH) on Labour's Health Bill. Networks fostered by the latter were clearly very important in garnering support for the smoking ban. As one of the key protagonists explained to us 'you need something that takes you away from the party politics, and of course an all-party group is an ideal thing to have'.

It is nonetheless often more ad hoc cross-party groupings which are most crucial in pushing for legislative change. These may be encouraged by the kinds of bodies already mentioned, with relationships built up across party lines between members with common interests through joint membership of select committees, public bill committees or APPGs. The growth of these formal mechanisms has hence boosted informal cross-party links. But other forms of connection can exist as well. For example one interviewee commented, again in the context of the Health Bill, on the importance of professional networks—suggesting that 'the links on medical matters between doctors, whether they were House of Lords or House of Commons, were close'. All of these kinds of informal groupings, once created, can use various official parliamentary mechanisms to assist their cause. At the backbench level, members may come together in the Commons to initiate early day motions (EDMs) or Backbench Business Committee debates, and in both chambers may gather support for private members' bills. As discussed in greater detail below, they can obviously also sponsor cross-party amendments. Where existing parliamentary networks are weak, pressure groups can have an important role in encouraging such action (as discussed in Chapter 7). One interviewee pointed out that 'that's where some of the outside groups are quite helpful in saying . . . "on that point, we've heard Lord such-and-such speak about it", you know, "he'd be worth approaching" '.

Most of these mechanisms facilitate cross-party contact specifically between backbenchers. But coordination and behind-the-scenes discussion between frontbenchers can be even more important—albeit often far more hidden. Under Labour there was more potential for these kinds of links than under the coalition, as there were two main opposition parties. Such relationships were particularly strong in the Lords, where the Conservatives and Liberal Democrats could potentially (depending on the behaviour of Crossbenchers and others) form a blocking majority against the government. Prior to 1999 there had been little incentive for opposition parties to coordinate in this way; Labour governments could be readily outnumbered in the Lords by the Conservatives alone (and indeed the role of Conservative whips was in part to prevent their members defeating the government too often); in contrast, even the combined forces of two opposition parties would usually be insufficient to defeat Conservative governments. But post-1999 the potential benefits of cooperation between the Conservatives and Liberal Democrats became clear. This occurred to a significant degree on policy issues where the two parties could find common ground, with one example being civil liberties—as illustrated by their joint work on the Identity Cards Bill. Subsequently under the coalition, with just one main opposition party, the primary opportunity for coordination was instead between Labour frontbenchers and key Crossbenchers in the Lords (as discussed particularly in Chapter 6). In addition, the opposition in both chambers has long had an incentive to pursue alliances—overt or covert—with discontented government backbenchers. In all of these cases a key mechanism of collaboration is the tabling of cross-party amendments. There may also be coordination of whipping arrangements between opposition parties, and more gentle forms of support such as speaking in support of each other in debate.

All of these kinds of contact can be explicitly organized, to some extent. But it is important to point out that some cross-party pressure on government instead occurs on an entirely ad hoc basis. In the course of their parliamentary duties, members clearly often listen to each other's speeches in debate, and sometimes read each other's contributions at earlier stages of a bill's passage. This may influence their own interventions. Members also read each other's amendments and may, sometimes without any formal coordination, choose to sign in support. Ultimately they may of course also decide to vote for such amendments. Most of these behaviours leave some trace of cross-party cooperation on the public record, whether actually coordinated or not. Although all are important, it is clearly the last of them that forms the ultimate threat to government.

Cross-Party Responses to the Case Study Bills

Previous chapters have reviewed the attitudes of distinct groups to the case study bills. To a large extent, cross-party attitudes are nothing but a summation of these responses. Where aspects of a bill were controversial with several different groupings, ministers would quickly be able to see the potential for hostile alliances to form. Likewise where a select committee raised concerns about a bill (e.g. the smoking provisions in the Health Bill, or the degree of compulsion in the Identity Cards Bill) the threat of such alliances coalescing later would also be obvious.

The degree to which there was clear evidence of cross-party disquiet on the bills varied widely. Some were plainly less controversial overall. Others provoked concern only from limited groupings. One example was the coalition's Savings Accounts and Health in Pregnancy Grant Bill, which has already been noted (see Chapter 4) as generating hostility on the Labour opposition benches that found little resonance elsewhere. Unlike the Welfare Reform Bill, where there was significant government backbench discomfort among Liberal Democrats (see Chapter 5), the junior coalition partner was relatively content with this bill. Its most high-profile element—the abolition of the Child Trust Fund—had appeared in the Liberal Democrat general election manifesto, as well as that of the Conservatives. In addition, of course, its certification as a money bill (see Chapter 4) meant that it was not given full consideration in the House of Lords—where cross-party alliances frequently form.

Other bills—or at least parts of them—provoked significant cross-party concern from the outset. This applied to several of the biggest arguments discussed in earlier chapters, including on Labour's Identity Cards Bill, the omission of deaths in custody from its Corporate Manslaughter and Corporate Homicide Bill, the extent of the smoking ban in the Health Bill, and key elements of the Welfare Reform Bill. Rather than review attitudes towards these bills, which readers can discern from evidence in earlier chapters, we give some brief examples here of how cross-party concerns can become evident from an early stage, and how this can appear from the government's point of view.

A useful illustration is provided by the objections raised over provisions in Labour's Employment Bill to allow expulsion of members of extremist parties from trade unions. The degree to which such concerns spanned party divides was already clear from the bill's initial introduction to the Lords. It otherwise enjoyed a good deal of cross-party agreement at second reading—for example Conservative frontbencher Baroness (Judith) Wilcox declared herself 'very supportive' of the key changes to the dispute resolution procedures, while from the Liberal Democrat frontbench Lord (Tim) Razzall indicated that his party 'broadly support[ed] the bill'.[4] But widespread concern was expressed about the government's decision—set out in clause 17—to remove all statutory limits on the ability of trade unions to expel members due to their political party affiliations in response to the *ASLEF v. UK* ruling. Baroness Wilcox expressed 'severe reservations' about this, concluding that the clause had 'a large potential for abuse', and could be 'the top of a very slippery slope'.[5] Former cabinet minister Lord (Norman) Fowler pressed the minister on whether the National Union of Journalists, of which he had long been a member, would now be able to expel him because he was a Conservative. Lord Razzall indicated his party's opposition to the clause, and deferred on the detail to his colleague Lord (Anthony) Lester of Herne Hill, whom he described as 'the world's foremost expert on human rights'.[6] Lester then set out carefully why he believed the proposal was flawed. Various other peers also spoke out against the clause, with one of the sharpest criticisms coming from respected Labour backbencher Lord (Bill) Morris of Handsworth, a former General Secretary of the Transport and General Workers' Union, who condemned it as 'barking mad'.[7]

This alarmingly broad range of forces spelled likely trouble ahead for ministers. Hence a government insider told us, 'we all came back from second reading in the Lords saying, "oh my god, we're going to have to rethink this"'. At later stages the pressure grew, with a report from the Joint Committee on Human Rights, of which Lester was a key member, and an amendment from him at Lords committee stage which had clear support across the House. In withdrawing this amendment to allow the minister to reconsider, Lester suggested slightly ominously that '[t]he fact that it is likely that both opposition parties will be taking a common position if the Government do not budge will, I hope, concentrate ministerial minds on finding a solution'.[8] As indicated in Chapter 8, a government amendment followed at report stage, resolving matters in Lester's favour.

Similar dynamics can be seen on several of the bills. The second reading debate is a prime opportunity for the breadth of opposition to government plans—where it exists—to be publicly expressed. Since government backbenchers, as discussed in Chapter 5, will frequently raise their concerns behind the scenes, open dissent from them at the early stages can demonstrate a significant depth of feeling, sometimes in response to ministerial intransigence. If mainstream backbench voices chime with those on the opposition benches (and in the Lords, with non-party peers) this may give ministers cause to rethink. Defending the government's position in such circumstances is a difficult job. Describing Lords second reading of one controversial bill, and referring (presumably) to the classic Hollywood film, one minister recalled reporting back to the Secretary of State that 'it was like Zulu—they were all coming at me!'. This was the first step in persuading those inside government that concessions would need to be made, and the bill was significantly changed by the time it left the Lords.

Cross-Party Amendments and their Motivations

Table 9.1 provides summary information about the numbers of amendments on the case study bills sponsored on a cross-party basis by non-government parliamentarians. Here we define 'cross-party' broadly, as members of any two distinct groups (including non-party parliamentarians) jointly signing an amendment. Fuller details of the types and frequency of different combinations are given subsequently, in Table 9.2. For comparison Table 9.1 also includes the number of non-government amendments proposed to each bill by members of a single party or group.[9] Putting these figures together we see that around one in six amendments were co-sponsored overall. But of course this does not capture the full extent of cross-party support for amendments—as already indicated, members may also speak or vote in favour of each other's amendments, or organize jointly behind the scenes. In addition, cross-party pressure on ministers can result from members of different groups proposing separate but similar amendments. This is not reflected in Table 9.1, but will be returned to below.

Table 9.1 demonstrates that while cross-party co-sponsorship is relatively commonplace, it varied quite a lot across the bills. On some there was little or no co-sponsorship: this is particularly seen with respect to the Saving Gateway Accounts Bill, the Budget Responsibility and National Audit Bill and the Savings Accounts and Health in Pregnancy Grant Bill. The first two were relatively uncontroversial; the third aroused fairly isolated resistance from the official opposition (which was alone responsible for 106 of the 108 amendments proposed). But as already noted this bill was not fully debated in the Lords, where the proportion of cross-party amendments is generally higher. Bills showing significant cross-party co-sponsorship included the Health Bill, the Public Bodies Bill, and the Welfare Reform Bill, while the number (if not the per cent) of co-sponsored amendments on the Identity Cards Bill was also high. But the bill with the greatest proportion of co-sponsored amendments overall, and by far the highest in the Commons, was the

Table 9.1 Single-group and cross-party amendments proposed by bill and chamber

	Commons			Lords			Total		
	Single group	Cross-party	Total	Single group	Cross-party	Total	Single group	Cross-party	Total
2005–10 parliament									
Identity Cards	291	16	307	396	76	472	687	92	779
Health	130	18	148	88	60	148	218	78	296
Corporate Manslaughter	152	19	171	147	11	158	299	30	329
Further Education	66	3	69	97	6	103	163	9	172
Employment	52	7	59	67	1	68	119	8	127
Saving Gateway Accounts	54	0	54	60	0	60	114	0	114
Energy	52	24	76	0	0	0	52	24	76
Total (2005–10)	797	87	884	855	154	1,009	1,652	241	1,893
2010–12 session									
Identity Documents	17	0	17	15	11	26	32	11	43
Savings Accounts	106	2	108	0	0	0	106	2	108
Budget Responsibility	43	0	43	47	2	49	90	2	92
Public Bodies	60	13	73	280	82	362	340	95	435
Welfare Reform	354	0	354	346	204	550	700	204	904
Total (2010–12)	580	15	595	688	299	987	1,268	314	1,582
Grand total	1,377	102	1,479	1,543	453	1,996	2,920	555	3,475

Note: Cross-party refers to parliamentarians from more than one party or non-party group (as defined in Chapter 6) co-sponsoring an amendment. All figures exclude amendments co-sponsored by the government.

Table 9.2 Cross-party character of non-government amendments proposed

	2005–10	2010–12	Total
Conservative & Crossbench	18	4	22
Conservative, Crossbench, & other	16	0	16
Conservative, Labour, Crossbench, & other	13	0	13
Conservative & Lib Dem	113	0	113
Labour & Conservative	11	4	15
Labour, Conservative, & Crossbench	4	6	10
Labour, Conservative & Lib Dem	7	3	10
Labour & Crossbench	5	134	139
Labour & Lib Dem	16	48	64
Labour, Lib Dem, & Crossbench	1	31	32
Labour & other	5	8	13
Lib Dem & Crossbench	1	28	29
Lib Dem & other	3	10	13
All other combinations	28	38	66
Total cross-party	241	314	555
Total single group	1,652	1,268	2,920
Grand total	1,893	1,582	3,475

Note: Definition of cross-party amendments as in Table 9.1. Within this table 'other' means any party or group other than Conservative, Labour, Liberal Democrat, Crossbench, or Bishop. Combinations sponsoring 10 or more amendments across both parliaments are spelt out, while the remainder are included in 'all other combinations'. All figures exclude amendments co-sponsored by the government.

Energy Bill (although the overall number of amendments was fairly small). From 2005 to 2010 the difference between the chambers was not as great as perhaps might be expected—15 per cent of Lords amendments were sponsored on a cross-party basis as compared to 10 per cent in the Commons. But under the coalition (when there was clearly much less opportunity for MPs to collaborate across party lines) the Commons figure dropped to 3 per cent, while the Lords figure exceeded 30 per cent.

Getting behind these figures, the different bills illustrate different types of cross-party coordination. On the Energy Bill various jointly sponsored amendments were proposed in Commons committee involving government backbenchers and opposition parties. We have seen that the committee on this bill was quite unusual, including many subject specialists who had worked together previously, while the bill itself dealt with fairly non-partisan topics. Some of these amendments resulted in concessions. For example a proposal from Labour backbencher Alan Whitehead that energy companies should be able to meet the requirements to address fuel poverty through new technologies, not just direct financial support, was backed by Liberal Democrat Simon Hughes and Conservative chair of the Environmental Audit Committee Tim Yeo (who was not a member of the public bill committee, but nonetheless signed the amendment). This was met by a government amendment at report.[10]

Table 9.1 shows that although the Health Bill was largely uncontroversial, there were numerous cross-party amendments—many of them on the smoking ban.

These obviously included the successful proposal from members of the Health Select Committee to move to a comprehensive ban (as discussed in Chapter 8). As seen in Chapter 6, a small cross-party group of backbench peers subsequently sought unsuccessfully to limit the ban. But there was also some cross-party coordination between the two opposition frontbenches in the Lords on lower-profile matters; relatively consensual changes were made, for example, on the regulation of controlled drugs.

As Table 9.2 shows, joint work by the two main opposition parties was the commonest form of co-sponsorship from 2005 to 2010. On some bills—a key example here being the Identity Cards Bill—these interventions were highly confrontational, with joint opposition amendments (sometimes also involving Crossbenchers or Labour backbenchers), sometimes culminating in Lords defeats. Later, on the large controversial bills under coalition, the high levels of co-sponsorship were largely accounted for by the Labour opposition working with non-party peers. Table 9.2 also shows that there were quite a large number of amendments under coalition co-sponsored by these groups with government backbenchers. These were largely Liberal Democrats, reflecting the junior partner's high propensity to express dissent through amendments (as discussed in Chapter 5).

In considering the dynamics of jointly sponsored amendments the different rules for sponsorship in the two chambers become important. In the Lords, an amendment can usually have up to four sponsors (or five, if a minister wishes to add their name).[11] In the Commons there is usually no upper limit on the number of members who can sign. In order to encourage the Speaker to select an amendment, MPs may therefore consider both the number of signatories and the degree of cross-party support to be important. In the Lords (where there is of course no selection of amendments), the only way of demonstrating breadth of support is through variety among the four names listed.

Motivations for cross-party amendments

In previous chapters we have explored the motivations behind non-government amendments, and discussed how these sometimes have objectives beyond changing the bill itself. Motivations include 'information seeking' (probing), 'signalling' targeted at the outside world, and mere political 'gameplaying'; some of these apply more to certain groups of parliamentarians than others. Cross-party amendments can potentially fall into various such categories, particularly given the diversity of cross-party alliances that may form. But the proportion sincerely targeted at legislative change is relatively high. Probing amendments, usually at the committee stage, tend to be uncoordinated and have no need to demonstrate wide support in order to gain the desired verbal ministerial response. Some cross-party signalling does occur: for example, under Labour when the two opposition parties wished to make the government appear isolated (e.g. on identity cards), and under coalition when Labour joined forces with Crossbenchers in order to signal that the government's policy was out of step with dispassionate expert opinion (e.g. on welfare). But in both cases working across party lines was also to some extent a sincere attempt to put pressure on the government to change policy direction.

Many parliamentarians emphasized in interview how cross-party sponsorship is a distinguishing feature of amendments seriously targeted at legislative change. As a Liberal Democrat frontbencher in the Lords explained, 'it depends whether you're serious about something. If you're serious about something you've got to join forces basically.' At the committee stage some accidental cross-party pressure may occur due to different groups tabling similar amendments, and cross-party alliances may start to form. More determined cross-party initiatives can then be pursued if necessary at report stage. Hence a frontbench Labour peer, speaking about the coalition period, told us 'report is the point at which you decide which ones you really want to push . . . in order to improve the bill', compared to amendments 'where you know you're never going to win them, but you want to make the political point'. He explained that the difference between the two is easily spotted, because the point-scoring amendments would be proposed solely in the name of the opposition, while those that were serious would be tabled on a cross-party basis, often led by a non-party peer. This dynamic was also emphasized by the previous Liberal Democrat interviewee, who suggested that it is 'partly a signal to the government, actually, that you're not serious if you're just putting [an amendment] in your own name'.

Given the number of stages in the legislative process at Westminster, the potential exists for a cross-party coalition around a topic to build and build—particularly (as applies in the majority of cases) where a bill moves from the Commons to the Lords. In the latter the chance of building a winning coalition against the government is clearly far greater. Interviewees speaking about the period of Labour government explained that the 'jackpot on any piece of legislation [was], you know, government backbencher, opposition, Crossbencher and, depending on the subject, a bishop', or that 'the real trick was to have four names: one Conservative, one Liberal Democrat, one Crossbench and one Labour'. Later, under coalition, a Labour frontbencher told us that 'it's become the conventional wisdom that if you want to win a vote against the government, you need to get a Crossbencher to move the amendment'.

The benefits of cross-party sponsorship

Although the last of these options clearly does not exist in the Commons, a similar general dynamic applies there on occasions when non-government parliamentarians are serious about achieving policy change. But this raises the question of why, when this is their aim, parliamentarians in both chambers put energy into pursuing cross-party sponsorship of their amendments. There are three fairly obvious interrelated reasons:

- First, cross-party sponsorship makes an amendment appear less partisan, and therefore more reasonable. If members of several groups are prepared to support a proposition, the government's argument may appear weaker, encouraging those both inside and outside parliament to conclude that the policy should be changed. If the sponsors are established 'experts' (such as members of a select committee), this clearly strengthens the case.

- Second, consequently, cross-party sponsorship may attract a wider range of other supporters to the amendment. Government backbenchers in particular may find it hard to 'break ranks' with their own group to support a hostile amendment, but the presence of a government backbench sponsor offers a degree of 'cover'. Likewise a Crossbench sponsor may encourage other Crossbenchers to look at an amendment carefully and consider supporting it, and so on. In the words of one Labour frontbencher who served in the Commons under coalition, when planning an amendment 'you've got to think: how am I going to make it easy for people to vote for this?'.

- This leads to the third and ultimate reason for seeking cross-party sponsorship of an amendment: the effect that it has government's thinking. Cross-party amendments demonstrate that there is a potential threat in the division lobbies. Speaking about the Commons, a civil servant who had served as a bill team manager commented that particular attention is paid to 'the number of MPs that sign up to something, and how much they are across party lines', adding that wide support for an amendment has the potential to 'send powerful messages' to government.

Parliamentarians are well aware of the last of these dynamics. For example a Lords frontbencher pointed out that wide support may serve as a persuasive device meaning that actual confrontation proves unnecessary:

At the beginning what you're trying to do is build a platform, so the government think 'bloody hell, I'd better do something about this, otherwise we're getting the Crossbenchers, plus the opposition, plus dissident backbenchers, etc.' . . . [but] a sensible minister never has to get to the point where you are having to make any overt sort of threat, because he actually sees the sense of what you're doing and is prepared to put the point to the Secretary of State or persuade his bill team that actually you're talking sense.

Of course, this is exactly the kind of dynamic seen on many of the successful initiatives discussed in earlier chapters, some of which we return to below.

Credit claiming and cross-party amendments

So cross-party amendments are disproportionately focused on seeking actual legislative change. But when this is the goal parliamentarians may need to be pragmatic about who gets the credit. This tension was expressed to us by several interviewees when discussing joint work between the opposition and government backbenchers in particular. A Liberal Democrat frontbencher, explaining why he spoke in support of a government backbench amendment to one of Labour's bills, rather than focusing on his own, said that this was because the MP concerned 'was a Labour backbencher trying to amend his own government's legislation and it was easier to piggy-back [on] that and try and entice him to put his amendment to the vote'. Describing an amendment to another bill in this period a Conservative frontbencher likewise said that 'it had to be done very tactically because if I'd led it as a Conservative amendment then the Labour MPs who supported it wouldn't have supported it', whereas 'because it was seen as [a Labour backbench] amendment, supported by us, then they would'.[12]

In the period of coalition similar dynamics applied, as expressed by a Labour opposition frontbencher:

> There is a balance to be struck between Labour having a voice on the one hand and, on the other hand, trying to make sure that you win. But it's slightly galling when you provide nine tenths of the vote or more but the only people who get the media are the Tory rebels. In the end, if you want to achieve a political victory, you just have to swallow your principles and accept that they're going to take the credit.

This form of working hence challenges conventional views not only about the lack of a cross-party mode in the UK parliament, but also about how the opposition behaves. If opposition were all about credit claiming, and external signalling (as presentations of Westminster often suggest), it would be counter-productive to get involved with such joint initiatives. But when frontbenchers have a genuine interest in achieving policy change, building cross-party alliances makes perfect sense. In contrast to the classic picture drawn by King (1976), this kind of activity is today relatively common. However, it may sometimes be hidden from view, with the official sponsors on the order paper not giving an accurate picture of the support for an amendment behind the scenes.

Notably, such hidden connections are not always about the opposition masking its amendments. Under coalition, a Liberal Democrat backbench MP reported working with Labour members, including 'trying to encourage them to do stuff as well so that it was coming from all directions'. Likewise on one of Labour's bills, a Conservative opposition frontbencher described tabling an amendment drafted by a Labour backbencher. The author of the amendment had privately 'made it quite clear that, although he agreed with every word of it—well, he'd written it—if it was pushed to a vote he wouldn't vote for it'. In both cases government backbenchers were seeking to exploit the opposition's 'issue politicization' function, by getting issues onto the public agenda and pressed quite vigorously—presumably with a view to building momentum for future policy change. Hence to some extent both opposition members' and government backbenchers' public behaviour may adhere to stereotypes, while privately there are more complex pressures, and relationships, at play.

Evidence of Cross-Party Influence on the Case Study Bills

We have established that, contrary to the picture painted by King (1976), and some subsequent scholars (e.g. Andeweg and Nijzink 1995), Westminster now has a fairly well-established 'cross-party mode' with respect to legislation. Indeed, it might be more accurate to say that it has various different cross-party modes, ranging from formal to informal, at front and backbench levels, between groups of different kinds, and across both chambers. And the ability to form cross-party alliances is ultimately what matters most in determining whether government bills pass through parliament unscathed. In this section we discuss change sparked by cross-party support for amendments, and then the role of potential cross-party alliances in parliament's 'power of anticipated reactions', as well as limitations on the ability of such alliances to affect policy outcomes.

Cross-party amendments and policy change

Table 9.3 again shows non-government amendments with cross-party sponsorship, this time alongside legislative strands demonstrating cross-party support.[13] In Chapters 3–6 we considered strands initiated by an amendment from the group concerned. We do the same here, indicating the number of strands initiated by cross-party amendments; but we also go further. There are at least two other ways in which a strand can be considered 'cross-party' in terms of the sponsors of amendments. First, it may contain amendments at different stages which are sponsored by different groups—for example starting in committee with government backbench amendments and being taken up at report stage by the opposition, or vice versa. Second, there may be two (or potentially more) strands pursued by different groups with very similar proposed policy effects. As set out in Appendix A, our rules for building strands did not permit separate amendments by different actors at the same stage within one strand, but where very similar strands from different actors existed we coded them as 'siblings'.[14] Table 9.3 includes both of these additional forms of support in the 'Cross-party (single-group initiated)' rows. We see that there were 246 strands initiated by a cross-party amendment, and a further 235 which demonstrated clear cross-party support in one of these other two ways. Of course there are further means of demonstrating cross-party support as well—for example if members organize behind the scenes in support of each other's amendments, speak in support of them, or ultimately vote for them. These are not captured in the table.

The table also does not fully capture the effect of formal cross-party networks, through the select committees. These were dealt with substantively in the previous chapter, where we used a different measure, of the number of strands containing agreed amendments that implemented select committee recommendations (of course this chapter also discussed other more subtle forms of influence by select committees). It is unusual for committee members to work together actively to pursue amendments as a group—though in some cases, most notably the successful action by the Commons Health Select Committee on the smoking ban, they do. The strength of support demonstrated by this group of signatories helped to force the dropping of Labour's manifesto line in favour of a wider ban. Due to the unusual nature of this amendment, it does appear in the table as a successful cross-party strand. But in cases where other actors pursued amendments similar to committee recommendations (which is more common), this is not automatically captured in the table unless the sponsors had cross-party characteristics. As indicated

Table 9.3 Cross-party amendments proposed and success of cross-party strands

	Amendments proposed by actor	Strands		% success	% of total successful strands in parliament
		Total strands	Of which successful		
2005–10 parliament					
Single group	1,652	798	36	5	21
Cross-party (cross-party initiated)	241	133	14	11	8
Cross-party (single-group initiated)	—	128	18	14	11
Total cross-party	—	261	32	12	19
Total for all non-govt actors	1,893	1,059	68	6	40
Total for all actors	2,389	1,161	169	15	100
2010–12 session					
Single group	1,268	585	30	5	23
Cross-party (cross-party initiated)	314	113	14	12	11
Cross-party (single-group initiated)	—	107	23	21	18
Total cross-party	—	220	37	17	28
Total for all non-govt actors	1,582	805	67	8	51
Total for all actors	1,972	889	131	15	100
Both parliaments					
Single group	2,920	1,383	66	5	22
Cross-party (cross-party initiated)	555	246	28	11	9
Cross-party (single-group initiated)	—	235	41	17	14
Total cross-party	—	481	69	14	23
Total for all non-govt actors	3,475	1,864	135	7	45
Total for all actors	4,361	2,050	300	15	100

Note: As in previous chapters the figures for single-group and cross-party amendments exclude any co-sponsored with the government; all amendments with a ministerial sponsor are included within the 'total for all actors'. Of the 555 cross-party-initiated amendments, 34 (6%) were agreed to, of which two (0.4% of the total) were neither subsequently overturned nor purely overturned an earlier amendment (as described in Chapter 3). 'Cross-party' is defined as joint involvement between non-government actors from different parties or non-party groups (as defined in Chapter 6).

in Chapter 8, the 12 strands where government responded directly to select committee recommendations (i.e. without pressure from non-government amendments) are
also excluded—as these are formally treated as government-initiated strands.

For comparison, Table 9.3 shows the total amendments and strands initiated by
single (party or non-party) groups, so that we can reflect on differences between
numbers and success rates of strands with and without cross-party support. As in
earlier chapters, we show the number of 'successful' strands (i.e. those resulting
directly in a change to the bill), and the proportion from each group that were successful. We see that 23 per cent of successful strands were cross-party in some sense.
We also see what looks like a substantial difference in levels of success between
single-group strands and those qualifying as cross-party. In 2005–10 the respective success rates were 5 per cent versus 12 per cent, and in 2010–12, 5 per cent
versus 17 per cent. These differences can be tested statistically using a chi squared
test, which shows them to be highly significant. The probability of such differences occurring randomly in either 2005–10, 2010–12, or overall (i.e. counting all
strands together) is in each case below 0.00001—that is, a less than one in 100,000
chance. We can very safely conclude that cross-party strands have a higher success
rate than single-group strands.[15]

There are various reasons for this to be the case. Many single-group strands start
and end with a (perhaps probing) amendment at just one stage. It is initiatives that
continue across several legislative stages which are more likely to collect cross-party
support, and to put pressure on government. Cross-party work is also more common in the Lords than the Commons, and this is where the government is most
vulnerable to policy challenge. Hence in many respects these results are, in fact,
unsurprising.[16] But we have also discussed the clear relationship between cross-
party work and sincerity in achieving legislative change. These figures suggest that
such working does pay off.

We have seen numerous examples throughout the book of coalitions coming
together across party lines to successfully push for changes. Key examples during
the period of Labour government include the following:

- The major compromise on deaths in custody in the Corporate Manslaughter
  and Corporate Homicide Bill, which followed government backbench
  Commons amendments, cross-party opposition Lords amendments, a high-
  profile intervention by Crossbencher Lord (David) Ramsbotham, plus reports
  from three select committees (see Chapters 5 and 6).

- Cross-party opposition pressure on costs and benefits in the Identity Cards
  Bill, which was resolved via an amendment proposed by government backbench MP Frank Dobson (see Chapter 5).

- Limiting the extent of compulsion in obtaining an ID card when applying
  for a passport in this same bill. As described in Chapter 6, change was pressed
  on the government by joint opposition amendments with some Labour backbench support, and finally resolved through the intervention of Crossbencher
  Lord (Robert) Armstrong.

- The further question in this bill of the scheme's potential extension to non-passport holders, resolved by the government conceding a Lords defeat on a joint opposition amendment, acknowledging that this was in line with the prior cross-party recommendations of a Commons select committee (see Chapters 5 and 8).

- Obviously, the cross-party amendment proposed by members of the Health Select Committee which helped force a change of policy on the smoking ban (also discussed in Chapter 8).

- The response on the matter of trade union membership in the Employment Bill, referred to above, which involved very similar amendments from Liberal Democrat Lord Lester and senior Labour backbencher Lord Morris of Handsworth, also with backing from a select committee (again see Chapter 8).

- The significant concessions on foundation degree franchising in response to Crossbencher Lord (Ron) Dearing's amendments on the Further Education and Training Bill, which enjoyed Conservative and Liberal Democrat front-bench and Labour backbench support (see Chapter 6).

- Less confrontationally than any of the above, the changes to the Energy Bill mentioned earlier in this chapter; the concession to government backbencher Jeff Ennis on age limits for tobacco sales on the Health Bill (described in Chapter 5), where Conservative frontbenchers had tabled similar amendments; likewise the concession to Stephen Ladyman on Carer's Allowance in the Saving Gateway Accounts Bill (also Chapter 5), where the Liberal Democrat frontbench had made related proposals.

In fact virtually every major change to the bills in this period shows clear evidence of cross-party support. In reverse, the failure of various initiatives can be traced to the lack of sufficient such support. The clearest example was the proposal from government backbencher John McDonnell to amend the Employment Bill (as discussed in Chapter 5), where despite a large backbench rebellion the amendment failed because the opposition supported the government. We also saw in Chapter 6 that Crossbench initiatives which lack determined opposition or government backbench support are largely doomed to fail. Both backbenchers and Crossbenchers are clearly important, and taken seriously by government; but neither group is likely to succeed on its own. Similarly, opposition initiatives which do not receive support from these groups will generally prove unsuccessful.

We have seen throughout the book how dynamics changed in important ways when the coalition entered power in 2010. The government was numerically stronger in the Lords, and could depend (rebels aside) on the votes of two of the three main parties. The opposition strengthened alliances with non-party peers, but otherwise options to put cross-party pressure on the government were greatly diminished. Various initiatives on the Welfare Reform Bill, in particular (as discussed in Chapter 6), showed little success. But again, changes that did occur invariably displayed cross-party support. This applied both on the relatively small changes to the Welfare Reform Bill, and the far more radical changes to the Public Bodies Bill. Particular examples, as described more fully in previous chapters, include:

- In the Welfare Reform Bill, extending the mobility component of the Personal Independence Payment Bill to care home residents, as initially pursued by the opposition and Liberal Democrat backbenchers, and resolved following the intervention of Crossbencher Lord (Colin) Low (discussed in Chapter 6).

- Likewise, concessions to Liberal Democrat backbencher Baroness (Celia) Thomas of Winchester regarding more general eligibility criteria for this benefit, which followed Labour frontbench amendments in the Commons (see Chapter 5).

- The more minor concessions in this bill on the qualifying period for Employment and Support Allowance, pursued by the opposition in the Commons, and Crossbench and government backbench peers, and resolved via opposition frontbench amendments drafted and supported by the government (discussed in Chapter 4).

- On the Public Bodies Bill, proposals by the Labour opposition frontbench to insert a sunset clause limiting the life of the bill; this was echoed by a similar Liberal Democrat backbench amendment, and reflected proposals from both the Delegated Powers and Regulatory Reform Committee (DPRRC) and the Commons Public Administration Select Committee (as described in Chapter 4).

- Changes regarding ministerial powers over bodies with judicial functions, driven by backbench Liberal Democrat Lord Lester, with amendments co-sponsored by a Crossbencher, a Labour frontbencher and a prominent Conservative backbencher, and again reflecting DPRRC concerns (see Chapter 5).[17]

- Reversal of the proposal to abolish the Chief Coroner, following intervention by Crossbencher Baroness (Ilora) Finlay, backed among others by Labour backbencher Baroness (Glenys) Thornton, and subsequently taken up in the Commons by Conservative backbench MP Andrew Percy (see Chapter 7).

- A similar reversal on the Youth Justice Board, following joint amendments from Crossbencher Lord Ramsbotham, with Labour and Conservative backbenchers, and concerns expressed by two Commons select committees (see Chapter 8).

- The removal of the forestry clauses, following an initiative led by backbench Liberal Democrat Lord (Tony) Greaves, with amendments co-sponsored by the Labour frontbench (also described in Chapter 7).

In many respects the Public Bodies Bill created a 'perfect storm' for parliamentary opposition, even under the coalition. It was an ill-prepared measure, introduced via the House of Lords, which generated resistance on all benches in both chambers, often backed by respected select committees. The biggest change of all on the bill reflected this dynamic: that is, the complete removal of schedule 7, which listed 150 bodies, along with clause 11 which allowed bodies in the schedule to be moved to any of the other schedules (making them eligible for merger, reform, or abolition) via secondary legislation. This provides our final example of change (not discussed in earlier chapters), showing cross-party work at its most effective.

Schedule 7 raised strong objections from both the Constitution Committee and the DPRRC, with the latter stating simply that '[i]f the House can find no over-riding reason or exceptional circumstances which justify the inclusion of clause 11 and Schedule 7, the Committee recommends that they should be removed from the Bill' (Delegated Powers and Regulatory Reform Committee 2010a: 3). The extent of cross-party concern about this element (as well as several of the other issues above) was patently clear from the second reading debate. As indicated in Chapter 5, contributions included a strong speech from Conservative backbencher Lord (Philip) Norton of Louth, a former chair of the Constitution Committee and academic specialist on parliament and the constitution. He read from the committee's scathing report, which claimed that the bill 'strikes at the very heart of our constitutional system', and suggested himself that '[t]he prime mischief in the Bill is to be found in Clause 11 and Schedule 7'.[18] At the committee stage, Norton tabled an 'intention to oppose' the clause, which was co-sponsored by Lord Greaves and the Labour frontbench, and also an intention to oppose the schedule, co-sponsored by Crossbench lawyer Lord (David) Pannick. In addition, over 70 amendments were tabled by non-government peers from all sides to remove specific bodies from schedule 7. This presented a huge challenge to ministers: not only was a senior backbench Conservative leading resistance with the backing of a fairly clear majority in the Lords, but the committee stage could have dragged on for many weeks in order to debate all of these other amendments. This latter procedural point was important. As one interviewee who was closely involved explained:

I don't think they signed up just to get rid of it for that reason but I think they realized: what's the point of having all these lengthy, lengthy debates on particular provisions of schedule 7, and then come to the motion that schedule 7 become part of the bill and have it deleted at that point . . . [when] it was fairly clear to the government that it would have lost schedule 7 anyway.

We were told by other interviewees that the government was very resistant to making such a large change to the bill, and that ministers were initially 'quite bullish', and intent on 'riding it out'. Although there was much open hostility, discussions behind the scenes were ultimately—as is often the case—crucial in changing the government's mind. In particular, we were told of an encounter between Cabinet Office minister Francis Maude, responsible for the bill, and former Conservative Lord Chancellor Lord (James) Mackay of Clashfern, who asked to meet with ministers to discuss his concerns. Mackay had not signed any of the amendments on this topic, and indeed did not speak at second reading or early in the committee debates; but he was widely seen as a very influential and respected voice on the Conservative benches. Various interviewees made comments to the effect that 'the most listened to person [in the Lords] is Lord Mackay of Clashfern', one suggesting that 'Mackay, in your top trumps set, is probably the most powerful card'. After this meeting, where ministers were urged to drop schedule 7, 'that was it, it was dropped'. The minister added his name to Norton's amendment, which was unanimously passed at committee stage. This avoided debate on the other numerous connected amendments.

There was some dispute among interviewees about the extent to which the Mackay meeting was pivotal. Asked whether it sparked the ministerial decision, one insider suggested that 'I think it was before that . . . we knew the game was up on schedule 7 early on'. Nonetheless, as well as providing a perfect example of cross-party pressure—including that wrought by select committees—this is a nice illustration of how visible on-the-record influence can often give only a partial impression of the true political dynamics and involvement. It also shows how influence often cannot be ascribed to any particular group. Numerous groups could claim credit for this parliamentary victory over government—some through visible influence and others not. When interviewing Labour parliamentarians, the change was cited several times as the opposition's biggest victory over the coalition. Yet it occurred on an amendment headed by a Conservative backbencher, backed by a Crossbencher and a Liberal Democrat backbencher, to implement the recommendations of a cross-party select committee.

Cross-party initiatives and anticipated reactions

In other chapters we have repeatedly emphasized the importance of anticipated reactions in the exercise of parliamentary power. Government works hard to second-guess the views of parliament, both through its 'handling strategies' when bills are being prepared for introduction, and more fundamentally when thinking through its policy priorities prior to legislation being drafted. We have seen that various groups are important to this thinking: government backbenchers are absolutely key; expert Crossbenchers can also be both pivotal in the Lords and influential on the views of others; the opposition meanwhile has the ability to attract negative publicity, and the capacity to defeat the government if it can achieve adequate support from these other groups. Since no single group on its own can force changes upon the government, it is ultimately the potential for cross-party coalitions to form that concerns ministers and civil servants the most.

This is clearest with respect to the Lords, where majorities against the government can fairly readily be built even without involvement of government backbenchers. But conscious planning, and careful negotiation, may enable ministers to minimize defeats. Under Labour, the number of Lords defeats was sometimes high—reaching a peak of 88 in the 2002–03 session. But it then fell gradually in the period to 2010. This was in part due to the government's changed policy agenda (with many prior defeats having been on high-profile civil liberties matters); but it also resulted from more careful Lords handling. A good deal of negotiation in the Lords takes place 'in the shadow' of potential government defeat. As an interviewee who served as a Lords whip under Labour explained, 'the whole job was trying to . . . reach an agreement with the Lib Dems on specific issues, or an agreement with the

Tories on specific issues, or persuading one or other of them to go home'. Another interviewee likewise described how in this period 'you need[ed] to give concessions to one party to prevent them going with the other' and hence 'had to work quite hard to get them to be with you rather than . . . voting against you'. Clearly this kind of conscious calculation goes on during the passage of a bill; but ministers will also be naturally sensitive to the risks of cross-party opposition at earlier stages, when formulating policy proposals. While coalition reduced the opportunities for cross-party resistance from the Lords, a similar dynamic returned post-2015.

In thinking through possible cross-party alliances, therefore, the Lords is clearly important to ministerial planning. But it is nonetheless ultimately alliances in the Commons—and specifically those involving government backbench MPs—that represent the biggest threat. Commons backbenchers matter because they can choose to side with the opposition. The opposition matters, because if it can win support from even some backbenchers then the government's Commons majority can come under threat. Ultimately the opposition's ability to force defeats in the Lords, sometimes with the support of others, merely allows it to put sensitive matters back onto the Commons agenda for government backbenchers to decide. This means that all groups, in both chambers, are crucial to some extent in the government's prior planning before bills are introduced.

The limits of cross-party influence

Undoubtedly, cross-party alliances present the biggest threat that ministers can face to their legislation in parliament. But not all cross-party initiatives succeed. While both chambers clearly matter fundamentally, it is far more difficult for opponents to build winning coalitions against the government when the Lords is excluded from full scrutiny of a bill. In most cases, this chamber is central to the success of cross-party alliances, and hence to achieving major policy changes. We see this in our sample through the bills which did not have full Lords consideration—the Savings Accounts and Health in Pregnancy Grant Bill, due to its money bill status, and the Energy Bill, due to the hasty 'wash-up' at the end of the 2005 parliament.

As was discussed in Chapter 4, opposition members failed to effect any change to the Savings Accounts and Health in Pregnancy Grant Bill, despite voicing fierce objections. On many matters it would have been difficult to build successful alliances even if the Lords had been involved. Liberal Democrat rebellions were unlikely and, as with the Welfare Reform Bill, there was a dominant rhetoric of 'austerity' and Lords amendments would probably have attracted claims of Commons' financial privilege (for discussion of these dynamics see Chapters 4–6). But the initiative by Labour backbencher Paul Goggins to protect the rights of 'looked-after' children attracted cross-party interest, and might well have resulted in an amendment had the bill been debated in the Lords. An even starker example is seen on the Energy Bill. Here a proposal to introduce an emissions performance standard for power stations failed, despite having impressive cross-party support. At the Commons committee stage three new clauses on this topic had been proposed—led by the Conservative frontbench, a Labour backbencher, and Liberal Democrat Simon Hughes. At report stage there were again several proposals, this time with mixed cross-party support, one of whose signatories included the Conservative and Liberal Democrat frontbench, 15 Labour backbenchers, plus minor party representatives. The government offered only a weak concessionary amendment, so this cross-party proposal was pushed to the vote—and only very narrowly defeated (by 252 votes to 244, with 27 Labour rebels). A government insider described this as 'a massive, massive push from parliament to ... introduce an emissions performance standard' which was only just fought off. Had the bill's parliamentary passage not been curtailed by the impending general election, and it proceeded to full debate in the Lords, this matter would almost certainly have been returned to, and the government forced to back down.

The House of Lords is very important to nurturing relationships across party lines, given its more clearly developed culture of cross-party work and in particular of cross-party amendments. This example provides a neat illustration of how it is also very important to the ability of cross-party groups to achieve policy change.

Conclusions

We have seen that cross-party working at Westminster is conventionally considered to be weak, or even non-existent. But recent changes have created greater opportunities and incentives for such connections to form. The select committees encourage subject specialization among parliamentarians, and create a parliamentary environment in which members generally work constructively across party lines. They do not propose or formally amend bills, but can nonetheless (as discussed in Chapter 8) have a significant impact on the legislative process. The House of Lords, unlike the House of Commons, has no inbuilt government majority, which allows coalitions of non-government parliamentarians to readily come together and press for policy change. There are various types of cross-party cooperation, ranging from the formal, such as that facilitated by the committees, to the informal—that is, networks between parliamentarians with common interests (which committees, and other bodies such as APPGs, can help to foster). Informal links can operate behind the scenes between parliamentarians in different parties, at both frontbench and backbench levels. Mechanisms such as EDMs and backbench debates meanwhile allow members to express their support for each other publicly. Where members openly agree across party lines, including in speeches on government bills, this offers ministers early indication of issues that they may need to reconsider. In the end, cross-party support for hostile amendments in the division lobbies is what ministers most fear.

Throughout the book there have been various examples of successful cross-party initiatives, some of which were briefly revisited in this chapter. In fact, virtually every significant change to the case study bills showed some evidence of cross-party support. We have seen that cross-party co-sponsorship of amendments is relatively common, but of course we know that non-government amendments are rarely accepted directly into bills. As in other chapters, we have therefore traced the sources of change implemented by analysing legislative strands, which often end with government concessionary amendments. The success rates of single-party and cross-party strands (broadly defined) demonstrate very clearly that cross-party initiatives have a far higher chance of success. There are various obvious reasons for this, but a key factor is the clear relationship between cross-party work and sincerity in achieving legislative change.

Where parliamentarians simply wish to 'probe', or to 'signal' their opposition, or where they wish to play partisan games, they rarely bother to seek cross-party sponsorship of their amendments. In contrast this becomes a priority when they are serious about achieving change. Cross-party amendments have various benefits: they make an issue look less partisan, demonstrate breadth of support, and indicate to ministers that there may be a need to reconsider. Ministers will likewise feel under pressure when different groups of parliamentarians table amendments on very similar topics, which may ultimately culminate in them joining forces. In 'handling' parliament, ministers and civil servants will be keen to avoid this occurring. Hence while all groups contribute to some extent to parliament's power of anticipated reactions, this is in large part because of their potential to form alliances each other.

We conclude that, far from being weak to non-existent, the 'cross-party mode' at Westminster is therefore now well developed and commonly used. While the growth of select committees and declining party cohesion were both important contributors, changes in the House of Lords have had a particularly profound effect in this regard. Because bills must usually pass through both chambers, the ability for Lords majorities to form against the government also serves to encourage cross-party links in the Commons. The incentives for opposition parties to build connections with disillusioned government backbenchers were always significant, but grew substantially as a result of the 1999 Lords reform. When opposition peers send controversial issues back to the Commons to consider, government will face a serious threat if members on its own benches choose to back the Lords. Conversely, when backbenchers want to pursue changes in policy, they can now far more easily place pressure on ministers, through encouraging dissent by peers.

A significant theme throughout this book has been the extent to which relationships at Westminster changed under the period of coalition government post-2010. Ironically, while the government itself became a cross-party alliance, the ability for non-government coalitions to form on a cross-party basis was weakened as a result. This particularly affected the Lords, where the coalition government was much stronger numerically than Labour had been pre-2010. Under Labour the two opposition parties had learned to work jointly in both chambers (and of course went on to form the coalition together). Labour opposition members had no equivalent option of building an alliance with another significant opposition party. Pursuing relationships with backbench Liberal Democrats brought limited rewards, as these members felt unable to stray too far from commitments in the coalition agreement on sensitive matters such as cuts to welfare benefits, particularly in a context of 'austerity'. Non-party peers meanwhile (as discussed in Chapter 6) provided only a rather 'soft' opposition. Consequently the effectiveness of cross-party work in this period declined. Nonetheless, cross-party groupings worked successfully to achieve some significant policy reversals in the Public Bodies Bill. The extent of this change can be traced to formation of very wide-ranging networks including the Labour opposition, non-party parliamentarians, and backbenchers from both sides of the coalition. Following the 2015 general election, the Lords returned to a state in which two main opposition parties (this time Labour and the Liberal Democrats) could seek to extract concessions from a single-party government.

Notes

1. The exception being the work referred to in Chapter 5, demonstrating that the government is more likely to give in to Lords defeats when there has been some support for the proposition among its own backbench peers (Russell 2013, Russell and Sciara 2008).
2. They were: Charles Hendry (Conservative), Anne Main (Conservative), Judy Mallaber (Labour), John Robertson (Labour), Paddy Tipping (Labour), Mike Weir (SNP), Alan Whitehead (Labour), and Phil Willis (Liberal Democrat) respectively.
3. These rules may be found on the parliamentary webpage devoted to the register of APPGs: http://www.publications.parliament.uk/pa/cm/cmallparty/memi01.htm [accessed 6 August 2015]. Other rules specify the need to include at least one member from the governing party and one from the official opposition, and at least two MPs one of whom must take up the role of chair.
4. House of Lords Hansard, 7 January 2008, columns 643, 646.
5. Ibid., columns 644–5.
6. Ibid., column 646.
7. Ibid., column 690.
8. House of Lords Hansard, 13 March 2008, column GC317.
9. Hence the 2,920 total for 'single group' is the total of the individual single-group totals in Chapters 4, 5, and 6. The 'cross-party' total does not add up to those from earlier chapters, as by definition many of these amendments were included in more than one 'with others' category.
10. However, clearly not all initiatives with cross-party support succeeded. As discussed later in the chapter, a similar set of new clauses on the Energy Bill, calling for an emissions performance standard, generated only a weak government concession—in part due to the curtailed scrutiny of this bill in the House of Lords.
11. The exception is a motion to disagree with the Commons during Lords consideration of Commons amendments, which only one member can sign.
12. For further indications of this dynamic, see Chapter 5.
13. Strands were introduced in Chapter 2. For further detail of how they were designed and constructed, see Appendix A.
14. As indicated in the appendix, this rule proved necessary in order to clearly delineate different strands; but of course strands are artificial constructs, and the full complexity of interrelationships between different actors' amendments would be difficult to capture in any scheme.
15. A methodological case can be made, once sibling strands are included, for comparing rates of strands considered 'not unsuccessful'—that is including those which were

neither strictly successful nor unsuccessful (as defined in Appendix A). This is because where sibling strands exist, a somewhat arbitrary judgement is sometimes required to determine which strand should be allocated any finally agreed amendments. In other published work (Russell et al. 2017) we have reviewed the likelihood of falling into this 'not unsuccessful' category, and similarly found a highly statistically significant difference between single-group and cross-party strands.

16. Nonetheless further statistical analysis suggests that the success of strands with cross-party support cannot be explained purely due to these other factors. A logistic regression testing the effect of cross-party support, strand length and impact of having included Lords stages on the success of strands found both of the former to be statistically significant ($p<0.001$), but not the latter. Repeating this analysis on the likelihood of being 'not unsuccessful' (see note 15) found all three factors to be statistically significant ($p<0.001$).

17. The paving amendment discussed in Chapter 5 was co-sponsored by Lord Lester and prominent Crossbencher Lord (David) Pannick. The follow-up amendment tabled alongside it was sponsored by Lester, Pannick, former Conservative chair of the Constitution Committee Lord (Philip) Norton of Louth, and Labour frontbencher Lord (Philip) Hunt of Kings Heath.

18. House of Lords Hansard, 9 November 2010, column 154, quoting Constitution Committee (2010: 5).

10

Conclusion

Parliamentary Power and the Legislative Process

This book has looked in detail at the legislative process at Westminster, and represents the largest such study conducted for 40 years. It has traced the passage of 12 government bills during the parliamentary sessions 2005–12, exploring the various mechanisms that make up the process, and also its political dynamics. The analysis has been structured by reviewing, in turn, the role of different groups of actors who participate: members of the government, opposition, government backbenchers, non-party parliamentarians, pressure groups, and select committees. In the previous chapter we considered the role of cross-party work. This final chapter draws the threads together, to reflect upon the contribution of parliament as a whole to the passage of government bills.

In Chapter 1 we set out a series of questions to be addressed in the book, which were returned to in various places in subsequent chapters. Here we sum up the evidence on those questions. A particular theme throughout has been the extent to which parliament really has influence on government legislation. As Chapter 1 indicated, both academic and popular commentators have often played down this role. Our study has shown the picture to be more complex than such accounts suggest. It is true that most changes made to government bills in parliament result from amendments proposed by ministers themselves; but the majority of substantive government amendments are traceable to pressure from non-government parliamentarians. More importantly, parliament has various other, more subtle forms of power beyond amending bills; we summarize these here. We also consider which parliamentary actors wield which forms of power, and how this all fits together at Westminster.

The chapter begins with the obvious question of how much visible change was wrought by parliament to the 12 case study bills. We then provide some brief general reflections from our interviewees, which emphasize parliament's far wider role in the process. This leads to a discussion of what we describe as the six 'faces' of parliamentary power. In this section we address one central question that was set out at the start of the book, of how much influence by legislative institutions operates through measurable on-the-record changes, versus through more subtle and less visible means. Our answer is relatively generic, and to some extent applicable to all legislatures. The subsequent section hence focuses more specifically on patterns

Legislation at Westminster. First edition. Meg Russell and Daniel Gover. © Meg Russell and Daniel Gover 2017. Published 2017 by Oxford University Press.

at Westminster, reflecting in turn on the distinct contributions of different actors, of the Commons and the Lords, and then on the changes to legislative dynamics during the period of coalition 2010–12. The chapter closes by returning to the overarching question of how influential Westminster is in the legislative process, and how and why this might be misunderstood, followed by some brief reflections about the future.

Changes Made to the Case Study Bills in Parliament

As outlined in Chapter 2, the most detailed previous study of the Westminster legislative process was conducted over 40 years ago by J. A. G. Griffith (1974). He looked at all bills passing through parliament during three sessions between 1967 and 1971, and at thousands of amendments proposed and made to all those bills. Our approach was rather different, though we built on his methods. By selecting a smaller sample of bills we could study the process in greater depth—including through drawing on extensive interviews. The 12 case studies were chosen as far as possible, given the small sample size, to be representative of the government bills considered by parliament during the period 2005–12 (for details see Appendix A). An important part of our analysis was tracing all amendments proposed to these bills—though we have also emphasized throughout the book that this gives only a partial picture of parliament's impact on the process. While other forms of legislative power may be more important, as further elaborated below, a review of visible changes to the 12 bills is an obvious place to start.

Chapter 2 set out how a total of 4,361 amendments were proposed, of which 964 were agreed, and 752 were ultimately incorporated into the legislation (as many were overturned or simply served to reverse previous amendments).[1] Of these amendments ultimately agreed, 728 (97 per cent) were proposed in the name of ministers. This clearly makes government look dominant in the process. But Griffith's landmark study showed how amendments sponsored by ministers frequently respond to points raised by non-government parliamentarians (including government backbenchers, opposition members, and non-party peers)—particularly through their own amendments. Indeed as discussed in Chapter 3, the government's own *Guide to Making Legislation* is now quite open about its use of such 'concessionary' amendments (Cabinet Office 2015: 153).

The dynamics of this concession-giving process have been a major theme throughout the book, with different chapters discussing the role of distinct groups of parliamentary actors in triggering such change. A key tool was our construction of legislative 'strands', linking similar amendments at different stages of the process (again, as detailed in Appendix A). Amendments are often agreed in a 'package' (some of which are minor and consequential), and the 752 which were agreed contributed to 300 distinct legislative strands. Although most of these changes to the bills were ultimately implemented through government amendments, just 165 of the 300 strands (55 per cent) were government-initiated (of which 12, as discussed in Chapter 8, responded to points raised by select committees).[2] The remainder began with amendments from non-government parliamentarians. The breakdown of these by bill is shown in Table 10.1. We also saw in Chapter 3 that a majority of government amendments had negligible policy substance—being either technical, or consequential on other amendments—and 57 of the 165 government-initiated strands implemented only this kind of minor change. Hence Table 10.1 also shows the total figures excluding technical-only strands, among which those initiated by non-government parliamentarians form the majority.

There is much nuance hidden in these basic summary figures. On the government side, we noted in Chapter 3 that even where substantive amendments from ministers initiate strands, these are often driven by the need to respond to external pressures, rather than by government changes of heart. The days of 'legislate as you go' observed in parliament in the 1980s appear to be long over (Miers and Brock 1993: 134). Indeed today's *Guide to Making Legislation* seeks explicitly to prohibit such an approach (Cabinet Office 2015: 152). Although these rules may not always be observed, at least the intent is clear. Conversely, it must be acknowledged that not all changes to bills initiated by non-government parliamentarians are greatly substantive. While purely technical changes originating from these groups are rare, we have noted at points in the book that substantive change can still range from that which is primarily procedural, to that which explicitly

Table 10.1 Successful strands by bill and whether government or non-government initiated

	All successful strands				Excluding technical-only			
	Govt	Non-govt	Total	% govt	Govt	Non-govt	Total	% govt
2005–10 parliament								
Identity Cards	12	28	40	30	10	27	37	27
Health	35	10	45	78	22	8	30	73
Corporate Manslaughter	19	8	27	70	14	8	22	64
Further Education	12	8	20	60	5	8	13	38
Employment	9	4	13	69	6	4	10	60
Saving Gateway Accounts	2	5	7	29	2	5	7	29
Energy	12	5	17	71	4	5	9	44
Total (2005–10)	101	68	169	60	63	65	128	49
2010–12 session								
Identity Documents	2	0	2	100	2	0	2	100
Savings Accounts	0	0	0	n/a	0	0	0	n/a
Budget Responsibility	1	6	7	14	0	6	6	0
Public Bodies	24	26	50	48	20	26	46	43
Welfare Reform	37	35	72	51	23	35	58	40
Total (2010–12)	64	67	131	49	45	67	112	40
Grand total	165	135	300	55	108	132	240	45

changes policy. Of the 135 successful strands sparked by non-government amendments, 43 (i.e. roughly one-third) fell into the former category. Examples include placing requirements on ministers to commission research or table reports on policy progress after a bill is passed, or to tighten up parliamentary oversight of any secondary legislation authorized by the bill. Notably, however, more than half of these procedural changes were concentrated on a single bill: the coalition's Welfare Reform Bill. This was the only major example in our sample where more than 30 per cent of non-government-initiated changes fell into the procedural category.[3]

Even purely policy-related changes can of course be relatively small. Examples given in earlier chapters included changes regarding time limits and eligibility rules in the Welfare Reform Bill and Saving Gateway Accounts Bill, those allowing an increased minimum age for the purchase of tobacco products in the Health Bill, tightening the definition of fuel poverty in the Energy Bill, and strengthening the independence of the new Office for Budget Responsibility in the Budget Responsibility and National Audit Bill. But as seen in previous chapters, a number of the policy changes made to bills were also far more major. Key examples included the extension of the new offence in the Corporate Manslaughter and Corporate Homicide Bill to include deaths in prison and police custody, and the introduction of a total (rather than partial) ban on smoking in public places in the Health Bill.

Labour's Identity Cards Bill and the coalition's Public Bodies Bill were both very significantly changed in parliament. Various aspects of the proposed identity card scheme were altered in response to parliamentarians' concerns, while fundamental changes were also made to restrict the degree of compulsion in the scheme, and ultimately to delay its implementation (allowing the 2010 coalition to scrap the cards via its Identity Documents Bill before they had begun being issued to the general population).[4] The Public Bodies Bill, described by one key interviewee as 'an extreme example of a bill that was manifestly unsatisfactory' when it was introduced after the 2010 election to implement the so-called 'bonfire of the quangos', was even more radically amended. Key changes included removal of the forestry provisions, the removal of schedule 7 which listed 150 bodies for potential future abolition, and the insertion of a 'sunset clause' limiting the lifetime of the bill's effects to five years. This ill-prepared bill demonstrated just how much resistance can be mounted by parliament when there has been inadequate prior consultation and negotiation on policy, and to what significant effect.

These examples of change raise various questions. One is the extent to which significant amendment of government bills in parliament can be seen as a 'good thing', or as an indication that the system is working well. On the one hand, clearly if ministers present parliament with ill-prepared measures such as the Public Bodies Bill most people would agree that parliament should ask difficult questions and if necessary force changes to improve the quality of policy. On the other hand, however, most would also agree that government should think through its policy thoroughly before presenting it to parliament, rather than introducing bills that are ill-considered or flawed. Such preparation might result in relatively few parliamentary amendments needing to be made. It is difficult, therefore, to interpret changes made in parliament as a sign of either 'success' or 'failure' in the system.

As there are various reasons why the number of amendments made may be high or low, it is also difficult to use such figures to draw conclusions about changes over time. In particular we have sought in places throughout the book to compare our results with those of Griffith (1974), but have noted that meaningful comparisons are extremely difficult. Aside from a certain lack of clarity in the detailed methods of the original study, and inevitable challenges of assessing relative substantiveness of amendments, legislative drafting styles and government preparedness have altered greatly over the intervening period. Preparation of policy is now far more open and consultative, and parliamentary counsel far better resourced. The number of minor drafting changes in parliament has almost certainly declined; the number of substantive changes may well have increased. But better government pre-planning means that the context for these changes is now also very different.

How Influential Is Parliament? Views from Interviewees

Our central focus in this chapter is parliament's influence in the legislative process. As set out in Chapter 1 (and detailed in the appendices), we conducted over 120 interviews with people closely involved in the process, in Westminster, Whitehall, and beyond. Quotations from these interviews have informed the analysis throughout the book, with respect to developments on particular bills and the contribution of specific actors. But we also asked all interviewees their opinion on one very central question: 'how influential is parliament on government legislation?'. Respondents were encouraged to interpret this question in their own ways, and it elicited a very wide range of answers. The responses cannot readily be sorted into clear-cut categories, and hence our interpretation here is purely qualitative. Nonetheless for indicative purposes, some of these comments are very illuminating.

Although there were many differences among interviewees, it was notable that those furthest from the lawmaking process tended to be the most sceptical about parliament's power—expressing views closer to those propagated by critical external commentators. For example, one outside group representative stated that he found the 'very question depressing beyond belief', and considered this 'testament to the weakness of parliamentary democracy and the strength of the party system and cabinet government'. Another suggested that 'largely, if it's a government bill, government has the whip hand', while a third described trying to influence bills through parliament as 'a frustrating process'. One Commons backbencher described parliament as 'normally not very influential', while another even suggested that its influence was 'nil, basically'.

This degree of negativity was rare, and there were various more ambivalent or nuanced responses. For example another backbencher replied 'well, not effective enough', while a Conservative peer with long ministerial experience observed that parliamentary influence on bills 'varies a great deal depending on the subject matter'. A Liberal Democrat MP likewise suggested that if seeking change to 'a manifesto commitment, a core policy that goes to the core of the sort of party it is, you ain't going to get very far', whereas on 'a new issue that's come up where people's positions aren't entrenched, you've got more traction'. These are thoughtful and broadly sensible reflections, but of course not supported by the extent of change to manifesto-based policy in the Identity Cards Bill, and particularly in the Health Bill.

If the executive did indeed have the whip hand, we might expect those who have the greatest experience working inside government to be the most dismissive of parliament and its power. It was therefore striking that among our interviewees the most strongly positive responses regarding parliamentary influence came from this group. This was primarily because such people chose to interpret the question in a different way—going beyond immediately visible change. For example when asked 'how influential is parliament on government legislation?' a former cabinet minister responded 'Enormously. It's a widespread illusion that it isn't.' Civil servants who had worked on bill teams very often spoke in similar terms. One described parliament as 'extremely influential', suggesting that it's 'not fully understood, either by the media or by the general public about how much influence parliament has'. Initial responses from other bill team officials included, respectively, 'very influential', 'massively influential', 'immensely', and '100 per cent'.

Further discussion with these government insiders showed that they took a wider view of the role of parliament, beyond simply considering its ability to amend bills during their passage (for further detail of this culture see particularly Chapter 3). A former minister suggested that parliament was 'more influential than many think it is because much of the influence is unseen'. The former cabinet minister already cited elaborated by saying 'just about all legislation is affected by parliament. It's a widespread and completely wrong myth that government goes ahead without parliament.' Likewise another interviewee with long cabinet experience responded to the question as follows:

I think much more than people might think, in that if you just focus on the narrow dialogue between parliament and government at the ... public bill stage of a bill, you ignore the fact that there's [often] been pre-legislative scrutiny, there's been a draft bill, but also ministers do take account of what they know the view of parliament is when they draft the bill. So, actually, it's a sort of progressive influence, and it gets crystallized at the public bill stage, but actually a lot of it happens long before then.

This echoed a comment from one of the bill team officials cited above, that 'it doesn't start and end with the bill itself; it's a constant dialogue with parliament that is influential on what happens'. Another such official went even further, claiming that 'civil servants do—as indeed do ministers—actually default to parliament, as being the basis for everything we do'.

The Six Faces of Parliamentary Power

These reflections illustrate, using words from some of those closest to the process, one of the central points emphasized in this book: that parliament exercises several distinct and complementary forms of power over government legislation. Some parliamentary power, as captured above in our amendment data, has immediate measurable effects; but much operates far more subtly, by changing the whole environment in which government operates, and the government's own behaviour. In this section we set out these forms of power generically, in terms likely to apply across legislative institutions—drawing on our examples from Westminster, and considering how it may compare to other similar bodies. In the subsequent section we go on to focus more specifically on Westminster dynamics, summarizing which groups of actors in parliament assert which kinds of power.

As indicated at various points throughout the book, it is common for legislative studies scholars to point out that parliamentary influence operates in subtle and complex ways (e.g. Arter 2006, Blondel 1970, 1995, Mezey 1979, Norton 1993). This is connected in part to the diverse roles played by legislative institutions: not only as decision-makers, but also representative bodies, national forums for debate, scrutineers and overseers of government action, and so on. But while various typologies of parliamentary functions have long existed (see e.g. Kreppel 2014, Loewenberg and Patterson 1979, Polsby 1975), there is no accepted typology of different forms of parliamentary power. Instead, scholars have tended simply to emphasize that power does not lie where you might think—at the decision-making stage on legislation. Instead, in defending the political importance of legislative bodies these authors often stress the centrality of different parliamentary *functions*, such as legitimation or representation (e.g. Judge 1993, Norton 1993, 2013, Tomkins 2003).

The risk with this approach is that parliaments may be unfairly characterized as powerless with respect to legislation. As this is clearly a core function of any 'legislature', the impression may even be created that such bodies are not properly doing their job. But our findings suggest otherwise with respect to Westminster—that parliament influences legislative outcomes significantly, in various interconnected ways. Below, we suggest that the different forms of influence identified and discussed in earlier chapters may be summarized as six distinct 'faces' of parliamentary power. Here we consciously borrow from the language of much of the power literature (e.g. Bachrach and Baratz 1962, Digeser 1992, Isaac 1987, Lukes 1974). Our first three faces bear some resemblance to those of Lukes, whose third face is particularly useful in a parliamentary setting. Some authors have characterized these as 'visible', 'hidden', and 'invisible' power respectively (e.g. Gaventa 2007).

We adopt the widely used conception of power as relational: describing A's capacity to exercise power over B. Lukes devised his scheme for a very different purpose, and it is associated with power as 'domination', which is commonly seen as negative. Nonetheless in more democratic settings the exercise of power by one actor over another may instead be positive (Haugaard 2012). In considering legislation, we are seeking to describe the power that parliament (i.e. A) exercises over government (i.e. B) in the process. Our final three faces maintain this same relational language but nonetheless interpret power more broadly, acknowledging the importance of 'power to' and 'power with', as a complement to the more commonly discussed 'power over' (Allen 1998, Isaac 1987).[5]

Our purpose in identifying these 'faces' is to contribute to legislative studies; we make no claim to contribute to the power literature itself, and draw on it only fairly loosely. The key point to illustrate is that parliamentary power takes various subtle and interconnected forms. Like any simple scheme that seeks to classify complex real-world phenomena, this sixfold categorization is no doubt imperfect. In particular, we do not suggest that the faces are wholly distinct; they are explicitly interlinked. We also acknowledge that when considering parliament's wider power over government, beyond legislation, additional faces apply.

Face 1: visible changes through amendments

The first face of parliamentary power is the most obvious and visible: the ability of parliament to get government to change policy direction, on the record, as evidenced through legislative amendments. This is consistent with the first face of power in much of the literature, which is focused on clear 'decision-making', overt conflict, and observable behaviour (Lukes 1974: 25). Legislative studies scholars have often sought to capture this kind of visible change in their studies (e.g. Damgaard and Jensen 2006, Kerrouche 2006, Maurer 1999, Olson 1994).

It is a lack of such change that is often lamented by those concerned about parliamentary powerlessness, including at Westminster. For example, the pressure group representatives cited in the previous section seemed to have in mind the difficulty of getting non-government amendments to bills agreed. We cited Dunleavy (2006: 325) in Chapter 5, complaining that while parliamentary defenders tend to 'talk up' the importance of backbench rebels, House of Commons defeats are in practice extremely rare. Even defenders of Westminster often suggest that its measurable impact on legislation is small. For example Norton (2013: 130) states that 'purely in terms of observable decision-making, there is little evidence of Parliament affecting policy outcomes regularly and significantly'.

Whether this claim is true depends partly on one's definition of 'observable'. As already indicated, and explained in Chapter 3, non-government amendments very rarely find their way directly into the bills that Westminster finally approves, and are far more commonly withdrawn, defeated, or (if agreed) subsequently overturned. But, as discussed above, government concessionary amendments are common. These allow government lawyers to be satisfied that legislation is technically correct, and ministers to avoid handing clear victories to their political opponents. But they nonetheless often implement changes proposed by non-government parliamentarians. This is 'observable' through very close study of the parliamentary record.

Such patterns have long been recognized (Blondel 1970), and have been demonstrated not only by our research but in earlier studies of Westminster (Griffith

1974, Thompson 2015) and of some other legislatures (e.g. Shephard and Cairney 2005, Tsebelis et al. 2001). These dynamics were freely acknowledged by our interviewees, as when a former minister suggested that 'bills can obviously be changed quite significantly, and most bills do get changed to a certain degree'. Indeed the passage of government legislation can depend on such changes; a former cabinet minister recalled the government realizing that, having introduced a bill to parliament (not one of our case studies), 'if we wanted any bill at all, we had to shift'. So 'we either had to pull the bill, or we had to make concessions'. The visible powers available to A, as parliament, extend not only to amending B's bill against its wishes, but also potentially to rejecting such a bill altogether; indeed A can *in extremis* even vote B out of office. Yet such visible conflict is rare. As Lukes (2005: 69) put it in the second edition of his text, 'power is a potentiality, not an actuality—indeed a potentiality that may never be actualized'.

Face 2: anticipated reactions, or 'generating fear'

This leads to the well-known power of 'anticipated reactions' (Friedrich 1968), whose importance has long been recognized by legislative studies scholars (e.g. Blondel 1970, Mayhew 1974, Mezey 1979, Norton 1993). Russell and Benton (2011: 88), using words from a parliamentarian about the power of select committees, referred to this as 'generating fear'. It is related, but not identical, to the second face articulated in much of the power literature—which is about the 'suppression of conflict' (Isaac 1987: 10), 'nondecision-making' (Lukes 1974: 18), and keeping controversial matters off the agenda.

The power of anticipated reactions operates in different ways throughout the legislative process. Concessionary amendments following the introduction of bills to parliament may be seen as a relatively visible, and last-minute example of such a response. Cases such as that referred to by the cabinet minister above, where bills are radically revised or even withdrawn, provide even more substantial examples.[6] If ministers realize that parliamentarians' concerns may lead a bill to be defeated, they will normally take preventative action. This leads some legislative specialists, in direct contrast to Dunleavy above, to ask '[w]hy does executive-initiated legislation *ever* get defeated?' (Saiegh 2011: 5, emphasis added). Where government does retreat, it will usually seek to do so in a way that minimizes embarrassment, and masks the extent of parliamentary power. Among our case studies the free vote offered on the smoking ban, when government faced likely Commons defeat on one of its manifesto policies, provides a clear example.

But even this kind of manoeuvre is undesirable from government's point of view, given the combination of reputational risks, time, and political capital which may need to be expended. It is thus far preferable to anticipate parliament's response at an earlier stage. Saiegh's answer to his own question was that government defeats result from imperfect information about the legislature's views. Normally governments will prefer to gather such information from the earliest stage. Chapter 3 described how in the UK a well-developed system of parliamentary 'handling strategies' has developed, whereby government thinks through parliament's likely response to bills systematically prior to their introduction, specifically to minimize the risk of conflict. This second-guessing of parliamentary actors' responses may lead its legislative ambitions to be trimmed. A clear example was seen in Chapter 5 with respect to the Housing Benefit changes omitted from the Welfare Reform Bill.

Parliamentary counsel ultimately have the job of getting bills ready for introduction to Westminster. One experienced interviewee from this group answered our central question by suggesting that parliament matters 'hugely', noting that often 'it's not obvious when a bill is going through parliament that parliament has necessarily changed it very much, but parliament's reactions or potential reactions will have been taken into account in framing the bill in the first place'. As he added, 'the sponsoring department will have a sense of what it thinks it can ask parliament, where it might need to concede, and what it shouldn't even ask because it would be too unacceptable'. This is clearly a form of influence that is often hidden from public view. If it operates effectively, conflict will be minimized, making the measurement of parliamentary influence through on-the-record change positively misleading.

Face 3: government internalizing what parliament will accept

Anticipated reactions do at least involve conscious decision-making, albeit behind the scenes. They may be researched through speaking with insiders. The third face, in contrast, is largely invisible—and even unconscious on the part of those affected. For Lukes (1974: 23) this was an 'insidious' power; it goes beyond behavioural aspects and active decision-making, to capture the power that A can exercise over B through 'influencing, shaping or determining his very wants'. But such influence can also be positive. It bears some resemblance to Joseph Nye's 'soft power' (2008: 95), which involves 'getting others to want the outcomes that you want' through enticement rather than coercion. When A and B are parliament and government respectively, such influence can be viewed as a natural and healthy consequence of interdependence between executive and legislative power.

We saw in Chapter 1 how comparative scholars tend to assume that legislatures in parliamentary systems are relatively weak, and largely 'reactive' to the executive's agenda rather than behaving as 'active' policy-makers (Mezey 1979, Polsby 1975). Among such systems Westminster is often considered to be at the weaker end (e.g. Martin and Vanberg 2011), and is frequently singled out for unfavourable comparison with the US Congress (e.g. Kreppel 2014). But this view, often propagated by scholars who are most familiar with the US system, arguably misunderstands the relationships between legislatures and executives in parliamentary democracies. The distinctive feature of these systems is the executive's accountability to the legislature, and ultimate dependence upon it (as potentially exercised by the confidence vote). In the language of principal–agent analysis now widely used in legislative studies, the legislature formally holds the power and is the principal, while the executive is its agent (Strøm 2003). The agent's role is to do what the principal desires; hence if the two adopt similar policy positions, it is quite possibly the agent that is adapting its behaviour. In presidential systems no such dependency relationship exists. Because the legislature and executive are directly and separately accountable to the voters, conflict between the two is far less hazardous. Higher levels of visible conflict in presidential systems are thus not necessarily a sign of greater legislative power.

In parliamentary systems there is a clear incentive for ministers to minimize disputes with the legislature. This dependency relationship is so ingrained that influence may often operate subconsciously, by ministers internalizing parliamentary desires. Government backbenchers and frontbenchers are after all generally drawn from the same party (or parties, in the case of coalition), share common interests, and understand each other well. Numerous opportunities exist for informal contact between them, and both must account to similar party forums outside parliament. At Westminster, most ministers are recruited from among backbenchers, and may ultimately return to that role. Hence while conscious planning may be needed to anticipate the reactions of parliamentarians from beyond the governing party (or parties), responsiveness to ministers' co-partisans can be more subtle and subconscious. This presents clear methodological challenges, but illustrates further how an emphasis on visible conflict may misunderstand, and underestimate, parliamentary power.

Face 4: issue politicization and agenda setting

A crucial distinguishing feature of legislatures is their public nature, and this is central to the fourth and fifth faces of parliamentary power. While governments may be subject to requirements such as freedom of information, much of their deliberation and decision-making nonetheless takes place privately and behind the scenes. Parliaments, in contrast, deliberate publicly and on the record. They provide a unique forum within which the executive is compelled to explain itself, including with respect to its legislation. To return to the words of Mill (1998 [1861]: 282), they have the ability to 'throw the light of publicity' on what the government does.

As Nye (2008: 95) puts it, '[p]olitical leaders have long understood the power that comes from setting the agenda and determining the framework of a debate'. In line with this, parliamentarians have a central role in deciding which issues reach public view. Hence Loewenberg and Patterson (1979: 60) emphasize that very often it is in the public arena of parliament that 'the agenda of politics is formulated'. Rather than being a 'power over' (as in faces 1–3) this is a 'power to'. In relational terms, it is the ability for A to draw attention to issues, including those that B might prefer to suppress or to ignore. Throughout the book we have emphasized this power at two stages of the legislative process, using two different terms: 'agenda setting' before a bill has been introduced, and 'issue politicization' when deciding which topics get greatest attention during its passage through parliament.

Standing orders in different parliaments give varying degrees of agenda control to non-government actors (Cox 2009, Döring 1995), and in comparative terms Westminster is often seen as relatively executive-controlled. This may be so when considering the introduction of bills, but not with respect to other agenda-setting opportunities. Outside the legislative process, questions and debates provide significant means both for opposition frontbenchers and for backbenchers from all parties to raise issues publicly. Party leaders have less control over speaking time than in many other parliaments (Russell and Paun 2007), and recent developments have further enhanced backbenchers' agenda access (Russell 2011).

Parliamentarians can use these different mechanisms to draw attention to issues at the early stages of the policy process, and encourage the government to act. Among our case studies we saw this most clearly with respect to the Corporate Manslaughter and Corporate Homicide Bill, where (as discussed in Chapter 5) parliamentary questions, early day motions (EDMs), and amendments to other government bills helped keep the matter on the agenda for years before the legislation was introduced. Notably, there had been significant executive resistance to this measure. Likewise private members' bills were used to encourage government to legislate for a smoking ban. Parliamentary mechanisms such as these are frequently dismissed as non-influential, since most cannot force decisions. But they can nonetheless focus public and media attention on issues, and crucially at Westminster, most also demand an on-the-record government response. In this context it seems wrong to dismiss such parliaments as necessarily merely 'reactive' (Mezey 1979).

While the government often has significant ability to choose what to legislate upon in parliamentary systems, it is again non-government parliamentarians who often determine which elements receive the greatest public attention once a bill has been introduced. Westminster's adversarial traditions give the opposition substantial control over what gets discussed within each bill, both through 'usual channels' negotiations and the fact that much of the debate is in practice structured around opposition amendments. They can also use media interventions to influence broader public debate. In addition, we saw examples of non-legislative mechanisms being deployed to highlight controversial issues within the case study bills. Hence parliament provided a forum for the politicization of the provisions in the Public Bodies Bill that allowed for the privatization of public forests, echoing and reinforcing external attention on the issue. This occurred not only through amendments, but also an opposition day debate and questions to the Prime Minister. These helped to spark a policy reversal.

Face 5: accountability and exposure

This leads to a second closely related parliamentary 'power to': in terms of subjecting government proposals to careful scrutiny, on the public record, often with the support of expert evidence. In relational terms, this is the power for A to require public explanations for decisions from B—of course, in an environment where it can ultimately be forced to reverse them if they fail to withstand such scrutiny.

Among parliamentary institutions, the legislative stages at Westminster are fairly typical. The government must set out the principles of a bill at the second reading in both chambers, and answer criticisms, and then respond on the detail during the committee stage (during which at Westminster it is often subject to numerous 'probing' amendments). At the report stage, once all of these debates have taken place, it may face further, more serious pressures from non-government amendments. As in other bicameral parliaments, these stages are subsequently repeated in the second chamber. In many comparator parliaments there is more input from specialist committees built into this process. Although Chapter 8 showed such input to be far from negligible, Westminster's lack of specialist legislation committees arguably weakens this power, and is a major reason for its classic presentation as an 'arena' rather than a 'transformative' legislature (Polsby 1975). Nonetheless, exposure in the Commons plenary is very challenging for ministers, given its public nature and MPs' increasing preparedness to speak out against the party line (as demonstrated for example in the 'responses' section of Chapter 5). The Lords meanwhile has no government majority, and contains numerous subject experts, many of whom have no requirement at all to follow a whip. Members in both chambers are supported by information and possible lines of questioning from pressure groups and other specialists, and their scrutiny is fully visible to the media.

Neither of these 'powers to' directly result in change; but they crucially underpin parliament's 'power over' government in the legislative process (i.e. the first three faces). Griffith (1974: 256) noted the 'undoubted importance' of parliament 'forcing Ministers to defend their policies and themselves'. The need to provide public responses, on topics largely determined by others, requires government to think through policy carefully in advance of it being introduced (faces 2 and 3). If ministers fail to do so, exposure may fuel resistance and potentially destabilizing policy reversals (face 1). Hence if a key power of parliament is 'generating fear', it is primarily through these issue politicization and exposure functions that it is generated. As the civil servants cited above who considered parliament to be 'extremely influential' stated, this influence comes 'through the level of scrutiny'. Another bill team official linked this directly to anticipated reactions, stating that 'it's like the law in general and the policeman walking the streets. You know it's illegal to steal so you don't steal for fear of being prosecuted. You know that parliament is going to give you a tough time, and therefore you prepare really well.'

Parliamentary functions such as these tend not to be presented as important to decision-making, but more often as separate, perhaps contributing to broader 'legitimation'. But they do more than simply legitimizing government's decisions by showing parliament's approval; they potentially change what those decisions were. Hence they are key to determining the legislation that gets agreed.

Face 6: counteractive pressure and support for the government

Finally, it should not be assumed that the exercise of parliamentary power in the legislative process is all about challenging the government. As already emphasized, if ministers are the agents of parliament, and prepare bills having sought carefully to take parliamentary opinion into account, it would clearly be wrong to gauge the legislature's impact solely through measuring amendments made. Parliament's power hence lies not only in blocking policy changes pursued by the government, but often in supporting them. This could be seen as reflecting a kind of 'power with'. In relational terms parliamentarians exercise counteractive influence in defending policy changes in government bills against other forces—that is A choosing to defend B, including sometimes against the counterclaims of C or D.

As discussed in Chapter 7, the notion of counteractive influence in the policy process is well recognized in the literature with respect to pressure groups (Austen-Smith and Wright 1994). This is a key reason why specialist scholars suggest that pressure group influence is very difficult to measure (Dür and De Bièvre 2007). It is understood that the success of one pressure group may often come through defending the status quo against other rival groups. In a parliamentary setting an obvious parallel exists in terms of one group of parliamentarians (usually members of the governing party, or parties) defending policy positions against claims from rival parliamentarians (particularly opposition members). Here the role of 'pivotal voters' (Krehbiel 1998) becomes clear. Sometimes policy will be wholly uncontroversial—several of the case study bills went through with relatively little complaint, including from the opposition. But where there is controversy there will be various groups in any parliamentary chamber that can potentially either deny the government its majority, or choose to defend its position. Any such defence takes place in an environment where non-government parliamentarians (particularly opposition members) have considerable agenda-setting power, and where ministers' claims must stand up to intense public scrutiny. The extent to which this kind of pressure poses a threat often depends on the voting decisions of the government's own backbenchers. At Westminster members are relatively independent of the whip in comparison to many other parliamentary (though not necessarily presidential) systems, and increasingly so. Their backing for ministers' positions must be viewed as an active choice—making parliament's decision to support the government a conscious exercise of power.[7]

The Political Dynamics of Influence at Westminster

The previous section explored the dynamics of parliamentary influence in a relatively generic way, setting out six faces of power that exist to varying degrees in all legislatures. It focused in detail on the question posed in Chapter 1 about the importance of visible versus less visible parliamentary power. In this section we return more specifically to Westminster, and other questions set out at the start of the book. We begin by reflecting upon the roles of different groups of actors in the legislative process. We then consider the differing roles of the Commons and the Lords, and the different dynamics under single-party government versus coalition.

Actors, motivations, and faces of power

Earlier chapters emphasized how different actors at Westminster have different incentives, and different motivations, during the legislative process. We also emphasized how distinct groups of actors wield subtly different, but interrelated, forms of power. In a very simplified and schematic way, the main findings are summarized in Table 10.2.

The starting point for ministers is of course primarily a wish to get their bills through parliament. Nonetheless we did see in Chapter 3 that government should not be viewed as monolithic, and that parliament often provides a forum for internal conflicts—including between departments, personalities, and the governing parties under coalition—ultimately to be resolved. Ministers are themselves drawn from parliament, and may even collude on occasion with other parliamentarians (particularly government backbenchers) in order to achieve their personal policy goals. Government amendments—unlike those from other parliamentarians—are only tabled if actually intended to pass, and they almost invariably do so. As already discussed, they dominate among the amendments which are agreed.

After ministers, the most visible parliamentary actors are members of the opposition. In Chapter 4 we discussed how this group has classically been seen as office-seeking rather than policy-seeking at Westminster (e.g. Andeweg 2013, Helms 2004, Uhr 2009). In line with the classic view, one of the opposition's primary powers remains that of issue politicization—i.e. determining which issues in bills will receive the greatest attention (face 4). In looking at opposition 'modes' we saw that some bills are received in a 'consensual mode', where opposition frontbenchers broadly support the government; others are received in 'acquiescent mode' or 'conflicted mode', where it is difficult to raise objections. But when opposition frontbenchers do wish to raise concerns, they are able to be more outspoken than government backbenchers, and can use parliamentary tools such as debates and questions, as well as the external media. For example it was the opposition that led the politicization of the forestry provisions in the Public Bodies Bill (mentioned above and discussed in Chapter 7).

The opposition's amendments are also a key tool of issue politicization. Opposition parties propose the great majority of amendments at Westminster—including 2,941 of the total 4,361 on the case study bills—making the opposition primarily responsible for which parts of bills get most attention. Extremely few such proposals are agreed, but many are not sincere attempts at policy change. A lot are simply 'information seeking' (i.e. probing), and essentially used to structure debate and demand answers on the record (face 5). Others serve purposes of 'signalling' to groups outside parliament, or 'gameplaying' to embarrass the government. We thus cannot interpret the numerous non-agreed opposition amendments as a sign of 'failure' (Russell, Gover, and Wollter 2016). Many contribute to parliament's wider powers.

Nonetheless, changes at Westminster have increased the potential for opposition party amendments to directly influence policy outcomes, and have thus altered these parties' incentives. In the post-1999 House of Lords, there is significant potential for the opposition to defeat the government on amendments. During the period 1999–2010 (and again post-2015), not only the main opposition party but also the

Table 10.2 Motivations and exercise of power by different actors at Westminster

	Actors					Chambers	
	Opposition	Govt backbench	Non-party	Select committees	Cross-party	Commons	Lords
Faces of power							
Visible, through amendments	***	**	*	n/a	***	**	***
Anticipated reactions	**	***	**	**	***	**	***
Government internalizing	*	***	*	*	*	***	*
Agenda setting & issue politicization	***	**	*	**	***	***	***
Accountability & exposure	**	**	***	***	**	**	***
Support for the government	*	***	**	**	**	***	*
Motivations for amendments							
Information seeking	***	*	**	n/a	—	n/a	n/a
Signalling	**	*	—	n/a	*	n/a	n/a
Gameplaying	**	—	—	n/a	—	n/a	n/a
Markers for the future	—	**	*	n/a	*	n/a	n/a
Legislative change	**	**	**	n/a	***	n/a	n/a

*** = major role; ** = medium role; * = minor role; — = minimal/no role

Liberal Democrats were effectively 'pivotal' in the Lords. In both chambers opposition parties can politicize issues in a very public arena, where other groups who are
potentially pivotal (Crossbenchers in the Lords, government backbenchers in the
Commons) form a crucial part of the audience.

While the opposition is classically seen as relatively non-influential in policy
terms, government backbench MPs have in contrast been viewed as the most
important group at Westminster, due to ministers' dependence on them to retain
a Commons majority (King 1976). Given their centrality in the primary chamber, government backbenchers are the ultimate pivotal voters in parliament overall. Their goal is usually to support the government and its programme. But with
increasing independence on the backbenches (Cowley 2005, 2015, Cowley and
Stuart 2014), open challenges from this group are more common than they used to
be. Ministers must work hard to retain backbench support.

Compared to the opposition, government backbenchers propose relatively
few amendments (there were 555 such proposals on the case study bills). Such
amendments are more likely to be sincere attempts at policy change, though
(as explored in Chapter 5) some perform an information seeking or signalling
function. Very often backbenchers' main concern is party priorities and audiences, with the legislative process used in part to hold the government to the
party's programme—what Martin and Vanberg (2008, 2011) called 'policing
the bargain'—or to encourage development of new policy (including through
amendments that we dubbed 'markers for the future'). Relatively few legislative
strands initiated by government backbenchers were agreed to the case study bills
(accounting for just 36 of the 300 strands agreed), but their success *rate* was relatively higher than that for the opposition (12 per cent compared to 7 per cent).[8]
Nonetheless, as seen in Table 10.3—which draws together figures from earlier
chapters—legislative strands initiated by opposition parties accounted for a far
higher number of changes (112) overall.

Table 10.3 Groups initiating successful legislative strands

	Alone		With others		Total	
	N	% of total	N	% of total	N	% of total
Opposition party*	88	29	24	8	112	37
Government backbench	18	6	18	6	36	12
Non-party	1	0	11	4	12	4
Cross-party	28	9	n/a	n/a	28	9
Select committee(s)	n/a	n/a	50	17	50	17
Government**	165	55	0	0	165	55
Total	300	100				

* Figures for 'alone' represent single opposition party, while opposition parties acting jointly are in the 'with
others' column.

** As in earlier chapters of the book, government 'alone' figures also include 12 cases where amendments were
proposed in direct response to select committee recommendations and a further six that responded to points
raised by non-government parliamentarians in debate.

This finding may at first appear counterintuitive, but is very much in line with what Griffith (1974) found. Explaining it helps to get to the heart of how influence works at Westminster. First, government backbenchers' primary influence on bills normally occurs prior to their introduction. Given this group's pivotal nature, ministers will always think carefully about backbenchers' likely response when planning their bills (face 2), and will also internalize backbenchers' desires to a large extent (face 3). Backbenchers can perform an agenda-setting function (face 4), in bringing matters to government attention for action. This under-researched dynamic was visible on the smoking provisions in the Health Bill, and even more so on the Corporate Manslaughter and Corporate Homicide Bill—which was resisted by senior figures in government, including the Prime Minister himself. Hence legislation is often introduced in a form which is acceptable to, and indeed actively welcomed by, backbenchers. But post-introduction, ministers are particularly attentive to concerns from this group. Consequently, so is the opposition, which will seek to exploit any divisions on the government side in order to achieve its own policy goals. Some opposition amendments are directly designed for this purpose; many others, by simply requiring government to explain its policy on the record, may expose weaknesses which raise backbench concerns. Ultimately this may well lead to government concessions.

Backbenchers often exert pressure relatively invisibly, with a natural inclination to raise concerns privately rather than publicly. Public statements of dissent act as a warning to ministers, sometimes demonstrating that private channels have failed. Backbench interviewees explained that a combination of behind-the-scenes discussions and the possibility of rebel votes, with one as an ultimate threat underlying the other, generally proves most effective in gaining ministers' attention. While there were various examples of rebel votes and rebel amendments on the case study bills, one of the most important backbench interventions may have been a private meeting. This involved former Lord Chancellor Lord (James) Mackay of Clashfern, who had neither spoken out publicly nor signed amendments, but helped to encourage ministers to drop schedule 7 from the Public Bodies Bill (see Chapter 9).

Ultimately, government backbenchers normally exercise power through deciding to support the government against the criticisms made by others (face 6). Of course, when there is backbench dissent, the potential does exist for ministers to gain support from the opposition on some policies. This was seen in the case of John McDonnell's amendments to the Employment Bill (as discussed in Chapter 5). But this is an uncomfortable—and ultimately risky—route to take when faced with dissent from more mainstream backbenchers. As our interviewee with close links to Tony Blair explained, 'even TB, in his most avant-garde moments of public-sector reform, blanched at the prospect that he was … going to get anything through parliament on the basis of Tory votes'; hence he concluded, 'your primary concern is your own backbenchers'.

Other groups at Westminster play increasingly important roles, particularly through facilitating informed debate and hence contributing to accountability and exposure (face 5). As explored in Chapter 6, the presence of non-party parliamentarians is very important to the tone of debate in the Lords. Members of this group require—and often explicitly demand—rational explanations, and will be unconvinced by party-political point-scoring. They hence encourage evidence-based debate and convincing ministerial explanations. This is boosted by their ability to influence the views of party parliamentarians, and potentially to cast pivotal votes. Occasionally non-party peers put issues onto the policy agenda (face 4), but more often they contribute to deciding the outcome on issues tabled by others. The government will often actively court their support (face 6).

Pressure groups and select committees (respectively the focus of Chapters 7 and 8) are also important in facilitating informed debate, as well as sometimes putting issues onto the agenda. Despite often being regarded as primarily focused on influencing government, pressure groups play an increasingly important role in Westminster legislative dynamics. They have the ability to mobilize members from all parties, inject greater evidence into parliamentary deliberations, and encourage independent thinking beyond the whip. Far from being peripheral, parliament provides an effective, and very public, safety net for them to pick up any outstanding problems not resolved in negotiations at earlier stages—even where they had previously engaged with government before bills were introduced. If legitimate pressure group concerns were previously ignored, they are likely to be heard, and acted upon, in parliament. Parliamentarians are also the final arbiters in disputes between different groups, which often seek to push policy in opposing directions.

The select committees, which have consistently grown in strength and profile since the 1970s (Kelso 2009, Norton 1998b, Russell 2011), have likewise brought a greater emphasis on evidence into parliamentary decision-making. By encouraging subject specialization among members they help to break down knee-jerk partisan hostilities. Committee reports—particularly those from the constitutional committees in the Lords which routinely report on bills, and any pre-legislative scrutiny committees—can contribute in important ways to agenda setting and issue politicization (face 4), inform legislative debate (face 5), and help to inspire non-government amendments (face 1). The Health Select Committee's unusual intervention on the smoking ban (described in Chapter 8) showed the potential that committees have to put evidence in front of parliament, and ultimately to trigger policy reversals. Where select committees, or pressure groups, support government policy, ministers will emphasize this to ease the passage of their bills (face 6).

This book was organized around distinct groups of parliamentary actors. But fundamentally, the subtle forms of influence exercised by these groups at Westminster cannot readily be disentangled. Each plays a complementary role, in influencing the initial policy agenda, forcing controversial issues in bills into the spotlight, proposing amendments, exposing government arguments to debate and evidence, and ultimately deciding whether to pass government legislation, amended or unamended. Where there is pressure for change, particularly on major matters, this generally requires a degree of cross-party backing to succeed. As seen in Chapter 9, amendments with cross-party support are the most likely to be sincere, and strands demonstrating such support have a far higher chance of extracting government concessions. Contrary to the classic view (e.g. Andeweg and Nijzink 1995, King 1976), there is hence a well-developed 'cross-party mode' (or indeed modes) at

Westminster. In the end, as a very public forum, one of parliament's most central functions is exposure (face 5), which in turn feeds its core power of anticipated reactions or 'generating fear' (face 2). All groups contribute to this; hence all must be considered to varying degrees in the 'handling' of government bills.

The Commons and the Lords

In addition to considering distinct actors, as presented in the different chapters of the book, an obvious question when thinking about influence at Westminster is the relative contribution of each of the two chambers. Because government lacks a majority in the House of Lords, and is frequently defeated there, it may be tempting (in line with face 1) to conclude that the Lords holds the greater power. But this kind of reasoning clearly becomes simplistic when considering the different interrelated faces of power.

Even some inside parliament adopt easy stereotypes when contemplating this question. Again, our interviews showed how levels of understanding vary in line with distance from the relevant processes. For example a Crossbench peer suggested that 'the House of Lords is massively influential but ... the Commons ... they're so strongly whipped and they follow their whip to the extent that they don't know what they're voting on, they really are not that influential'. Likewise, a Liberal Democrat peer commented that 'the Commons, it seems to me, is very largely uninfluential ... on virtually all pieces of legislation'.

But these comments only make sense if viewing parliamentary influence narrowly, in terms of on-the-record change. Our analysis suggests very different conclusions. Ultimately, the influence of the two chambers cannot be separated—they operate as an interconnected system. In the words of a Commons official, under the usual scenario where a bill starts in that chamber and then moves to the Lords, the 'degree of uncertainty increases as you go through the process'. The primary job in the Commons is 'holding the line on all of the points that the opposition have made', which will generally be possible given the government's majority. But in the Lords often 'the cracks start to appear'. The government knows that it faces possible defeat if it doesn't compromise, and may make concessions to peers on inessential points in order to ease the bill's passage. But on the central issues ministers' greatest concern remains the views of pivotal voters in the primary chamber: that is, its own backbench MPs. Describing this dynamic from the point of view of the opposition, an experienced Commons frontbencher explained:

If you're at the point in the Commons where you can push the government in that way, but the government will be able to resist, then the chances are very high that the Lords will force the government to look at it again. Because that's actually how our constitution works: the Lords will have noted the extent of the disquiet expressed on a cross-party basis in the Commons, and therefore are likely to focus on it.

As earlier chapters have emphasized, this gives the Lords a crucial issue politicization function (face 4). On most bills the chamber's ultimate weapon—which is wielded particularly by the opposition—is the ability to put controversial matters back onto the Commons' agenda for decision.[9] Unlike the Commons, the Lords offers no immediate threat to the government, as it does not enjoy the power of the confidence vote—making it an environment where confrontation is less risky. But if defeats occur, the likely reactions of government backbenchers in the Commons are key. Where backbench opinion is solid, ministers will stand their ground; where there is known dissent, they are much more likely to back down. This was seen very explicitly on the Identity Cards Bill, as described in Chapter 5. The dispute between the two chambers over costs was ultimately resolved by an amendment from Labour backbencher Frank Dobson. Less visibly, the government accepted a Lords defeat on compulsion, rather than risk putting this to its MPs. Likewise the successful Crossbench-led Lords defeats to extend the Corporate Manslaughter and Corporate Homicide Bill to deaths in custody tapped into known Commons backbench dissent (Chapter 6); on the Public Bodies Bill the government chose to overturn some of its own amendments (e.g. over abolition of the Chief Coroner—see Chapter 7) rather than risk asking discontented Conservative MPs to back its position against the Lords.

Where government backbenchers have insufficient sympathy for the Lords' position, the chamber can fairly readily be overridden. This occurred, for example, on Lord Best's concerns over the so-called 'bedroom tax' in the Welfare Reform Bill (Chapter 6), where the hoped-for Liberal Democrat Commons rebellion did not occur. Changes seemingly forced by the Lords are thus in fact victories for parliament as a whole, as they must always be approved by the primary chamber; the Commons remains the final arbiter on big issues of legislative principle. After our study period the same dynamic was clearly seen on the 2015 Conservative government's Lords defeat on cuts to tax credits. This followed concerns expressed by backbench Conservative MPs, and initially sparked an angry response from ministers. But following the defeat, the government quietly dropped the proposal.

In terms of faces of power, we have seen that parliamentary 'handling strategies' were first developed for the Lords, and only later extended to the Commons. But this does not imply that the Lords is the more powerful chamber. Much government effort goes into anticipating and assuaging the concerns of peers (face 2). But what matters most to ministers is ensuring that they retain support of the Commons, and particularly the government backbenchers within it. As demonstrated by ministerial comments in Chapter 3, these demands are more instinctively understood (face 3).

The 2010 coalition

A remaining question set out in Chapter 1, and addressed in various places throughout the book, is the extent to which dynamics changed during the period of coalition government 2010–12. Conventional wisdom holds that parliaments are more powerful in an environment of coalition, as the need for bargaining to maintain the support of different government parties is greater (e.g. Norton 1990a, Polsby 1975, Taagepera and Shugart 1989). Hence when comparing 'majoritarian' and 'consensus' democracies, Lijphart (1999: 12) suggests that '[i]n multi-party parliamentary systems, cabinets—which are often coalition cabinets—tend to be much less dominant'. But again, the visible indicators of strength used in the comparative literature, such as government longevity in office, are often fairly crude.

At Westminster the norm has been single-party government (making Britain Lijphart's classic exemplar of a 'majoritarian' democracy), and this has contributed to parliament being seen as weak. Yet there is little sign that the period of coalition strengthened parliament. A central reason was the 2010 government's numerically greater strength in the Lords. Indeed, it might even be argued that the key shift at Westminster took place not in 2010, but in 1999, when the new 'no overall control' House of Lords gave far greater power to the centre party. This challenged majoritarianism at Westminster (Russell 2013). Subsequently the Lords was greatly weakened by coalition, and the reduction from two opposition parties to one also limited the opposition's ability to demonstrate broad-based resistance to government plans. Labour peers became dependent on alliances with non-party peers, who were far less assertive than the previously pivotal Liberal Democrats had been.

Beyond the Lords, our analysis shows that coalition also changed backbench behaviour. Labour backbenchers had relatively little interest pre-2010 in 'signalling' to the outside world, whereas Liberal Democrats frequently used their amendments to publicly distance themselves from the Conservatives. Chapter 5 showed that the number of such amendments was very high, but their effect on legislative outcomes (particularly on the Welfare Reform Bill) fairly small. There was little sign of the pattern noted in the comparative literature, whereby the junior coalition partner 'polices the bargain', by holding the larger party to their policy agreements (Martin and Vanberg 2008, 2011). Indeed, the behaviour of Labour backbenchers under single-party government better fitted this model—as seen above with respect to the Corporate Manslaughter and Corporate Homicide Bill. This again demonstrates the risks of conflating visible conflict with policy power: accountability to backbenchers under single-party government may be less visible, but is not necessarily any less effective than the kind of public 'signalling' that occurs under coalition. Of course the coalition period was brief; behaviour might develop differently should such arrangements become more commonplace at Westminster. Notably, the Liberal Democrats are widely seen as having been outmanoeuvred by the larger party in the initial coalition deal (Bale 2012, Fox 2010, Hayton 2014). Their amendments hence often sought to pull the government to the left, rather than defending the agreements made. Such mistakes would not necessarily be repeated.

The creation of the coalition government was obviously only the latest in a long line of changes at Westminster, as emphasized throughout the book and already touched on in this chapter. In terms of strengthening parliament, the most important changes may have occurred previously. As well as the 1999 Lords reform these included the development of the select committees, evidence-taking by Commons public bill committees, more frequent pre-legislative scrutiny, greater agenda access for backbenchers, declining party cohesion, and growing pressure group engagement. All of these occurred alongside, and are likely to have encouraged, more careful consultation and pre-parliamentary preparation of government bills. Even before some of these changes had taken place, one well-qualified observer looking back at over

40 years at Westminster had characterized parliament as 'more effective and much more significant in the politics of [the UK] than ever before' (Ryle 2005: 8). Ours was not a longitudinal study and, for various reasons already discussed, our results are not directly comparable with the last similar results from decades ago (Griffith 1974). But our conclusions are certainly not incompatible with Ryle's judgement.

Parliament as Legislator: Perceptions and Reality

This book's opening chapter reviewed common perceptions about parliament(s) and the legislative process. Popular accounts often present Westminster as little more than a 'rubber stamp', acquiescent to whatever the government demands. Academic accounts tend to be more nuanced, but nonetheless to play down Westminster's policy-making role. We saw that recent textbooks in both law and politics suggest that the British parliament shouldn't be seen as a 'lawmaker' (Harlow and Rawlings 2009: 141), and that it is 'misunderstood if viewed as a legislator' (Moran 2015: 111). Specialist scholars who argue for parliament's importance tend instead to base this on its other functions, for example of representation, accountability, and legitimation (e.g. Judge 1993, Norton 1993, 2013, Tomkins 2003). Our final question is hence whether popular perceptions fit reality.

Assessing these claims again depends crucially on how we define our terms. It is undeniable that most law is written in Whitehall. Legislative drafting is a skilled job, and becomes ever more so as the complexity of the statute book increases. Most words that appear in statutes were carefully crafted by parliamentary counsel, working under instructions from government departments. Decisions about which policy proposals appear in government bills are ultimately made by ministers and civil servants in those same departments, in consultation with central actors in the Treasury and 10 Downing Street. To that extent, the formulation of legislation is indeed 'overwhelmingly a government-centred activity' (Norton 2013: 77).

But following careful and detailed study, this book has shown that parliament's influence on government legislation is extensive, and is exerted in various different ways throughout the policy process. Ideas for policies in bills are frequently urged upon government by parliamentarians (often working in conjunction with pressure groups). Mechanisms such as debates, private members' bills, and EDMs—generally presented as weak, and as quite distinct from the legislative process—play an important part in setting the policy agenda. So do select committees. During the policy formulation stage, and indeed later, after bills have been introduced, parliamentarians publicly test the arguments, and continue using these mechanisms to influence the detail. In formulating major bills, ministers will always be careful to consult inside their own parliamentary party; and at the drafting stage, the ability to get a bill through parliament is paramount to government planning. If all of this fails, and objections are raised which can potentially garner majority support in parliament, bills often go on to be amended. This usually occurs in an outwardly consensual way, via government concessionary amendments.

In today's Westminster ill-prepared proposals, such as the Public Bodies Bill, will be tested hard—and are liable to be substantially changed during their parliamentary passage.[10] Consequently the norm is now for extensive government consultation prior to legislative introduction, to ensure that bills can proceed successfully through parliament. In considering such bills, parliamentarians are well-supported by evidence, including from pressure groups and through the select committees, and are alert to media and public opinion. Where government policy enjoys public support, it may proceed relatively unimpeded. But increasingly, government backbench MPs are willing to speak out against ill-considered proposals, and may be supported in doing so by the House of Lords. The complex set of 'pivotal voters' across the two chambers enhances parliament's ability to 'generate fear'.

The popular perception is that the lack of visible conflict between parliament and government indicates parliamentary acquiescence in the face of a dominant executive. But, as already emphasised, this is to misunderstand the fundamental dynamics in a parliamentary system of government. In such systems, of which Westminster is often presented as the quintessential case, the executive depends on parliament for its survival. Parliament is the 'principal' and the executive its 'agent' (Strøm 2003), with the job of the agent being to implement the principal's wishes. Hence the flow of power may well operate in the opposite direction to that which is commonly assumed. As McGann (2006: 454–5) observes, 'if the legislature was to find an agent that perfectly implemented its wishes, then [it might appear] ... that the legislature was a rubber stamp'.

The role of parliament hence includes, but goes far further than, the 'legitimation' that is often emphasized by its defenders, important though that is. Indeed the functions of legitimation, representation, scrutiny, and accountability cannot be separated—as the literature sometimes implicitly suggests—from the policy-making function. Parliament is ultimately the decision-maker, whose day-to-day role is to oversee those implementing policy decisions on its behalf. Delegation does not require the principal to give up control, but to entrust most decisions to the agent, while maintaining the ability to reclaim power, and to punish the agent, if its wishes are ignored. In this light it is wholly appropriate to describe Westminster as a 'legislator'.

The perception of parliamentary power and the reality are hence very different, and it is valuable to reflect upon why. The six faces of power offer a partial explanation. If we focus only on the first face—that is, visible conflict and policy change at the decision-making stage—parliament may appear ineffective. Much power may instead be exercised behind the scenes, and by mutual agreement. But legitimacy problems can result, as some scholars have pointed out, if publics consequently cannot see and appreciate the effects of their democratic institutions. For example Häge and Kaeding (2007: 358) have suggested that behind-the-scenes agreements between the executive and legislators, while both extensive and important in policy terms, are 'counterproductive' to the European Parliament being viewed as an open, democratically legitimate institution.

A key point, emphasized by pressure group scholars, is that it is difficult to spot influence when it is denied by those whose behaviour it changes (Dür 2008). This problem clearly applies to parliament, where if government reverses policy in response to parliamentary pressure, ministers will often prefer to conceal this in order to save face. But the challenges can be even greater than this, because in parliaments those exercising influence may also profit from playing down their role.

Opposition politicians may see greater electoral advantage in decrying executive dominance and intransigence than in emphasizing policy victories. Notably the strongest denunciations of parliamentary ineffectiveness (such as the words from William Hague in chapter 1) often emanate from those in opposition, and are greedily picked up and propagated by journalists. Meanwhile at the heart of government—as demonstrated by the interview quotations earlier in this chapter—those closest to the process often privately see things very differently.

In their analysis of the long-established 'parliamentary decline thesis' Flinders and Kelso (2011: 249) suggested that 'the dominant public, media and academic perception of an eviscerated and sidelined parliament provides a misleading caricature of a more complex institution', adding that 'promotion and reinforcement of this caricature by scholars arguably perpetuates and fuels public disengagement and disillusionment with politics'. While many legislative studies scholars reject such easy stereotypes, the trend in political science towards privileging approaches that provide replicable, quantitative results may contribute to this problem. Our quantitative results have challenged to some extent the common view that the executive controls the legislative process; but our qualitative results demonstrate that there is much about legislative influence which is subtle and immeasurable. These forms of influence, recognized by the expert scholars of decades ago, have received relatively little recent attention. Given the challenges that parliaments have in communicating their own achievements, scholars have a public duty to conduct cool-headed analysis, based on the widest possible evidence, in order to promote better public understanding of these most central democratic institutions.

A Note on the Future

We have concluded that the Westminster parliament performs its role as a legislator far better than many—even some of those working inside the system—would assume or readily admit. But it would be wrong to leave the reader with an impression that we consider the system to be perfect. Democratic institutions by their nature are messy and complex, and indeed likely to result in disappointment for those who find themselves on the losing side in policy debates (Flinders 2012, Hay 2007, Russell 2005, Stoker 2006). In addition there are various well-rehearsed ways in which Westminster's role in the legislative process could be enhanced.

One such case was discussed in Chapter 8, where we noted how establishment of specialist legislation committees in the House of Commons (see Russell, Morris, and Larkin 2013), or even simply greater use of select committee amendments (Procedure Committee 2009), could help to strengthen the scrutiny process and make it more evidence-based. Others have, for example, proposed improvements to the management of witnesses by public bill committees (Levy 2010). Such changes would bring Westminster more closely into line with other legislatures that are viewed as having stronger committee systems, including across continental Europe and in the USA. Many overseas legislatures also send bills for committee scrutiny before they are debated in plenary, which is seen by scholars as strengthening oversight (though it may simultaneously weaken transparency).

Numerous wider-ranging changes have been proposed. For example the Hansard Society has supported introducing a 'legislative standards committee' to ensure that government bills are well justified, and that they are introduced in good shape (Fox and Korris 2010). It has also proposed strengthening the private members' bill process (Brazier and Fox 2010), and this cause has recently been taken up by the House of Commons Procedure Committee (2016a, 2016b). Ironically, there are risks that if parliament becomes more effective in its scrutiny of primary legislation, government may seek to bypass this through greater use of secondary legislation, and calls for clearer regulation of the boundary between the two have become increasingly insistent since the 2015 tax credits controversy (Constitution Committee 2016, Delegated Powers and Regulatory Reform Committee 2016, Fox and Blackwell 2014). The House of Lords Constitution Committee (2004) has already conducted one wholesale review of the legislative process, which for example proposed more pre- and post-legislative scrutiny, and in late 2016 it announced another.[11]

In addition, the wider stability of the system depends on further reform to the composition of the House of Lords. Irrespective of whether large-scale Lords reform proceeds, the current unregulated system of appointments, which has allowed the chamber's size to grow inexorably, is an increasingly obvious problem (Political and Constitutional Reform Committee 2013, Russell 2013, Russell and Semlyen 2015).[12] The Lords has a fragile existence, and faces constant claims of illegitimacy; yet we have seen that it plays a very major legislative role. Unless its membership is put onto a more secure basis, gradual decline in the Lords' de facto power due to legitimacy concerns, or even its 'packing' to create a government majority, could do great damage to the valuable system of parliamentary influence documented in this book.

While much at Westminster works surprisingly well, there hence remains considerable room for improvement and need for vigilance.

Notes

1. For our definition of amendments—which differs slightly from that of the parliamentary authorities—see Appendix A.
2. We also noted in Chapter 3 that six government-initiated strands responded to points previously raised by non-government parliamentarians in debate. As strands are defined as groups of amendments, we have classified these 18 throughout as 'government-initiated', but this could be seen as overstating government influence. Of course, with these strands excluded, the proportion of successful strands which were government-initiated would drop to less than half.
3. On the Saving Gateway Accounts Bill there were just five successful non-government-initiated strands, three of which were procedural (60 per cent); on the Energy Bill there were again five such strands, two of which were procedural (40 per cent).

4. In their study of 'blunders' in British government, King and Crewe (2013: 236) note that thanks to parliamentary intervention, the Identity Cards Act 'as it finally reached the statute book was not quite the one that ministers had had in mind'. They also note that the change from a partial to a total ban on smoking in public places resulted from the intervention of MPs, citing this as a highly successful policy. It is therefore both strange and disappointing that they title one of their chapters 'a peripheral parliament', even suggesting that parliament is so 'irrelevant' that it 'might as well not exist' (361).

5. The designation of parliament as A and government as B does not rule out the possibility that government also exercises forms of power over parliament. In a multifaceted arrangement, power may operate in both directions; but it is parliament's power that interests us here.

6. Of course, none of our bills were withdrawn (indeed our sampling explicitly excluded bills which did not get royal assent), but such major backtracking does occur. Russell and Cowley (2016: 126) give examples of the coalition's House of Lords Reform Bill and the Brown government's Post Office privatization proposals, noting that 'other similar examples can be found during all recent governments'.

7. We again emphasize below how this is a power usually exercised by parliamentarians on the government side. Nonetheless, at times parliament may choose to support a policy position on a nonpartisan basis—as occurred in the free vote to extend the scope of the smoking ban. Here parliamentarians supporting (and supported by) the health lobby could be seen as successfully counteracting the claims of parliamentarians supporting (and supported by) the tobacco lobby.

8. As indicated in Chapter 5, a statistically significant difference at $p<0.01$.

9. As discussed in Chapter 2, under the terms of the Parliament Acts the House of Commons can ultimately override the House of Lords' position on bills which started in the Commons. However, this power is very rarely used, and usually agreement on policy is instead reached through negotiation.

10. In terms of change over time, it is interesting to reflect on the prospects for such ill-prepared measures. For example, Butler, Adonis, and Travers (1994) chart the parliamentary passage of the legislation providing for the so-called 'poll tax' in the late 1980s. The select committees considered the topic too hot to handle; and despite a backbench Commons rebellion the Lords ultimately let it through. Following public mass protests, the policy was subsequently dropped. It is difficult to imagine the poll tax being approved at Westminster today.

11. As summarized in the committee's call for evidence, available at: http://www.parliament.uk/documents/lords-committees/constitution/Legislative-process-2016/Final-Call-for-Evidence-Legislative-process.pdf [accessed 23 October 2016].

12. In late 2016 two committees began investigation into this matter—the House of Commons Public Administration and Constitutional Affairs Committee (http://www.parliament.uk/business/committees/committees-a-z/commons-select/public-administration-and-constitutional-affairs-committee/inquiries/parliament-2015/house-of-lords-16-17/ [accessed 10 April 2017]), and a newly established Lord Speaker's Committee on the Size of the House [of Lords] (http://www.parliament.uk/size-of-house-committee [accessed 10 April 2017]). Reports from both committees were still awaited as this book went to press.

Methodology

This appendix outlines our research methodology. We first explain the criteria against which we selected the 12 case study bills. We then elaborate on how we collected and coded the data on amendments and strands that underpins our research. Finally we discuss how we selected interviewees and used our interview data.

Selection of Case Study Bills

The 12 case study bills were designed to be a fair cross-section of the principal type of government legislation considered by parliament—that is, 'primary' legislation beyond certain types of narrowly financial measures. We focused on government bills, rather than private members' bills, because they dominate legislative activity at Westminster and are far more likely to become law. We focused on primary (rather than 'secondary' or 'delegated') legislation because this is the vehicle for most substantial policy changes, and because secondary legislation goes through a very different parliamentary process.

We began by collecting basic data about all government bills introduced into parliament during the period 2005–12, using information available on the parliamentary website such as the *Sessional Information Digest* from each parliamentary session. Because our investigation sought to examine the usual bicameral scrutiny process on legislation, we excluded financial bills known as 'bills of aids and supplies', which by strong convention are not amended at all by the Lords.[1] We also excluded five bills that did not receive royal assent. This left us with a total of 170 bills, of which 132 were from the 2005–10 parliament and 38 from the 2010–12 session (single counting those 'carried over' between sessions, and including four introduced in 2010–12 that received royal assent in 2012–13).

From these we selected our case study bills with reference to several key variables. To allow meaningful comparisons between the two periods of government, we sought variation not only across the whole sample of 12 bills, but also within the selections for each parliament. Given the relatively small number of bills (seven drawn from 2005–10 and five from 2010–12), it was clearly not possible for these samples to be fully representative in every respect. Nevertheless, we sought to ensure that they reflected the diversity of bills considered by parliament as far as possible.

The variables that we selected against were as follows.

- *Session*. In the 2005–10 parliament, bills were distributed fairly evenly across the five sessions, with the exception of 2005–06 which featured roughly double the number of bills. We therefore selected one bill from each of these sessions, plus one additional bill from 2005–06. We also included one bill that was introduced in this session and carried over into 2006–07. For the 2010–12 session this variable was clearly not relevant, but (as indicated in Chapter 2) we chose bills that were introduced at various points throughout the session.

- *Sponsoring department.* The Treasury was the highest-legislating department in each parliament (even following removal of bills of aids and supplies), followed by the Home Office. We selected three bills from each of these departments. The remaining case study bills were selected from six separate government departments with lower legislation rates.

- *House of introduction.* During this period, two-thirds of relevant bills were introduced in the Commons, and one-third in the Lords. We selected eight Commons-starting bills, and four starting in the Lords.

- *Draft bill.* Using analysis produced by the House of Commons Library, we identified all the bills for which at least some provisions had been published in draft. Around one-fifth of bills during this period met this criterion, of which we selected two.

- *Length.* The bills were placed into five roughly equal-sized categories, based on the number of pages as introduced (1–10, 11–25, 26–50, 51–125, and 126+ pages). We selected at least one bill from each of these categories.

- *Profile and controversy.* From each parliament we selected some examples of high-profile 'flagship' bills, and some other lower-profile examples. We accounted for controversy largely through number of defeats on the bill in the House of Lords. Approximately half of bills suffered Lords defeats, and this was reflected in our sample.

Amendments and Strands

We collected information about every amendment (including new clauses and schedules) proposed to the case study bills in a database. Basic data about each amendment is included in the 'amendment papers' published before debate in each chamber. From these we recorded information such as the text of each amendment, its parliamentary sponsors (to which we added information about their party/group and whether they were frontbench or backbench), and the chamber and legislative stage at which it was proposed. We then used transcripts of parliamentary proceedings (primarily Hansard) to collect additional information about how MPs and peers responded to the amendments, and read the text of each amendment against the bill (and pre-existing statute when necessary) to record a description of its policy effect. This description was used to code each amendment for how 'substantive' a change it represented, on a three-point scale (as described in Chapter 3).

In most cases, what constituted an 'amendment' was straightforward, and in line with the records of the parliamentary authorities. In a small number of cases, however, we made judgements that resulted in differences from the official record. First, we counted the 66 'intentions to oppose' a clause in any of the bills at Lords committee stage as amendments. As the *Companion to the Standing Orders* states, 'an amendment to leave out a clause or Schedule in committee is not technically an amendment, but a statement of intention to oppose' it (House of Lords 2015: 133). However, these statements are listed on the Lords amendment papers, and in most respects function like amendments. Second, during the Commons Consideration of Lords Amendments (CCLA) and Lords Consideration of Commons Amendments (LCCA) stages MPs and peers table 'motions' that may include several different changes. We disaggregated these into separate proposals, and counted as an amendment any that represented a change to the other chamber's decision.[2] This treatment was necessary in order to construct legislative strands, as described below. Third, in one case the Commons Deputy Speaker formally deemed a Lords amendment to be disagreed to without this being put to the House, on the basis that it involved so-called 'unwaivable' financial privilege. Although this was not technically an amendment, it in effect overturned the Lords amendment, so is included in our figures.

Having recorded information about amendments we then placed each into a legislative strand. The purpose of strands was to record the connections between amendments that sought the same or a very similar change at different legislative stages, allowing us to trace how proposals were pursued across the entire parliamentary process and whether they ultimately resulted in change. Because bills at Westminster can 'ping-pong' repeatedly between the two chambers, as explained in Chapter 2, amendments may be proposed at an unrestricted number of stages. Table A.1 presents data on the 'length' of strands, measured by the number of legislative stages at which an amendment was recorded. Over two-thirds of strands lasted only one stage, while under 1 per cent proceeded beyond four stages. The longest strands occurred on the issue of deaths in custody in the Corporate Manslaughter and Corporate Homicide Bill (13 legislative stages) and compulsion on registering for an ID card when applying for a passport in the Identity Cards Bill (14 stages).

We allowed each amendment to be assigned to only one strand. At any legislative stage, a strand could contain only one proposal (e.g. a lead amendment and consequential amendments) by only one actor (e.g. an individual parliamentarian, or a group acting together)— except for government amendments, most obviously where a government concession was made at the same legislative stage. Where more than one actor pursued the same change at the same stage through separate amendments, we placed these in separate strands. This was because proposals from distinct groups of actors that sought similar change at one stage often went on to develop in different directions at later stages, making this rule necessary in order to reliably record connections later on. In such cases it was not always straightforward to determine which amendments to link to at future stages. We based these decisions on the amendments' effect and drafting, as well as their sponsors. Where strands sought essentially

Table A.1 Strand lengths (i.e. number of legislative stages)

Legislative stages	Strands (N)	Cumulative %
1	1,405	68.5
2	429	89.5
3	149	96.7
4	49	99.1
5	9	99.6
6	5	99.8
7	2	99.9
8	0	99.9
9	0	99.9
10	0	99.9
11	0	99.9
12	0	99.9
13	1	100.0
14	1	100.0
Grand total	**2,050**	

identical changes, they were coded as 'siblings'. As discussed in Chapter 9, this was useful to identify patterns of cross-party pressure which would otherwise be masked by our strict coding rules. But because sibling strands did need to be essentially identical (not just similar) in their aims, our figures if anything downplay cross-party pressure.

The rules for legislative strands are illustrated by Figure A.1. This shows three strands related to the smoking ban in the Health Bill. Strand A concerned the application of the ban to vehicles; it was pursued at three stages, but none of the amendments were agreed to. Strand B was also three stages long, and concerned a different topic: the ability for additional places to be designated as subject to the ban. In this case the final amendment was a government concession, showing how a strand initiated by the opposition resulted in legislative change. Strand C concerned essentially the same matter as strand B, and so these two strands were coded as siblings. Comparing the amendments in strands B and C at Lords committee highlights some typical coding dilemmas. Either could have been placed in a strand with the initial amendment, but ultimately the opposition frontbench-led amendment was included in strand B for two reasons. First, its supporters were more similar to those in the initial amendment—despite some additional Crossbench support. Second, because the altered

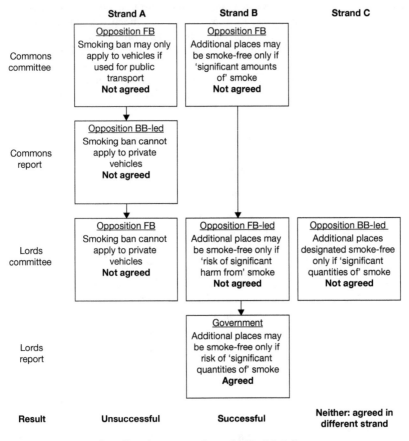

Figure A.1 Examples of legislative strands on the Health Bill

drafting appeared specifically to respond to the minister's reasons for rejecting the earlier amendment (as described on page 79). Likewise, the government concession could have been included in either strand. However, adding it to strand B kept it with the amendment that initiated this cause at Commons committee stage.

Once constructed, each strand was coded for key attributes. These included which actor(s) initiated it, whether others joined at other stages, whether it had siblings, which chamber(s) it was pursued in, and its outcome. The latter of these requires particular explanation. Returning to the examples above, strand A contained no agreed amendment, so was coded as 'unsuccessful'. Strand B, by contrast, contained an agreed amendment that was not subsequently overturned, so was coded as 'successful'. However, as strand C illustrates, not all strands fit into either of these categories. Where a strand was not itself successful but was resolved by a separate successful strand concerning the same matter, it was coded as being 'neither successful nor unsuccessful'. This allowed us to record its influence without double-counting the number of successful strands overall. Strands were also counted as being 'neither successful nor unsuccessful' where there was clear evidence of a non-legislative change in government policy, but this was used very sparingly and applied to only nine strands.

The outcome of strands on the case study bills is presented in Table A.2. As can be seen, around three-quarters of strands were 'unsuccessful', while around one-sixth were 'successful', and one-tenth were 'neither successful nor unsuccessful'.

Where a strand was successful we subsequently recorded the type of legislative change that it achieved (i.e. whether it concerned policy substance, procedure, or was purely technical). The creation of strands also enabled us to code some additional attributes of amendments, including in the case of those 'agreed to' whether they were subsequently overturned by another amendment, and in the case of government amendments, whether they responded to earlier non-government proposals.

Clearly, some of our coding required judgement—particularly with respect to strands, but also amendments. This always introduces the risk of subjectivity by the researcher, or

Table A.2 Outcome of strands by chamber

	Commons only		Lords only		Both Houses		Total	
	N	%	N	%	N	%	N	%
2005–10 parliament								
Successful	57	13	81	16	31	13	169	15
Neither	15	3	17	3	7	3	39	3
Unsuccessful	358	83	401	80	194	84	953	82
Total	430	100	499	100	232	100	1,161	100
2010–12 session								
Successful	42	16	59	13	30	19	131	15
Neither	9	4	121	26	7	4	137	15
Unsuccessful	206	80	292	62	123	77	621	70
Total	257	100	472	100	160	100	889	100
Both parliaments								
Successful	99	14	140	14	61	16	300	15
Neither	24	3	138	14	14	4	176	9
Unsuccessful	564	82	693	71	317	81	1,574	77
Total	687	100	971	100	392	100	2,050	100

inconsistency between different members of the research team (four separate researchers were involved, with two conducting most of the coding). In order to minimize such risks, we worked from a detailed coding handbook, and difficult cases were discussed among the team. Given the volume of amendments, double-coding (whereby each case is independently considered by two researchers) was impractical; but all coding was checked by at least one other researcher.

Interviews

An important part of our analysis was more qualitative. For each bill we gathered key background information, such as details of previous government consultations, manifesto and other commitments, and notable external reports or campaigns. But the most important qualitative data came from our interviews. We conducted roughly 10 interviews for each of the 12 case study bills, amounting to more than 120 in total. For each bill we approached at least one person who had served as a minister, one who had held an opposition portfolio, one civil servant from the bill team, one outside group representative and one backbencher. On each bill we ensured that we had a spread of interviewees from the Commons and the Lords. During the 2005–10 parliament and 2010–12 session respectively we also sought a spread among political parties (e.g. including Liberal Democrat as well as Conservative opposition frontbenchers from the 2005–10 parliament). Some interviewees had experience relevant to more than one bill. A small number of interviewees contributed more general (i.e. non bill-specific) expertise. These included representatives of parliamentary counsel and clerks in both chambers. Hence not all interviewees can be neatly assigned to individual bills, and there is clearly some overlap. In general, we conducted more interviews on bigger and/or more controversial bills than on smaller less controversial ones. A full list of interviewees is given in Appendix B.

Clearly different actors may have their own biases (e.g. opposition members may suggest that the government behaved improperly, or vice versa). Hence we use interview quotations with care, either to illustrate points which our own broader research (e.g. interviews with others, and study of the parliamentary record) shows to be correct, or in places explicitly to illustrate the view of the particular actor concerned. All interviews were conducted on a confidential basis, and no interviewee is identified by name in the text. However, parliamentarians give their formal responses to government bills on the public record, and we also quote extensively from Hansard throughout the book. Off-the-record interviews provided a rich source of additional information from these actors, and an essential source from those who operate behind the scenes—such as clerks and civil servants.

Notes

1. These bills implement the government's taxation and spending decisions (e.g. in Finance Bills or Supply and Appropriation Bills), and can be identified by their 'enactment formula'. We did not exclude 'money bills' (unless also bills of aids and supplies): although these are also not amended by the Lords, they are only certified as such once they have completed their Commons passage, taking account of amendments passed in that House. The inclusion of one money bill within the sample allowed illustration of some of the tensions that can occur over this process.

2. For example, on the Corporate Manslaughter and Corporate Homicide Bill, Lord Ramsbotham tabled a motion stating that the House 'do insist on its Amendments 2, 3, 5, 6 and 10, do disagree with the Commons in their Amendments 10K to 10N in lieu and do propose the following amendments in lieu of Commons Amendments 10K to 10N' (House of Lords Hansard, 17 July 2007, column 138). This is counted as 11 amendments in our database: five to insist on amendments rejected by the Commons, four to reject government amendments that had been passed by the Commons, and two new amendments proposed.

APPENDIX B

List of Interviewees

The research for this book included over 120 interviews with parliamentarians and others closely involved in the process. Our primary interviewees are listed below. Note that in some cases individuals were interviewed more than once. In addition, the book draws in places on other interviews conducted for related projects, and hence quotations in the text cannot necessarily be ascribed to any of those listed below. We are very grateful for the cooperation of all of our interviewees.

Interviewees Who Served in the Commons During the Study Period

Kevin Barron
Charles Clarke
John Denham
Andrew Dismore
Caroline Flint
Paul Goggins
Kate Green
Dominic Grieve
David Hanson
Charles Hendry
Patricia Hewitt
Meg Hillier
Mark Hoban
Martin Horwood
Simon Hughes
Stephen Ladyman
Andrew Lansley (now Lord Lansley)
Kerry McCarthy
Pat McFadden
Mark Oaten
Bill Rammell
Joan Ruddock
Barry Sheerman
Jack Straw
Gerry Sutcliffe
Richard Taylor
Stephen Timms
Jon Trickett
Mike Weir

Alan Whitehead
Stephen Williams
Jenny Willott
Sir George Young (now Lord Young of Cookham)
Plus one Liberal Democrat MP who did not wish to be named.

Interviewees Who Served in the Lords During the Study Period

Lord (Andrew) Adonis
Baroness (Joyce) Anelay of St Johns
Lord (Robert) Armstrong of Ilminster
Lord (John) Attlee
Lord (Willy) Bach
Baroness (Liz) Barker
Lord (Steve) Bassam of Brighton
Lord (Richard) Best
Lord (Tim) Clement-Jones
Lord (Bryan) Davies of Oldham
Baroness (Ilora) Finlay of Llandaff
Lord (Mike) German
Lord (Tony) Greaves
Baroness (Tanni) Grey-Thompson
Baroness (Dianne) Hayter of Kentish Town
Lord (Terence) Higgins
Baroness (Patricia) Hollis of Heigham
Lord (Greville) Howard of Rising
Earl (Freddie) Howe
Lord (Philip) Hunt of Kings Heath
Lord (David) Hunt of Wirral
Lord (Archy) Kirkwood
Lord (Jim) Knight
Lord (Anthony) Lester of Herne Hill
Lord (James) Mackay
Baroness (Patricia) Morris of Bolton
Lord (Michael) Naseby
Baroness (Pauline) Neville-Jones
Lord (Dick) Newby
Lord (Philip) Norton of Louth
Lord (David) Pannick
Lord (Maurice) Peston
Lord (Andrew) Phillips of Sudbury
Lord (David) Ramsbotham
Lord (Tim) Razzall
Bishop of Ripon and Leeds (John Packer)
Baroness (Jan) Royall of Blaisdon
Lord (James) Sassoon
Lord (David) Steel of Aikwood

Lord (Tom) Strathclyde
Lord (John) Taylor
Baroness (Celia) Thomas of Winchester
Lord (Andrew) Turnbull
Baroness (Muriel) Turner of Camden
Baroness (Joan) Walmsley
Lord (Norman) Warner
Baroness (Diana) Warwick of Undercliffe
Lord (Larry) Whitty

Outside Group Representatives

Janet Allbeson
Deborah Arnott
Adrian Coles
Matthew Downie
Sophie Farthing
Andrew Gall
Emily Holzhausen
Isobel Larkin
Eric Metcalfe
Sam Royston
Abbie Shelton
Jonathan Stearn
Vivienne Stern
Sarah Veale
Christopher Walden
Kate Webb

Government and Parliamentary Officials

Two senior members of the Office of the Parliamentary Counsel
One further Cabinet Office official
Eleven bill team civil servants
One departmental special adviser
One senior special adviser from 10 Downing Street
Five parliamentary officials

Bibliography

Abbott, D. (2011), 'The Dead Hand of the Whips', *Guardian*, 15 February 2011.

Allen, A. (1998), 'Rethinking Power', *Hypatia*, 13(1), 21–40.

Andeweg, R. B. (2013), 'Parties in Parliament: The Blurring of Opposition' in W. C. Müller & H. M. Narud, eds, *Party Governance and Party Democracy* (New York: Springer).

Andeweg, R. B. and Nijzink, L. (1995), 'Beyond the Two-Body Image: Relations between Ministers and MPs' in H. Döring, ed, *Parliaments and Majority Rule in Western Europe* (Mannheim: University of Mannheim).

Arter, D. (1985), 'The Nordic Parliaments: Patterns of Legislative Influence', *West European Politics*, 8(1), 55–70.

Arter, D. (2003), 'Committee Cohesion and the "Corporate Dimension" of Parliamentary Committees: A Comparative Analysis', *Journal of Legislative Studies*, 9(4), 73–87.

Arter, D. (2006), 'Questioning the Mezey Question: An Interrogatory Framework for the Comparative study of Legislatures', *Journal of Legislative Studies*, 12(3–4), 462–82.

Austen-Smith, D. and Wright, J. R. (1994), 'Counteractive Lobbying', *American Journal of Political Science*, 38(1), 25–44.

Bach, S. (2008), 'Senate Amendments and Legislative Outcomes in Australia, 1996–2007', *Australian Journal of Political Science*, 43(3), 395–423.

Bachrach, P. and Baratz, M. S. (1962), 'Two Faces of Power', *American Political Science Review*, 56(4), 947–52.

Bagehot, W. (2001 [1867]), *The English Constitution* (Oxford: Oxford University Press).

Baldwin, N. (1990), 'The House of Lords' in M. Rush, ed, *Parliament and Pressure Politics* (Oxford: Clarendon).

Bale, T. (2012), 'The Black Widow Effect: Why Britain's Conservative–Liberal Democrat Coalition Might Have an Unhappy Ending', *Parliamentary Affairs*, 65(2), 323–37.

Barrett, A. W. (2008), 'Are All Presidential Legislative Successes Really Victories? Examining the Substance of Legislation', *White House Studies Compendium*, 5, 101–9.

Barrett, A. W. and Eshbaugh-Soba, M. (2007), 'Presidential Success on the Substance of Legislation', *Political Research Quarterly*, 60(1), 100–12.

Baumgartner, F. R. and Jones, B. D. (1993), *Agendas and Instability in American Politics* (Chicago: University of Chicago Press).

Benton, M. and Russell, M. (2012), 'Assessing the Impact of Parliamentary Oversight Committees: The Select Committees in the British House of Commons', *Parliamentary Affairs*, 66(4), 772–97.

Bevir, M. (2008), 'The Westminster Model, Governance and Judicial Reform', *Parliamentary Affairs*, 61(4), 559–77.

Binderkrantz, A. S. (2014), 'Legislatures, Lobbying, and Interest Groups' in S. Martin, T. Saalfeld, & K. Strom, eds, *The Oxford Handbook of Legislative Studies* (Oxford: Oxford University Press).

Binderkrantz, A. S., Christiansen, P. M., and Pedersen, H. H. (2015), 'Interest Group Access to the Bureaucracy, Parliament, and the Media', *Governance*, 28(1), 95–112.

Blackburn, R. and Kennon, A. (2003), *Griffith and Ryle on Parliament: Functions, Practice and Procedures* (London: Sweet & Maxwell).

Blondel, J. (1970), 'Legislative Behaviour: Some Steps Towards a Cross-National Measurement', *Government and Opposition*, 5(1), 67–85.

Blondel, J. (1995), *Comparative Government: An Introduction* (London: Prentice Hall).

Bogdanor, V. (2004), 'The Constitution and the Party System in the Twentieth Century', *Parliamentary Affairs*, 57(4), 717–33.

Bowler, S., Farrell, D. M., and Katz, R. S. (1999), *Party Discipline and Parliamentary Government* (Columbus: Ohio State University Press).

Bown, F. (1994), 'Influencing the House of Lords: The Role of the Lords Spiritual 1979–1987', *Political Studies*, 42(1), 105–19.

Brand, J. (1992), *British Parliamentary Parties: Policy and Power* (Oxford: Clarendon).

Brazier, A. and Fox, R. (2010), 'Enhancing the Backbench MP's Role as a Legislator: The Case for Urgent Reform of Private Members Bills', *Parliamentary Affairs*, 63(1), 201–11.

Brazier, A., Kalitowski, S., and Rosenblatt, G. (2008), *Law in the Making: Influence and Change in the Legislative Process* (London: Hansard Society).

Bromhead, P. A. (1958), *The House of Lords and Contemporary Politics, 1911–1957* (London: Routledge & Kegan Paul).

Brunner, M. (2012), *Parliaments and Legislative Activity: Motivations for Bill Introduction* (Wiesbaden: Springer VS).

Butler, D., Adonis, A., and Travers, T. (1994), *Failure in British Government: The Politics of the Poll Tax* (Oxford: Oxford University Press).

Butt, R. (1969), *The Power of Parliament* (London: Constable).

Cabinet Office (2003), *Government Response to the Public Administration Select Committee's Fourth Report of Session 2002–2003 'Government by Appointment: Opening up the Patronage State' (HC 165)*, Cm 6056 (London: Stationery Office).

Cabinet Office (2015), *Guide to Making Legislation (July 2015)* (London: Stationery Office).

Cairney, P. (2007), 'A "Multiple Lenses" Approach to Policy Change: The Case of Tobacco Policy in the UK', *British Politics*, 2(1), 45–68.

Cairney, P. (2009), 'The Role of Ideas in Policy Transfer: The Case of UK Smoking Bans Since Devolution', *Journal of European Public Policy*, 16(3), 471–88.

Cairney, P. (2012), *Understanding Public Policy: Theories and Issues* (Basingstoke: Palgrave Macmillan).

Calmfors, L. and Wren-Lewis, S. (2011), 'What Should Fiscal Councils Do?', *Economic Policy*, 26(68), 649–95.

Capano, G. and Giuliani, M. (2001), 'Governing without Surviving? An Italian Paradox: Law-Making in Italy, 1987–2001', *Journal of Legislative Studies*, 7(4), 13–36.

Centre for Social Justice (2009), *Dynamic Benefits: Towards Welfare That Works* (London: Centre for Social Justice).

Chubb, B. (1957), 'The Independent Member in Ireland', *Political Studies*, 5(2), 131–9.

Collard, S. and McKay, S. (2006), 'Closing the Savings Gap? The Role of the Saving Gateway', *Local Economy*, 21(1), 25–35.

Conservative Party (2010), *Invitation to Join the Government of Britain: The Conservative Manifesto 2010* (London: Conservative Party).

Conservative Party and Liberal Democrats (2010), 'Conservative Liberal Democrat Coalition Negotiations: Agreements Reached', [https://www.conservatives.com/~/media/Files/Downloadable%20Files/agreement.ashx, accessed 2 April 2017].

Constitution Committee (2004), *Parliament and the Legislative Process (Fourteenth Report of Session 2003–04), Vol. I*, HL 173-I (London: House of Lords).

Constitution Committee (2005), *Identity Cards Bill (Third Report of Session 2005–06)*, HL Paper 44 (London: House of Lords).

Constitution Committee (2010), *Public Bodies Bill (Sixth Report of Session 2010–11)*, HL Paper 51 (London: House of Lords).

Constitution Committee (2011), *Money Bills and Commons Financial Privilege (Tenth Report of Session 2010–11)*, HL Paper 97 (London: House of Lords).

Constitution Committee (2016), *Delegated Legislation and Parliament: A Response to the Strathclyde Review (Ninth Report of Session 2015–16)*, HL Paper 116 (London: House of Lords).

Copus, C., Clark, A., and Bottom, K. (2008), 'Multi-Party Politics in England: Small Parties, Independents, and Political Associations in English Local Politics' in M. Reiser & E. Holtmann, eds, *Farewell to the Party Model? Independent Local Lists in East and West European Countries* (Wiesbaden: VS Verlag für Sozialwissenschaften).

Costar, B. and Curtin, J. (2004), *Rebels with a Cause: Independents in Australian Politics* (Sydney: UNSW Press).

Cowley, P. (2002), *Revolts and Rebellions: Parliamentary Voting under Blair* (London: Politico's).

Cowley, P. (2005), *The Rebels: How Blair Mislaid his Majority* (London: Politico's).

Cowley, P. (2006), 'Making Parliament Matter?' in P. Dunleavy, R. Heffernan, P. Cowley, & C. Hay, eds, *Developments in British Politics 8* (Basingstoke: Palgrave).

Cowley, P. (2015), 'The Coalition and Parliament' in A. Seldon & M. Finn, eds, *The Coalition Effect 2010–2015* (Cambridge: Cambridge University Press).

Cowley, P. and Stuart, M. (2006), *Dissension Amongst the Parliamentary Labour Party, 2005–2006: A Data Handbook* (Nottingham: University of Nottingham).

Cowley, P. and Stuart, M. (2009), 'There Was a Doctor, a Journalist and Two Welshmen: the Voting Behaviour of Independent MPs in the United Kingdom House of Commons, 1997–2007', *Parliamentary Affairs*, 62(1), 19–31.

Cowley, P. and Stuart, M. (2012), *The Bumper Book of Coalition Rebellions* (Nottingham: University of Nottingham).

Cowley, P. and Stuart, M. (2014), 'In the Brown Stuff? Labour Backbench Dissent under Gordon Brown, 2007–2010', *Contemporary British History*, 28(1), 1–23.

Cox, G. W. (2009), 'The Organization of Democratic Legislatures' in D. A. Wittman & B. R. Weingast, eds, *The Oxford Handbook of Political Economy* (Oxford: Oxford University Press).

Crewe, E. (2015), *The House of Commons: An Anthropology of MPs at Work* (London: Bloomsbury Academic).

Crick, B. (1964), *The Reform of Parliament* (London: Wiedenfeld & Nicolson).

Damgaard, E. and Jensen, H. (2006), 'Assessing Strength and Weakness in Legislatures: The Case of Denmark', *Journal of Legislative Studies*, 12(3–4), 426–42.

Delegated Powers and Regulatory Reform Committee (2010a), *Government Amendments and Response: Public Bodies Bill [HL] (Sixth Report of Session 2010–12)*, HL Paper 62 (London: House of Lords).

Delegated Powers and Regulatory Reform Committee (2010b), *Public Bodies Bill [HL] (Fifth Report of Session 2010–12)*, HL Paper 57 (London: House of Lords).

Delegated Powers and Regulatory Reform Committee (2016), *Special Report: Response to the Strathclyde Review (Twenty-fifth Report of Session 2015–16)*, HL Paper 119 (London: House of Lords).

Denver, D., Carman, C., and Johns, R. (2012), *Elections and Voters in Britain* (Basingstoke: Palgrave).

Department of Health (2003), *Response to the Health Select Committee Fifth Report of the Session 2002–03 on the Control of Entry Regulations and Retail Pharmacy Services in the UK*, CM 5896 (London: Stationery Office).

Department of Health (2005), *Consultation on the Smokefree Elements of the Health Bill* (London: Department of Health).

Digeser, P. (1992), 'The Fourth Face of Power', *Journal of Politics*, 54(4), 977–1007.

Dorey, P. (2014), *Policy Making in Britain* (London: Sage).

Döring, H. (1995), 'Time as a Scarce Resource: Government Control of the Agenda' in H. Döring, ed, *Parliaments and Majority Rule in Western Europe* (New York: St. Martin's Press).

Drewry, G. (1985a), 'Introduction' in G. Drewry, ed, *The New Select Committees: A Study of the 1979 Reforms* (Oxford: Clarendon).

Drewry, G., ed (1985b), *The New Select Committees: A Study of the 1979 Reforms* (Oxford: Clarendon).

Drewry, G. and Brock, J. (1993), 'Government Legislation: An Overview' in D. Shell & D. Beamish, eds, *The House of Lords at Work: A Study Based on the 1988–1989 Session* (Oxford: Clarendon).

Dunleavy, P. (2005), 'Facing up to Multi-Party Politics: How Partisan Dealignment and PR Voting Have Fundamentally Changed Britain's Party Systems', *Parliamentary Affairs*, 58(3), 503–32.

Dunleavy, P. (2006), 'The Westminster Model and the Distinctiveness of British Politics' in P. Dunleavy, R. Heffernan, P. Cowley, & C. Hay, eds, *Developments in British Politics 8* (Basingstoke: Palgrave).

Dür, A. (2008), 'Measuring Interest Group Influence in the EU: A Note on Methodology', *European Union Politics*, 9(4), 559–76.

Dür, A. and De Bièvre, D. (2007), 'The Question of Interest Group Influence', *Journal of Public Policy*, 27(1), 1–12.

Edmonds, T. and Kennedy, S. (2010), *Savings Accounts and Health in Pregnancy Grant Bill (Bill 73 of 2010–11) (RP10/66)* (London: House of Commons Library).

Education and Skills Committee (2006), *Further Education (Fourth Report of Session 2005–06)*, HC 649 (London: House of Commons).

Ekins, R. (2012), *The Nature of Legislative Intent* (Oxford: Oxford University Press).

Engle, G. (1983), '"Bills Are Made to Pass as Razors Are Made to Sell": Practical Constraints on the Preparation of Legislation', *Statute Law Review*, 4(2), 7–23.

Erskine May (2011), *Erskine May's Treatise on the Law, Privileges, Proceedings and Usage of Parliament*, 24th edn (London: LexisNexis).

Finlayson, A. (2009), 'Financialisation, Financial Literacy and Asset-Based Welfare', *British Journal of Politics and International Relations*, 11(3), 400–21.

Fisher, J. (2008), 'Whither the Parties?' in R. Hazell, ed, *Constitutional Futures Revisited* (Basingstoke: Palgrave).

Flinders, M. (2012), *Defending Politics: Why Democracy Matters in the 21st Century* (Oxford: Oxford University Press).

Flinders, M. and Curry, D. (2008), 'Bi-constitutionality: Unravelling New Labour's Constitutional Orientations', *Parliamentary Affairs*, 61(1), 99–121.

Flinders, M. and Kelso, A. (2011), 'Mind the Gap: Political Analysis, Public Expectations and the Parliamentary Decline Thesis', *British Journal of Politics and International Relations*, 13(2), 249–68.

Forestry Commission England and Department for Environment, Food and Rural Affairs (2011), *The Future of the Public Forest Estate in England: A Public Consultation* (Bristol: Forestry Commission).

Foster, A. (2005), *Realising the Potential: A Review of the Future Role of Further Education Colleges* (London: Department for Education and Skills).

Foster, D. H. (2015), 'Going "Where Angels Fear to Tread": How Effective Was the Backbench Business Committee in the 2010–2012 Parliamentary Session?', *Parliamentary Affairs*, 68(1), 116–34.

Fox, R. (2010), 'Five Days in May: A New Political Order Emerges', *Parliamentary Affairs*, 63(4), 607–22.

Fox, R. and Blackwell, J. (2014), *The Devil Is in the Detail: Parliament and Delegated Legislation* (London: Hansard Society).

Fox, R. and Korris, M. (2010), *Making Better Law: Reform of the Legislative Process from Policy to Act* (London: Hansard Society).

Friedrich, C. J. (1968), *Constitutional Government and Democracy: Theory and Practice in Europe and America* (Waltham, MA: Blaisdell Publishing).

Gaventa, J. (2007), 'Levels, Spaces and Forms of Power' in F. Berenskoetter & M. J. Williams, eds, *Power in World Politics* (Abingdon: Routledge).

Gay, O. (2016), 'The Regulation of Lobbyists' in A. Horne & A. Le Sueur, eds, *Parliament: Legislation and Accountability* (Oxford: Hart).

Giddings, P. (1985), 'What Has Been Achieved? The New Select Committees' in G. Drewry, ed, *The New Select Committees: A Study of the 1979 Reforms* (Oxford: Clarendon).

Gobert, J. (2005), 'The Politics of Corporate Manslaughter: The British Experience', *Flinders Journal of Law Reform*, 8(1), 1–38.

Gover, D. and Kenny, M. (2016), *Finding the Good in EVEL: An Evaluation of 'English Votes for English Laws' in the House of Commons* (Edinburgh: Centre on Constitutional Change).

Gover, D. and Russell, M. (2015), 'The House of Commons' "Financial Privilege" on Lords Amendments: Perceived Problems and Possible Solutions', *Public Law*, 1, 12–22.

Grant, W. (2000), *Pressure Groups and British Politics* (Basingstoke: Palgrave).

Greenberg, D. (2011), *Laying Down the Law: A Discussion of the People, Processes and Problems That Shape Acts of Parliament* (London: Sweet & Maxwell).

Greenberg, D. (2013), 'The Realities of the Parliament Act 1911' in D. Feldman, ed, *Law in Politics, Politics in Law* (Oxford: Hart).

Griffith, J. A. G. (1974), *Parliamentary Scrutiny of Government Bills* (London: Allen & Unwin).

Häge, F. M. and Kaeding, M. (2007), 'Reconsidering the European Parliament's Legislative Influence: Formal vs. Informal Procedures', *Journal of European Integration*, 29(3), 341–61.

Hansard Society (1992), *Making the Law: The Report of the Hansard Society Commission on the Legislative Process* (London: Hansard Society).

Hansard Society (2014), *PMQs: Tuned in or Turned off? Public Attitudes to Prime Minister's Questions* (London: Hansard Society).

Hansard Society (2016), *Audit of Political Engagement 13: The 2016 Report* (London: Hansard Society).

Hansen, E. (2010), 'The Parliamentary Behaviour of Minor Parties and Independents in Dáil Éireann', *Irish Political Studies*, 25(4), 643–60.

Harlow, C. and Rawlings, R. (2009), *Law and Administration* (Cambridge: Cambridge University Press).

Haugaard, M. (2012), 'Rethinking the Four Dimensions of Power: Domination and Empowerment', *Journal of Political Power*, 5(1), 33–54.

Hawes, D. (1992), 'Parliamentary Select Committees: Some Case Studies in Contingent Influence', *Policy & Politics*, 20, 227–36.

Hawes, D. (1993), *Power on the Back Benches? The Growth of Select Committee Influence* (Bristol: SAUS).

Hay, C. (2007), *Why We Hate Politics* (Cambridge: Polity).

Hayton, R. (2014), 'Conservative Party Statecraft and the Politics of Coalition', *Parliamentary Affairs*, 67(1), 6–24.

Hazell, R., ed (2008), *Constitutional Futures Revisited: Britain's Constitution to 2020* (Basingstoke: Palgrave).

Hazell, R., Paun, A., Chalmers, M., Yong, B., and Haddon, C. (2009), *Making Minority Government Work: Hung Parliaments and the Challenges for Westminster and Whitehall* (London: Constitution Unit).

Health Committee (2003), *The Control of Entry Regulations and Retail Pharmacy Services in the UK (Fifth Report of Session 2002–03)*, HC 571 (London: House of Commons).

Health Committee (2005a), *Smoking in Public Places (First Report of Session 2005–06), Vol. I*, HC 485-I (London: House of Commons).

Health Committee (2005b), *Smoking in Public Places (First Report of Session 2005–06), Vol. III*, HC 485-III (London: House of Commons).

Heidar, K. and Koole, R. (2000), 'Parliamentary Party Groups Compared' in K. Heidar & R. Koole, eds, *Parliamentary Party Groups in European Democracies: Political Parties Behind Closed Doors* (London: Routledge).

Helms, L. (2004), 'Five Ways of Institutionalizing Political Opposition: Lessons from the Advanced Democracies', *Government and Opposition*, 39(1), 22–54.

Helms, L. (2008), 'Studying Parliamentary Opposition in Old and New Democracies: Issues and Perspectives', *Journal of Legislative Studies*, 14(1–2), 6–19.

Herman, V. (1972), 'Backbench and Opposition Amendments to Government Legislation' in D. Leonard & V. Herman, eds, *The Backbencher and Parliament* (London: Macmillan).

Hiebert, J. L. (2006), 'Parliament and the Human Rights Act: Can the JCHR Help Facilitate a Culture of Rights?', *International Journal of Constitutional Law*, 4(1), 1–38.

Hindmoor, A., Larkin, P., and Kennon, A. (2009), 'Assessing the Influence of Select Committees in the UK: The Education and Skills Committee, 1997–2005', *Journal of Legislative Studies*, 15(1), 71–89.

HM Government (2010), *The Coalition: Our Programme for Government* (London: Stationery Office).

HM Inspectorate of Prisons (1999), *Suicide Is Everyone's Concern: A Thematic Review by HM Chief Inspector of Prisons for England and Wales* (London: HM Inspectorate of Prisons for England and Wales).

HM Treasury (2010), *Budget 2010: The Red Book* (London: HM Treasury).

Home Affairs Committee (1996), *Identity Cards (Fourth Report of Session 1995–96)*, HC 172 (London: House of Commons).

Home Affairs Committee (2004), *Identity Cards (Fourth Report of Session 2003–04), Vol. I*, HC 130-I (London: House of Commons).

Home Affairs and Work and Pensions Committees (2005), *Draft Corporate Manslaughter Bill (First Joint Report of Session 2005–06), Vol. I*, HC 540-I (London: House of Commons).

Home Office (1995), *Identity Cards: A Consultation Document*, CM 2879 (London: Home Office).

Home Office (2000a), *Corporate Manslaughter: A Summary of Responses to the Home Office's Consultation in 2000* (London: Home Office).

Home Office (2000b), *Reforming the Law on Involuntary Manslaughter: The Government's Proposals* (London: Home Office).

Home Office (2002), *Entitlement Cards and Identity Fraud: A Consultation Paper*, CM 5557 (London: Home Office).

House of Lords (2015), *Companion to the Standing Orders and Guide to the Proceedings of the House of Lords*, 24th edn (London: House of Lords).

House of Lords Legislation Office (2016), *House of Lords: Public Bill Sessional Statistics for Session 2015–2016* (London: House of Lords).

Howlett, M. and Ramesh, M. (2003), *Studying Public Policy: Policy Cycles and Policy Subsystems* (Oxford: Oxford University Press).

Hunt, M., Hooper, H., and Yowell, P. (2012), *Parliaments and Human Rights: Redressing the Democratic Deficit* (London: AHRC).

Independent Review of Personal Mobility in State Funded Residential Care (2011), *Independence, Choice and Control: DLA and Personal Mobility in State-funded Residential Care* (the '*Low Review*') (London: Leonard Cheshire Disability).

Isaac, J. C. (1987), 'Beyond the Three Faces of Power: A Realist Critique', *Polity*, 20(1), 4–31.

John, P. (2012), *Analysing Public Policy* (Abingdon: Routledge).

Johnson, N. (1997), 'Opposition in the British Political System', *Government and Opposition*, 32(4), 487–510.

Joint Committee on Conventions (2006), *Conventions of the UK Parliament (Report of Session 2005–06), Vol. II*, HL Paper 265-II HC 1212-II (London: House of Lords and House of Commons).

Joint Committee on Human Rights (2006), *Legislative Scrutiny: Corporate Manslaughter and Corporate Homicide Bill (Twenty-seventh Report of Session 2005–06)*, HL Paper 246, HC 1625 (London: House of Lords and House of Commons).

Joint Committee on Human Rights (2011), *Legislative Scrutiny: Public Bodies Bill; Other Bills (Seventh Report of Session 2010–11)*, HL Paper 86, HC 725 (London: House of Lords and House of Commons).

Jordan, A. G. and Maloney, W. A. (2007), *Democracy and Interest Groups: Enhancing Participation?* (Basingstoke: Palgrave).

Judge, D. (1993), *The Parliamentary State* (London: Sage).

Justice Committee (2011), *The Proposed Abolition of the Youth Justice Board (Tenth Report of Session 2010–12)*, HC 1547 (London: House of Commons).

Kaiser, A. (2008), 'Parliamentary Opposition in Westminster Democracies: Britain, Canada, Australia and New Zealand', *Journal of Legislative Studies*, 14(1–2), 20–45.

Kasack, C. (2004), 'The Legislative Impact of the European Parliament Under the Revised Co-Decision Procedure: Environmental, Public Health and Consumer Protection Policies', *European Union Politics*, 5(2), 241–60.

Kavanagh, D. and Cowley, P. (2010), *The British Election of 2010* (Basingstoke: Palgrave).

Kelly, R. (2011), *Pre-Legislative Scrutiny (SN/PC/2822)* (London: House of Commons Library).

Kelly, R. (2015a), *Carry-over of Public Bills (SN/PC/03236)* (London: House of Commons Library).

Kelly, R. (2015b), *Pre-Legislative Scrutiny Under the Coalition Government: 2010–2015 (SN/05859)* (London: House of Commons Library).

Kelly, R. (2016), *Short Money (SN/PC/1663)* (London: House of Commons Library).

Kelly, R. and Yousaf, S. (2014), *All-Party Groups (SN/PC/06409)* (London: House of Commons Library).

Kelso, A. (2009), *Parliamentary Reform at Westminster* (Manchester: Manchester University Press).

Kerrouche, E. (2006), 'The French Assemblée Nationale: The Case of a Weak Legislature?', *Journal of Legislative Studies*, 12(3), 336–65.

Kettell, S. and Cairney, P. (2010), 'Taking the Power of Ideas Seriously—The Case of the United Kingdom's 2008 Human Fertilisation and Embryology Bill', *Policy Studies*, 31(3), 301–17.

King, A. (1976), 'Modes of Executive–Legislative Relations: Great Britain, France and West Germany', *Legislative Studies Quarterly*, 1(1), 11–36.

King, A. (2007), *The British Constitution* (Oxford: Oxford University Press).

King, A. and Crewe, I. (2013), *The Blunders of Our Governments* (London: Oneworld).

Kinnock, N. (2011), 'Leading the Opposition' in N. Fletcher, ed, *How to Be in Opposition: Life in the Political Shadows* (London: Biteback).

Klug, F. and Wildbore, H. (2007), 'Breaking New Ground: The Joint Committee on Human Rights and the Role of Parliament in Human Rights Compliance', *European Human Rights Law Review*, 3, 231–50.

Knill, C. and Tosun, J. (2012), *Public Policy: A New Introduction* (Basingstoke: Palgrave).

Krehbiel, K. (1998), *Pivotal Politics: A Theory of U.S. Lawmaking* (Chicago: University of Chicago Press).

Kreppel, A. (1999), 'What Affects the European Parliament's Legislative Influence? An Analysis of the Success of EP Amendments', *Journal of Common Market Studies* 37(3), 521–37.

Kreppel, A. (2014), 'Typologies and Classifications' in S. Martin, T. Saalfeld, & K. Strom, eds, *The Oxford Handbook of Legislative Studies* (Oxford: Oxford University Press).

Kubala, M. (2011), 'Select Committees in the House of Commons and the Media', *Parliamentary Affairs*, 64(2), 694–713.

Labour Party (2001), *Ambitions for Britain: Labour's Manifesto 2001* (London: Labour Party).

Labour Party (2004), *National Policy Forum Report to Labour Party Annual Conference* (London: Labour Party).

Labour Party (2005), *Britain Forward Not Back: The Labour Party Manifesto 2005* (London: Labour Party).

Law Commission (1996), *Legislating the Criminal Code: Involuntary Manslaughter*, HC 171 (London: Stationery Office).

Laws, D. (2016a), *Coalition* (London: Biteback).

Laws, S. (2016b), 'What Is Parliamentary Scrutiny of Legislation for?' in A. Horne & A. Le Sueur, eds, *Parliament: Legislation and Accountability* (Oxford: Hart).

Leach, R., Coxall, B. and Robins, L. (2011), *British Politics* (Basingstoke: Palgrave).

Levy, J. (2010), 'Public Bill Committees: An Assessment Scrutiny Sought; Scrutiny Gained', *Parliamentary Affairs*, 63(3), 534–44.

Liaison Committee (2010), *The Work of Committees in Session 2008–09 (Second Report of Session 2009–10)*, HC 426 (London: House of Commons).

Liberal Democrats (2010), *Liberal Democrat Manifesto 2010* (London: Liberal Democrats).

Lijphart, A. (1999), *Patterns of Democracy: Government Forms and Performance in Thirty-Six Countries* (New Haven: Yale University Press).

Lijphart, A. (2012), *Patterns of Democracy: Government Forms and Performance in Thirty-Six Countries*, 2nd edn (New Haven: Yale University Press).

Littleboy, C. and Kelly, R. (2005), *Pepper v Hart (SN/PC/392)* (House of Commons Library).

Loewenberg, G. and Patterson, S. C. (1979), *Comparing Legislatures* (Lanham: University Press of America).

Low, S. (1904), *The Governance of England* (London: T. Fisher Unwin).

LSE (2005), *The Identity Project: An Assessment of the UK Identity Cards Bill and its Implications* (London: London School of Economics).

Lukes, S. (1974), *Power: A Radical View* (Hong Kong: Macmillan).

Lukes, S. (2005), *Power: A Radical View*, 2nd edn (Basingstoke: Palgrave).

Lynskey, J. J. (1970), 'The Role of British Backbenchers in the Modification of Government Policy', *Western Political Quarterly*, 23(2), 333–47.

McGann, A. (2006), 'Social Choice and Comparing Legislatures: Constitutional versus Institutional Constraints', *Journal of Legislative Studies*, 12(4), 443–61.

Manow, P. and Burkhart, S. (2007), 'Legislative Self-Restraint under Divided Government in Germany, 1976–2002', *Legislative Studies Quarterly*, 32(2), 167–91.

Martin, L. W. and Vanberg, G. (2008), 'Coalition Government and Political Communication', *Political Research Quarterly*, 61(3), 502–16.

Martin, L. W. and Vanberg, G. (2011), *Parliaments and Coalitions: The Role of Legislative Institutions in Multiparty Governance* (Oxford: Oxford University Press).

Mattson, I. and Strøm, K. (2004), 'Committee Effects on Legislation' in H. Döring & M. Hallerberg, eds, *Patterns of Parliamentary Behaviour: Passage of Legislation Across Western Europe* (Aldershot: Ashgate).

Maurer, L. M. (1999), 'Parliamentary Influence in a New Democracy: The Spanish Congress', *Journal of Legislative Studies*, 5(2), 24–45.

Mayhew, D. R. (1974), *Congress: The Electoral Connection* (New Haven: Yale University Press).

Mezey, M. L. (1979), *Comparative Legislatures* (Durham: Duke University Press).

Mezey, M. L. (1991), 'Parliaments and Public Policy: An Assessment' in D. M. Olson & M. L. Mezey, eds, *Legislatures in the Policy Process* (Cambridge: Cambridge University Press).

Miers, D. and Brock, J. (1993), 'Government Legislation: Case-Studies' in D. Shell & D. Beamish, eds, *The House of Lords at Work: A Study Based on the 1988–1989 Session* (Oxford: Clarendon).

Mill, J. S. (1998 [1861]), *On Liberty and Other Essays* (Oxford: Oxford University Press).

Moran, M. (2015), *Politics and Governance in the UK* (London: Palgrave).

Morgan, J. P. (1975), *The House of Lords and the Labour Government 1964–1970* (London: Oxford University Press).

Mulley, J. and Kinghorn, H. (2016), 'Pre-Legislative Scrutiny in Parliament' in A. Horne & A. Le Sueur, eds, *Parliament: Legislation and Accountability* (Oxford: Hart).

National Committee of Inquiry into Higher Education (1997), *Higher Education in the Learning Society* (London: HM Stationery Office).

Newson, N. and Kelly, R. (2011), *Wash-up 2010 (LLN 2011/007)* (London: House of Lords Library).

Norton, P. (1975), *Dissension in the House of Commons 1945–74* (London: Macmillan).

Norton, P. (1978), *Conservative Dissidents* (London: Temple Smith).

Norton, P. (1980), *Dissension in the House of Commons, 1974–1979* (Oxford: Clarendon).

Norton, P. (1990a), 'Legislatures in Perspective', *West European Politics*, 13(3), 143–52.

Norton, P. (1990b), 'Public Legislation' in M. Rush, ed, *Parliament and Pressure Politics* (Oxford: Clarendon).

Norton, P. (1993), *Does Parliament Matter?* (New York: Harvester Wheatsheaf).

Norton, P. (1998a), 'The Institution of Parliaments' in P. Norton, ed, *Parliaments and Governments in Western Europe* (London: Frank Cass).

Norton, P. (1998b), 'Nascent Institutionalisation: Committees in the British Parliament' in L. D. Longley & R. H. Davidson, eds, *The New Roles of Parliamentary Committees* (London: Frank Cass).

Norton, P. (1999), 'The United Kingdom: Parliament under Pressure' in P. Norton, ed, *Parliaments and Pressure Groups in Western Europe* (London: Frank Cass).

Norton, P. (2000), 'The United Kingdom: Exerting Influence from within' in K. Heidar & R. Koole, eds, *Parliamentary Party Groups in European Democracies: Political Parties behind Closed Doors* (London: Routledge).

Norton, P. (2003), 'Cohesion without Discipline: Party Voting in the House of Lords', *Journal of Legislative Studies*, 9(4), 57–72.

Norton, P. (2008), 'Making Sense of Opposition', *Journal of Legislative Studies*, 14(1–2), 236–50.

Norton, P. (2013), *Parliament in British Politics* (Basingstoke: Palgrave).

Nye, J. (2008), 'Public Diplomacy and Soft Power', *Annals of the American Academy of Political and Social Science*, 616(1), 94–109.

Oaten, M. (2009), *Screwing up: How One MP Survived Politics, Scandal and Turning 40* (London: Biteback).

O'Dowd, J. (2010), 'Parliamentary Scrutiny of Bills' in M. Maccarthaigh & M. Manning, eds, *The Houses of the Oireachtas: Parliament in Ireland* (Dublin: Institute of Public Administration).

Office of Fair Trading (2003), *The Control of Entry Regulations and Retail Pharmacy Services in the UK: A Report of an OFT Market Investigation* (London: Office of Fair Trading).

Olson, D. M. (1994), *Democratic Legislative Institutions: A Comparative View* (Armonk: M.E. Sharpe).

Olson, D. M. (2003), 'Cohesion and Discipline Revisited: Contingent Unity in the Parliamentary Party Group', *Journal of Legislative Studies*, 9(4), 164–78.

Olson, D. M. and Mezey, M. L. (1991), 'Parliaments and Public Policy' in D. M. Olson & M. L. Mezey, eds, *Legislatures in the Policy Process* (Cambridge: Cambridge University Press).

Olson, M. D. (1965), *The Logic of Collective Action: Public Goods and the Theory of Groups* (Cambridge, MA: Harvard University Press).

Page, E. C. (2001), *Governing By Numbers: Delegated Legislation and Everyday Policy-Making* (Oxford: Hart).

Page, E. C. (2002), 'The Insider/Outsider Distinction: An Empirical Analysis', *British Journal of Politics and International Relations*, 1(2), 205–14.

Page, E. C. (2003), 'The Civil Servant as Legislator: Law Making in British Administration', *Public Administration*, 81(4), 651–79.

Page, E. C. (2006), 'The Origins of Policy' in M. Moran, M. Rein, & R. E. Goodin, eds, *Oxford Handbook of Public Policy* (Oxford: Oxford University Press).

Page, E. C. (2009), 'Their Word Is Law: Parliamentary Counsel and Creative Policy Analysis', *Public Law*, 4, 790–811.

Parry, K. and Kelly, R. (2012), *Limitations on the Number of Ministers and the Size of the Payroll vote (SN/PC/03378)* (London: House of Commons Library).

Partington, A. (2006), *Church and State: The Contribution of the Church of England Bishops to the House of Lords During the Thatcher Years* (Milton Keynes: Paternoster).

Partington, A. and Bickley, P. (2007), *Coming off the Bench: The Past, Present and Future of Religious Representation in the House of Lords* (London: Theos).

Parvin, P. (2007), *Friend or Foe? Lobbying in British Democracy* (London: Hansard Society).

Pettai, V. and Madise, U. (2006), 'The Baltic Parliaments: Legislative Performance from Independence to EU Accession', *Journal of Legislative Studies*, 12(3), 291–310.

Political and Constitutional Reform Committee (2013), *House of Lords Reform: What Next? (Ninth Report of Session 2013–14, Volume I)* (London: House of Commons).

Polsby, N. W. (1975), 'Legislatures' in F. Greenstein & N. Polsby, eds, *Handbook of Political Science* (Reading, MA: Addison-Wesley).

Procedure Committee (2009), *Tabling of Amendments by Select Committees (Fifth Report of Session 2008–09)*, HC 1104 (London: House of Commons).

Procedure Committee (2013), *Committee of Selection and Membership of General Committees: Corrected Transcript of Oral Evidence*, HC 216-I (London: House of Commons).

Procedure Committee (2016a), *Private Members' Bills (Third Report of Session 2015–16)*, HC 684 (London: House of Commons).

Procedure Committee (2016b), *Private Members' Bills: Observations on the Government Response to the Committee's Third Report of Session 2015–16 HC 684 (Second Report of Session 2016–17)*, HC 701 (London: House of Commons).

Public Accounts Committee (2011), *The Youth Justice System in England and Wales: Reducing Offending by Young People (Twenty-First Report of Session 2010–11)*, HC 721 (London: House of Commons).

Public Accounts Committee (2013), *Universal Credit: Early Progress (Thirtieth Report of Session 2013–14)*, HC 619 (London: House of Commons).

Public Accounts Committee (2014), *Personal Independence Payment (First Report of Session 2014–15)*, HC 280 (London: House of Commons).

Public Administration Select Committee (2003), *Government by Appointment: Opening up the Patronage State (Fourth Report of Session 2002–03)*, Vol. I, HC 165-I (London: House of Commons).

Public Administration Select Committee (2011), *Smaller Government: Shrinking the Quango State (Fifth Report of Session 2010–11)*, HC 537 (London: House of Commons).

Quinn, T. (2013), 'From Two-Partism to Alternating Predominance: The Changing UK Party System, 1950–2010', *Political Studies*, 61(2), 378–400.

Rhodes, R. A. W. and Marsh, D., eds (1992), *Policy Networks in British Government* (Oxford: Clarendon).

Richardson, J. J. (1993), 'Interest Group Behaviour in Britain: Continuity and Change' in J. J. Richardson, ed, *Pressure Groups* (Oxford: Oxford University Press).

Richardson, J. J. and Jordan, A. G. (1979), *Governing under Pressure: The Policy Process in a Post-Parliamentary Democracy* (Oxford: Martin Robertson).

Rogers, R. and Walters, R. (2015), *How Parliament Works*, 7th edn (Abingdon: Routledge).

Rose, R. (1980), *Do Parties Make a Difference?* (Chatham: Chatham House).

Rush, M., ed (1990), *Parliament and Pressure Politics* (Oxford: Clarendon).

Rush, M. (2005), *Parliament Today* (Manchester: Manchester University Press).

Rush, M. and Ettinghausen, C. (2002), *Opening up the Usual Channels* (London: Hansard Society).

Russell, M. (2000), *Reforming the House of Lords: Lessons from Overseas* (Oxford: Oxford University Press).

Russell, M. (2005), *Must Politics Disappoint?* (London: Fabian Society).

Russell, M. (2010), 'A Stronger Second Chamber? Assessing the Impact of House of Lords Reform in 1999, and the Lessons for Bicameralism', *Political Studies*, 58(5), 866–85.

Russell, M. (2011), ' "Never Allow a Crisis to Go to Waste": The Wright Committee Reforms to Strengthen the House of Commons', *Parliamentary Affairs*, 64(4), 612–33.

Russell, M. (2013), *The Contemporary House of Lords: Westminster Bicameralism Revived* (Oxford: Oxford University Press).

Russell, M. (2014), 'Parliamentary Party Cohesion: Some Explanations from Psychology', *Party Politics*, 20(5), 712–23.

Russell, M. and Benton, M. (2011), *Selective Influence: The Policy Impact of House of Commons Select Committees* (London: Constitution Unit).

Russell, M. and Cowley, P. (2016), 'The Policy Power of the Westminster Parliament: The "Parliamentary State" and the Empirical Evidence', *Governance*, 29(1), 121–37.

Russell, M. and Gover, D. (2014), *Demystifying Financial Privilege: Does the Commons' Claim of Financial Primacy on Lords Amendments Need Reform?* (London: Constitution Unit).

Russell, M., Gover, D., and Wollter, K. (2016), 'Does the Executive Dominate the Westminster Legislative Process?: Six Reasons for Doubt', *Parliamentary Affairs*, 69(2), 286–308.

Russell, M., Gover, D., Wollter, K., and Benton, M. (2017), 'Actors, Motivations and Outcomes in the Legislative Process: Policy Influence at Westminster', *Government and Opposition*, 52(1), 1–27.

Russell, M., Morris, R. M., and Larkin, P. (2013), *Fitting the Bill: Bringing Commons Legislation Committees into Line with Best Practice* (London: Constitution Unit).

Russell, M. and Paun, A. (2007), *The House Rules?: International Lessons for Enhancing the Autonomy of the House of Commons* (London: Constitution Unit).

Russell, M. and Sciara, M. (2007), 'Why Does the Government Get Defeated in the House of Lords? The Lords, the Party System and British Politics', *British Politics*, 2(3), 299–322.

Russell, M. and Sciara, M. (2008), 'The Policy Impact of Defeats in the House of Lords', *British Journal of Politics and International Relations*, 10(4), 571–89.

Russell, M. and Sciara, M. (2009), 'Independent Parliamentarians en masse: The Changing Nature and Role of the "Crossbenchers" in the House of Lords', *Parliamentary Affairs*, 62(1), 32–52.

Russell, M. and Semlyen, T. (2015), *Enough Is Enough: Regulating Prime Ministerial Appointments to the Lords* (London: Constitution Unit).

Ryle, M. (2005), 'Forty Years on and a Future Agenda' in P. Giddings, ed, *The Future of Parliament: Issues for a New Century* (Basingstoke: Palgrave).

Saalfeld, T. (2003), 'The United Kingdom: Still a Single "Chain of Command"? The Hollowing Out of the "Westminster Model"' in K. Strøm, W. C. Müller, & T. Bergman, eds, *Delegation and Accountability in Parliamentary Democracies* (Oxford: Oxford University Press).

Sabatier, P. A. and Jenkins-Smith, H. C. (1993), *Policy Change and Learning: An Advocacy Coalition Approach* (Boulter: Westview).

Saiegh, S. M. (2011), *Ruling by Statute: How Uncertainty and Vote Buying Shape Lawmaking* (Cambridge: Cambridge University Press).

Schleiter, P. and Belu, V. (2016), 'The Decline of Majoritarianism in the UK and the Fixed-term Parliaments Act', *Parliamentary Affairs*, 69(1), 36–52.

Scott, J. (2008), 'Modes of Power and the Re-conceptualization of Elites', *Sociological Review*, 56(s1), 25–43.

Seaward, P. and Silk, P. (2003), 'The House of Commons' in V. Bogdanor, ed, *The British Constitution in the Twentieth Century* (Oxford: Oxford University Press).

Seeberg, H. B. (2013), 'The Opposition's Policy Influence through Issue Politicisation', *Journal of Public Policy*, 33(1), 89–107.

Sharman, C. (1999), 'The Representation of Small Parties and Independents in the Senate', *Australian Journal of Political Science*, 34(3), 353–61.

Shaw, M. (1979), 'Conclusion' in J. D. Lees & M. Shaw, eds, *Committees in Legislatures* (Oxford: Martin Robertson).

Shaw, M. (1998), 'Parliamentary Committees: A Global Perspective' in L. D. Longley & R. H. Davidson, eds, *The New Roles of Parliamentary Committees* (London: Frank Cass).

Shell, D. (1992), *The House of Lords* (Hemel Hempstead: Harvester Wheatsheaf).

Shell, D. (2000), 'Labour and the House of Lords: A Case Study in Constitutional Reform', *Parliamentary Affairs*, 53(2), 290–310.

Shell, D. (2007), *The House of Lords* (Manchester: Manchester University Press).

Shell, D. and Beamish, D., eds (1993), *The House of Lords at Work: A Study Based on the 1988–1989 Session* (Oxford: Clarendon).

Shephard, M. and Cairney, P. (2005), 'The Impact of the Scottish Parliament in Amending Executive Legislation', *Political Studies*, 53(2), 303–19.

Sieberer, U. (2006), 'Party Unity in Parliamentary Democracies: A Comparative Analysis', *Journal of Legislative Studies*, 12(2), 150–78.

Smookler, J. (2006), 'Making a Difference? The Effectiveness of Pre-Legislative Scrutiny', *Parliamentary Affairs*, 59(3), 522–35.

Steven, M. H. M. (2011), *Christianity and Party Politics: Keeping the Faith* (Abingdon: Routledge).

Stoker, G. (2006), *Why Politics Matters: Making Democracy Work* (Basingstoke: Palgrave).

Strøm, K. (2003), 'Parliamentary Democracy and Delegation' in K. Strøm, W. Müller, & T. Bergman, eds, *Delegation and Accountability in Parliamentary Democracies* (Oxford: Oxford University Press).

Taagepera, R. and Shugart, M. S. (1989), *Seats and Votes: The Effects and Determinants of Electoral Systems* (New Haven: Yale University Press).

Thompson, L. (2013), 'More of the Same or a Period of Change? The Impact of Bill Committees in the Twenty-First Century House of Commons', *Parliamentary Affairs*, 66(3), 459–79.

Thompson, L. (2015), *Making British Law: Committees in Action* (Basingstoke: Palgrave).

Tomkins, A. (2003), 'What Is Parliament For?' in N. Bamforth & P. Leyland, eds, *Public Law in a Multi-layered Constitution* (Oxford: Hart).

Torrance, M. (2012), *Select Committees in the House of Lords (LLN 2012/031)* (London: House of Lords Library).

Treasury Committee (2007), *Financial Inclusion Follow-up: Saving for All and Shorter Term Saving Products (Thirteenth Report of Session 2006–07)*, HC 504 (London: House of Commons).

Treasury Committee (2010), *Office for Budget Responsibility (Fourth Report of Session 2010–11)*, *Vol. I*, HC 385-I (London: House of Commons).

Tsebelis, G. (2002), *Veto Players: How Political Institutions Work* (Princeton: Princeton University Press).

Tsebelis, G., Jensen, C. B., Kalandrakis, A., and Kreppel, A. (2001), 'Legislative Procedures in the European Union: An Empirical Analysis', *British Journal of Political Science*, 31(4), 573–99.

Tsebelis, G. and Kalandrakis, A. (1999), 'The European Parliament and Environmental Legislation: The Case of Chemicals', *European Journal of Political Research*, 36(1), 119–54.

Tsebelis, G. and Money, J. (1997), *Bicameralism* (Cambridge: Cambridge University Press).

Uhr, J. (2009), 'Parliamentary Opposition Leadership' in H. Patapan, P. 't. Hart, & J. Kane, eds, *Dispersed Democratic Leadership* (Oxford: Oxford University Press).

Vibert, F. (2007), *The Rise of the Unelected: Democracy and the New Separation of Powers* (Cambridge: Cambridge University Press).

Waldron, J. (1999), *Law and Disagreement* (Oxford: Oxford University Press).

Walkland, S. A. (1979), 'Government Legislation in the House of Commons' in S. A. Walkland, ed, *The House of Commons in the Twentieth Century* (Oxford: Clarendon).

Walters, R. (2003), 'The House of Lords' in V. Bogdanor, ed, *The British Constitution in the Twentieth Century* (Oxford: Oxford University Press).

Ward, P. (2005), *The Identity Cards Bill (RP05/43)* (London: House of Commons Library).

Weeks, L. (2009), 'We Don't Like (to) Party. A Typology of Independents in Irish Political Life, 1922–2007', *Irish Political Studies*, 24(1), 1–27.

Welsh Affairs Committee (2007), *Legislative Competence Orders in Council (Second Report of Session 2006–07)*, HC 175 (London: House of Commons).

White, H. (2015), *Select Committees under Scrutiny: The Impact of Parliamentary Committee Inquiries on Government* (London: Institute for Government).

Whitley, E. A., Hosein, I. R., Angell, I. O., and Davies, S. (2007), 'Reflections on the Academic Policy Analysis Process and the UK Identity Cards Scheme', *Information Society*, 23(1), 51–8.

Wood, D. M. (1991), 'The House of Commons and Industrial Policy' in D. Olson & M. Mezey, eds, *Legislatures in the Policy Process* (Cambridge: Cambridge University Press).

Work and Pensions Committee (2010), *Changes to Housing Benefit Announced in the June 2010 Budget (Second Report of Session 2010–11)*, *Vol. I*, HC 469-I (London: House of Commons).

Work and Pensions Committee (2011), *Changes to Housing Benefit Announced in the June 2010 Budget: Government Response to the Committee's Second Report of Session 2010–11 (Fourth Special Report of Session 2010–11)*, HC 845 (London: House of Commons).

Work and Pensions Committee (2014), *Universal Credit Implementation: Monitoring DWP's Performance in 2012–13 (Fifth Report of Session 2013–14)*, HC 1209 (London: House of Commons).

Wren-Lewis, S. (2011), 'Fiscal Councils: The UK Office for Budget Responsibility', *DICE Report*, 9(3), 50–3.

Wright, T. (2004), 'Prospects for Parliamentary Reform', *Parliamentary Affairs*, 57(4), 867–76.

Yong, B. (2012), 'The Coalition in Parliament' in R. Hazell & B. Yong, eds, *The Politics of Coalition: How the Conservative–Liberal Democrat Government Works* (Oxford: Hart).

Zander, M. (2015), *The Law-Making Process* (Oxford: Hart).

Zubek, R. (2011), 'Negative Agenda Control and Executive–Legislative Relations in East Central Europe, 1997–2008', *Journal of Legislative Studies*, 17(2), 172–92.

Index